## Rumiko Takahashi

The spotlight on Rumiko Takahashi's career began in 1978 when she won an honorable mention in Shogakukan's annual New Comic Artist Contest for *Those Selfish Aliens*. Later that same year, her boy-meets-alien comedy series, *Urusei Yatsura*, was serialized in *Weekly Shonen Sunday*. This phenomenally successful manga series was adapted into anime format and spawned a TV series and half a dozen theatrical-release movies, all incredibly popular in their own right. Takahashi followed up the success of her debut series with one blockbuster hit after another—*Maison Ikkoku* ran from 1980 to 1987, *Ranma ½* from 1987 to 1996, and *Inuyasha* from 1996 to 2008. Other notable works include *Mermaid Saga*, *Rumic Theater*, and *One-Pound Gospel*.

Takahashi won the prestigious Shogakukan Manga Award twice in her career, once for *Urusei Yatsura* in 1981 and the second time for *Inuyasha* in 2002. A majority of the Takahashi canon has been adapted into other media such as anime, live-action TV series, and film. Takahashi's manga, as well as the other formats her work has been adapted into, have continued to delight generations of fans around the world. Distinguished by her wonderfully endearing characters, Takahashi's work adeptly incorporates a wide variety of elements such as comedy, romance, fantasy, and martial arts. While her series are difficult to pin down into one simple genre, the signature style she has created has come to be known as the "Rumic World." Rumiko Takahashi is an artist who truly represents the very best from the world of manga.

# RIN-NE

## VOLUME 11
## Shonen Sunday Edition

STORY AND ART BY
**RUMIKO TAKAHASHI**


Original Japanese edition "KYOUKAI NO RINNE"
published by SHOGAKUKAN Inc.

Translation/Christine Dashiell
Touch-up Art & Lettering/Evan Waldinger
Design/Yukiko Whitley, Shawn Carrico
Editor/Mike Montesa



Printed in Canada

Published by VIZ Media, LLC
P.O. Box 77010
San Francisco, CA 94107

10 9 8 7 6 5 4 3 2 1
First printing, March 2013

www.viz.com

WWW.SHONENSUNDAY.COM

PARENTAL ADVISORY
RIN-NE is rated T+ for Older Teen and is recommended for ages 16 and up.
FOR OLDER TEEN
ratings.viz.com

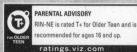

# RIN-NE

### Story and Art by
## Rumiko Takahashi

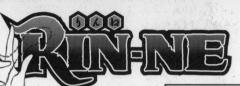

RIN-NE りんね

# Characters

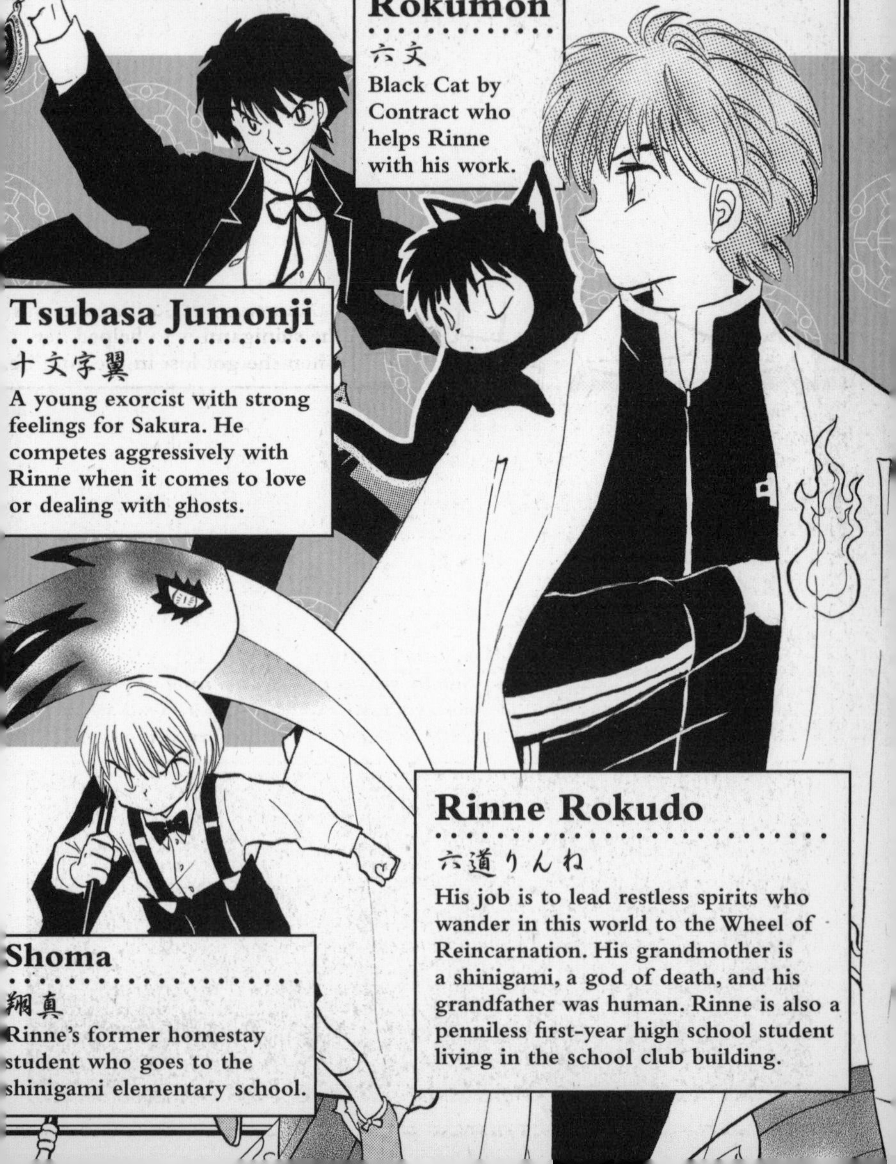

## Rokumon

六文

Black Cat by Contract who helps Rinne with his work.

## Tsubasa Jumonji

十文字翼

A young exorcist with strong feelings for Sakura. He competes aggressively with Rinne when it comes to love or dealing with ghosts.

## Rinne Rokudo

六道りんね

His job is to lead restless spirits who wander in this world to the Wheel of Reincarnation. His grandmother is a shinigami, a god of death, and his grandfather was human. Rinne is also a penniless first-year high school student living in the school club building.

## Shoma

翔真

Rinne's former homestay student who goes to the shinigami elementary school.

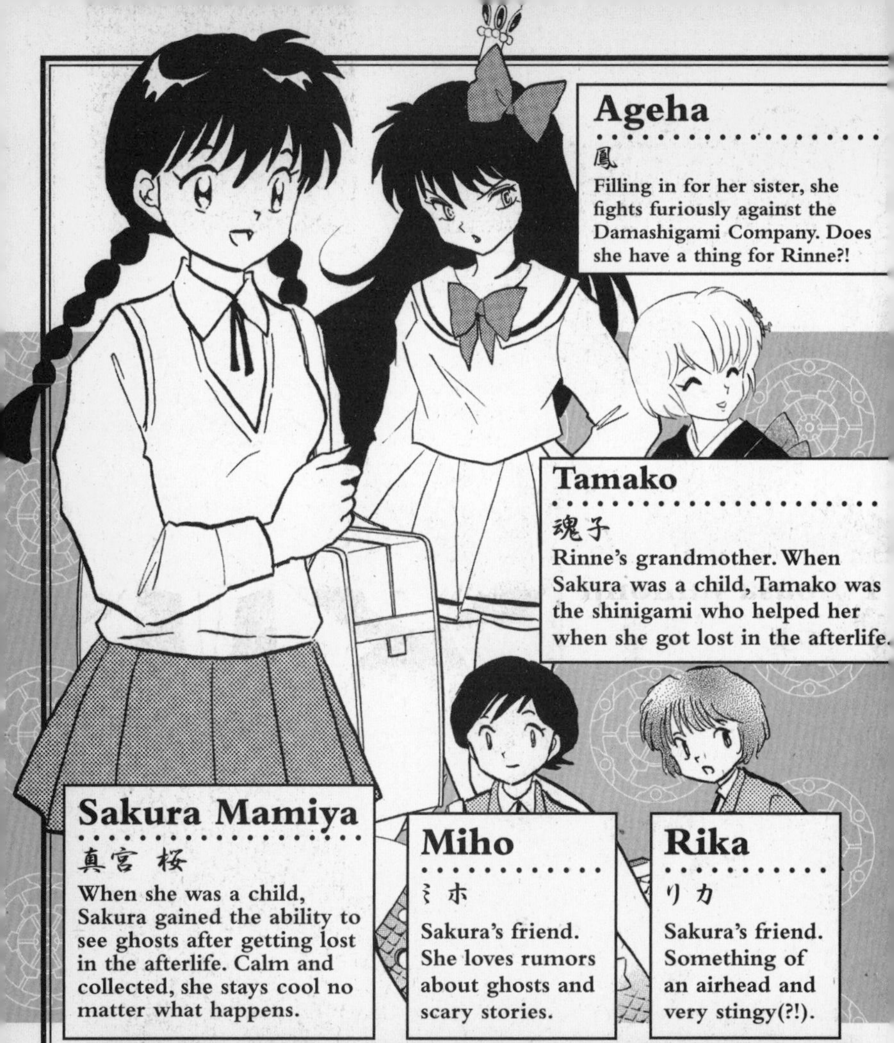

## Ageha

鳳

Filling in for her sister, she fights furiously against the Damashigami Company. Does she have a thing for Rinne?!

## Tamako

魂子

Rinne's grandmother. When Sakura was a child, Tamako was the shinigami who helped her when she got lost in the afterlife.

## Sakura Mamiya

真宮 桜

When she was a child, Sakura gained the ability to see ghosts after getting lost in the afterlife. Calm and collected, she stays cool no matter what happens.

## Miho

ミホ

Sakura's friend. She loves rumors about ghosts and scary stories.

## Rika

リカ

Sakura's friend. Something of an airhead and very stingy(?!).

## The Story So Far

Together, Sakura, the girl who can see ghosts, and Rinne the shinigami (sort of) spend their days helping spirits that can't pass on reach the afterlife, and deal with all kinds of strange phenomena at their school.

After getting caught up in a troublesome employee relations problem between Ageha and her Black Cat Oboro, Rinne clashes with his rival, the shingami clerk Kain and his Black Cat Suzu, in a squabble over Rinne's shinigami membership dues. From the shingami world to the schoolyard, there are plenty of ghostly matters to deal with.

# Contents

# CHAPTER 99: BLINDING CANDY

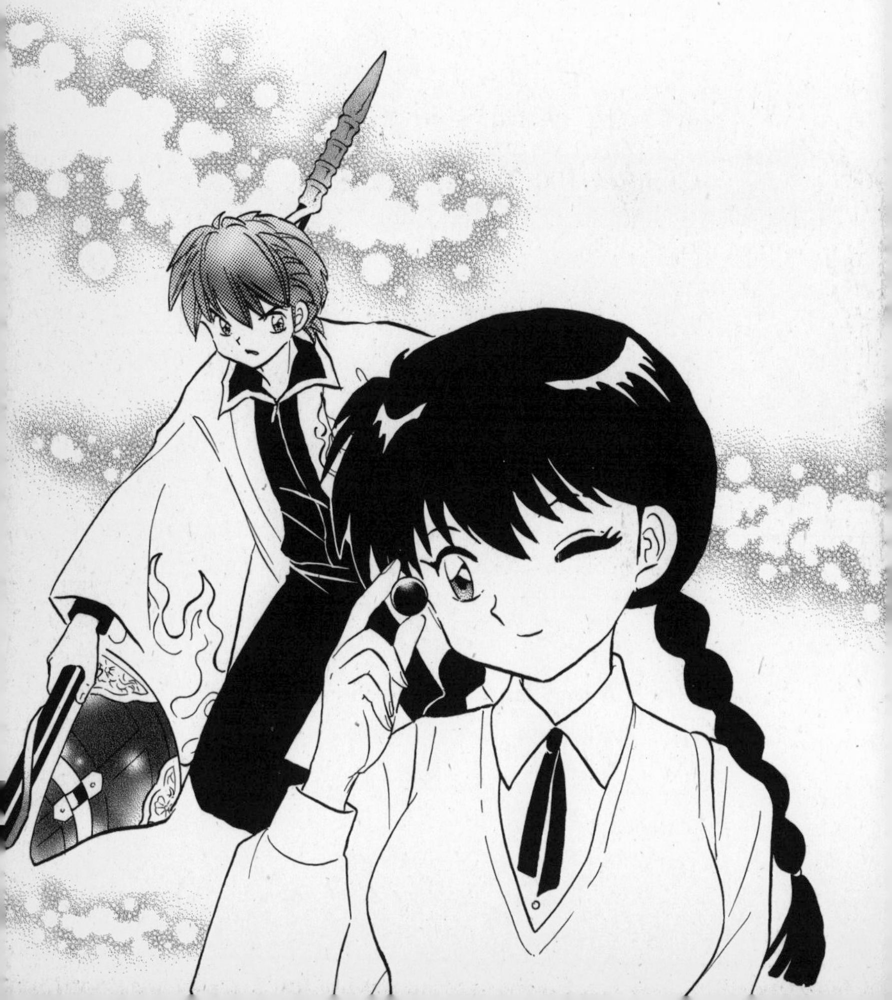

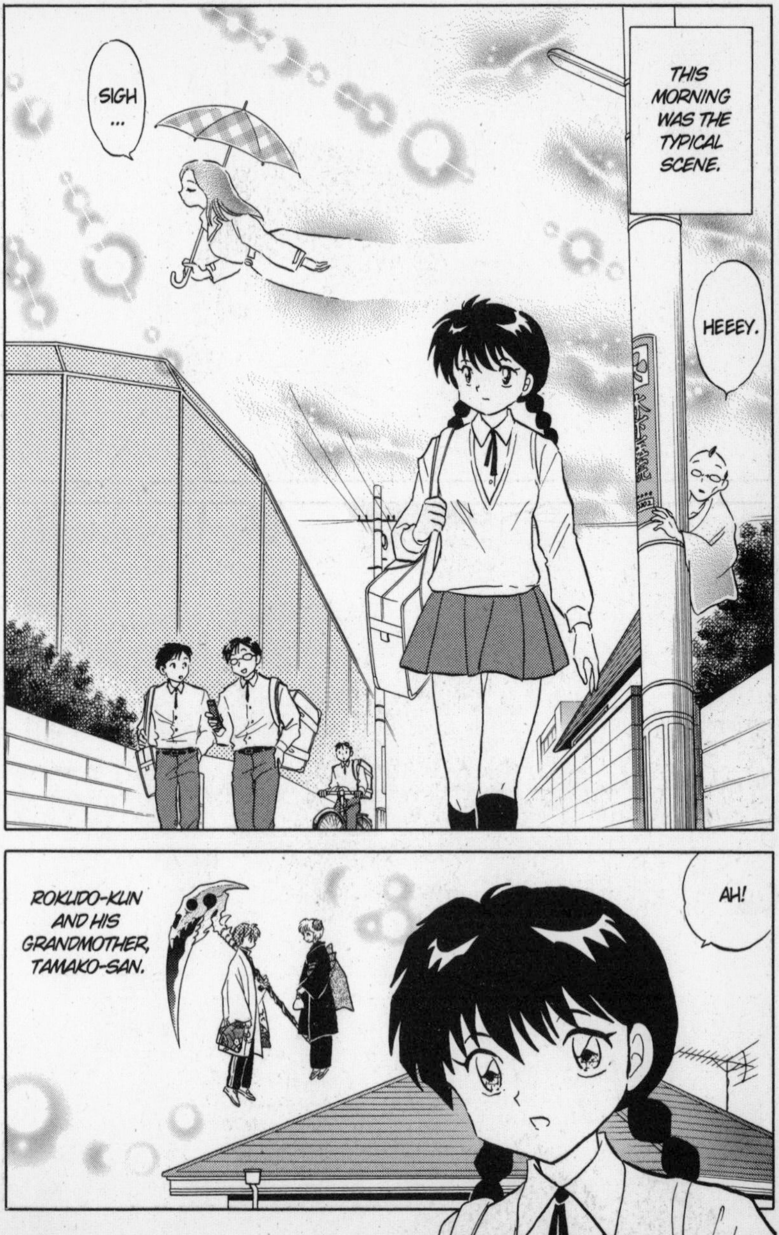
THIS MORNING WAS THE TYPICAL SCENE.
HEEEY.
SIGH ...
AH!
ROKUDO-KUN AND HIS GRANDMOTHER, TAMAKO-SAN.

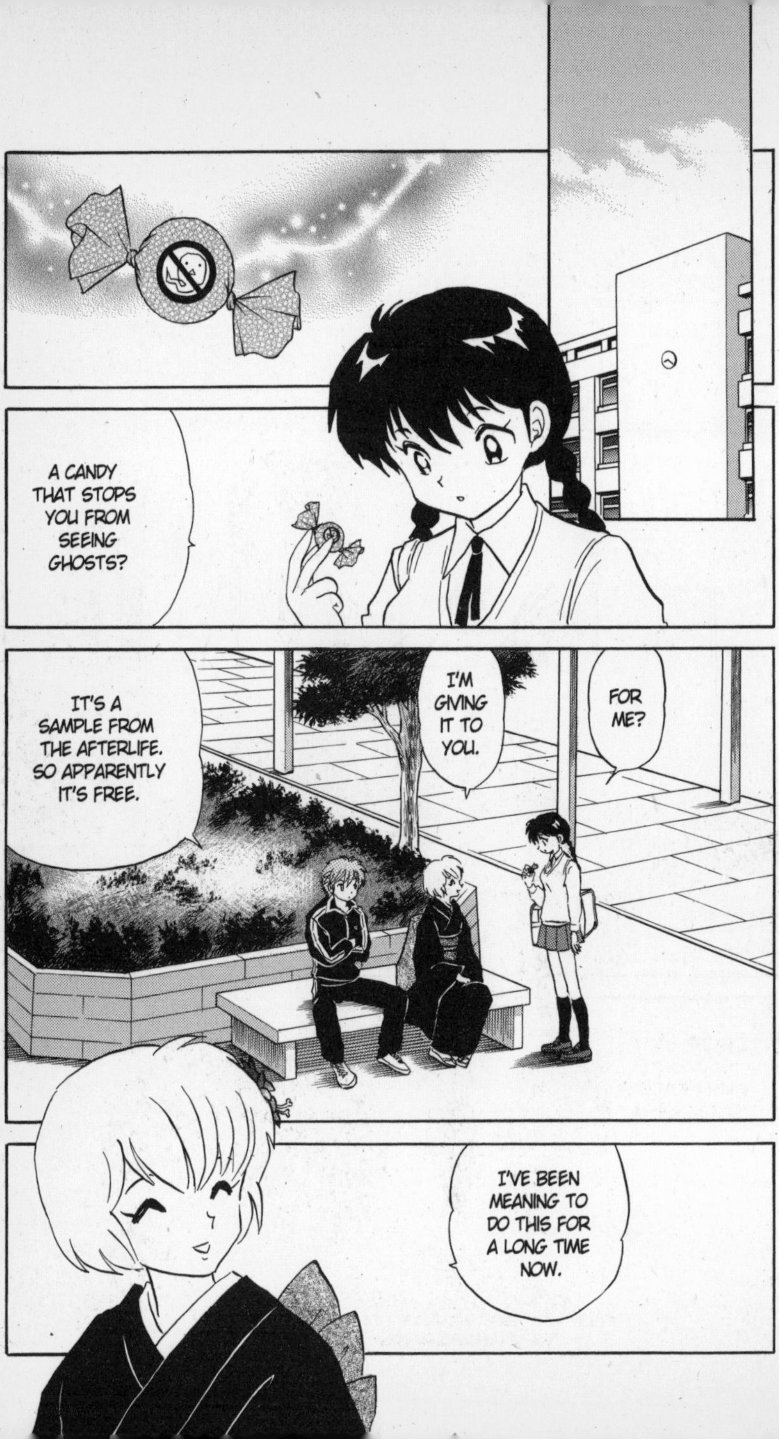
A CANDY THAT STOPS YOU FROM SEEING GHOSTS?
FOR ME?
I'M GIVING IT TO YOU.
IT'S A SAMPLE FROM THE AFTERLIFE. SO APPARENTLY IT'S FREE.
I'VE BEEN MEANING TO DO THIS FOR A LONG TIME NOW.

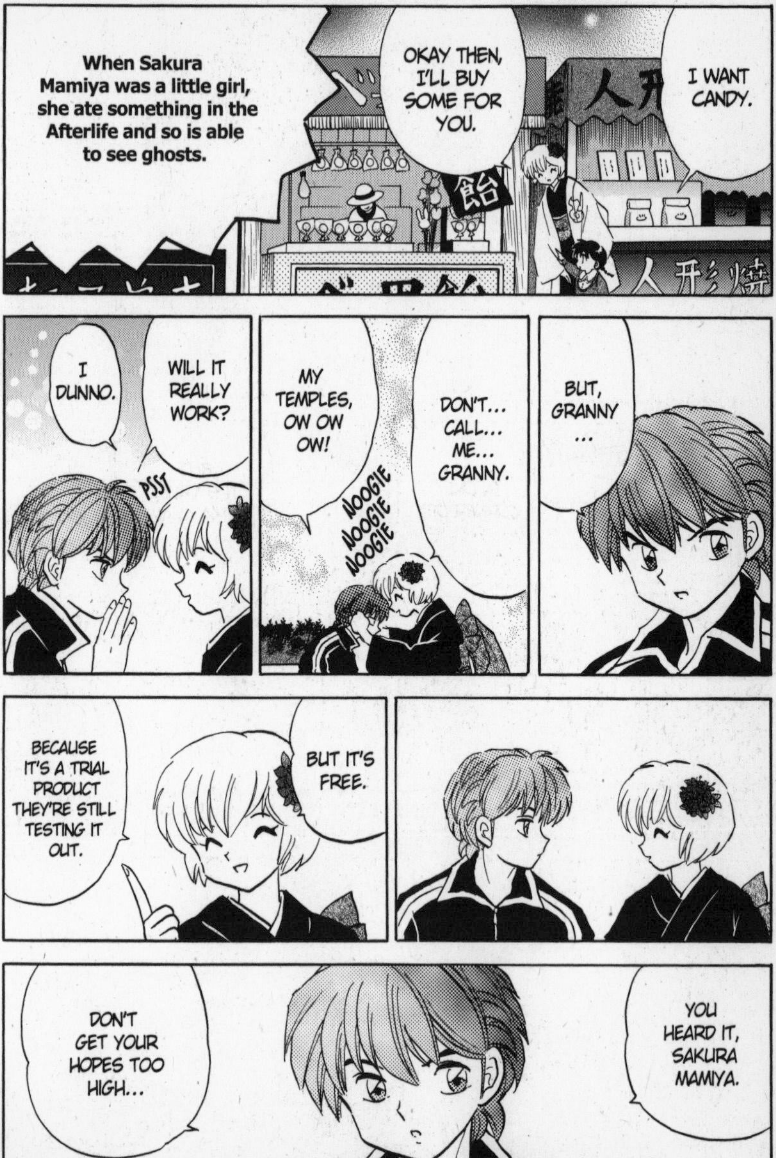
I WANT CANDY.
OKAY THEN, I'LL BUY SOME FOR YOU.
When Sakura Mamiya was a little girl, she ate something in the Afterlife and so is able to see ghosts.
BUT, GRANNY...
DON'T... CALL... ME... GRANNY.
MY TEMPLES, OW OW OW!
NOOGIE NOOGIE NOOGIE
WILL IT REALLY WORK?
I DUNNO.
PSST
BUT IT'S FREE.
BECAUSE IT'S A TRIAL PRODUCT THEY'RE STILL TESTING IT OUT.
YOU HEARD IT, SAKURA MAMIYA.
DON'T GET YOUR HOPES TOO HIGH...

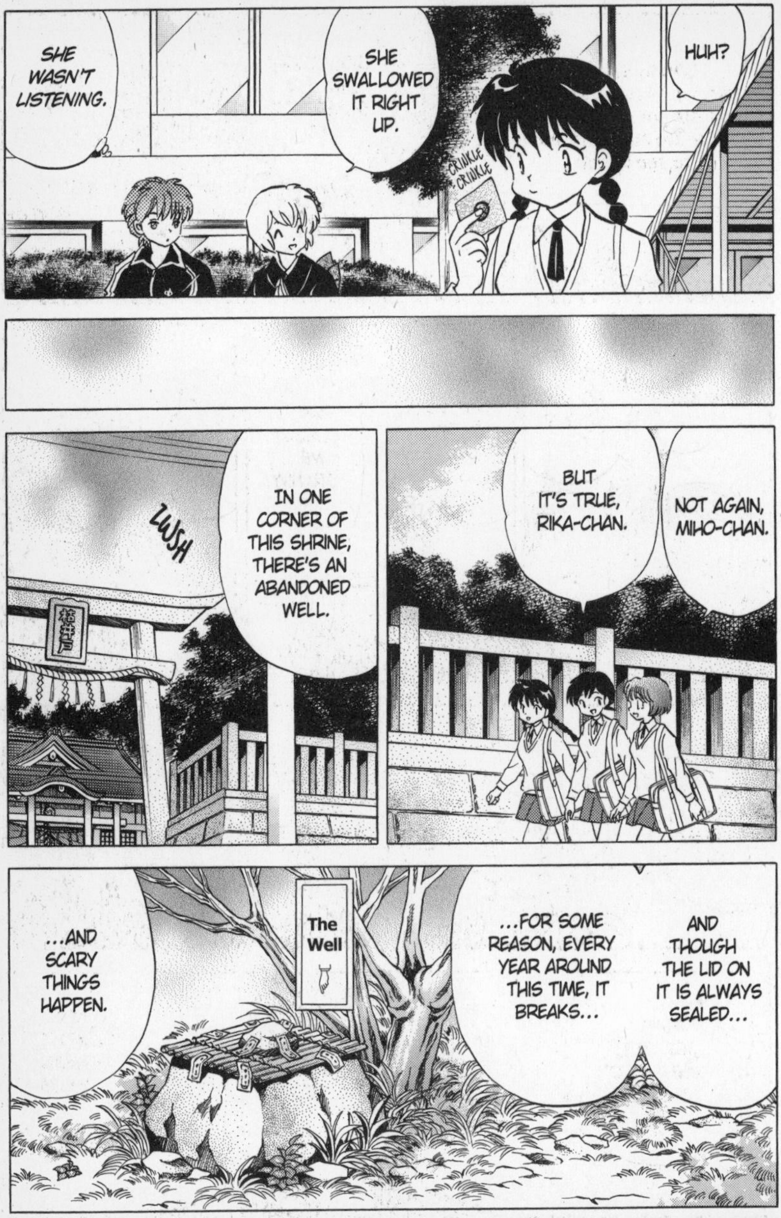
HUH?
CRINKLE CRINKLE
SHE SWALLOWED IT RIGHT UP.
SHE WASN'T LISTENING.
NOT AGAIN, MIHO-CHAN.
BUT IT'S TRUE, RIKA-CHAN.
IN ONE CORNER OF THIS SHRINE, THERE'S AN ABANDONED WELL.
ZWSH
AND THOUGH THE LID ON IT IS ALWAYS SEALED...
...FOR SOME REASON, EVERY YEAR AROUND THIS TIME, IT BREAKS...
The Well
...AND SCARY THINGS HAPPEN.

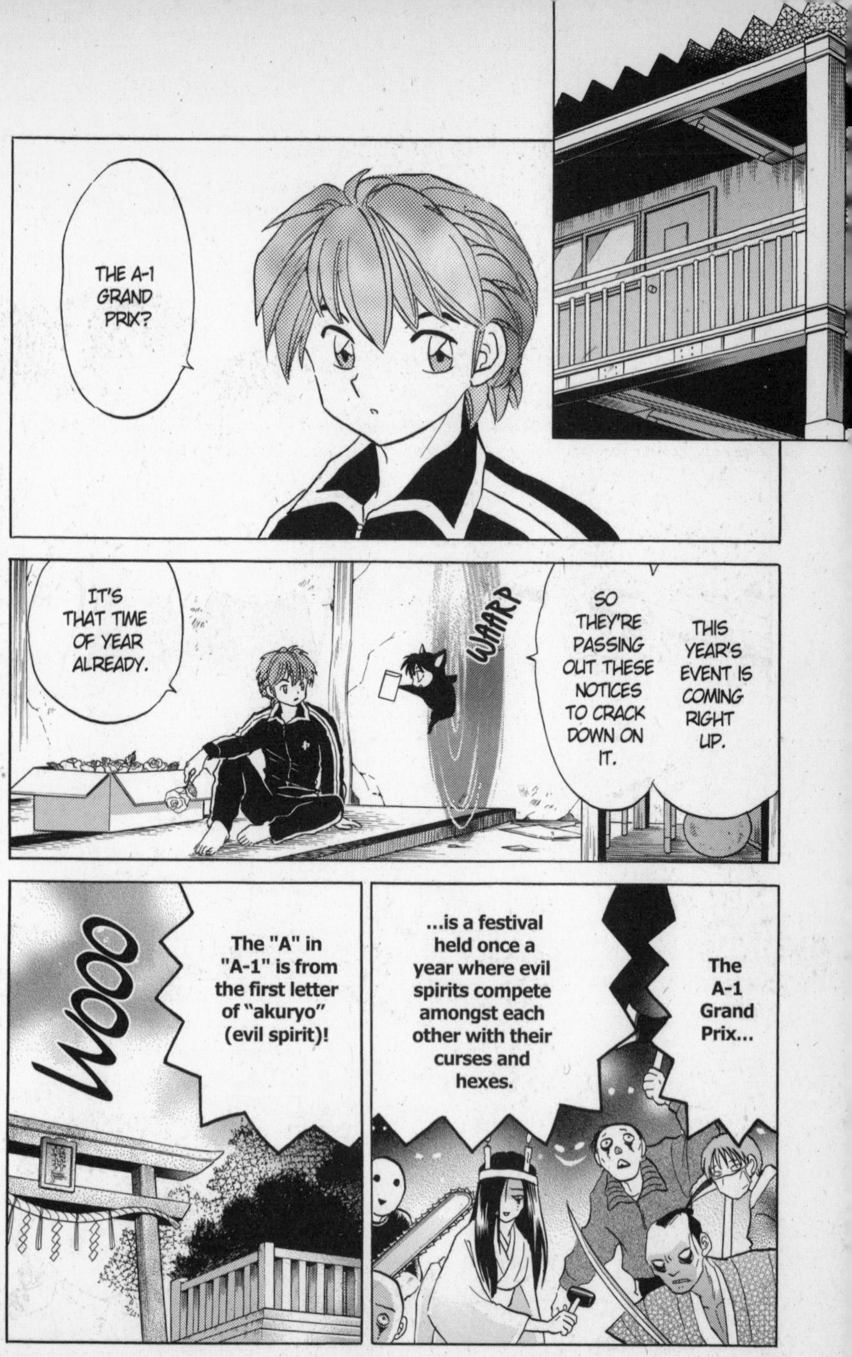
THE A-1 GRAND PRIX?
THIS YEAR'S EVENT IS COMING RIGHT UP.
SO THEY'RE PASSING OUT THESE NOTICES TO CRACK DOWN ON IT.
WAARP
IT'S THAT TIME OF YEAR ALREADY.
The A-1 Grand Prix...
...is a festival held once a year where evil spirits compete amongst each other with their curses and hexes.
The "A" in "A-1" is from the first letter of "akuryo" (evil spirit)!
WOOO

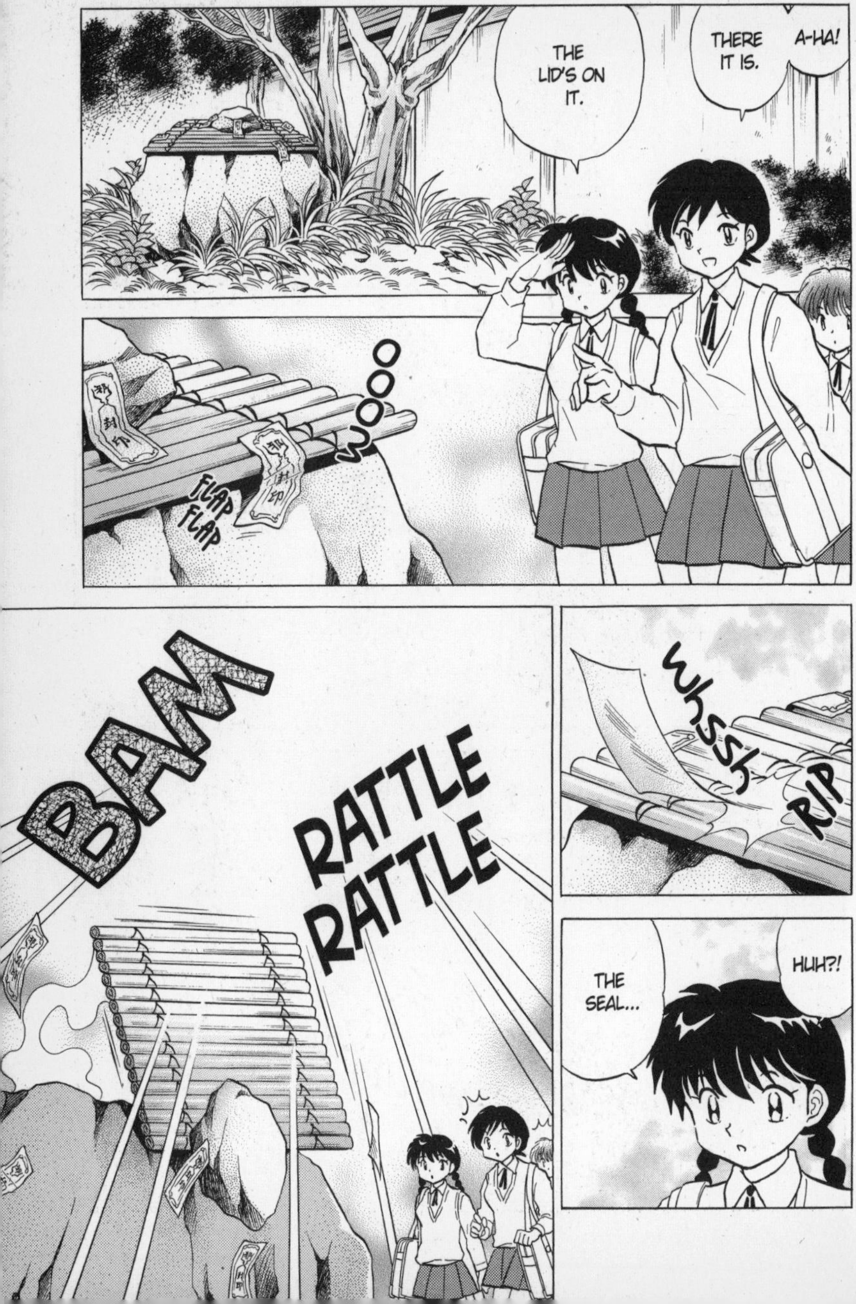
A-HA!
THERE IT IS.
THE LID'S ON IT.
WOOOO
FLAP FLAP
WHSSSH
RIP
HUH?!
THE SEAL...
BAM
RATTLE RATTLE

EEEK! SCARYYY!
THE LID CAME OFF!!
ZOOM
I AM ENTRY NUMBER 4, THE OCHIMUSHA.
I SHALL CURSE YOU.
THRUM THRUM THRUM

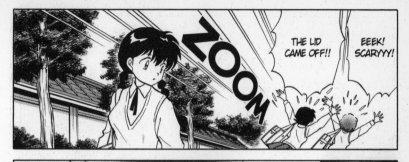

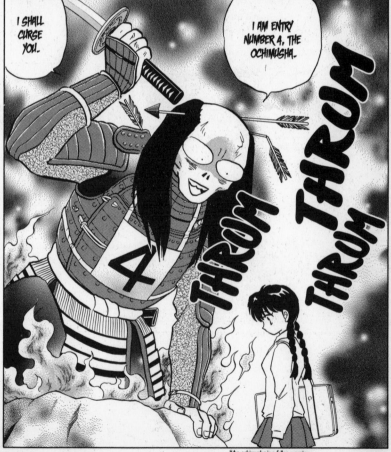

*An *ochimusha* is a fallen warrior

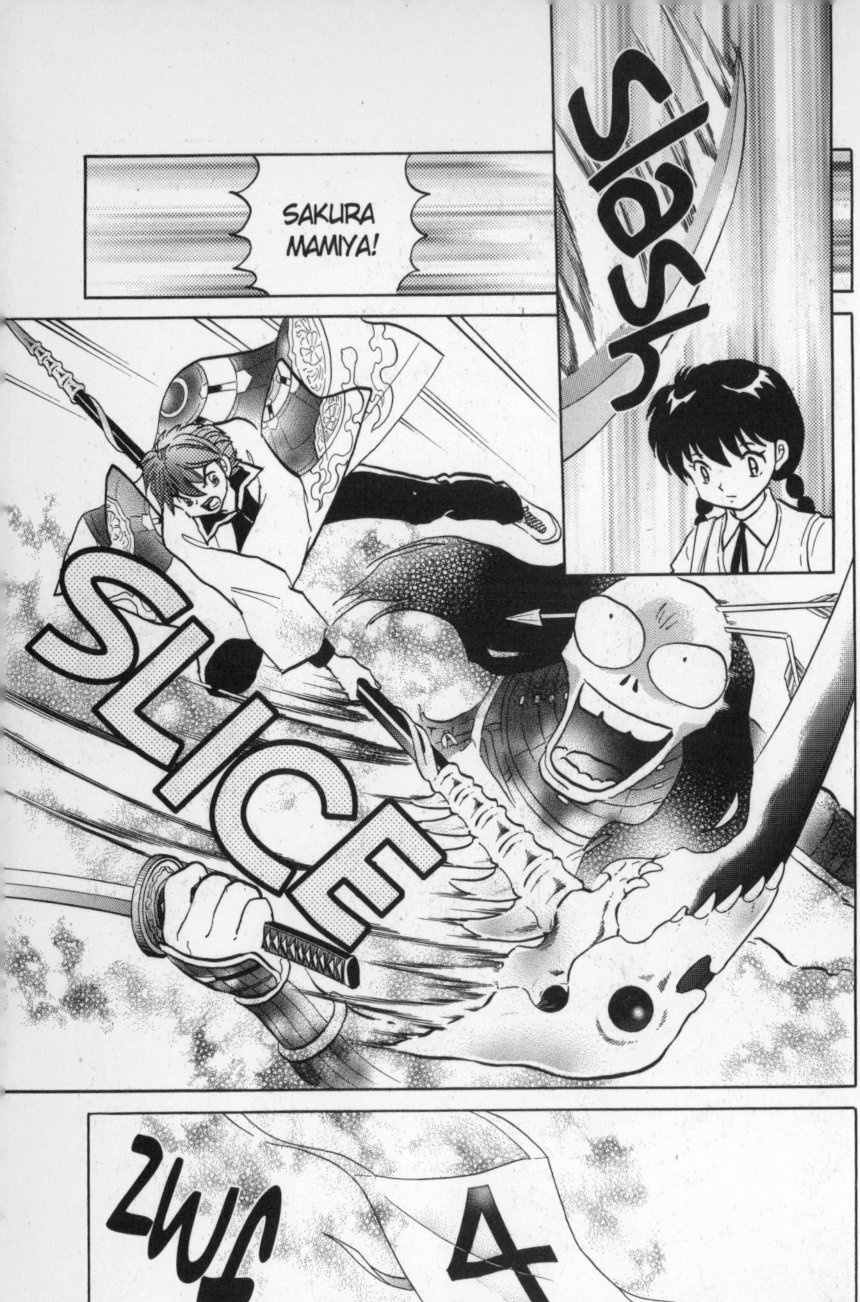
Slash
SAKURA MAMIYA!
SLICE

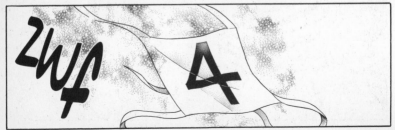

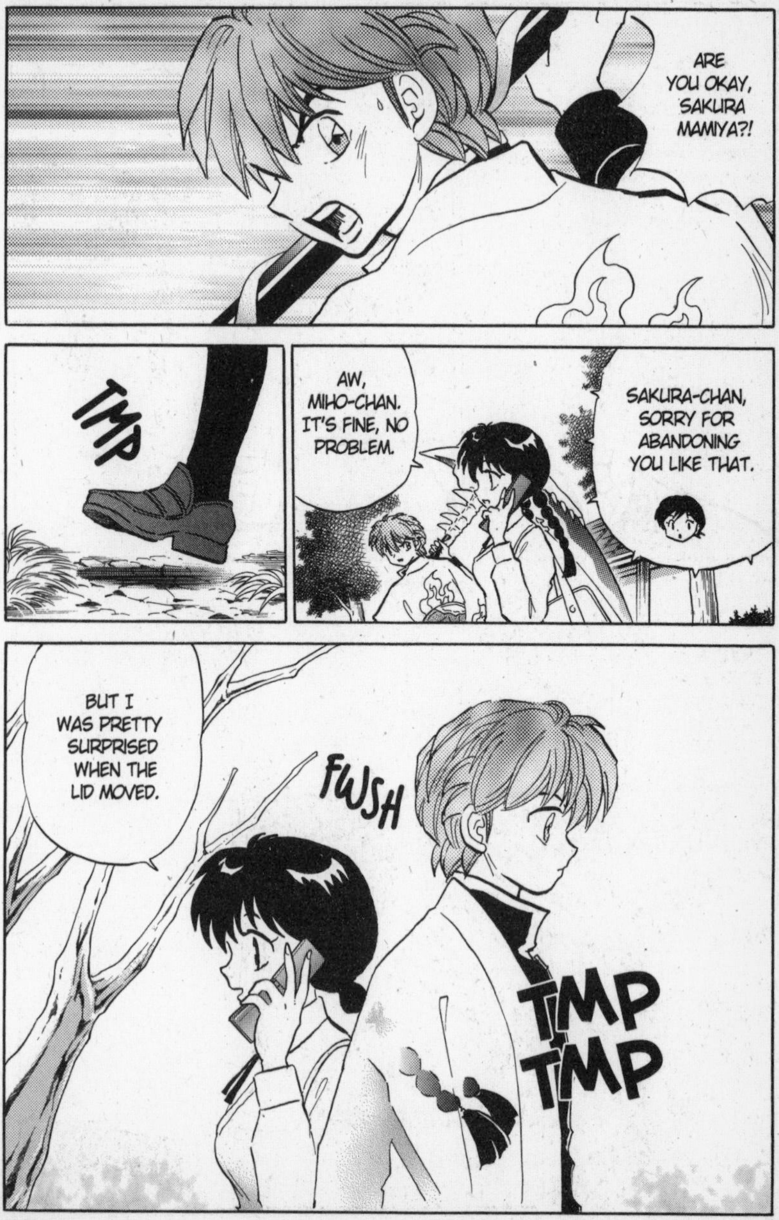
ARE YOU OKAY, SAKURA MAMIYA?!
SAKURA-CHAN, SORRY FOR ABANDONING YOU LIKE THAT.
AW, MIHO-CHAN. IT'S FINE, NO PROBLEM.
TMP
BUT I WAS PRETTY SURPRISED WHEN THE LID MOVED.
FWSH
TMP TMP

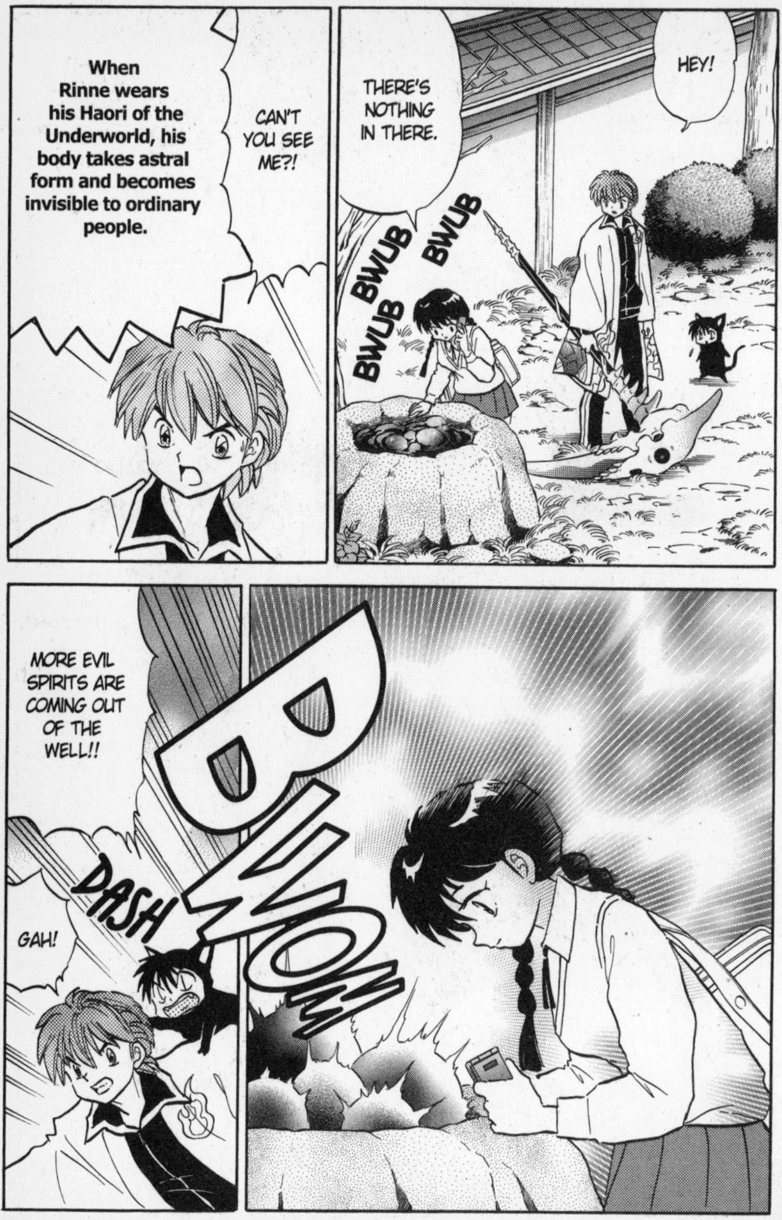
HEY!
THERE'S NOTHING IN THERE.
BWUB BWUB
BWUB BWUB
CAN'T YOU SEE ME?!
When Rinne wears his Haori of the Underworld, his body takes astral form and becomes invisible to ordinary people.
BWOW
MORE EVIL SPIRITS ARE COMING OUT OF THE WELL!!
DASH
GAH!

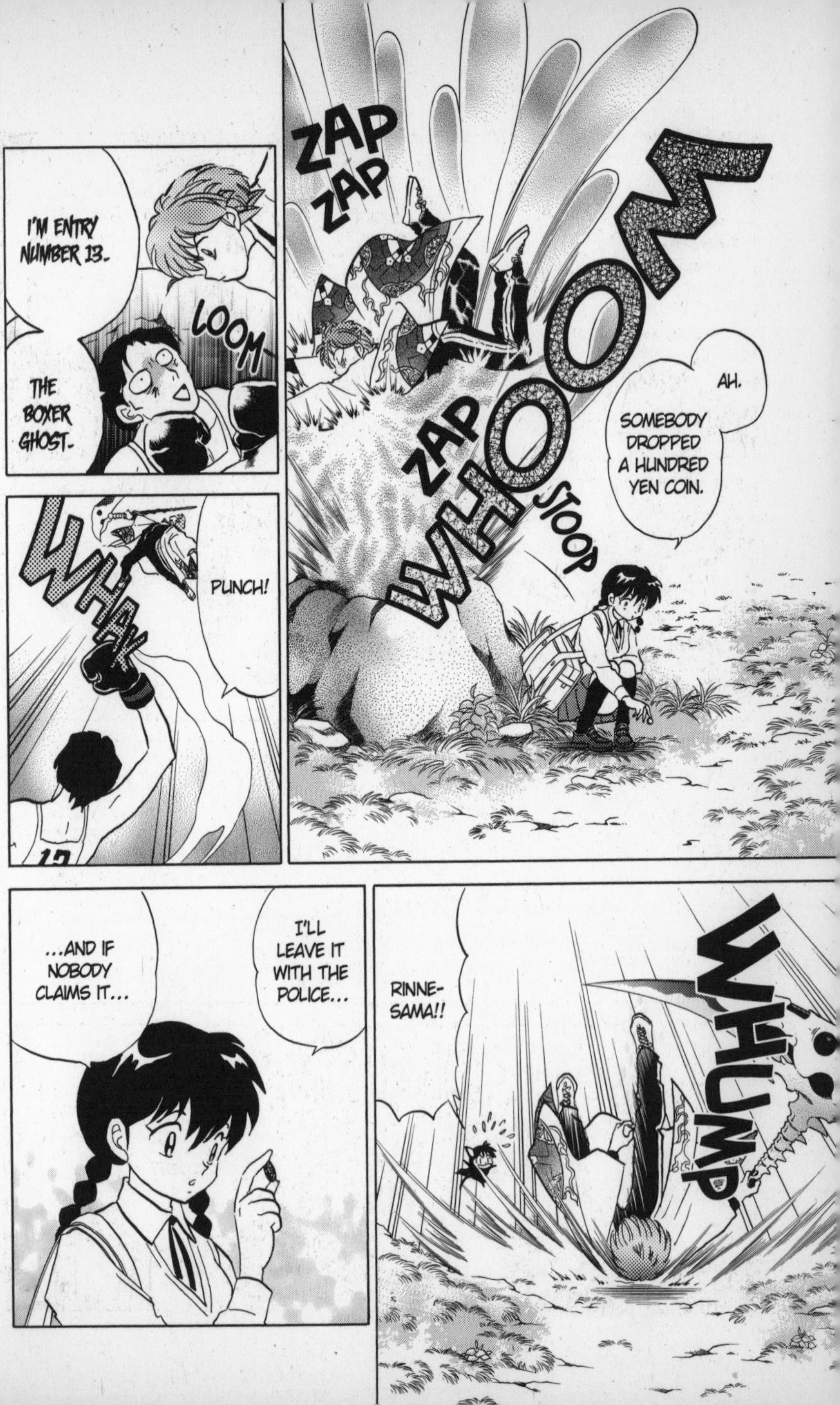
WHOOOOM
ZAP ZAP
ZAP
AH.
SOMEBODY DROPPED A HUNDRED YEN COIN.
ZAP ZAP
STOOP
I'M ENTRY NUMBER 13.
LOOM
THE BOXER GHOST.
WHAM
PUNCH!
RINNE-SAMA!!
WHUMP
I'LL LEAVE IT WITH THE POLICE...
...AND IF NOBODY CLAIMS IT...

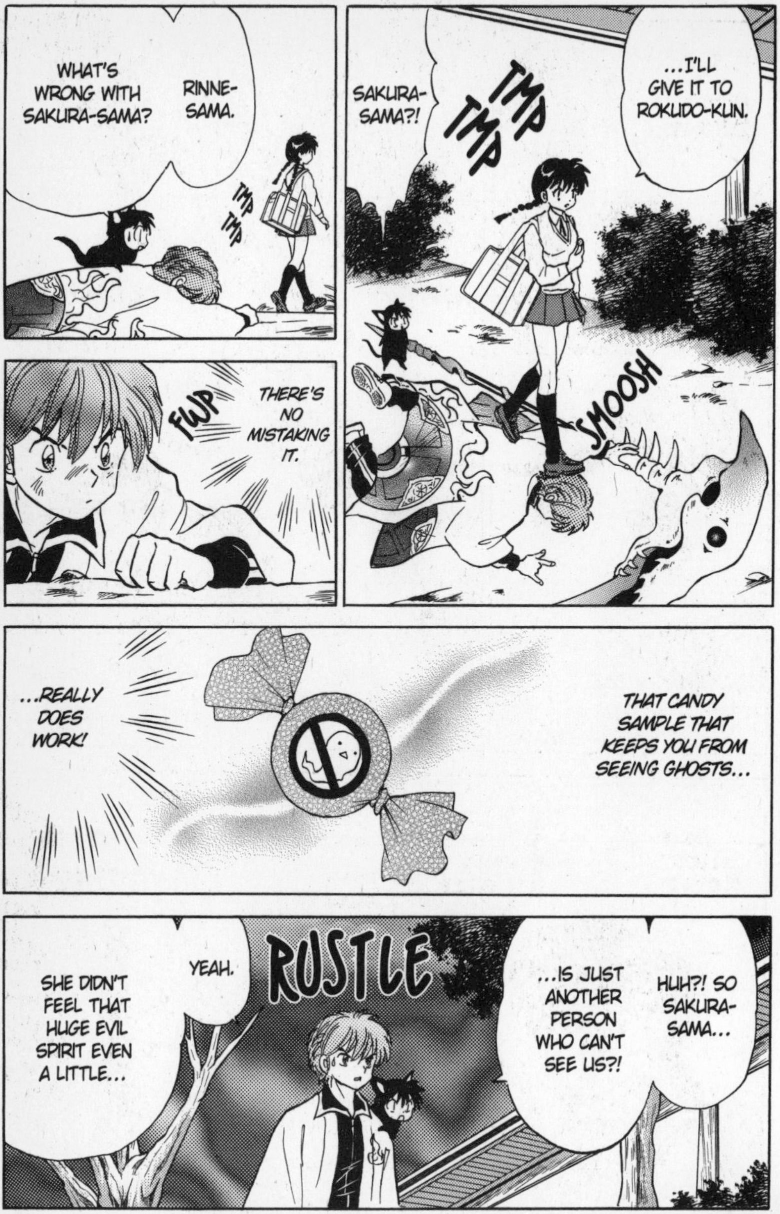
...I'LL GIVE IT TO ROKUDO-KUN.
TMP TMP
SAKURA-SAMA?!
SMOOSH
RINNE-SAMA.
WHAT'S WRONG WITH SAKURA-SAMA?
TMP TMP
THERE'S NO MISTAKING IT.
FWP
THAT CANDY SAMPLE THAT KEEPS YOU FROM SEEING GHOSTS...
...REALLY DOES WORK!
HUH?! SO SAKURA-SAMA...
...IS JUST ANOTHER PERSON WHO CAN'T SEE US?!
RUSTLE
YEAH.
SHE DIDN'T FEEL THAT HUGE EVIL SPIRIT EVEN A LITTLE...

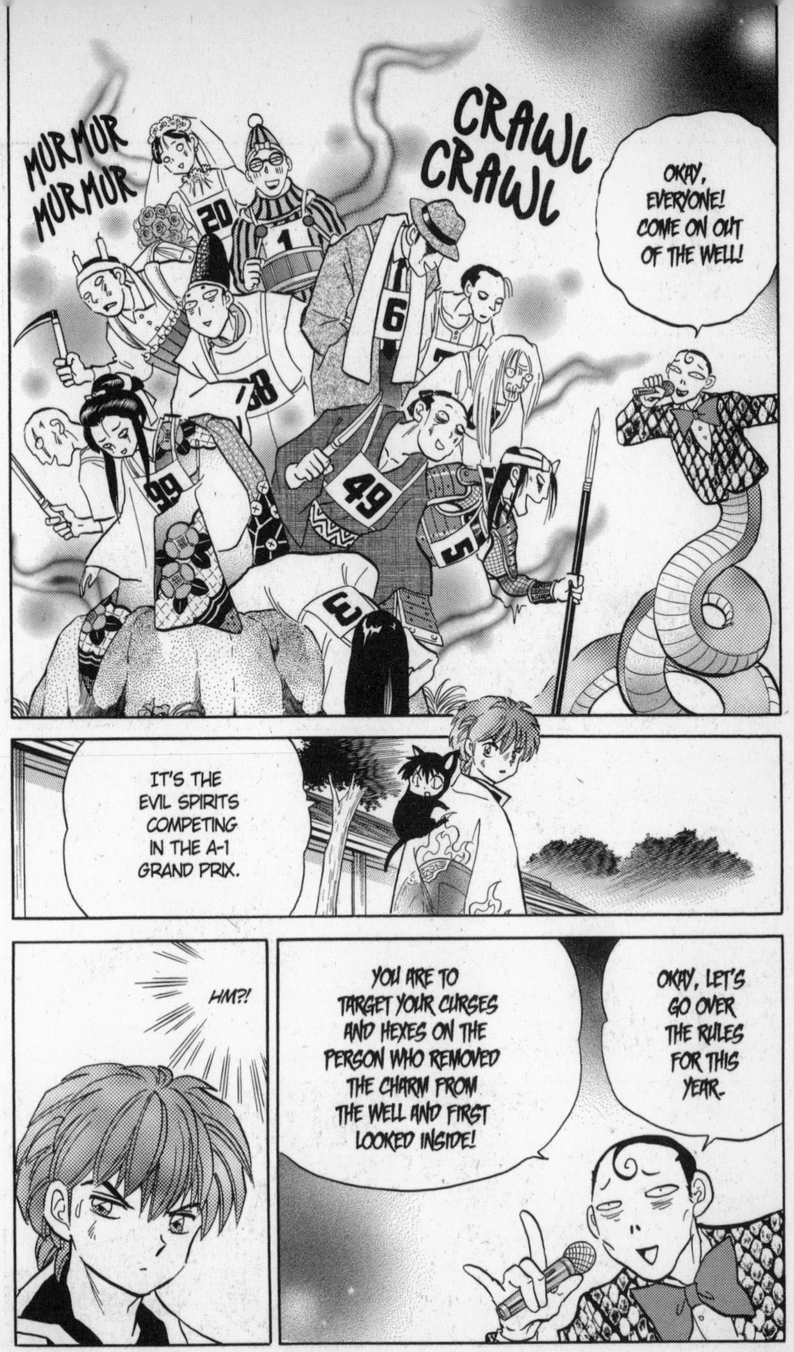
OKAY, EVERYONE! COME ON OUT OF THE WELL!
CRAWL CRAWL
MURMOR MURMOR
IT'S THE EVIL SPIRITS COMPETING IN THE A-1 GRAND PRIX.
OKAY, LET'S GO OVER THE RULES FOR THIS YEAR.
YOU ARE TO TARGET YOUR CURSES AND HEXES ON THE PERSON WHO REMOVED THE CHARM FROM THE WELL AND FIRST LOOKED INSIDE!
HM?!

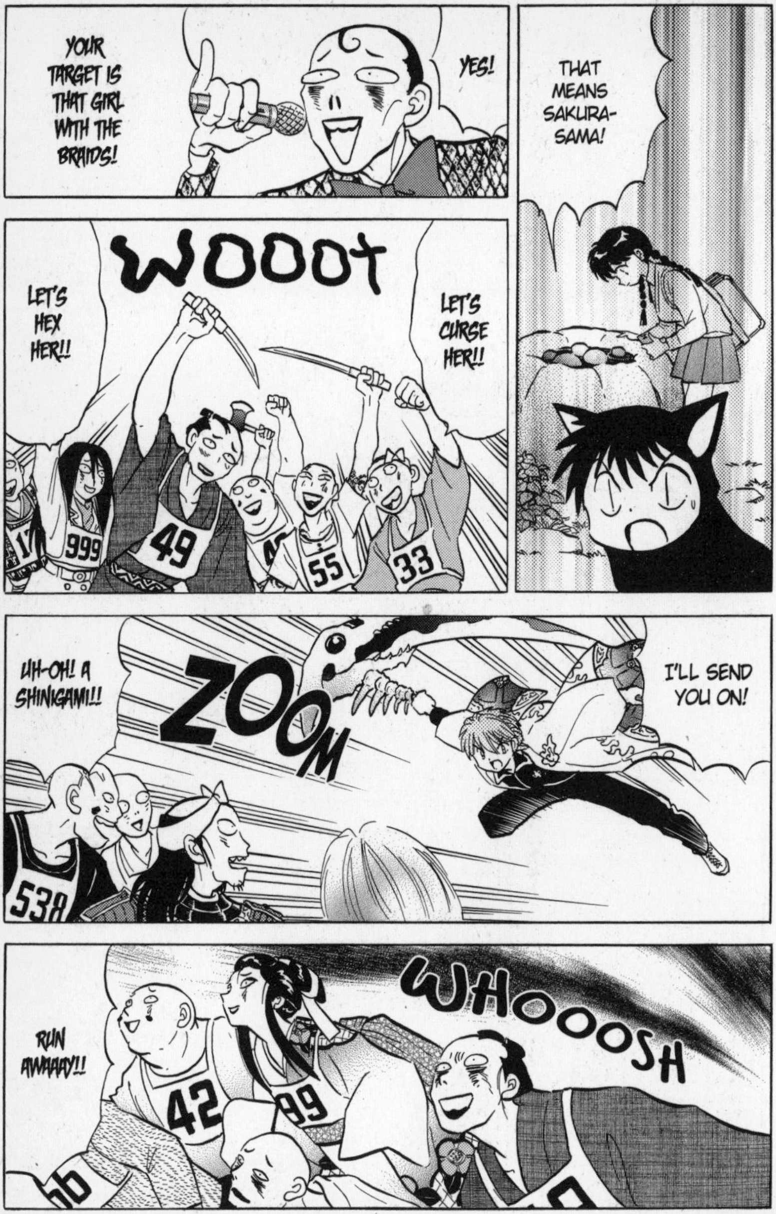
THAT MEANS SAKURA-SAMA!
YOUR TARGET IS THAT GIRL WITH THE BRAIDS!
YES!
LET'S CURSE HER!!
WOOOT
LET'S HEX HER!!
999
49
55
33
I'LL SEND YOU ON!
ZOOM
UH-OH! A SHINIGAMI!!
538
WHOOOSH
RUN AWAAAY!!
42
99

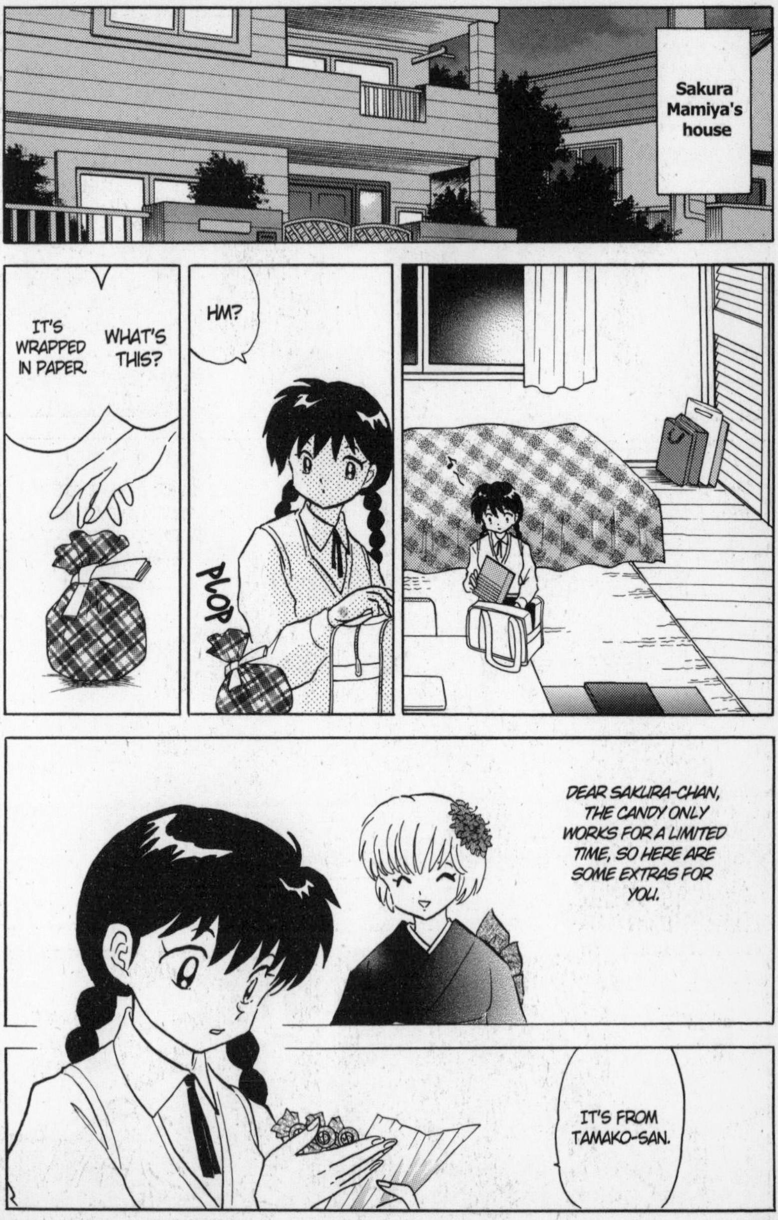
Sakura Mamiya's house
HM?
PLOP
WHAT'S THIS?
IT'S WRAPPED IN PAPER.
DEAR SAKURA-CHAN, THE CANDY ONLY WORKS FOR A LIMITED TIME, SO HERE ARE SOME EXTRAS FOR YOU.
IT'S FROM TAMAKO-SAN.

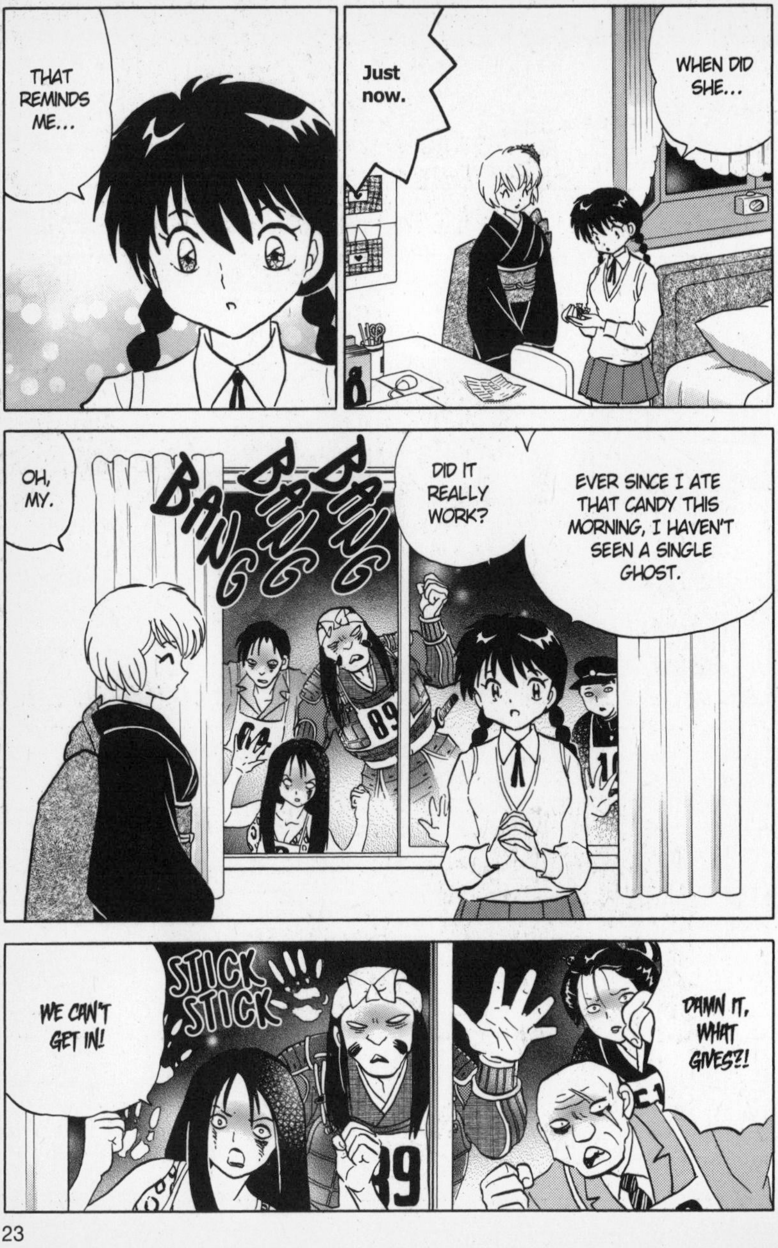
WHEN DID SHE...
Just now.
THAT REMINDS ME...
EVER SINCE I ATE THAT CANDY THIS MORNING, I HAVEN'T SEEN A SINGLE GHOST.
DID IT REALLY WORK?
BANG BANG BANG
OH, MY.
DAMN IT, WHAT GIVES?!
STICK STICK
WE CAN'T GET IN!

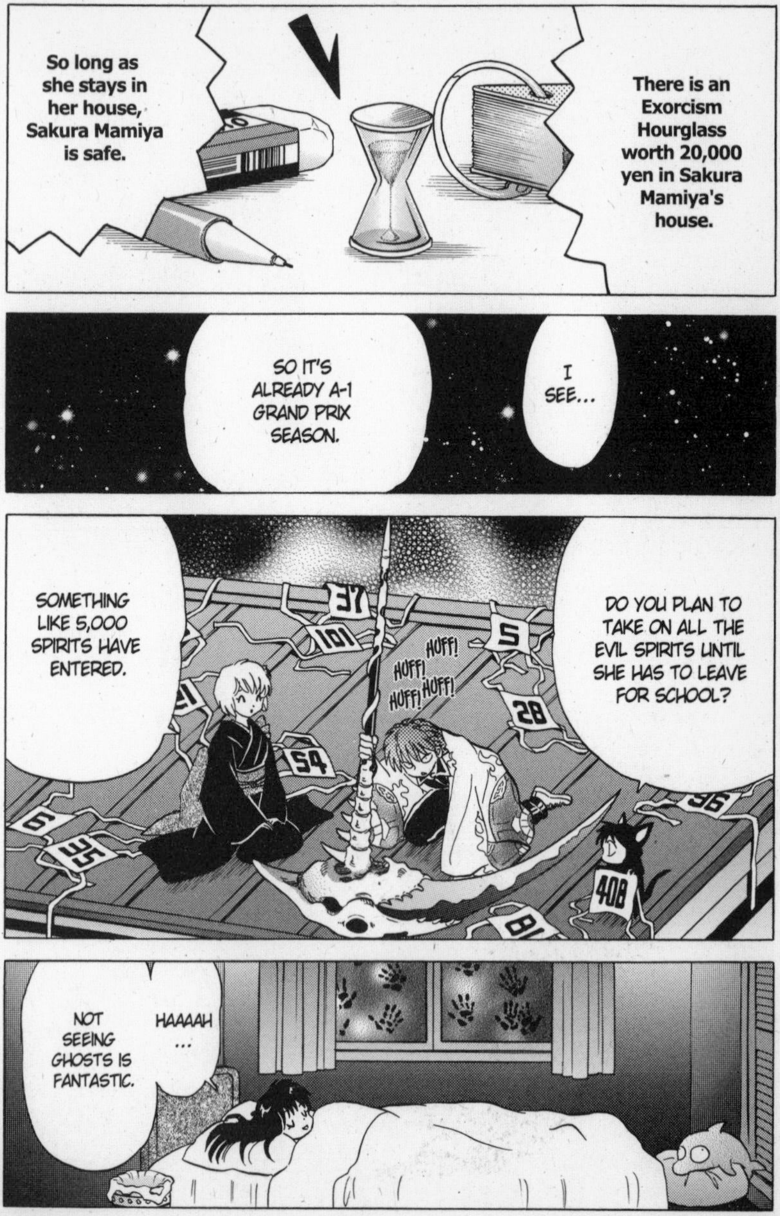

There is an Exorcism Hourglass worth 20,000 yen in Sakura Mamiya's house.
So long as she stays in her house, Sakura Mamiya is safe.
I SEE...
SO IT'S ALREADY A-1 GRAND PRIX SEASON.
DO YOU PLAN TO TAKE ON ALL THE EVIL SPIRITS UNTIL SHE HAS TO LEAVE FOR SCHOOL?
HUFF! HUFF! HUFF! HUFF!
SOMETHING LIKE 5,000 SPIRITS HAVE ENTERED.
HAAAAH ...
NOT SEEING GHOSTS IS FANTASTIC.

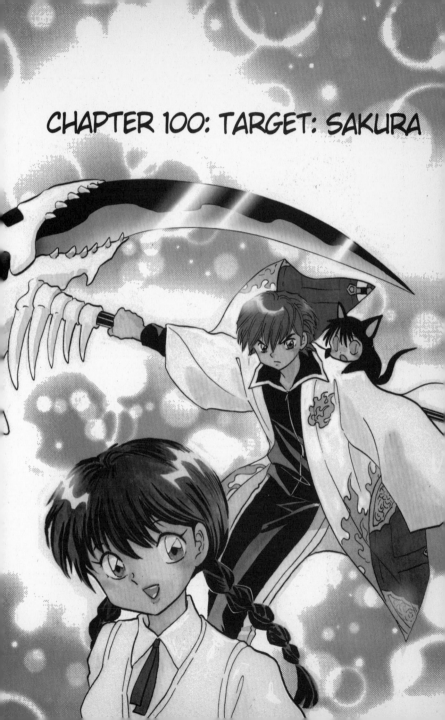

# CHAPTER 100: TARGET: SAKURA

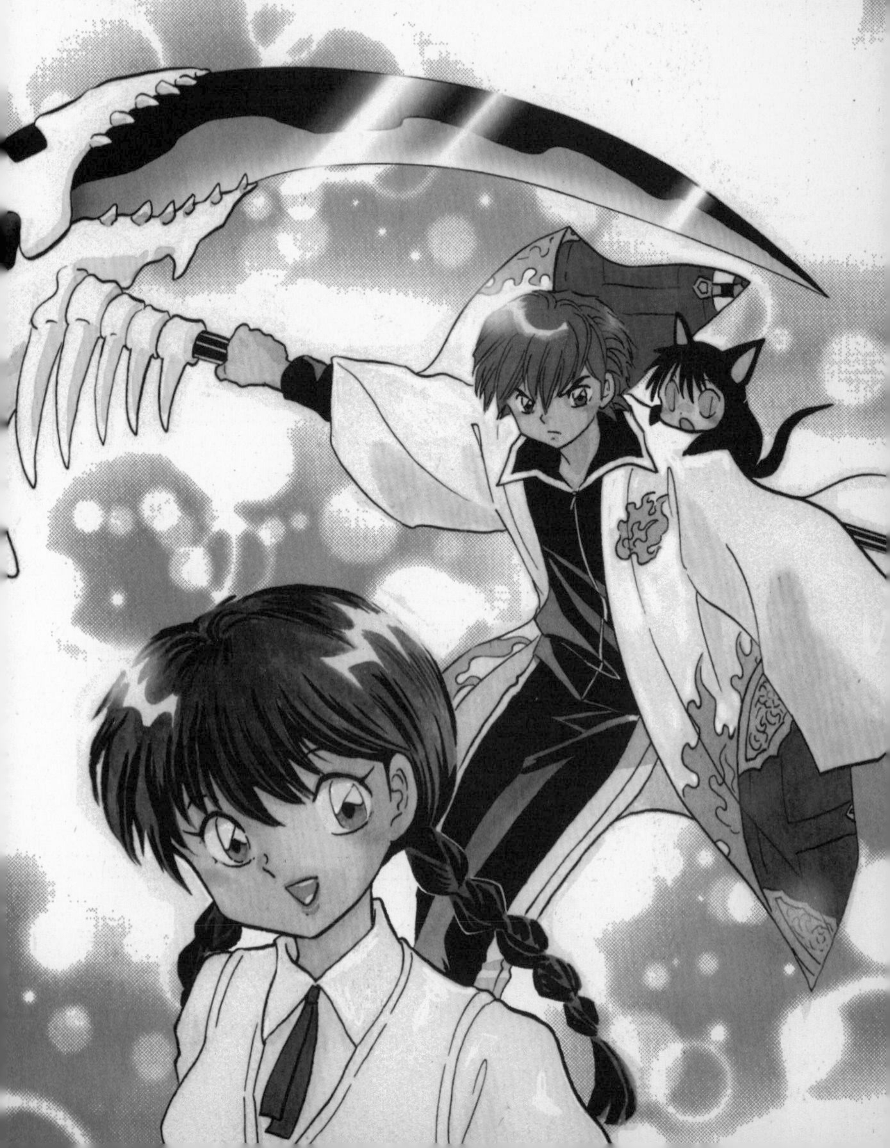

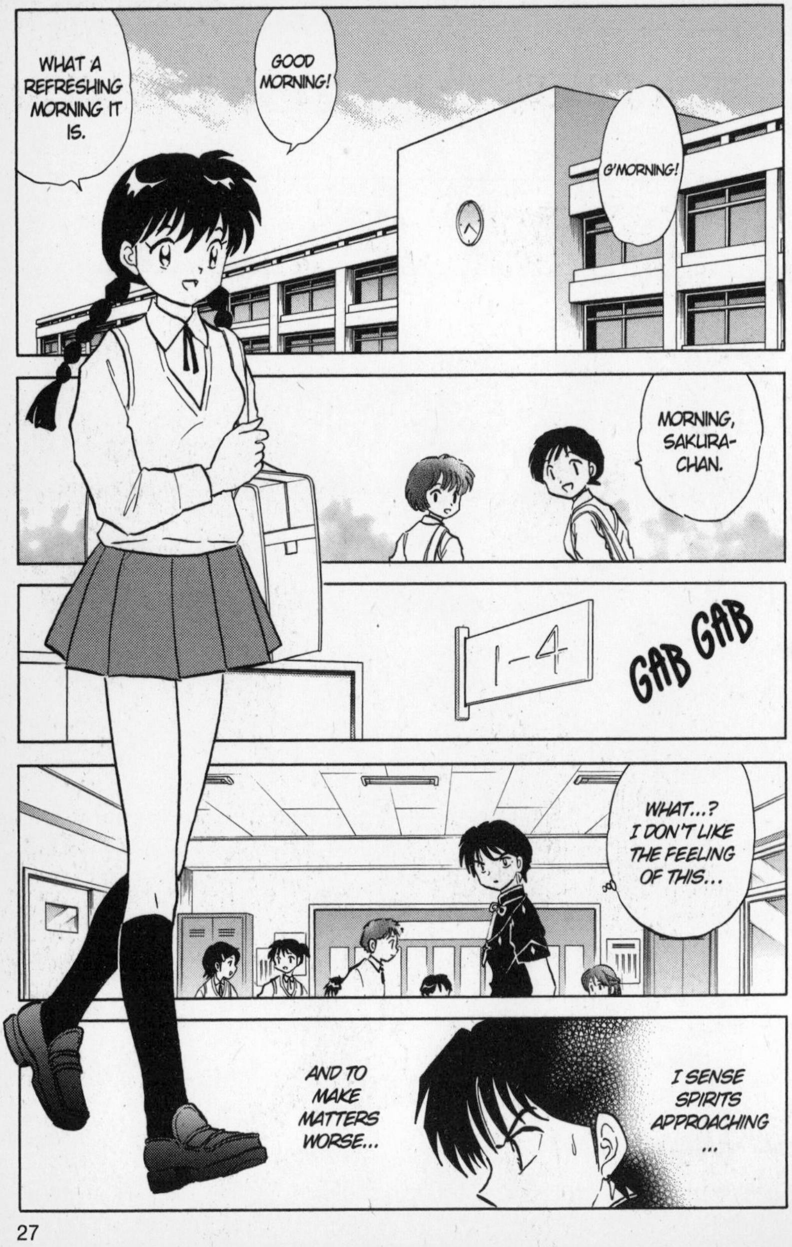
G'MORNING!
GOOD MORNING!
WHAT A REFRESHING MORNING IT IS.
MORNING, SAKURA-CHAN.
1-4
GAB GAB
WHAT...? I DON'T LIKE THE FEELING OF THIS...
I SENSE SPIRITS APPROACHING ...
AND TO MAKE MATTERS WORSE...

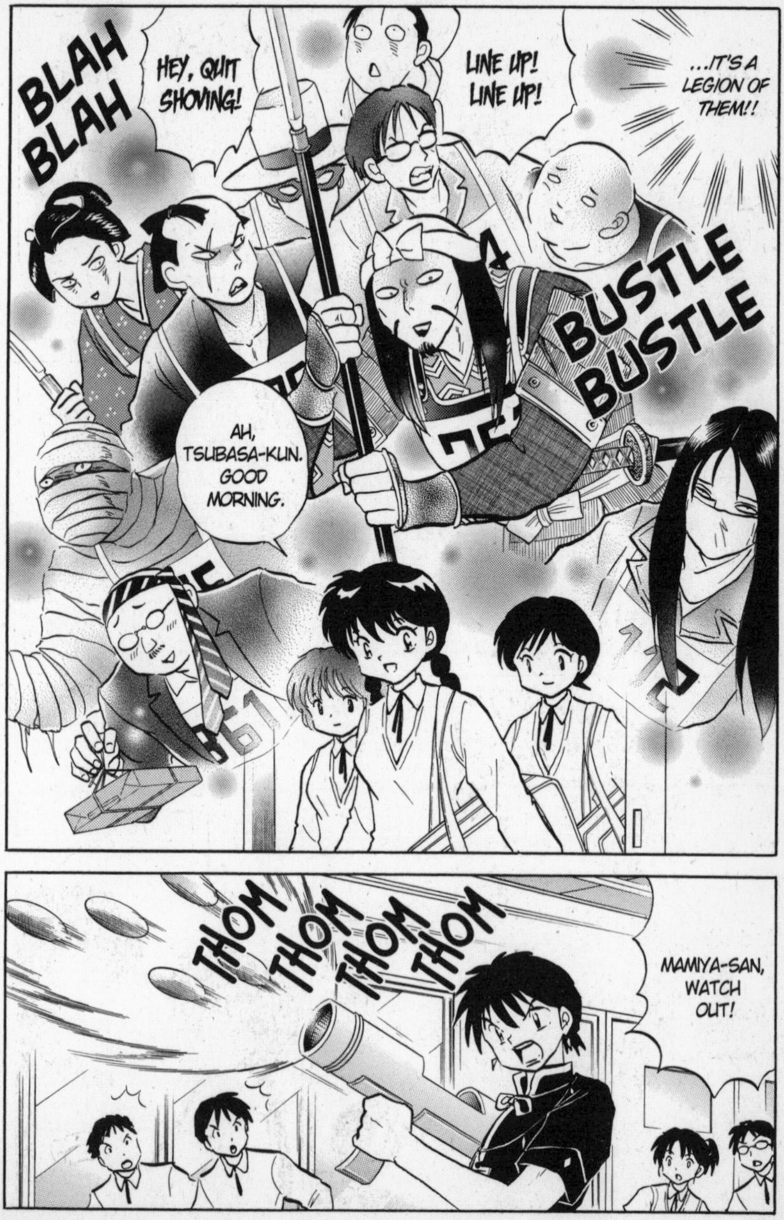
...IT'S A LEGION OF THEM!!
LINE UP! LINE UP!
HEY, QUIT SHOVING!
BLAH BLAH
BUSTLE BUSTLE
AH, TSUBASA-KUN. GOOD MORNING.
MAMIYA-SAN, WATCH OUT!
THOM THOM THOM THOM

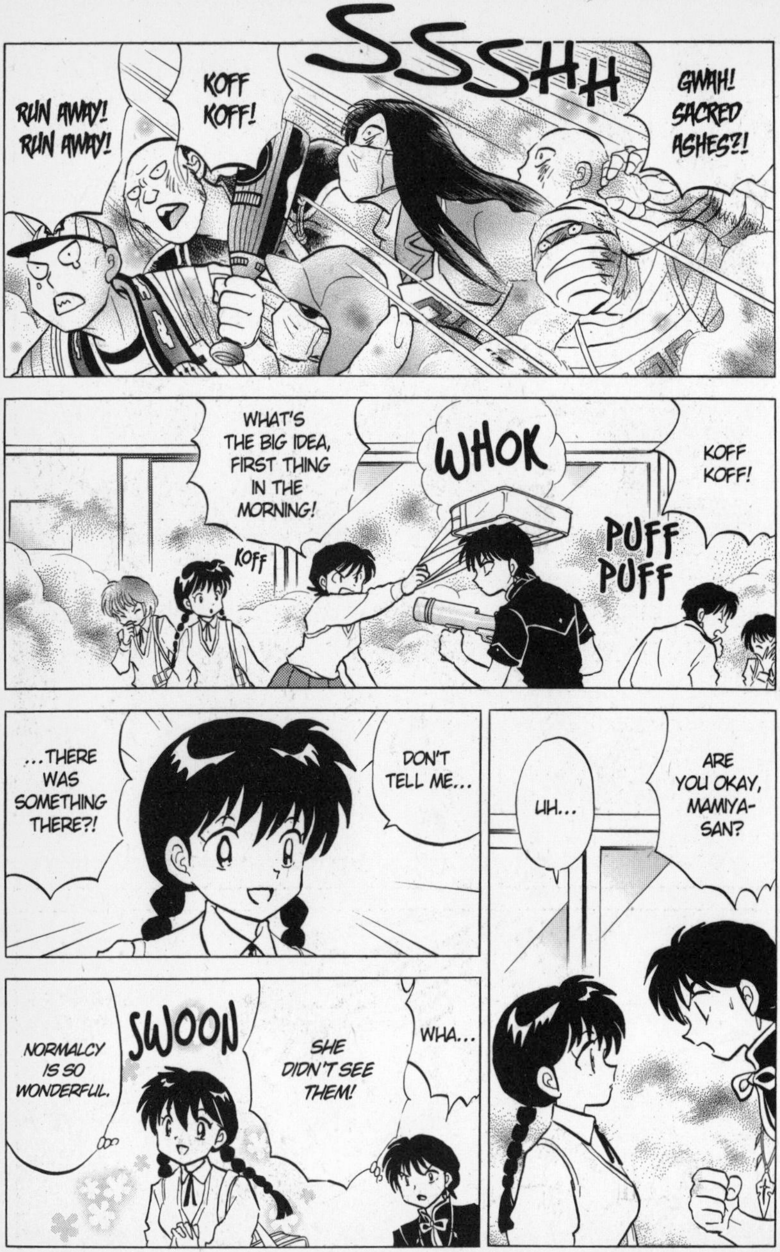
GWAH! SACRED ASHES?!
SSSHH
KOFF KOFF!
RUN AWAY! RUN AWAY!
KOFF KOFF!
PUFF PUFF
WHOK
WHAT'S THE BIG IDEA, FIRST THING IN THE MORNING!
KOFF
ARE YOU OKAY, MAMIYA-SAN?
UH...
DON'T TELL ME...
...THERE WAS SOMETHING THERE?!
WHA...
SHE DIDN'T SEE THEM!
SWOON
NORMALCY IS SO WONDERFUL.

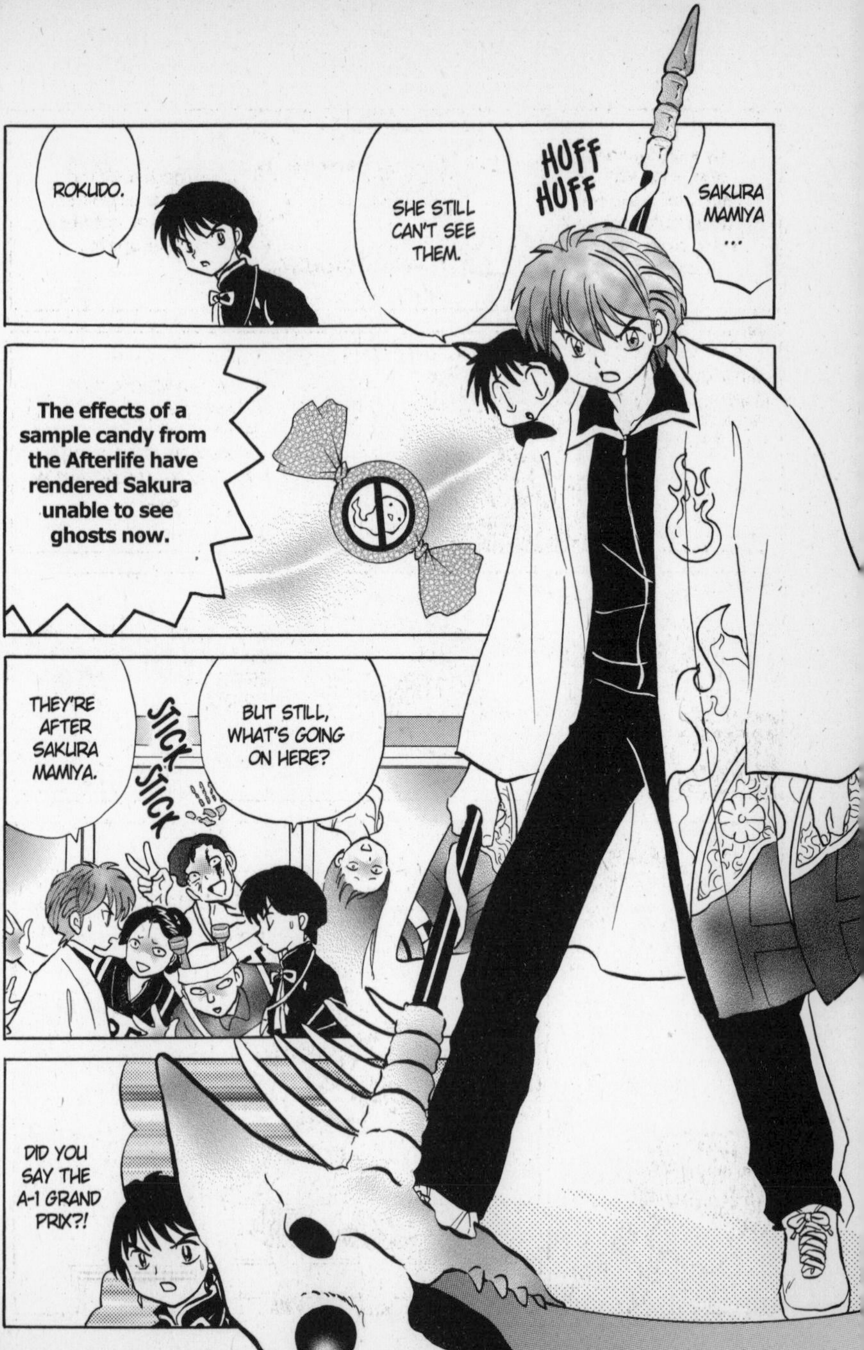
SAKURA MAMIYA ...
HUFF HUFF
SHE STILL CAN'T SEE THEM.
ROKUDO.
The effects of a sample candy from the Afterlife have rendered Sakura unable to see ghosts now.
BUT STILL, WHAT'S GOING ON HERE?
STICK STICK
THEY'RE AFTER SAKURA MAMIYA.
DID YOU SAY THE A-1 GRAND PRIX?!

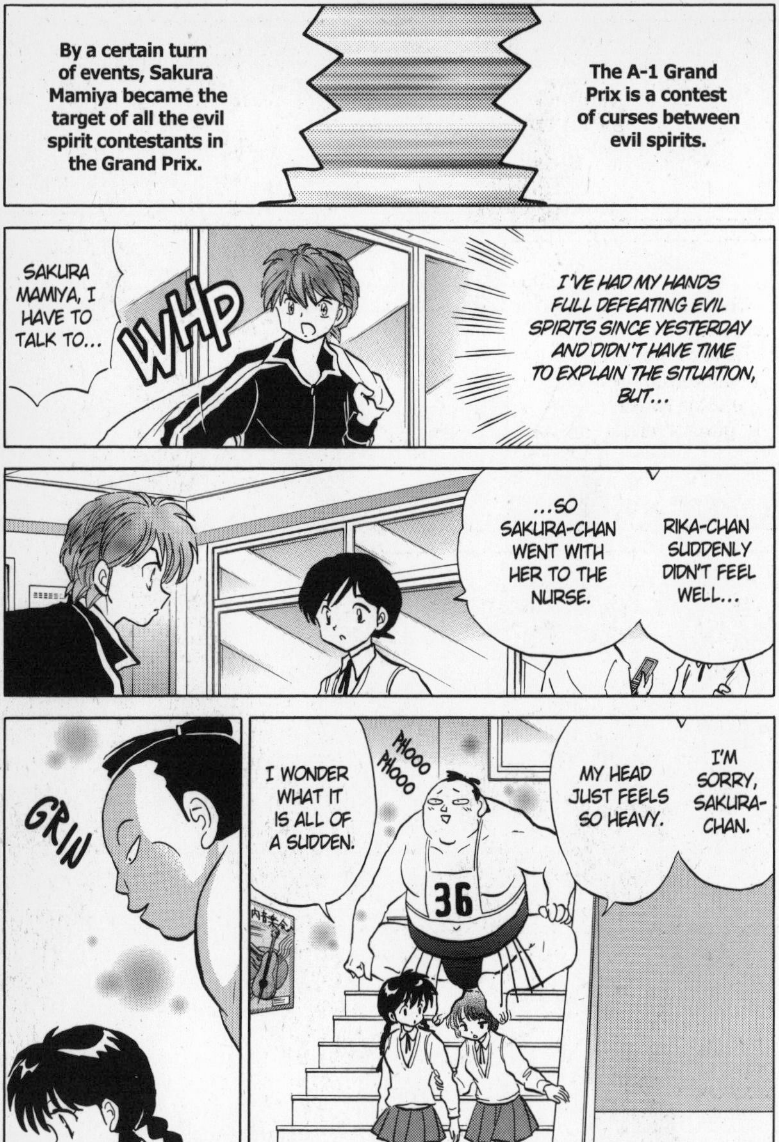
The A-1 Grand Prix is a contest of curses between evil spirits.
By a certain turn of events, Sakura Mamiya became the target of all the evil spirit contestants in the Grand Prix.
I'VE HAD MY HANDS FULL DEFEATING EVIL SPIRITS SINCE YESTERDAY AND DIDN'T HAVE TIME TO EXPLAIN THE SITUATION, BUT...
WHP
SAKURA MAMIYA, I HAVE TO TALK TO...
RIKA-CHAN SUDDENLY DIDN'T FEEL WELL...
...SO SAKURA-CHAN WENT WITH HER TO THE NURSE.
I'M SORRY, SAKURA-CHAN.
MY HEAD JUST FEELS SO HEAVY.
PHOOO PHOOO
I WONDER WHAT IT IS ALL OF A SUDDEN.
36
GRIN

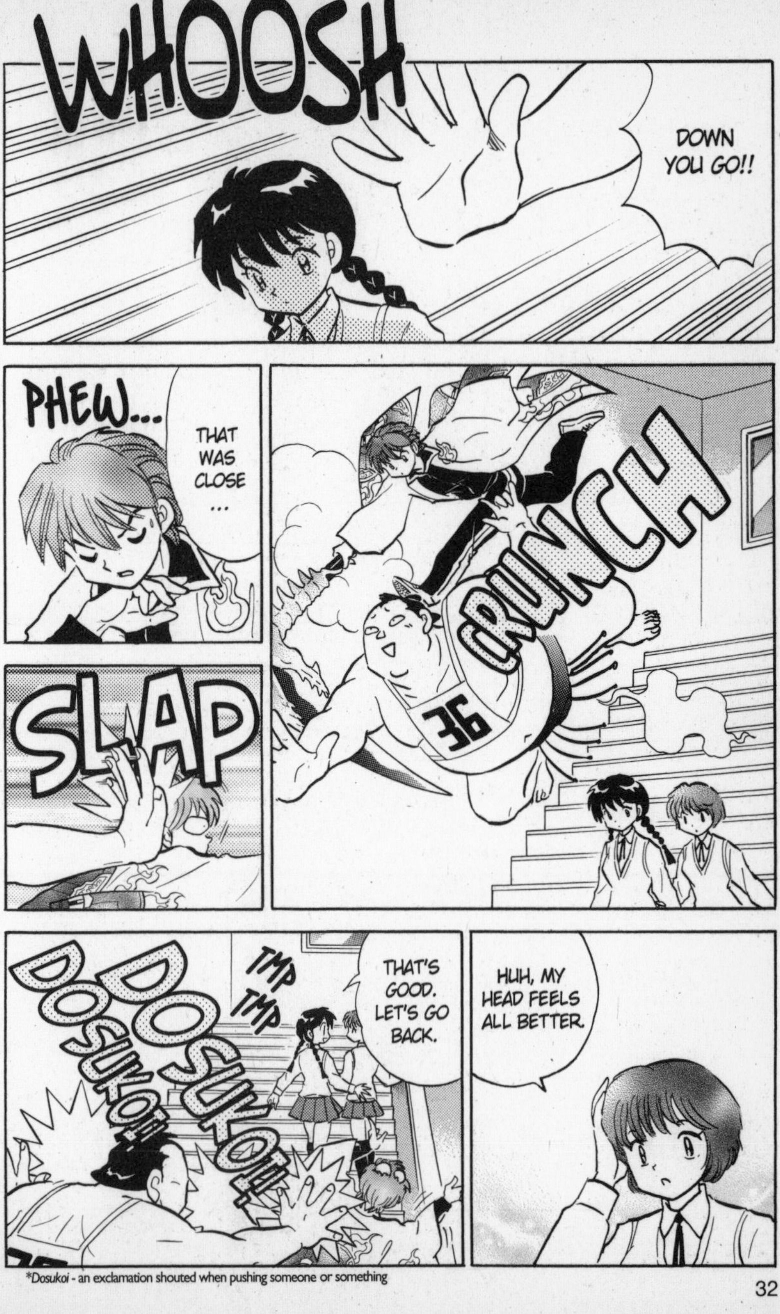
WHOOSH
DOWN YOU GO!!
CRUNCH
PHEW...
THAT WAS CLOSE ...
SLAP
HUH, MY HEAD FEELS ALL BETTER.
THAT'S GOOD. LET'S GO BACK.
TMP TMP
DOSUKOI!!
DOSUKOI!!

*Dosukoi - an exclamation shouted when pushing someone or something

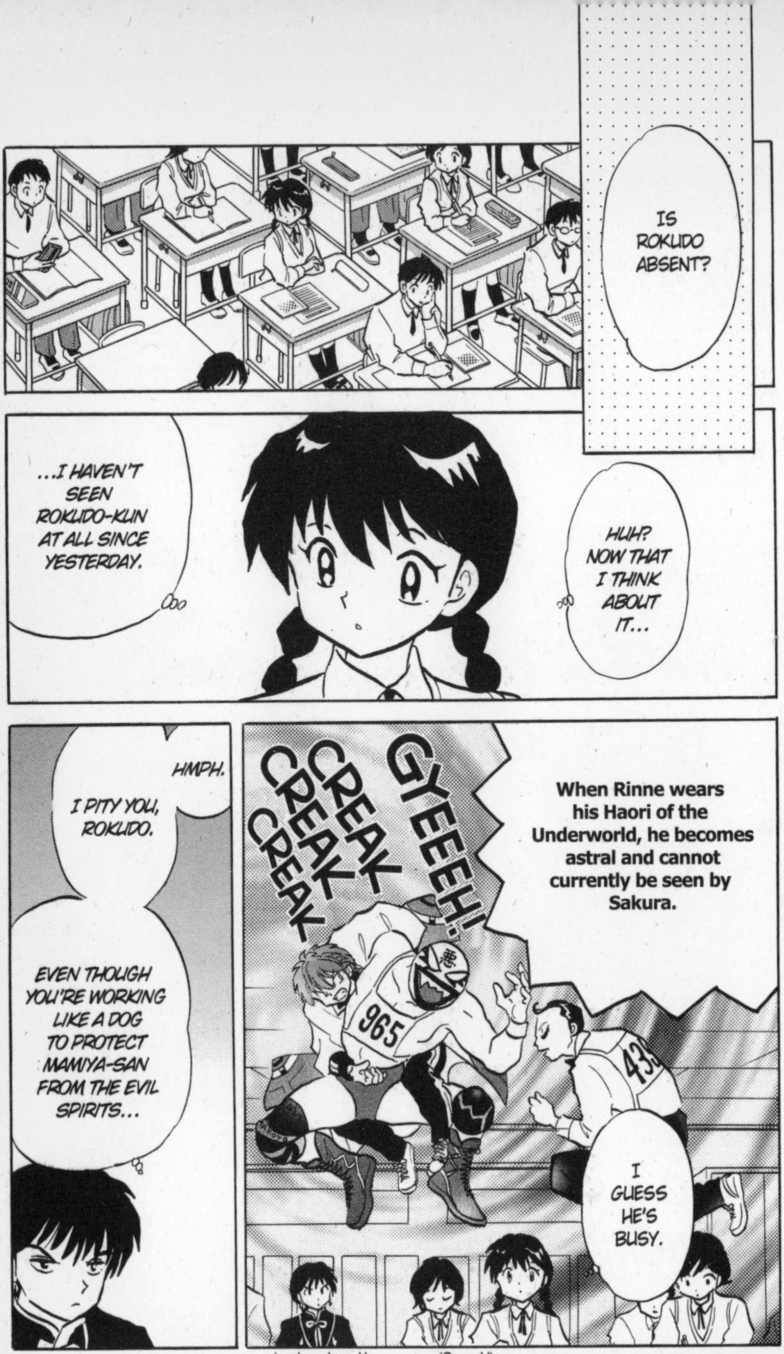
IS ROKUDO ABSENT?
HUH? NOW THAT I THINK ABOUT IT...
...I HAVEN'T SEEN ROKUDO-KUN AT ALL SINCE YESTERDAY.
GYEEEEH!
CREAK CREAK CREAK
When Rinne wears his Haori of the Underworld, he becomes astral and cannot currently be seen by Sakura.
965
I GUESS HE'S BUSY.
HMPH.
I PITY YOU, ROKUDO.
EVEN THOUGH YOU'RE WORKING LIKE A DOG TO PROTECT MAMIYA-SAN FROM THE EVIL SPIRITS...

(creak creak creak) (Gyeeeh!)

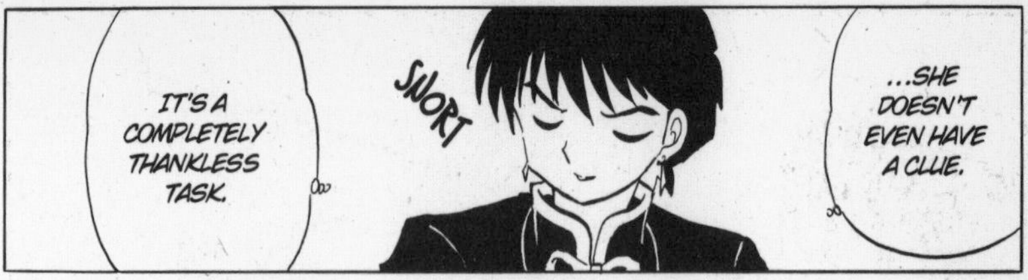
...SHE DOESN'T EVEN HAVE A CLUE.
SNORT
IT'S A COMPLETELY THANKLESS TASK.

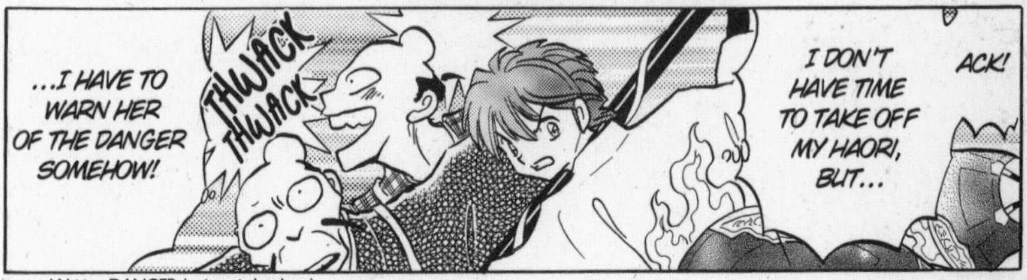
ACK!
I DON'T HAVE TIME TO TAKE OFF MY HAORI, BUT...
THWACK THWACK
...I HAVE TO WARN HER OF THE DANGER SOMEHOW!

Writing: DANGER (written in katakana)

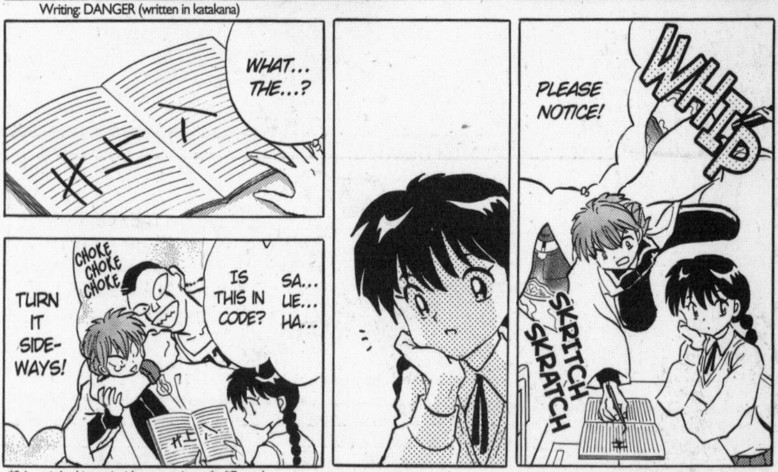
PLEASE NOTICE!
WHIP
SKRITCH SKRATCH
WHAT... THE...?
SA... LIE... HA...
IS THIS IN CODE?
CHOKE CHOKE CHOKE
TURN IT SIDEWAYS!

*Sakura is looking at it sideways so it reads differently

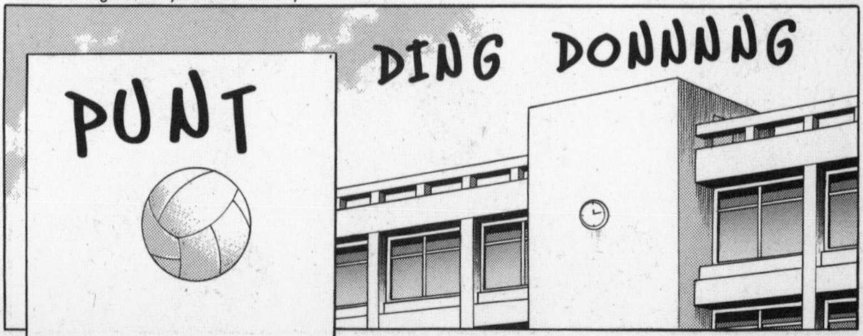
DING DONNNNG
PUNT

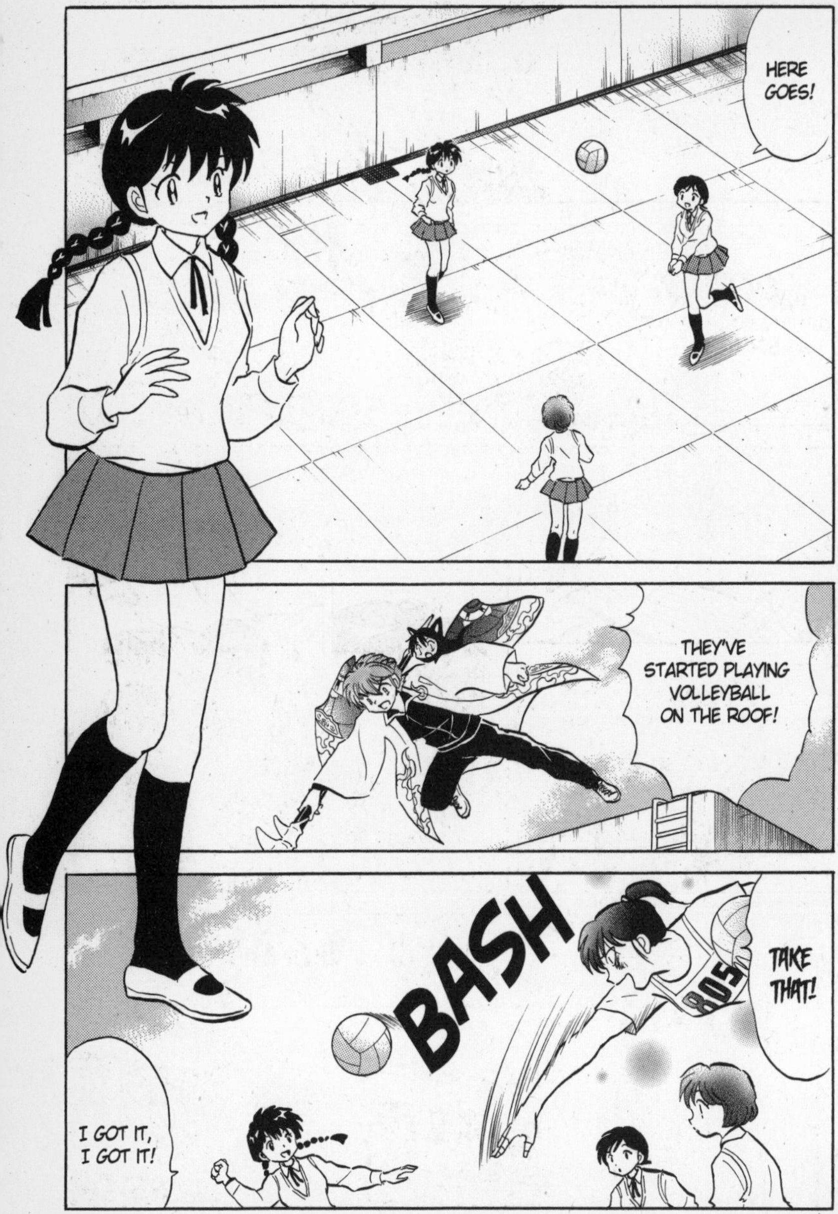
HERE GOES!
THEY'VE STARTED PLAYING VOLLEYBALL ON THE ROOF!
TAKE THAT!
BASH
I GOT IT, I GOT IT!

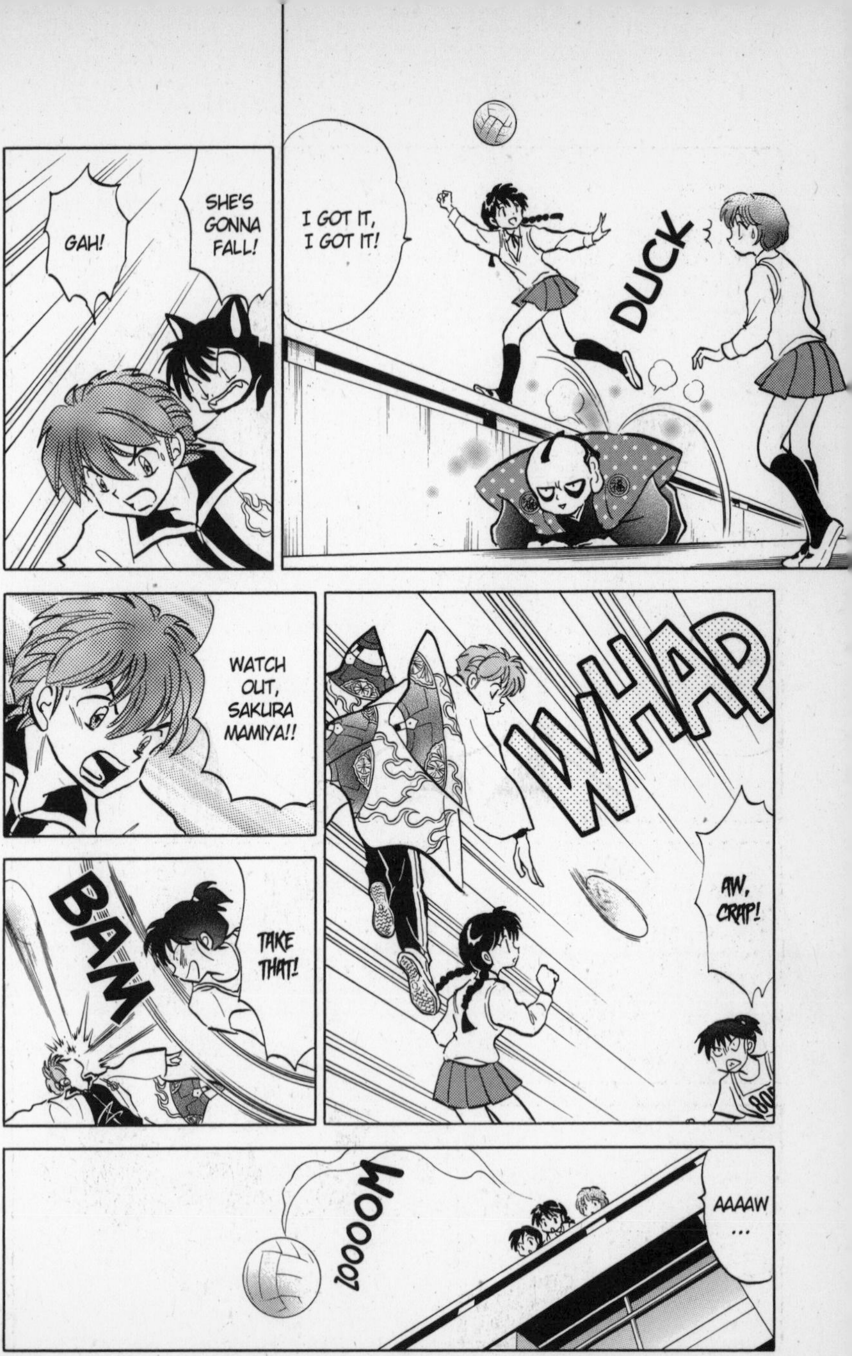
I GOT IT, I GOT IT!
DUCK
SHE'S GONNA FALL!
GAH!
WHAP
AW, CRAP!
WATCH OUT, SAKURA MAMIYA!!
TAKE THAT!
BAM
AAAAW ...
WOOOO!

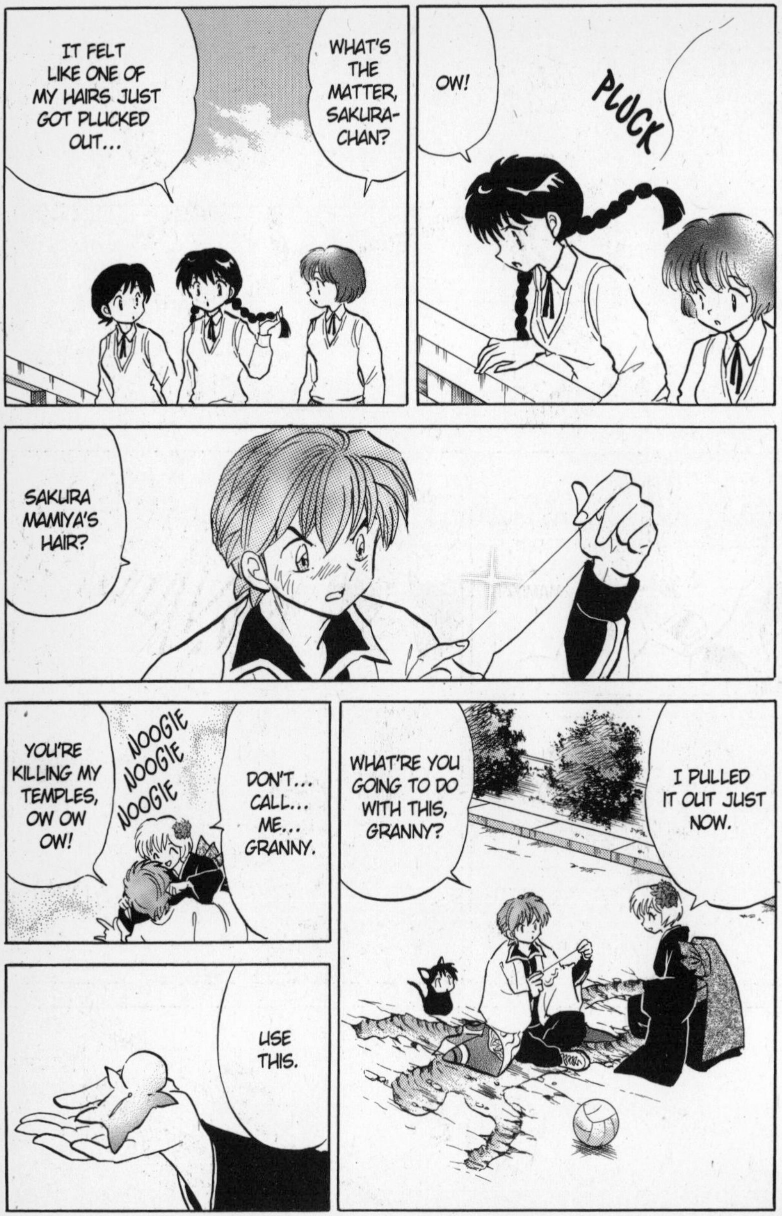
PLUCK
OW!
WHAT'S THE MATTER, SAKURA-CHAN?
IT FELT LIKE ONE OF MY HAIRS JUST GOT PLUCKED OUT...
SAKURA MAMIYA'S HAIR?
I PULLED IT OUT JUST NOW.
WHAT'RE YOU GOING TO DO WITH THIS, GRANNY?
DON'T... CALL... ME... GRANNY.
NOOGIE NOOGIE NOOGIE
YOU'RE KILLING MY TEMPLES, OW OW OW!
USE THIS.

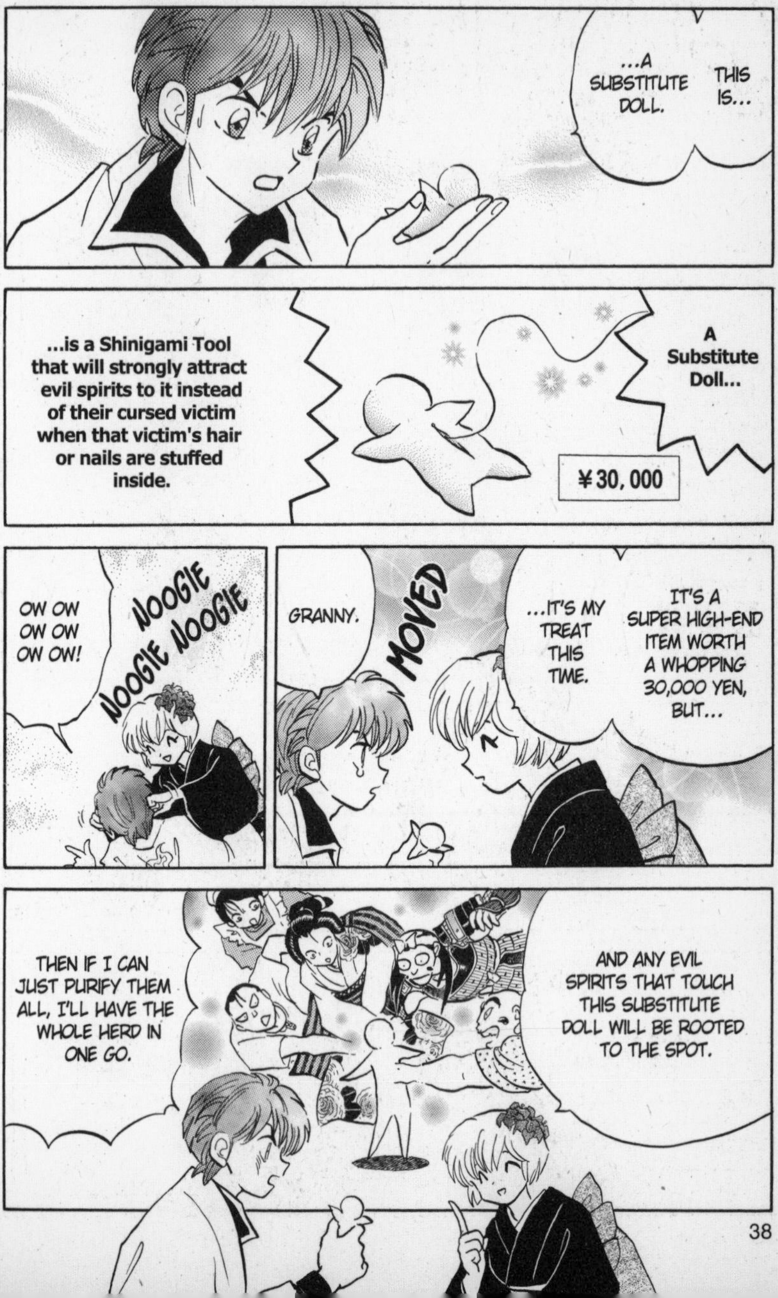
THIS IS... ...A SUBSTITUTE DOLL.
A Substitute Doll...
¥30,000
...is a Shinigami Tool that will strongly attract evil spirits to it instead of their cursed victim when that victim's hair or nails are stuffed inside.
IT'S A SUPER HIGH-END ITEM WORTH A WHOPPING 30,000 YEN, BUT...
...IT'S MY TREAT THIS TIME.
MOVED
GRANNY.
NOOGIE NOOGIE NOOGIE
OW OW OW OW OW OW!
AND ANY EVIL SPIRITS THAT TOUCH THIS SUBSTITUTE DOLL WILL BE ROOTED TO THE SPOT.
THEN IF I CAN JUST PURIFY THEM ALL, I'LL HAVE THE WHOLE HERD IN ONE GO.

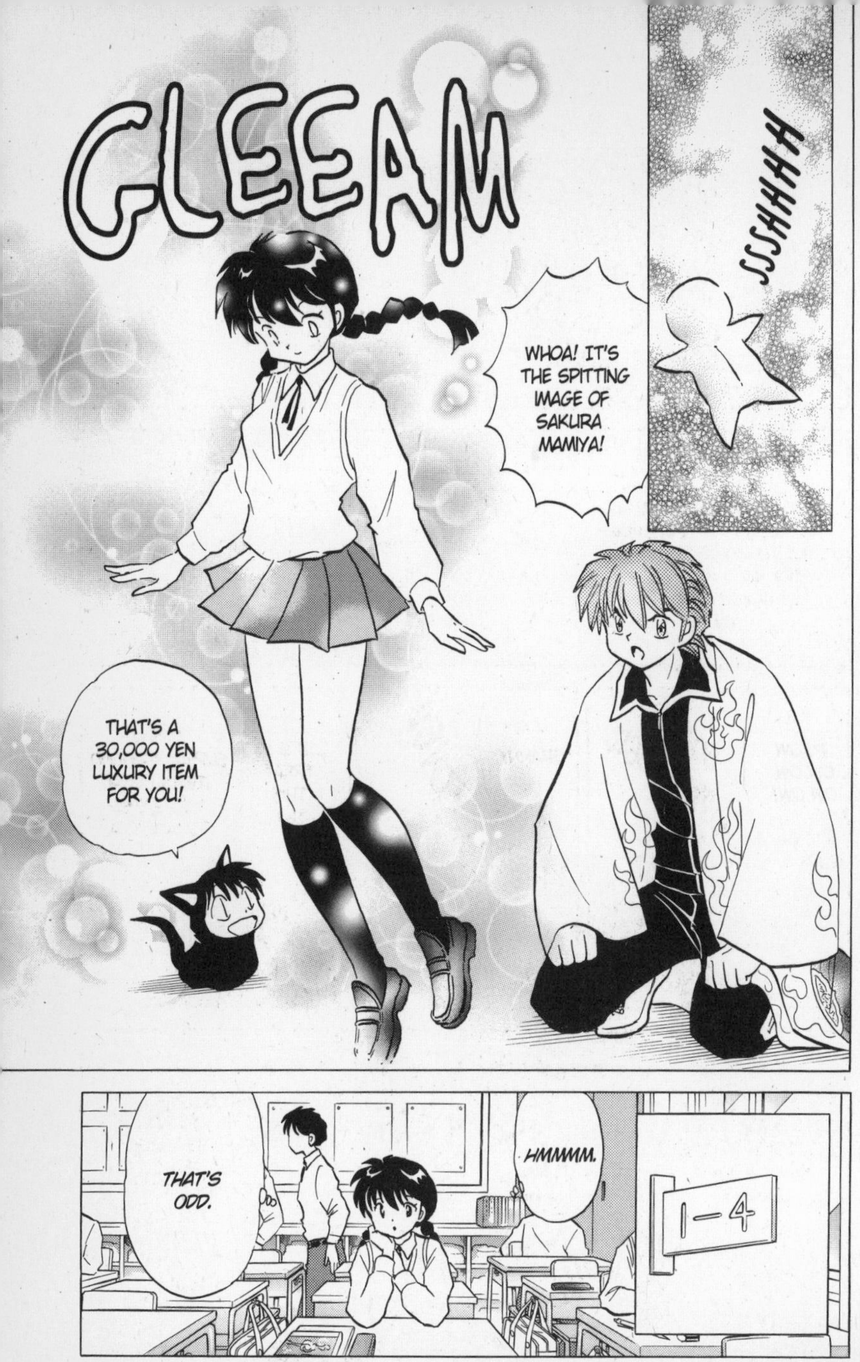
SSHHHHH
GLEEAM
WHOA! IT'S THE SPITTING IMAGE OF SAKURA MAMIYA!
THAT'S A 30,000 YEN LUXURY ITEM FOR YOU!
1-4
HMMMM.
THAT'S ODD.

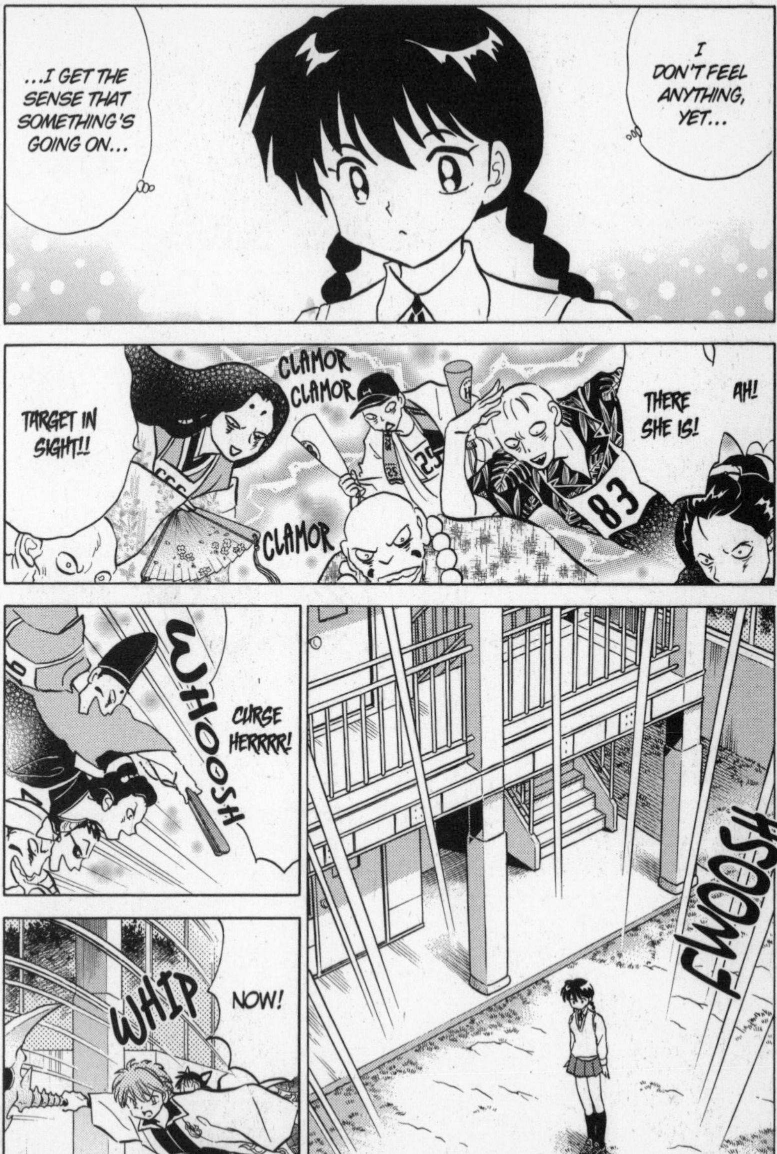
I DON'T FEEL ANYTHING, YET...
...I GET THE SENSE THAT SOMETHING'S GOING ON...
AH!
THERE SHE IS!
CLAMOR CLAMOR
CLAMOR
TARGET IN SIGHT!!
FWOOSH
CURSE HERRRR!
WHOOSH
NOW!
WHIP

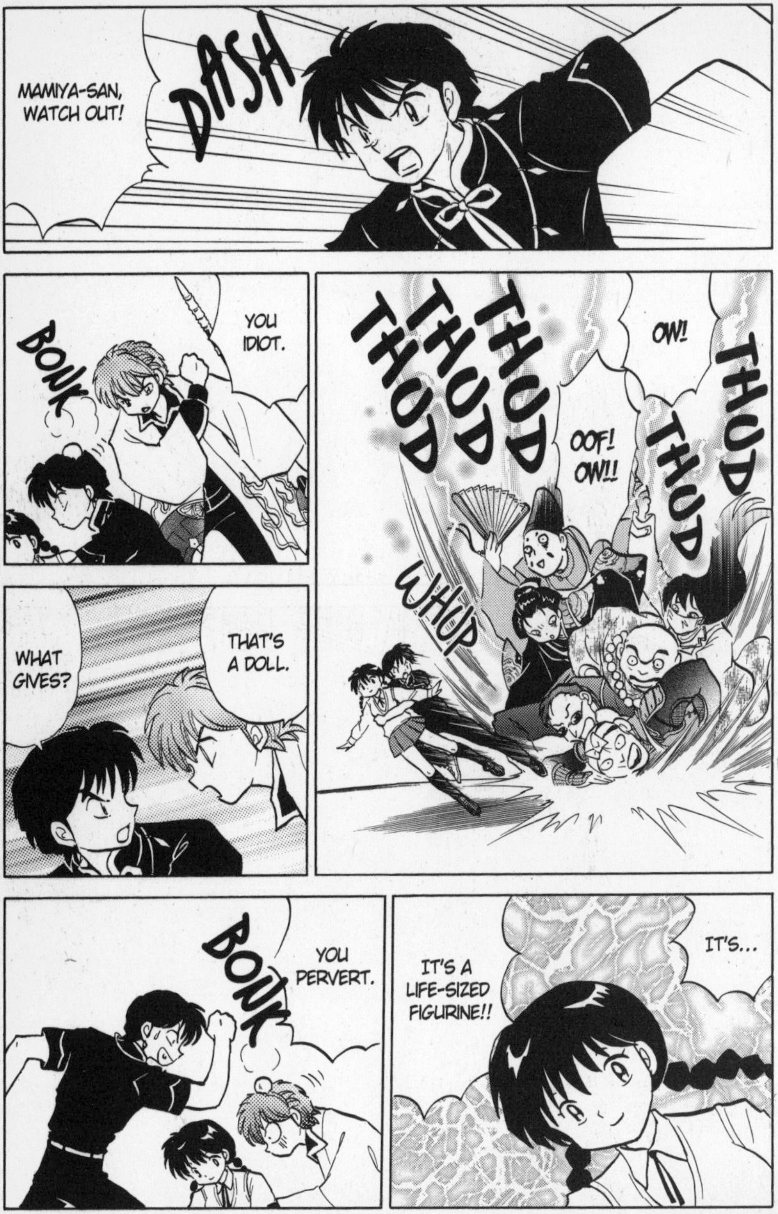
DASH
MAMIYA-SAN, WATCH OUT!
THUD THUD
OW!
THUD THUD THUD
OOF! OW!!
WHUP
YOU IDIOT.
BONK
THAT'S A DOLL.
WHAT GIVES?
IT'S...
IT'S A LIFE-SIZED FIGURINE!!
YOU PERVERT.
BONK

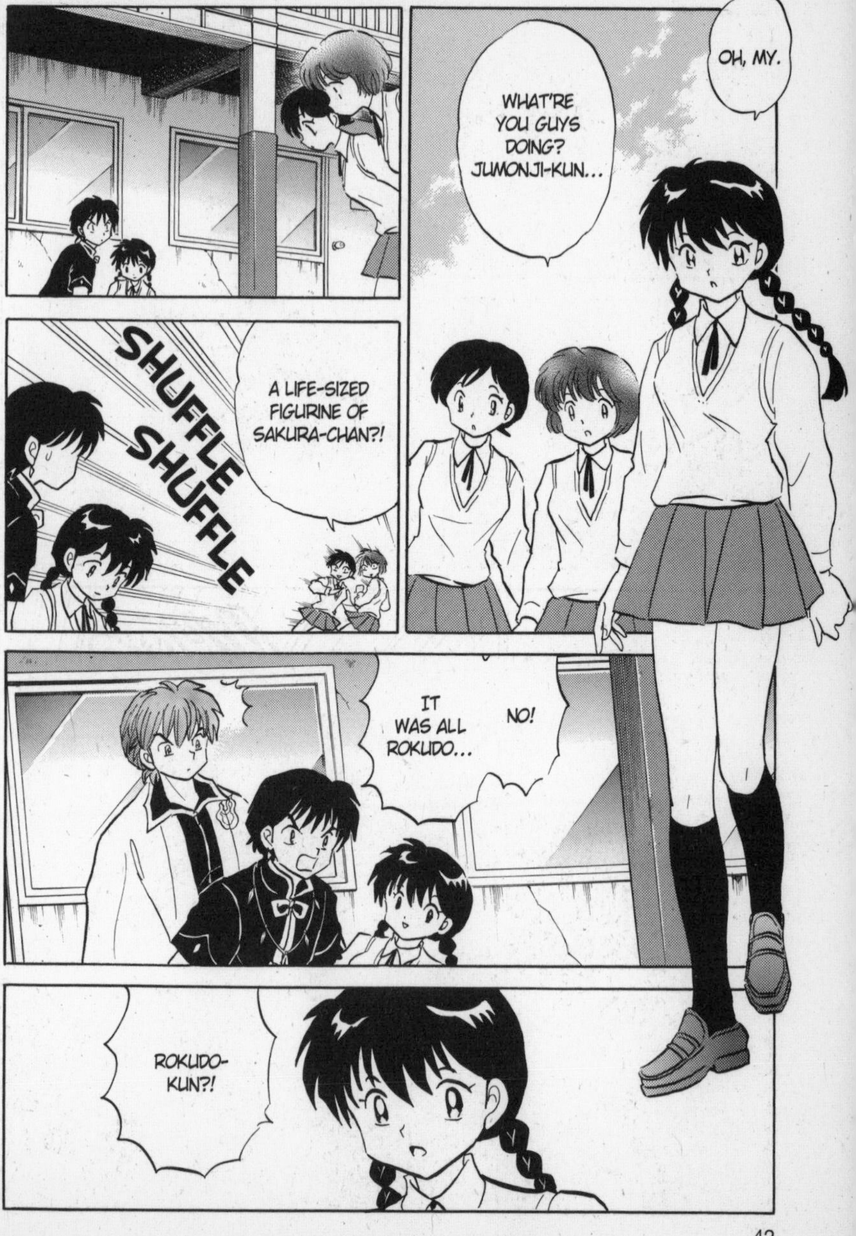
OH, MY.
WHAT'RE YOU GUYS DOING? JUMONJI-KUN...
A LIFE-SIZED FIGURINE OF SAKURA-CHAN?!
SHUFFLE SHUFFLE
NO!
IT WAS ALL ROKUDO...
ROKUDO-KUN?!

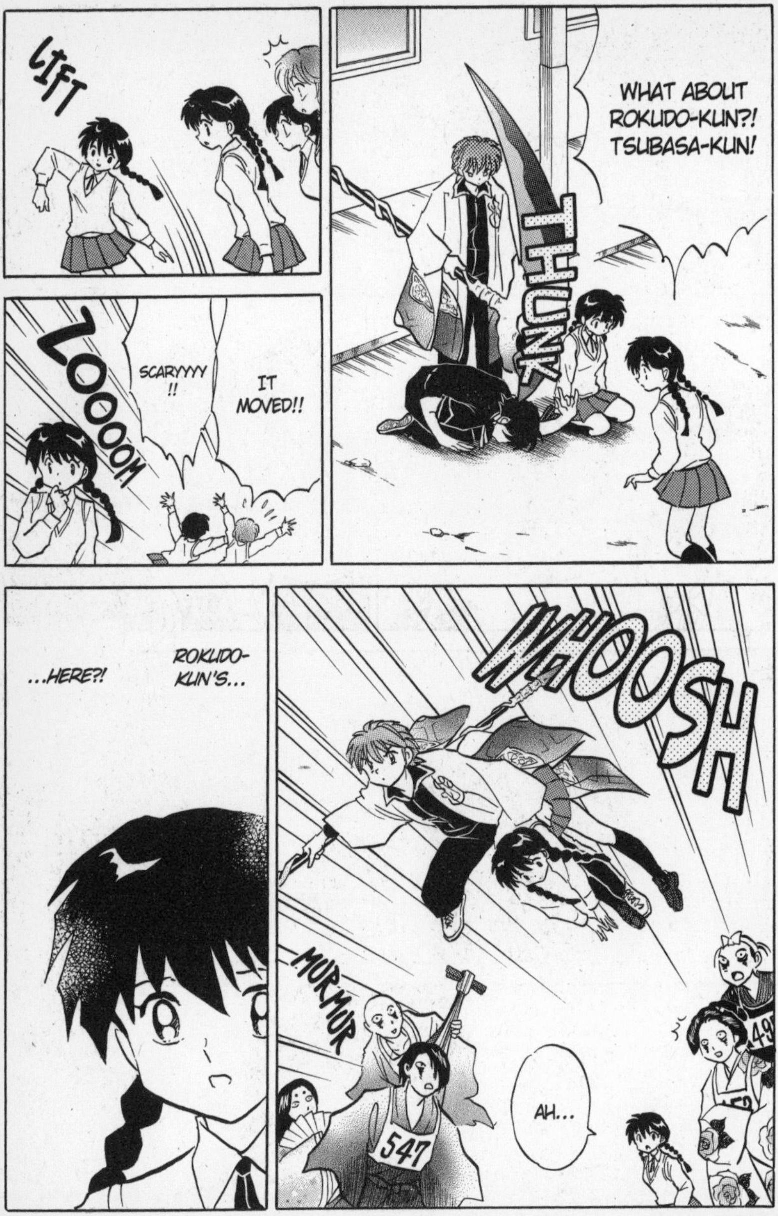
WHAT ABOUT ROKUDO-KUN?! TSUBASA-KUN!
THUNK
LIFT
ZOOOOOM
IT MOVED!!
SCARYYYY!!
WHOOSH
MURMUR
AH...
ROKUDO-KUN'S...
...HERE?!

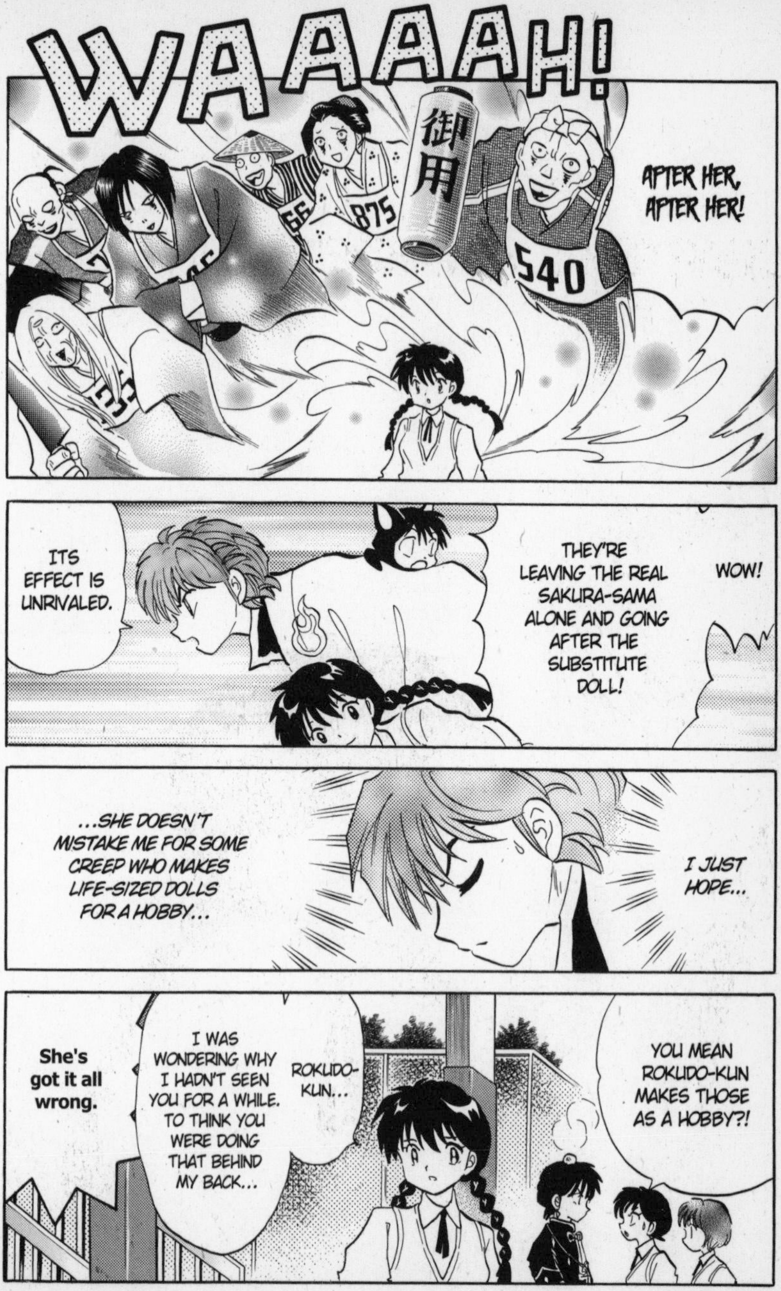
WAAAAH!
AFTER HER, AFTER HER!
WOW!
THEY'RE LEAVING THE REAL SAKURA-SAMA ALONE AND GOING AFTER THE SUBSTITUTE DOLL!
ITS EFFECT IS UNRIVALED.
I JUST HOPE...
...SHE DOESN'T MISTAKE ME FOR SOME CREEP WHO MAKES LIFE-SIZED DOLLS FOR A HOBBY...
YOU MEAN ROKUDO-KUN MAKES THOSE AS A HOBBY?!
ROKUDO-KUN...
I WAS WONDERING WHY I HADN'T SEEN YOU FOR A WHILE. TO THINK YOU WERE DOING THAT BEHIND MY BACK...
She's got it all wrong.

# CHAPTER 101: WHERE'D RINNE GO?

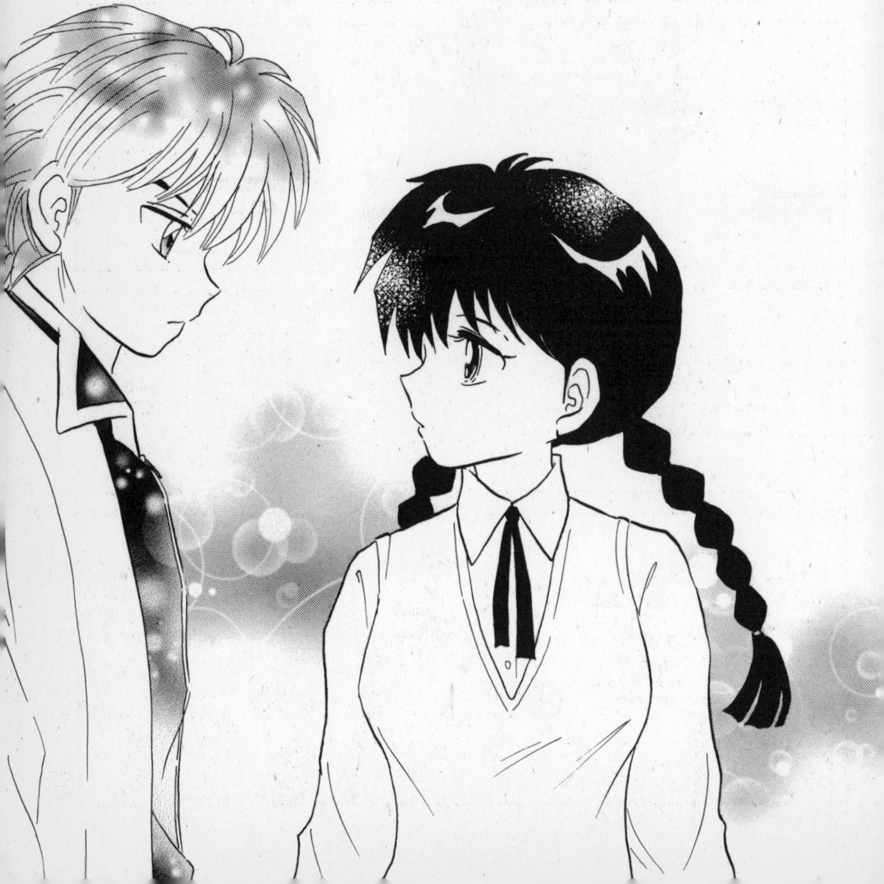

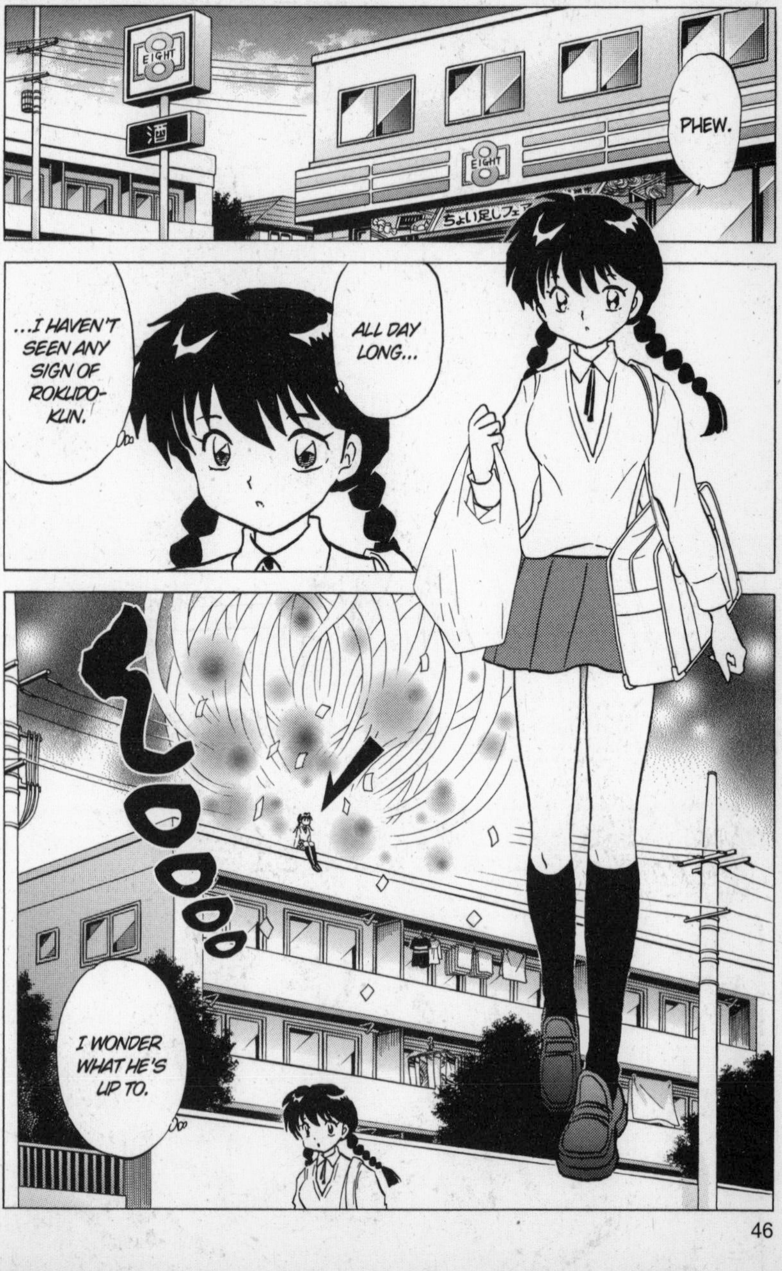
EIGHT
酒
EIGHT
ちょい足しフェ
PHEW.
ALL DAY LONG...
...I HAVEN'T SEEN ANY SIGN OF ROKUDO-KUN.
I WONDER WHAT HE'S UP TO.

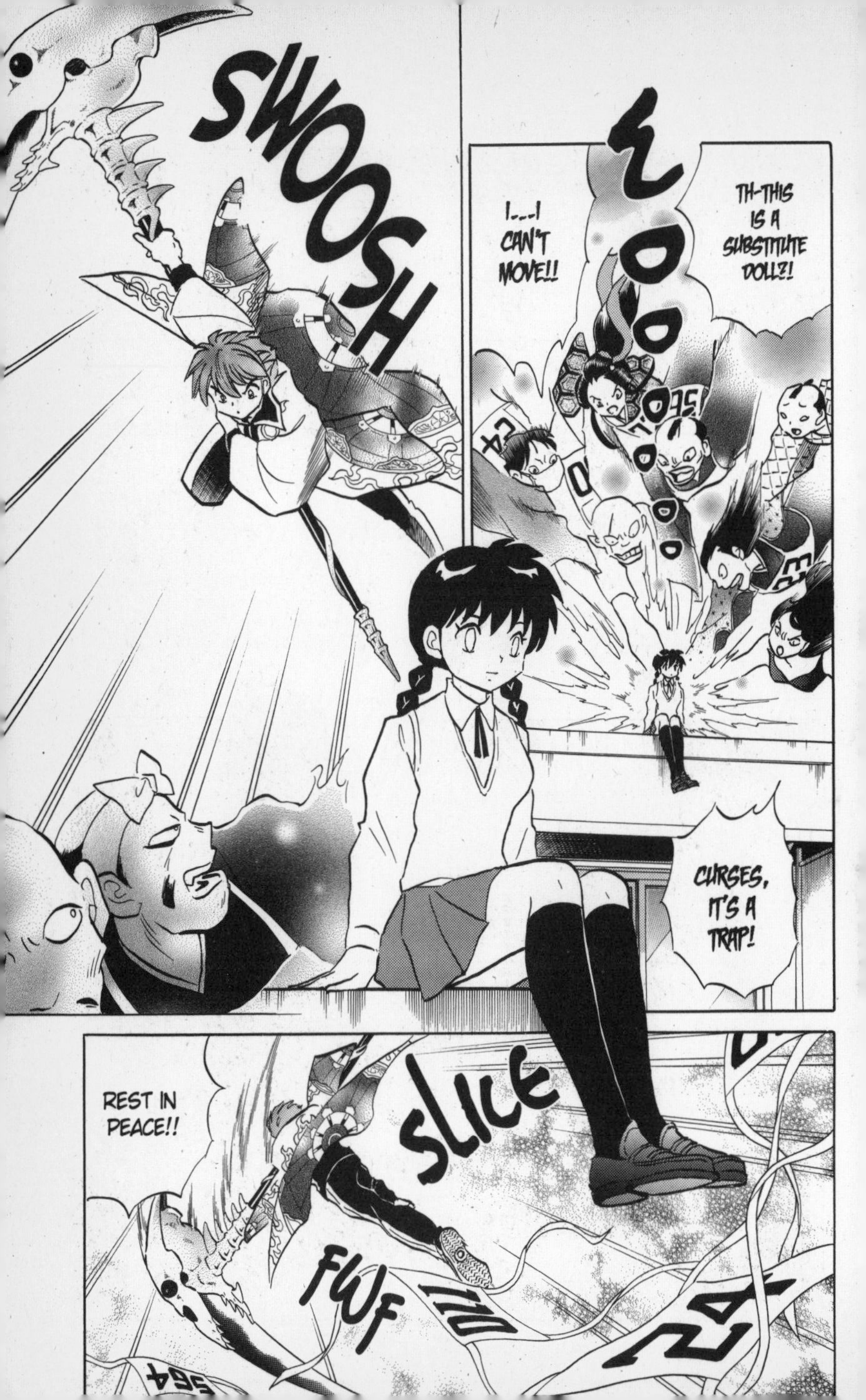
TH-THIS IS A SUBSTITUTE DOLL?!
I...I CAN'T MOVE!!
CURSES, IT'S A TRAP!
SWOOSH
REST IN PEACE!!
SLICE
FWF

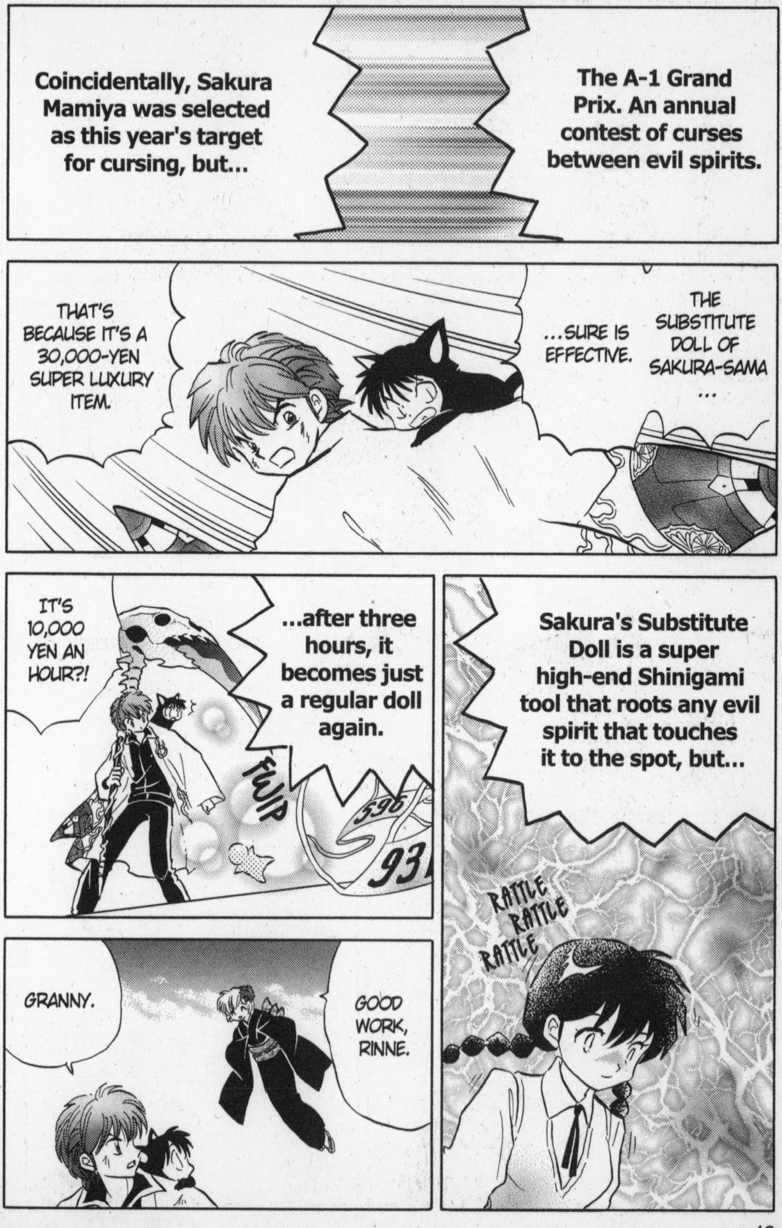
The A-1 Grand Prix. An annual contest of curses between evil spirits.
Coincidentally, Sakura Mamiya was selected as this year's target for cursing, but...
THE SUBSTITUTE DOLL OF SAKURA-SAMA ...
...SURE IS EFFECTIVE.
THAT'S BECAUSE IT'S A 30,000-YEN SUPER LUXURY ITEM.
Sakura's Substitute Doll is a super high-end Shinigami tool that roots any evil spirit that touches it to the spot, but...
RATTLE RATTLE RATTLE
...after three hours, it becomes just a regular doll again.
FWIP
IT'S 10,000 YEN AN HOUR?!
GOOD WORK, RINNE.
GRANNY.

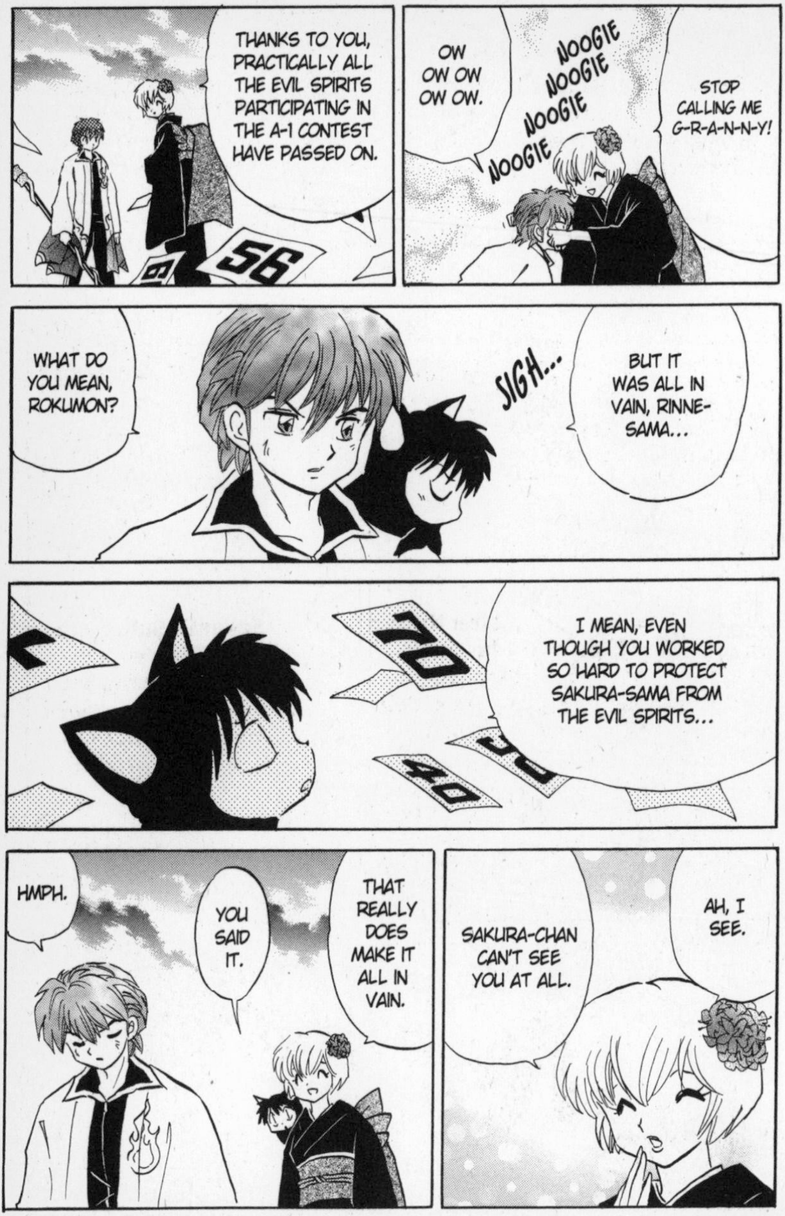
STOP CALLING ME G-R-A-N-N-Y!
NOOGIE NOOGIE NOOGIE NOOGIE
OW OW OW OW OW.
THANKS TO YOU, PRACTICALLY ALL THE EVIL SPIRITS PARTICIPATING IN THE A-1 CONTEST HAVE PASSED ON.
56
BUT IT WAS ALL IN VAIN, RINNE-SAMA...
SIGH...
WHAT DO YOU MEAN, ROKUMON?
I MEAN, EVEN THOUGH YOU WORKED SO HARD TO PROTECT SAKURA-SAMA FROM THE EVIL SPIRITS...
70
40
AH, I SEE.
SAKURA-CHAN CAN'T SEE YOU AT ALL.
THAT REALLY DOES MAKE IT ALL IN VAIN.
YOU SAID IT.
HMPH.

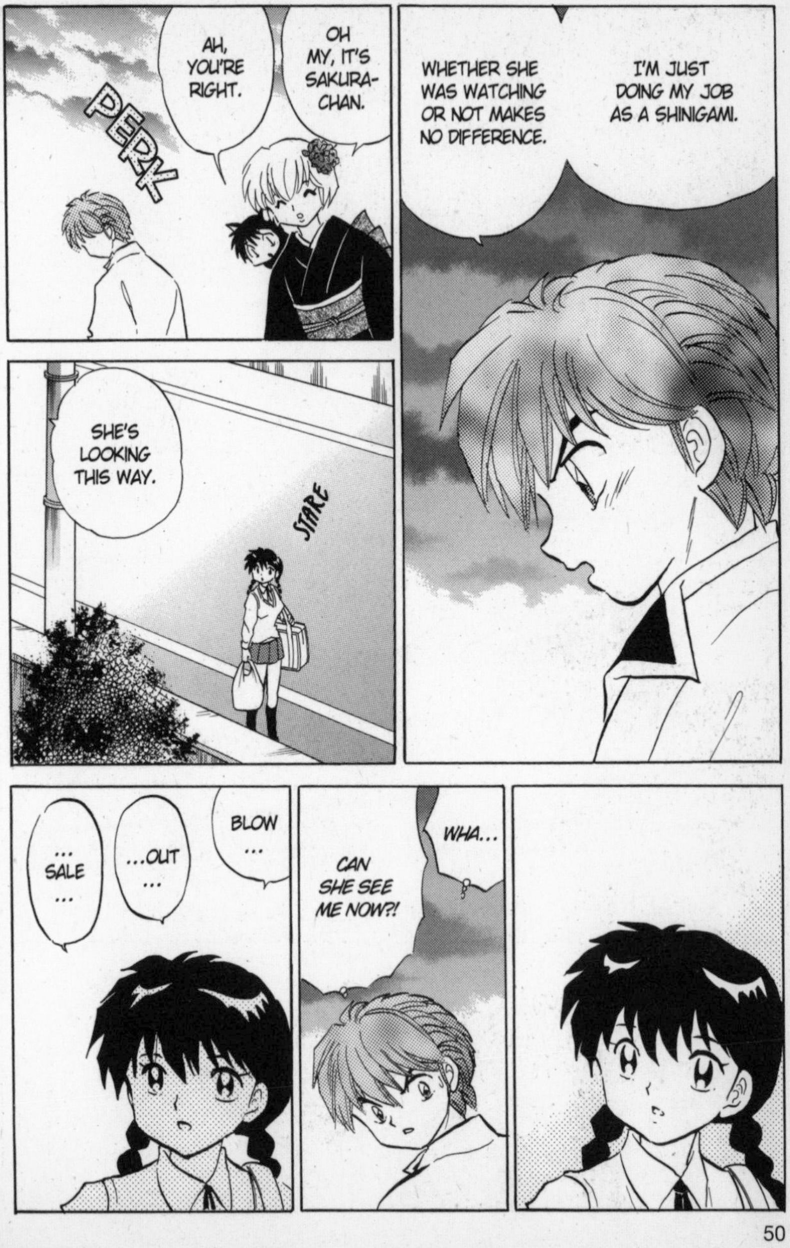
I'M JUST DOING MY JOB AS A SHINIGAMI.
WHETHER SHE WAS WATCHING OR NOT MAKES NO DIFFERENCE.
OH MY, IT'S SAKURA-CHAN.
AH, YOU'RE RIGHT.
PERK
SHE'S LOOKING THIS WAY.
STARE
WHA...
CAN SHE SEE ME NOW?!
BLOW ...
...OUT ...
... SALE ...

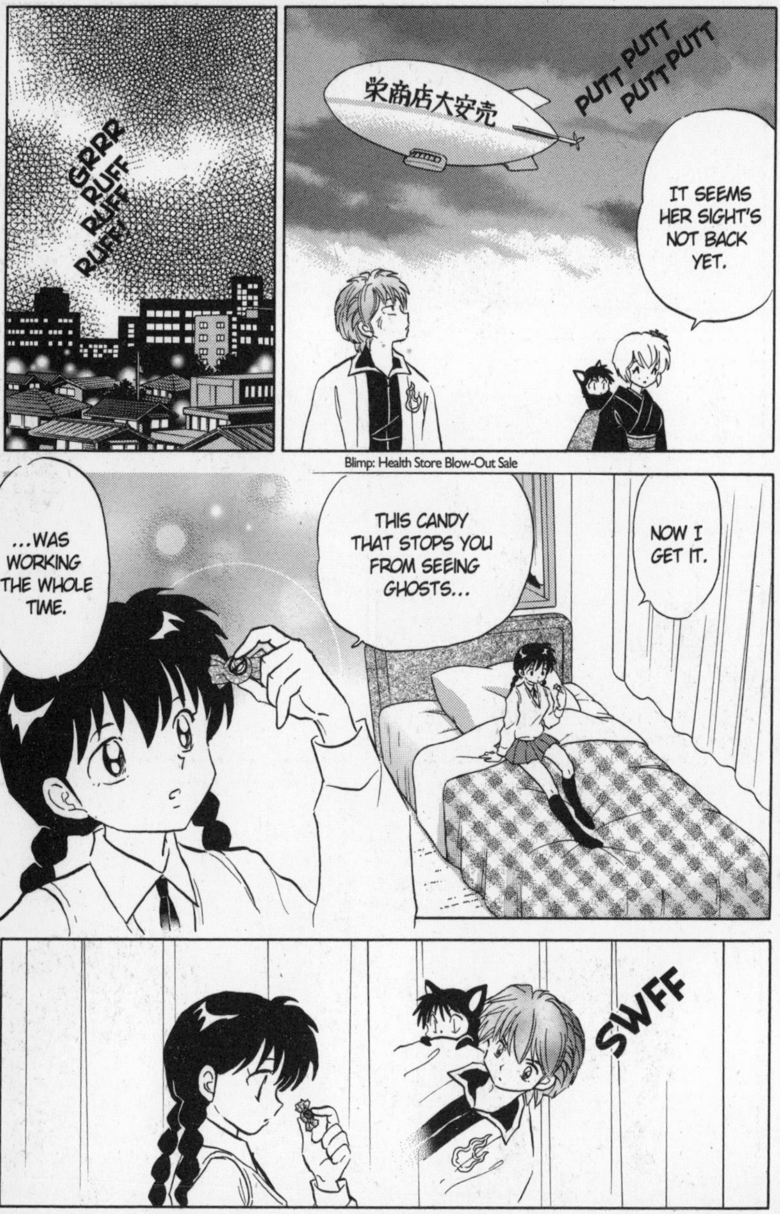
栄商店大安売
PUTT PUTT PUTT PUTT
IT SEEMS HER SIGHT'S NOT BACK YET.
GRRR RUFF RUFF RUFF
NOW I GET IT.
THIS CANDY THAT STOPS YOU FROM SEEING GHOSTS...
...WAS WORKING THE WHOLE TIME.
SWFF
Blimp: Health Store Blow-Out Sale

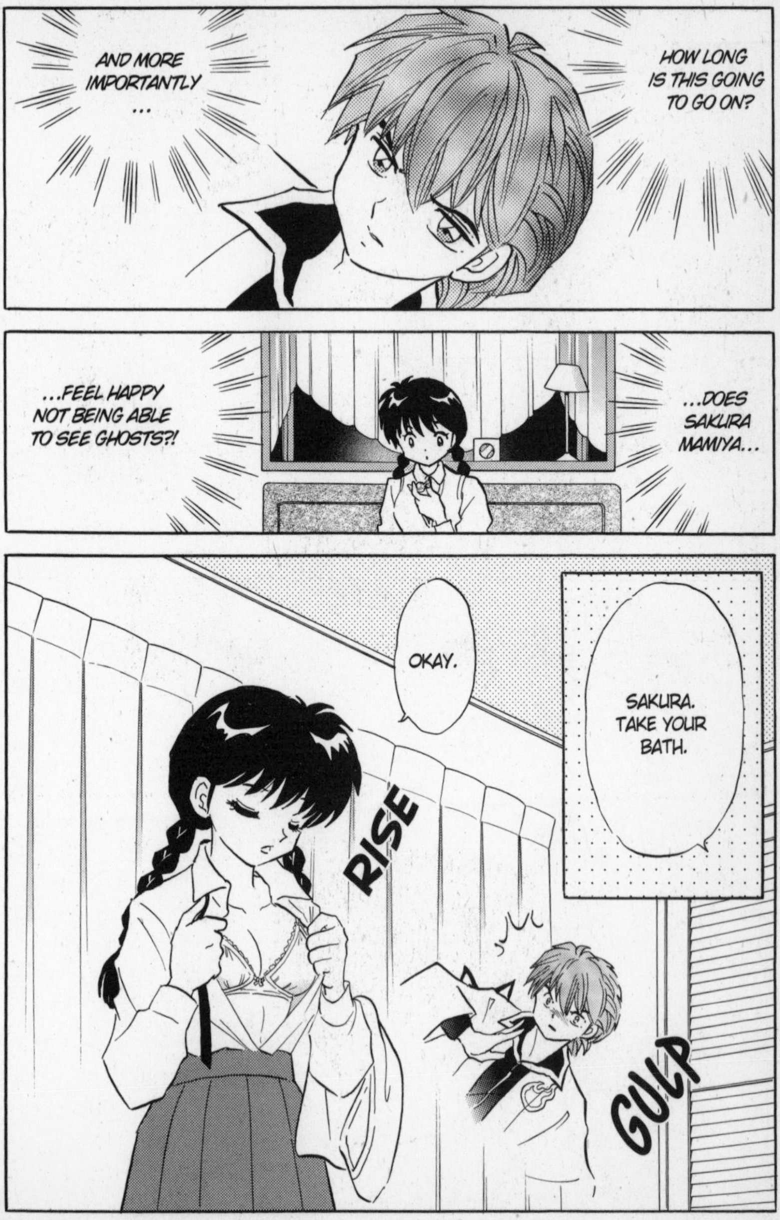
HOW LONG IS THIS GOING TO GO ON?
AND MORE IMPORTANTLY ...
...DOES SAKURA MAMIYA...
...FEEL HAPPY NOT BEING ABLE TO SEE GHOSTS?!
SAKURA. TAKE YOUR BATH.
OKAY.
RISE
GULP

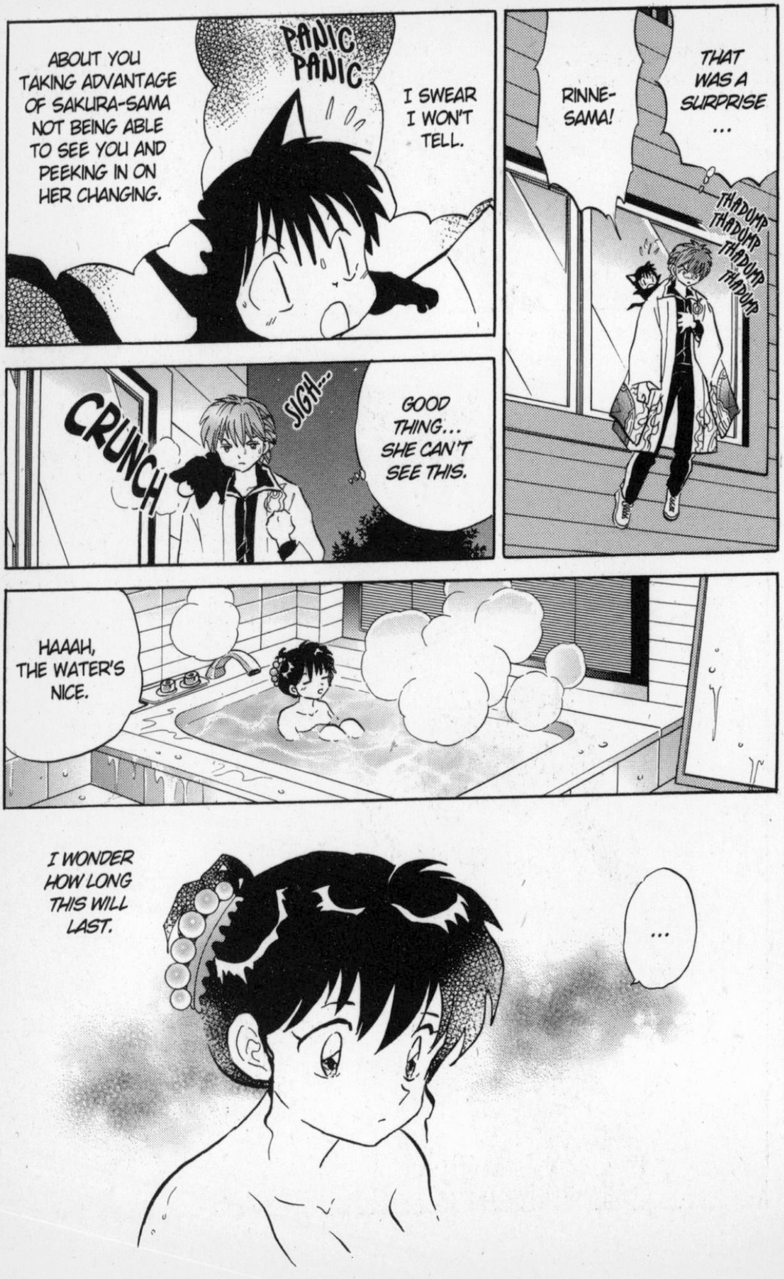
THAT WAS A SURPRISE ...
RINNE-SAMA!
THADUMP THADUMP THADUMP THADUMP
I SWEAR I WON'T TELL.
PANIC PANIC
ABOUT YOU TAKING ADVANTAGE OF SAKURA-SAMA NOT BEING ABLE TO SEE YOU AND PEEKING IN ON HER CHANGING.
GOOD THING... SHE CAN'T SEE THIS.
SIGH...
CRUNCH
HAAAH, THE WATER'S NICE.
...
I WONDER HOW LONG THIS WILL LAST.

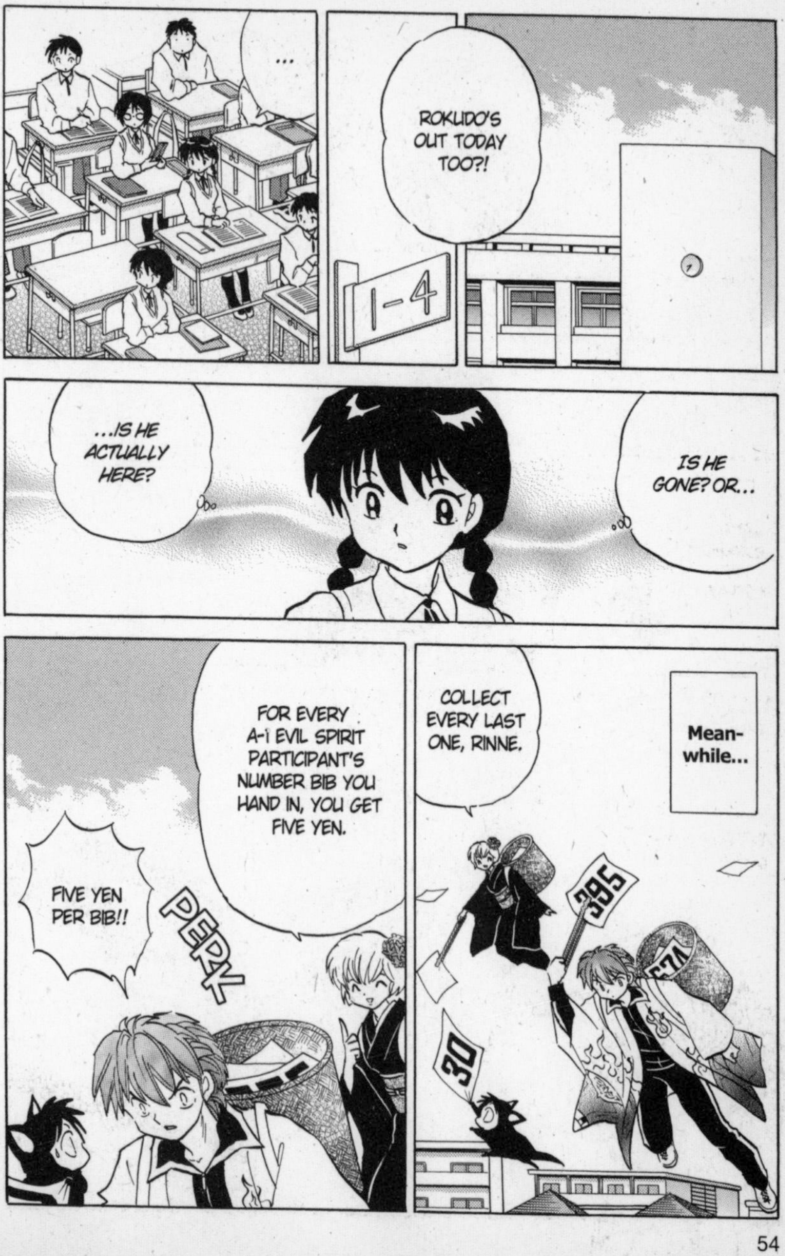
ROKUDO'S OUT TODAY TOO?!
1-4
...
IS HE GONE? OR...
...IS HE ACTUALLY HERE?
Mean-while...
COLLECT EVERY LAST ONE, RINNE.
FOR EVERY A-1 EVIL SPIRIT PARTICIPANT'S NUMBER BIB YOU HAND IN, YOU GET FIVE YEN.
PERK
FIVE YEN PER BIB!!

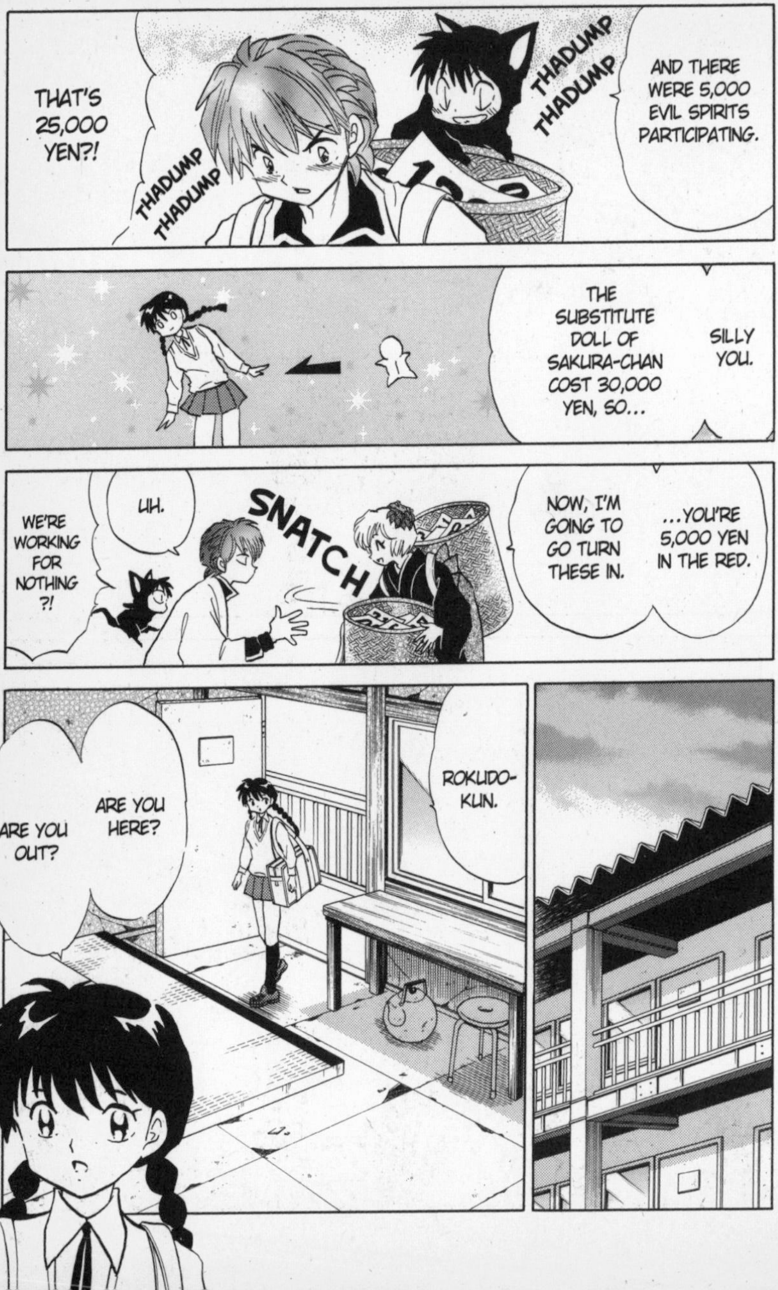
AND THERE WERE 5,000 EVIL SPIRITS PARTICIPATING.
THADUMP THADUMP
THADUMP THADUMP
THAT'S 25,000 YEN?!
SILLY YOU.
THE SUBSTITUTE DOLL OF SAKURA-CHAN COST 30,000 YEN, SO...
...YOU'RE 5,000 YEN IN THE RED.
NOW, I'M GOING TO GO TURN THESE IN.
SNATCH
UH.
WE'RE WORKING FOR NOTHING ?!
ROKUDO-KUN.
ARE YOU HERE?
ARE YOU OUT?

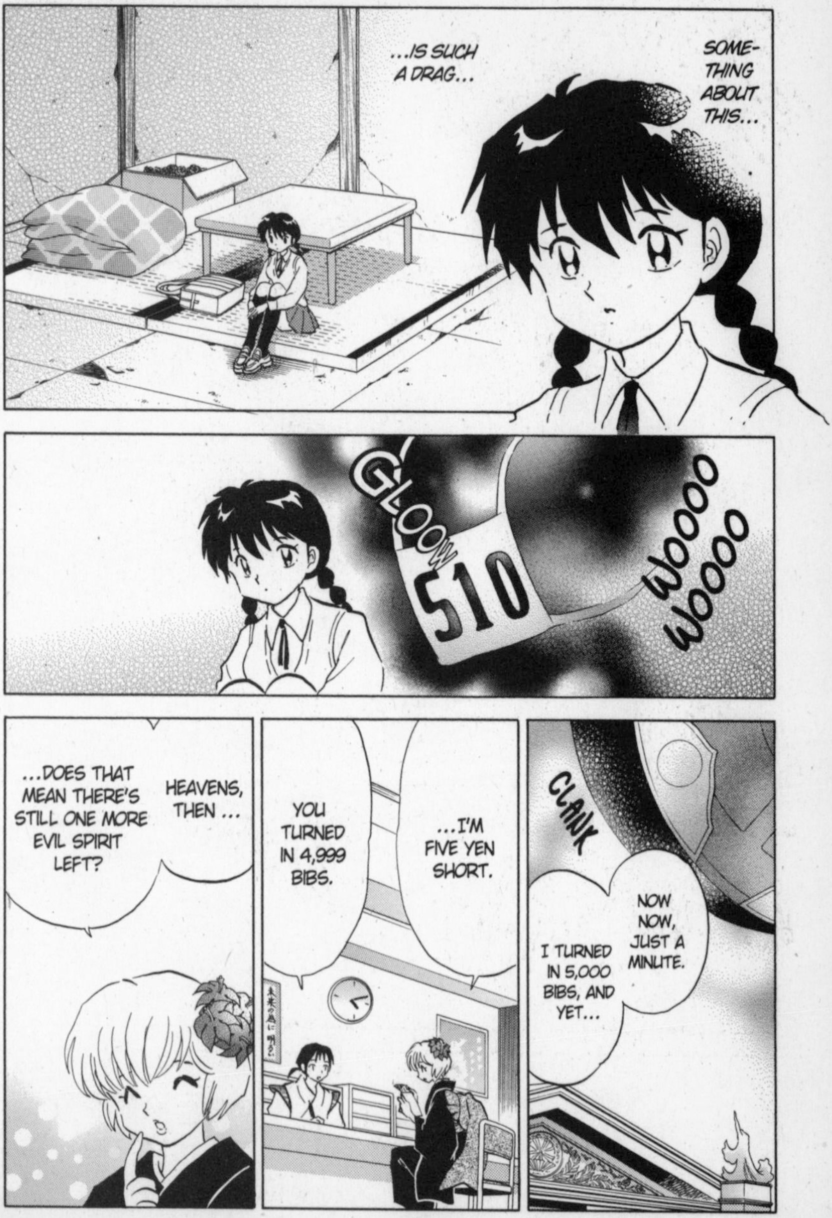
SOME-THING ABOUT THIS...
...IS SUCH A DRAG...
WOOOO WOOOO
GLOOW
510
CLANK
NOW NOW, JUST A MINUTE.
I TURNED IN 5,000 BIBS, AND YET...
...I'M FIVE YEN SHORT.
YOU TURNED IN 4,999 BIBS.
HEAVENS, THEN ...
...DOES THAT MEAN THERE'S STILL ONE MORE EVIL SPIRIT LEFT?

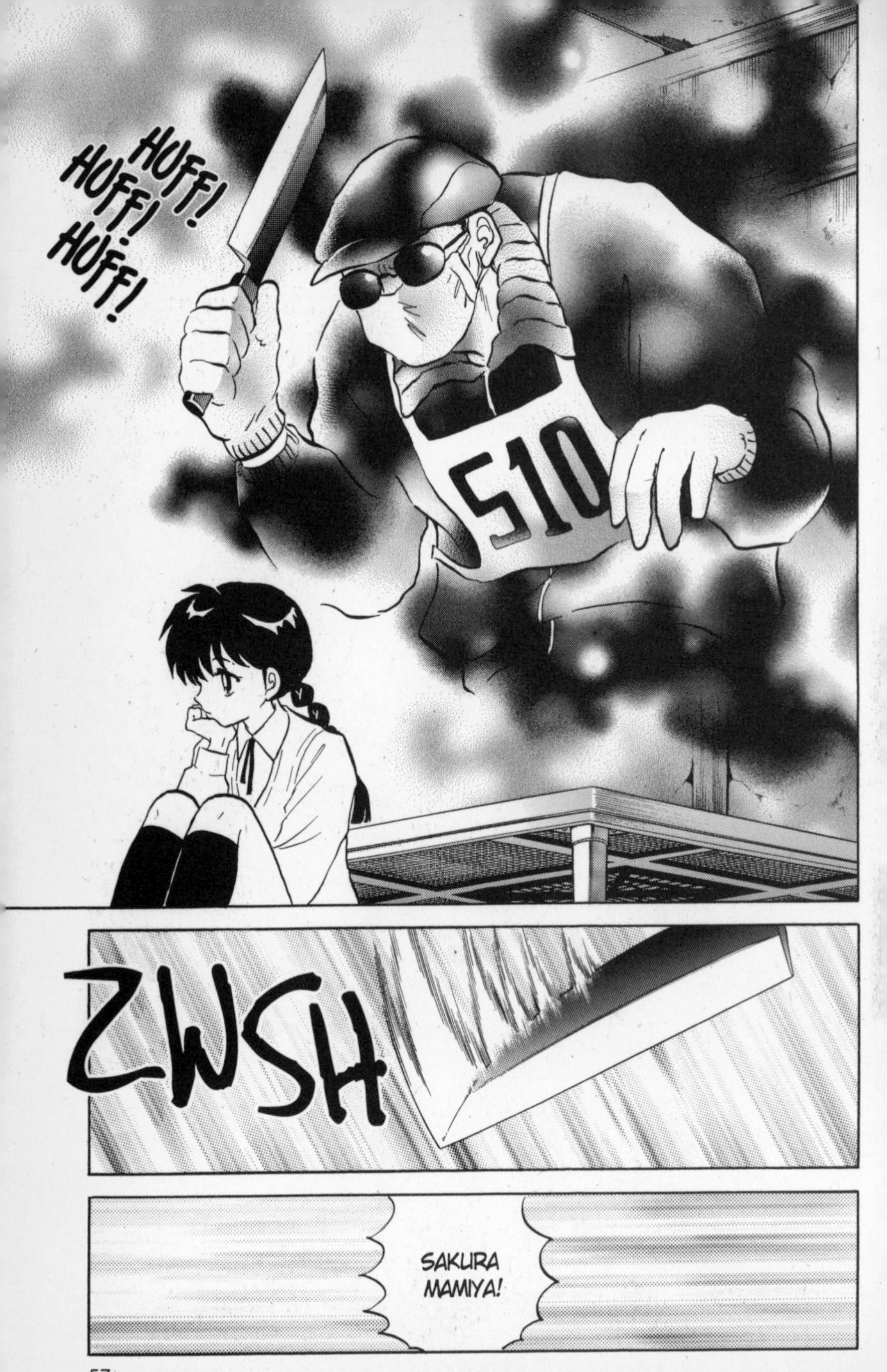
HUFF! HUFF! HUFF!
510
ZWSH
SAKURA MAMIYA!

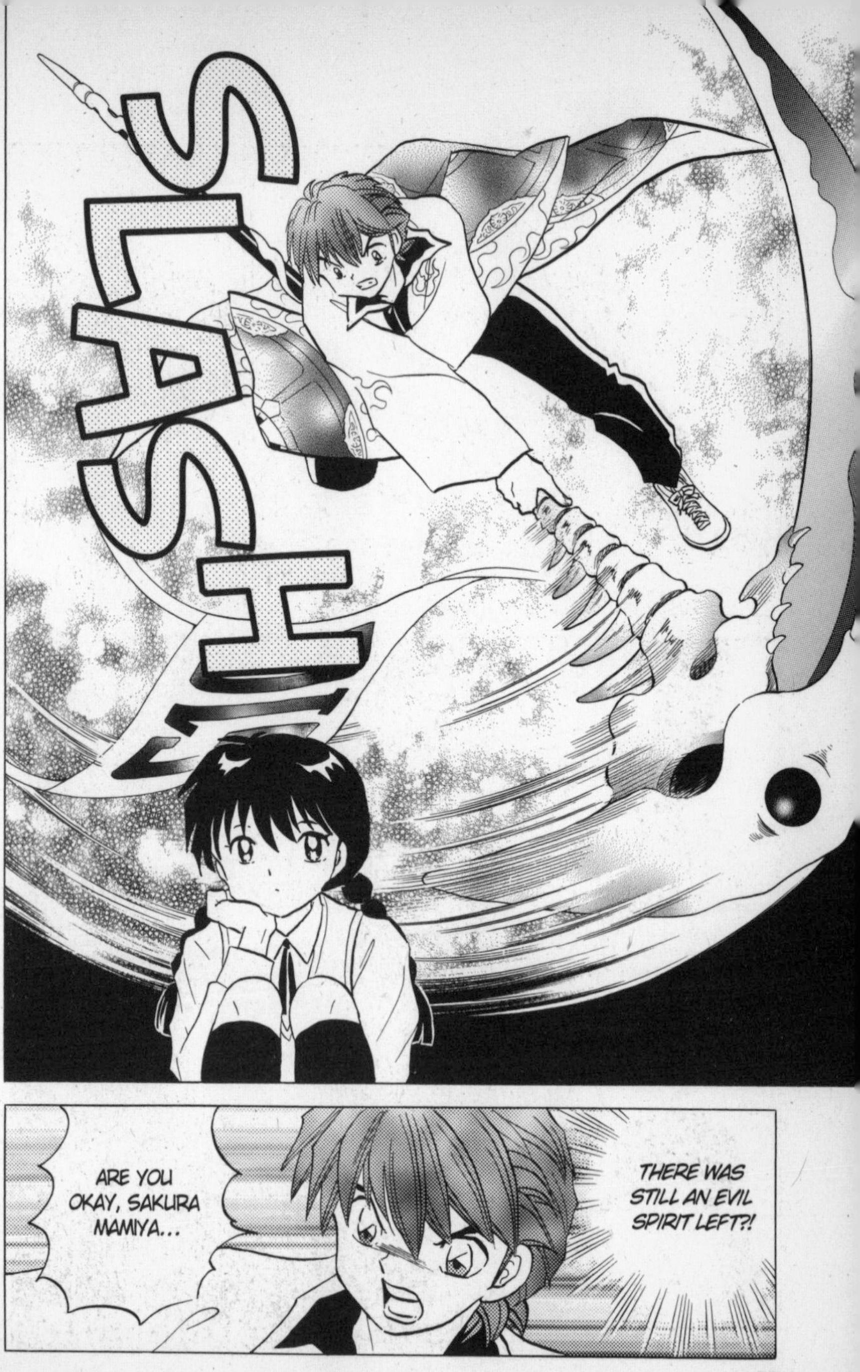
SLASH
THERE WAS STILL AN EVIL SPIRIT LEFT?!
ARE YOU OKAY, SAKURA MAMIYA...

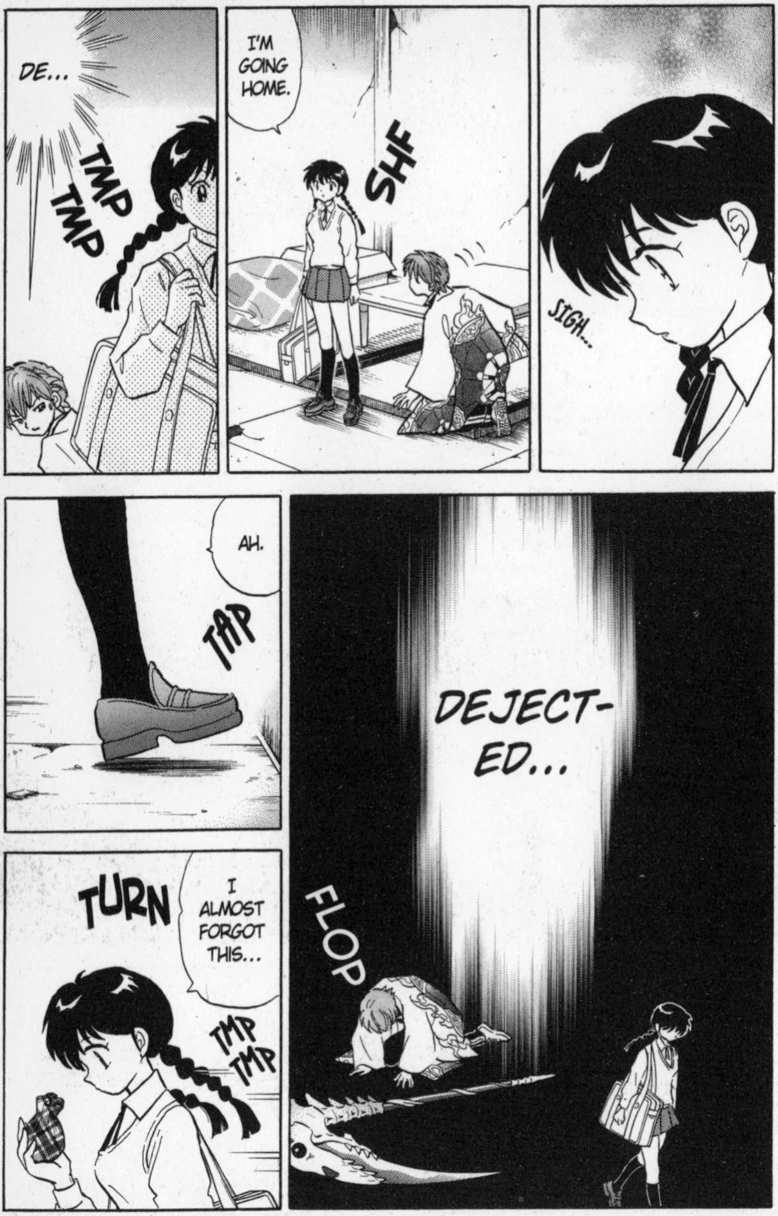
SIGH...
I'M GOING HOME.
SHF
DE...
TMP TMP
DEJECT-ED...
FLOP
AH.
TAP
TURN
I ALMOST FORGOT THIS...
TMP TMP

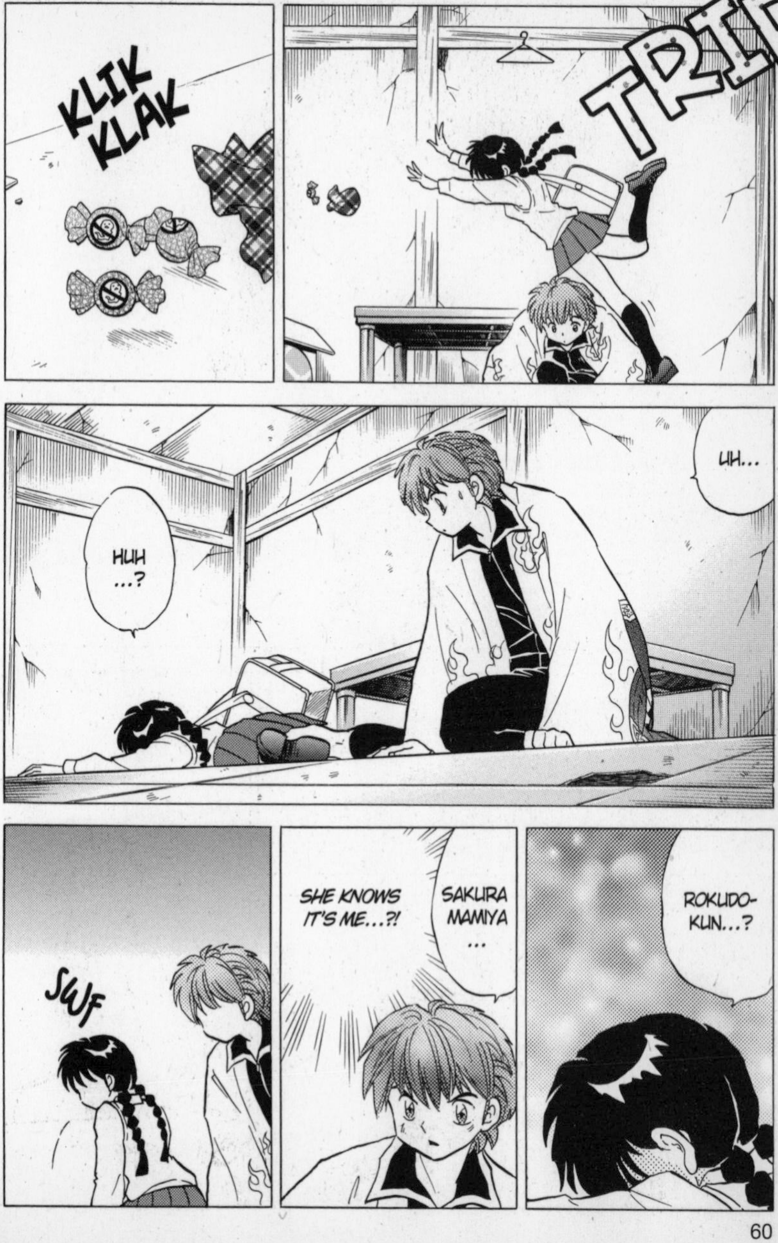
TRIP
KLIK KLAK
UH...
HUH ...?
ROKUDO-KUN...?
SAKURA MAMIYA ...
SHE KNOWS IT'S ME...?!
SWF

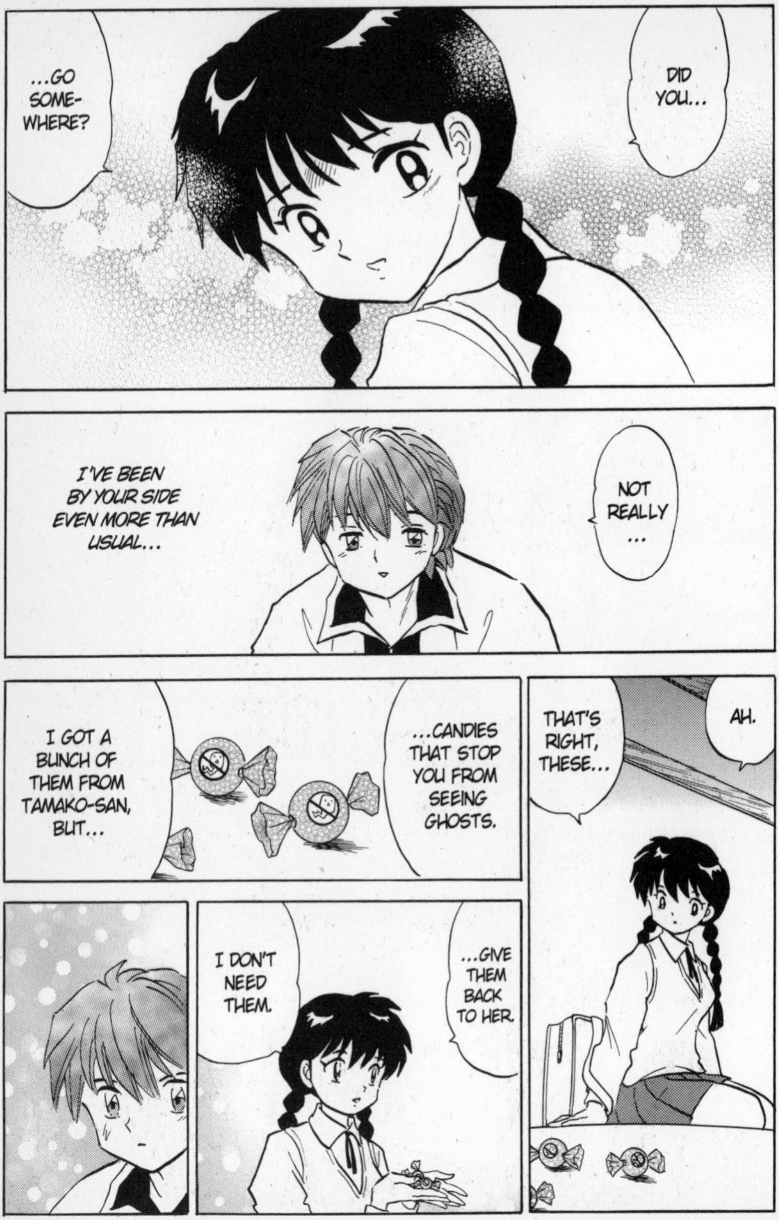
DID YOU...
...GO SOME-WHERE?
NOT REALLY ...
I'VE BEEN BY YOUR SIDE EVEN MORE THAN USUAL...
AH.
THAT'S RIGHT, THESE...
...CANDIES THAT STOP YOU FROM SEEING GHOSTS.
I GOT A BUNCH OF THEM FROM TAMAKO-SAN, BUT...
...GIVE THEM BACK TO HER.
I DON'T NEED THEM.

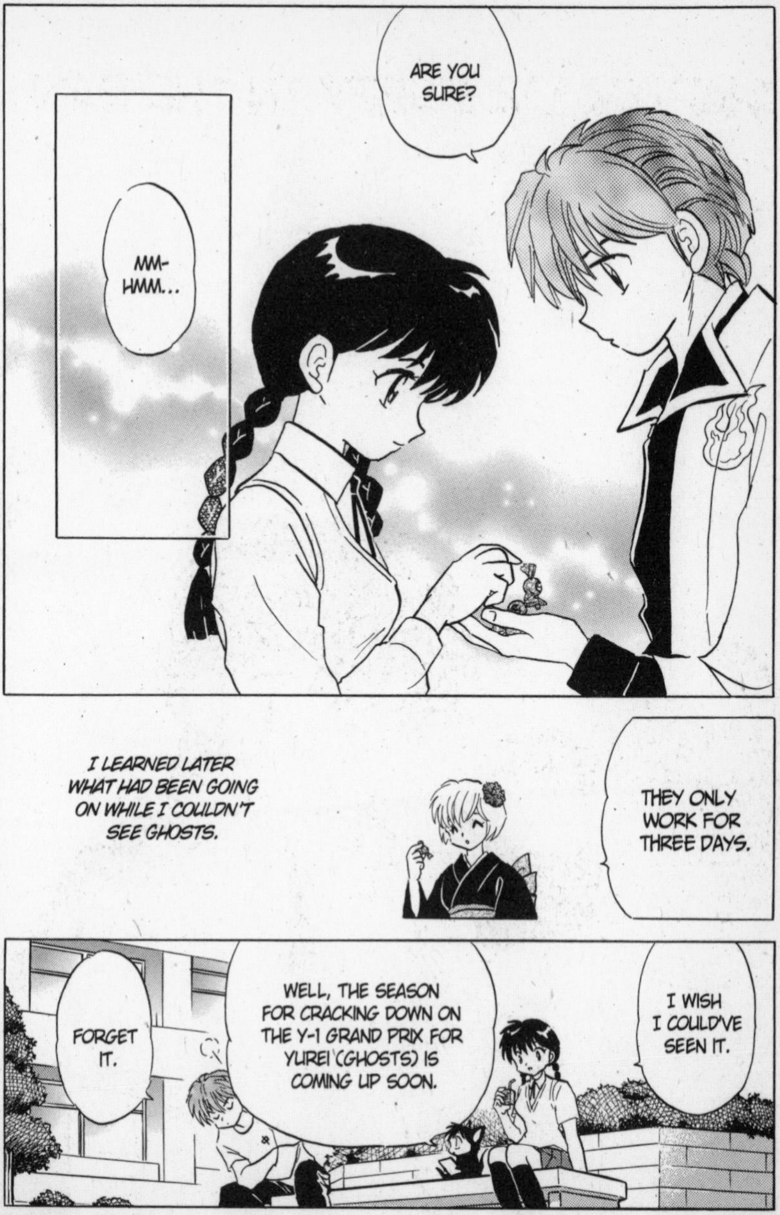
ARE YOU SURE?
MM-HMM...
THEY ONLY WORK FOR THREE DAYS.
I LEARNED LATER WHAT HAD BEEN GOING ON WHILE I COULDN'T SEE GHOSTS.
I WISH I COULD'VE SEEN IT.
WELL, THE SEASON FOR CRACKING DOWN ON THE Y-1 GRAND PRIX FOR YUREI (GHOSTS) IS COMING UP SOON.
FORGET IT.

# CHAPTER 102: PUPPY IN THE RAIN

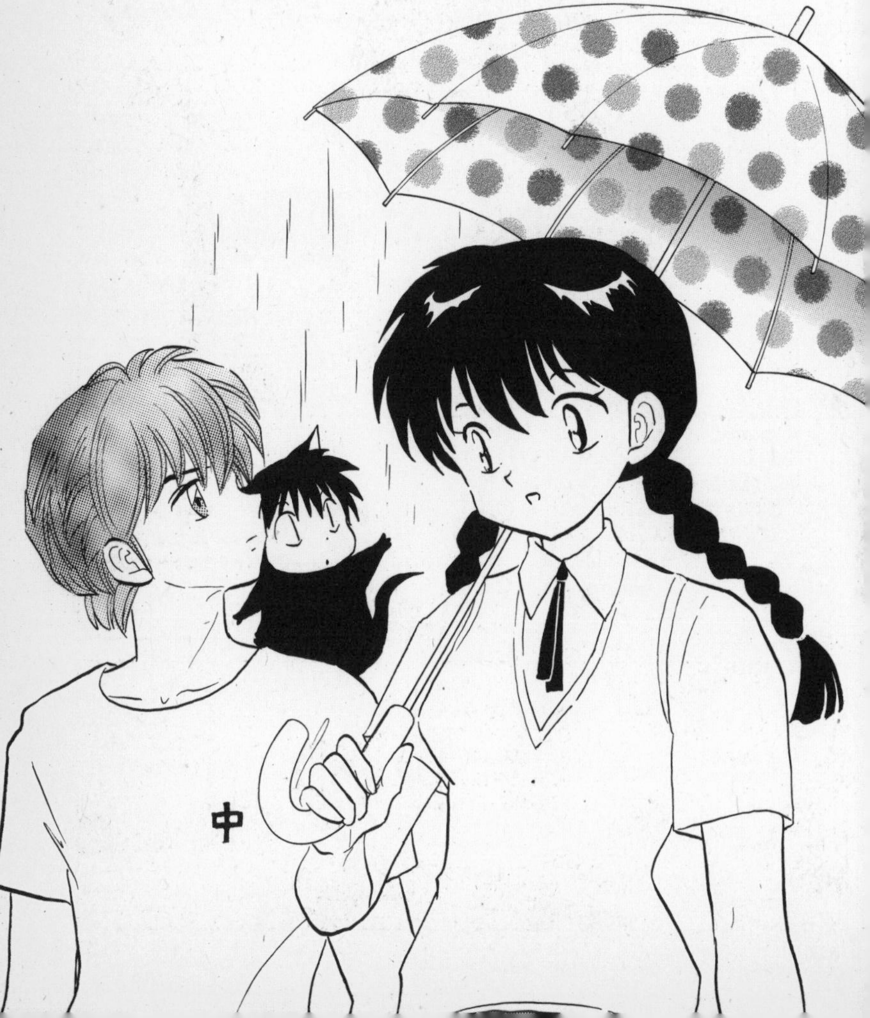
中

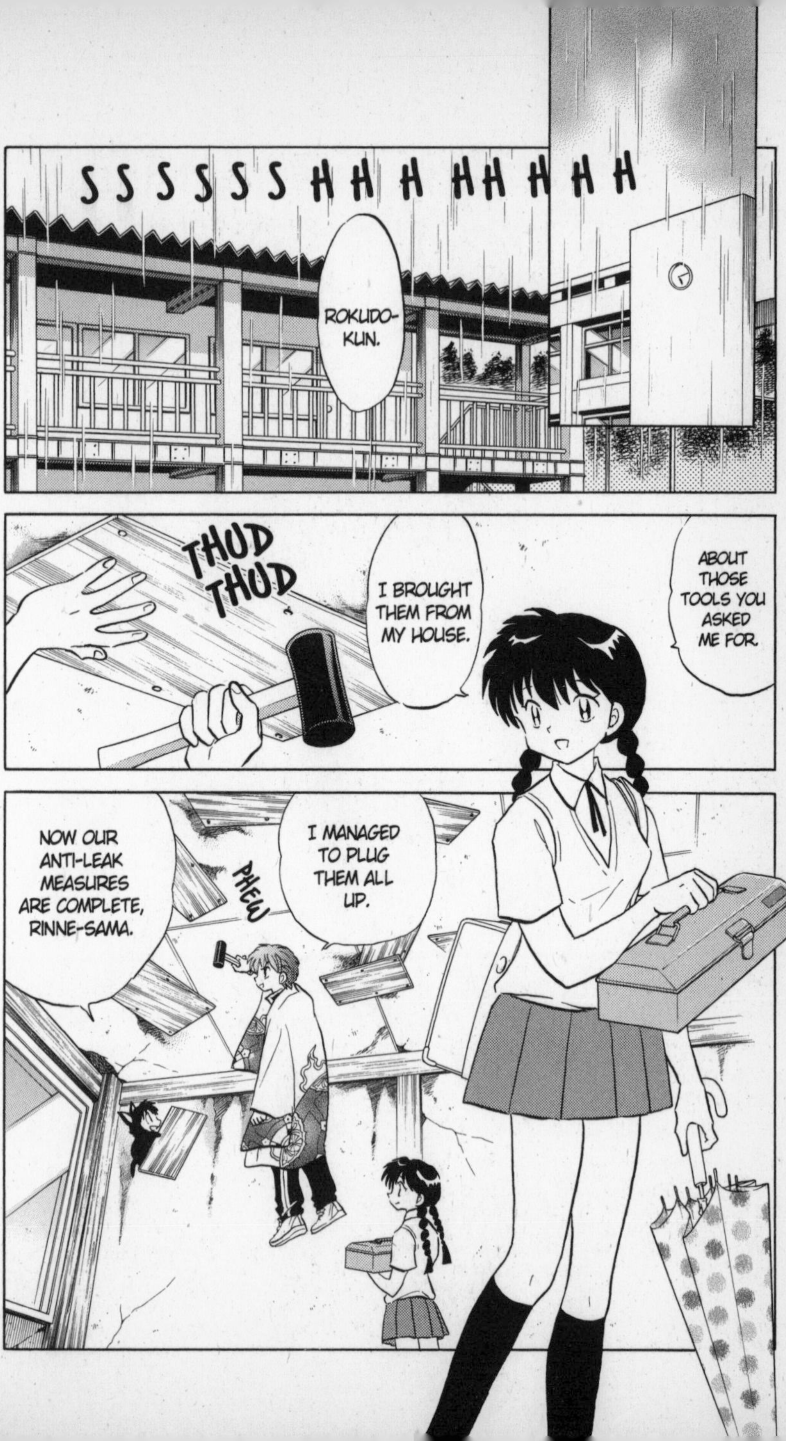
SSSSSHHHHHHH
ROKUDO-KUN.
ABOUT THOSE TOOLS YOU ASKED ME FOR.
I BROUGHT THEM FROM MY HOUSE.
THUD THUD
I MANAGED TO PLUG THEM ALL UP.
PHEW
NOW OUR ANTI-LEAK MEASURES ARE COMPLETE, RINNE-SAMA.

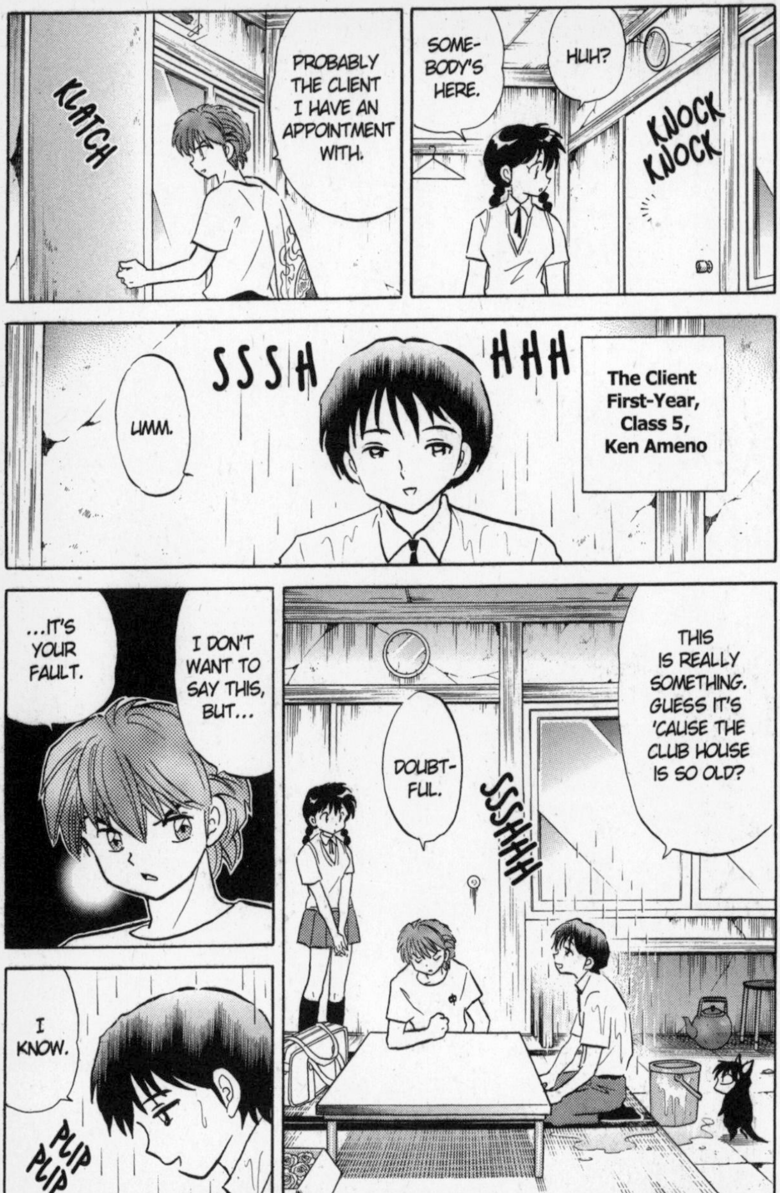
KNOCK KNOCK
HUH?
SOME-BODY'S HERE.
PROBABLY THE CLIENT I HAVE AN APPOINTMENT WITH.
KLATCH
The Client
First-Year, Class 5, Ken Ameno
SSSH HHH
UMM.
THIS IS REALLY SOMETHING. GUESS IT'S 'CAUSE THE CLUB HOUSE IS SO OLD?
SSSHHH
DOUBT-FUL.
I DON'T WANT TO SAY THIS, BUT...
...IT'S YOUR FAULT.
I KNOW.
PLIP PLIP

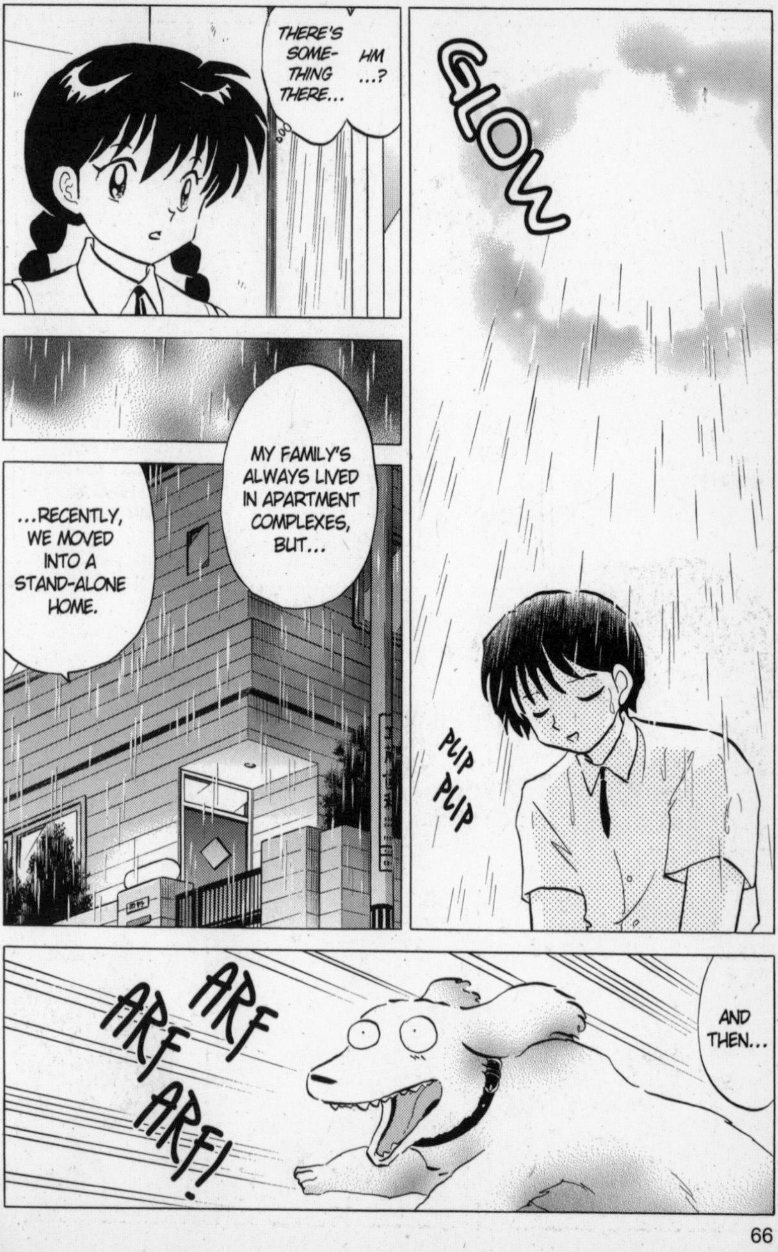
GLOW
PLIP PLIP
THERE'S SOME-THING THERE...
HM ...?
MY FAMILY'S ALWAYS LIVED IN APARTMENT COMPLEXES, BUT...
...RECENTLY, WE MOVED INTO A STAND-ALONE HOME.
AND THEN...
ARF ARF ARF!

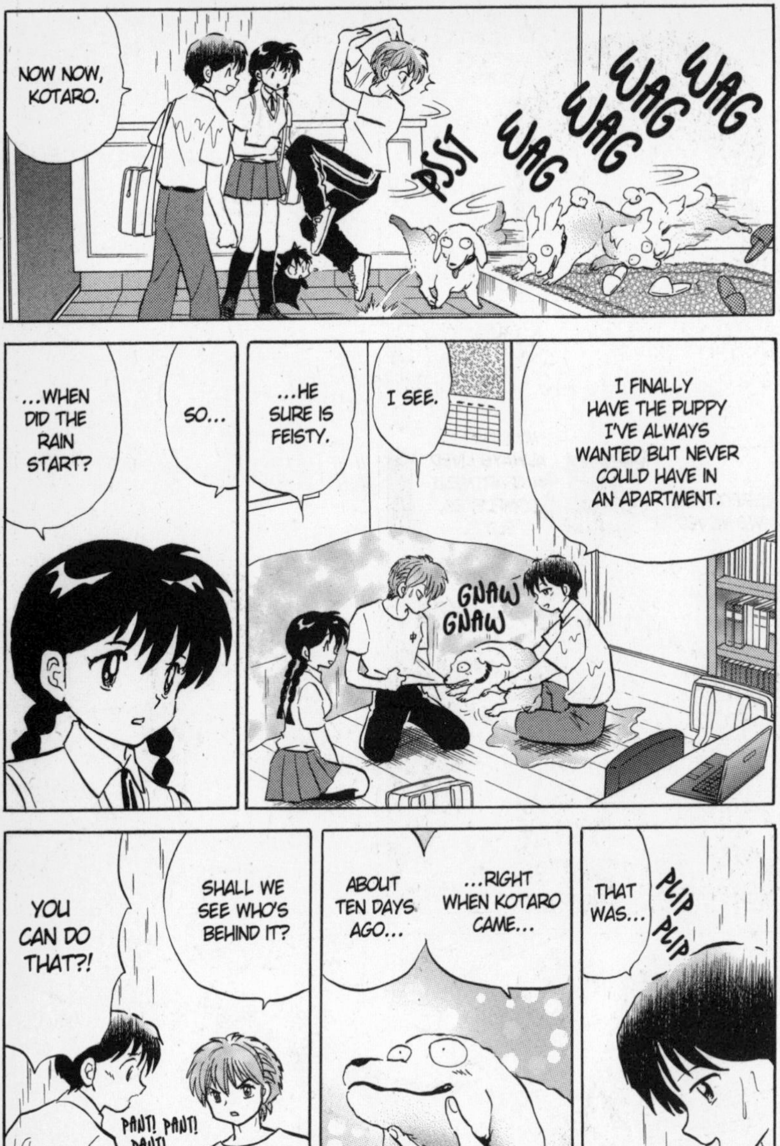
WAG WAG WAG WAG
PSST
NOW NOW, KOTARO.
I FINALLY HAVE THE PUPPY I'VE ALWAYS WANTED BUT NEVER COULD HAVE IN AN APARTMENT.
I SEE.
...HE SURE IS FEISTY.
GNAW GNAW
SO...
...WHEN DID THE RAIN START?
THAT WAS...
PLIP PLIP
...RIGHT WHEN KOTARO CAME...
ABOUT TEN DAYS AGO...
SHALL WE SEE WHO'S BEHIND IT?
YOU CAN DO THAT?!
PANT! PANT! PANT!

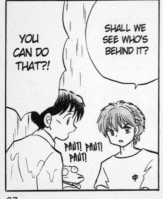

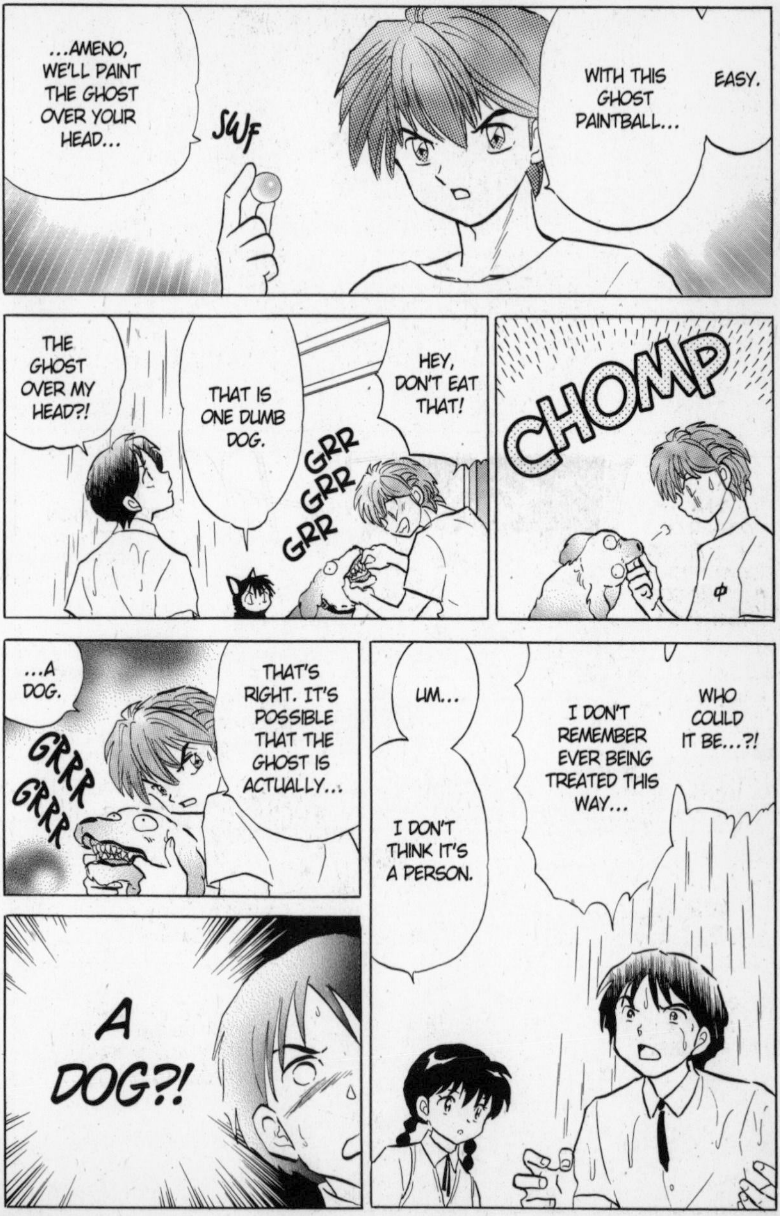
EASY.
WITH THIS GHOST PAINTBALL...
SWF
...AMENO, WE'LL PAINT THE GHOST OVER YOUR HEAD...
CHOMP
HEY, DON'T EAT THAT!
GRR GRR GRR
THAT IS ONE DUMB DOG.
THE GHOST OVER MY HEAD?!
WHO COULD IT BE...?!
I DON'T REMEMBER EVER BEING TREATED THIS WAY...
UM...
I DON'T THINK IT'S A PERSON.
THAT'S RIGHT. IT'S POSSIBLE THAT THE GHOST IS ACTUALLY...
...A DOG.
GRRR GRRR
A DOG?!

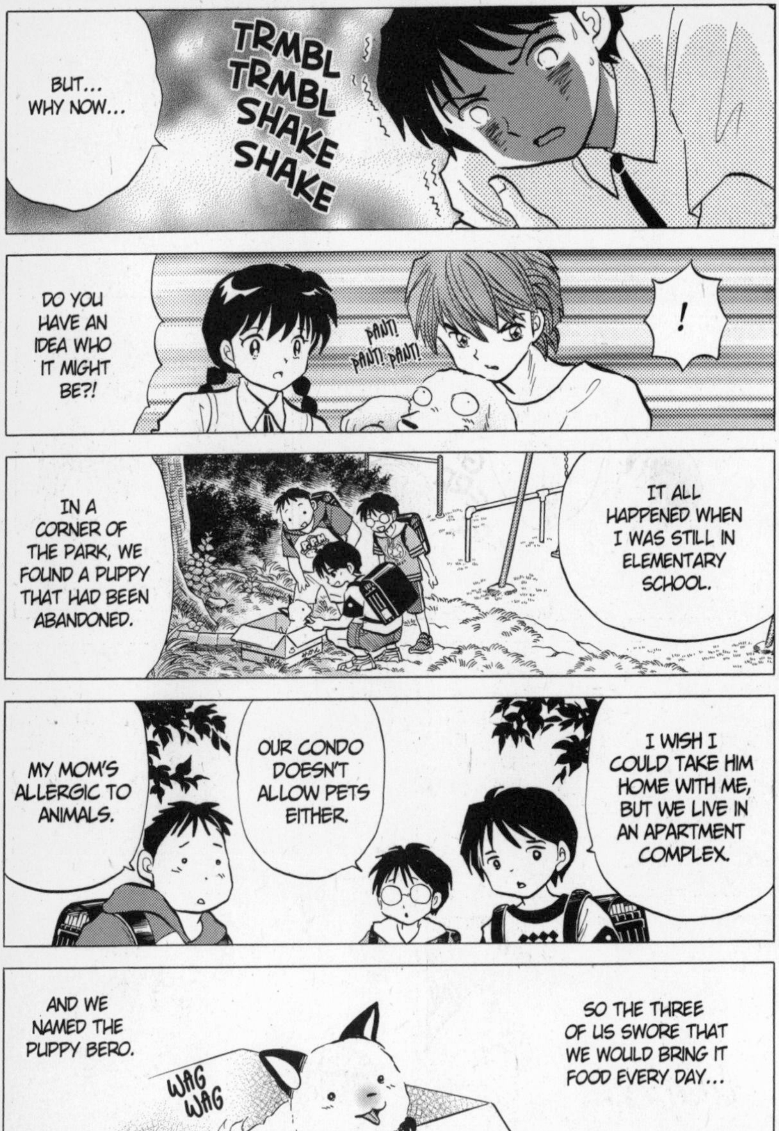
TRMBL TRMBL SHAKE SHAKE
BUT... WHY NOW...
!
PANT! PANT! PANT!
DO YOU HAVE AN IDEA WHO IT MIGHT BE?!
IT ALL HAPPENED WHEN I WAS STILL IN ELEMENTARY SCHOOL.
IN A CORNER OF THE PARK, WE FOUND A PUPPY THAT HAD BEEN ABANDONED.
I WISH I COULD TAKE HIM HOME WITH ME, BUT WE LIVE IN AN APARTMENT COMPLEX.
OUR CONDO DOESN'T ALLOW PETS EITHER.
MY MOM'S ALLERGIC TO ANIMALS.
SO THE THREE OF US SWORE THAT WE WOULD BRING IT FOOD EVERY DAY...
WAG WAG
AND WE NAMED THE PUPPY BERO.

*Bero means "tongue" or "lick"

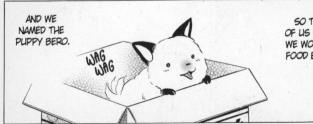

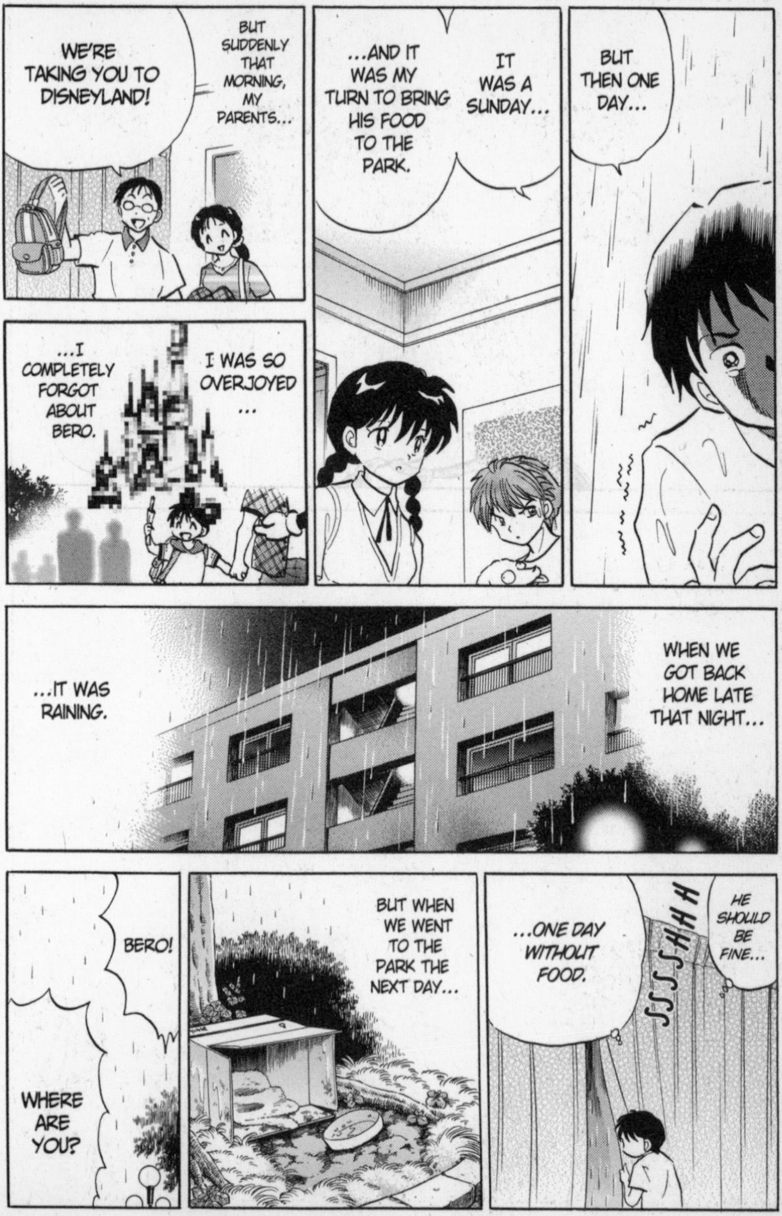
BUT THEN ONE DAY...
IT WAS A SUNDAY...
...AND IT WAS MY TURN TO BRING HIS FOOD TO THE PARK.
BUT SUDDENLY THAT MORNING, MY PARENTS...
WE'RE TAKING YOU TO DISNEYLAND!
I WAS SO OVERJOYED...
...I COMPLETELY FORGOT ABOUT BERO.
WHEN WE GOT BACK HOME LATE THAT NIGHT...
...IT WAS RAINING.
HE SHOULD BE FINE...
SSSSHHHH
...ONE DAY WITHOUT FOOD.
BUT WHEN WE WENT TO THE PARK THE NEXT DAY...
BERO!
WHERE ARE YOU?

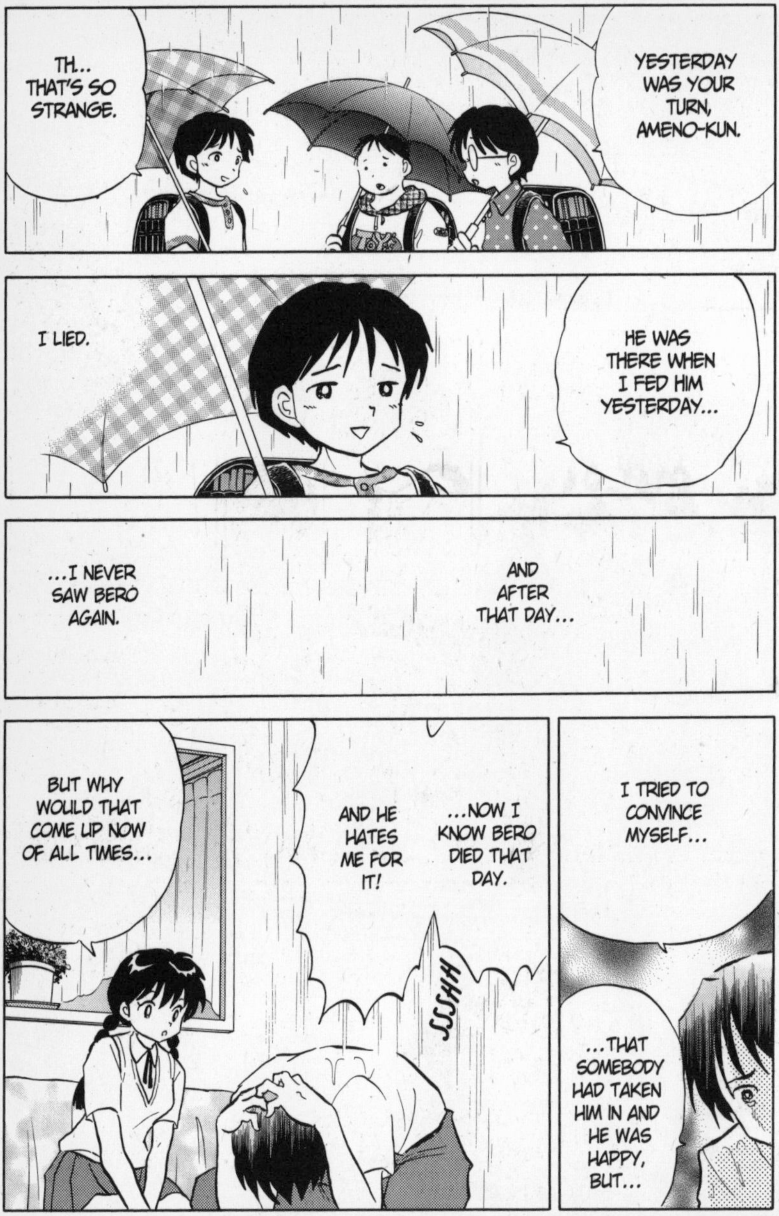
YESTERDAY WAS YOUR TURN, AMENO-KUN.
TH... THAT'S SO STRANGE.
HE WAS THERE WHEN I FED HIM YESTERDAY...
I LIED.
AND AFTER THAT DAY...
...I NEVER SAW BERO AGAIN.
I TRIED TO CONVINCE MYSELF...
...THAT SOMEBODY HAD TAKEN HIM IN AND HE WAS HAPPY, BUT...
...NOW I KNOW BERO DIED THAT DAY.
AND HE HATES ME FOR IT!
SSSHH
BUT WHY WOULD THAT COME UP NOW OF ALL TIMES...

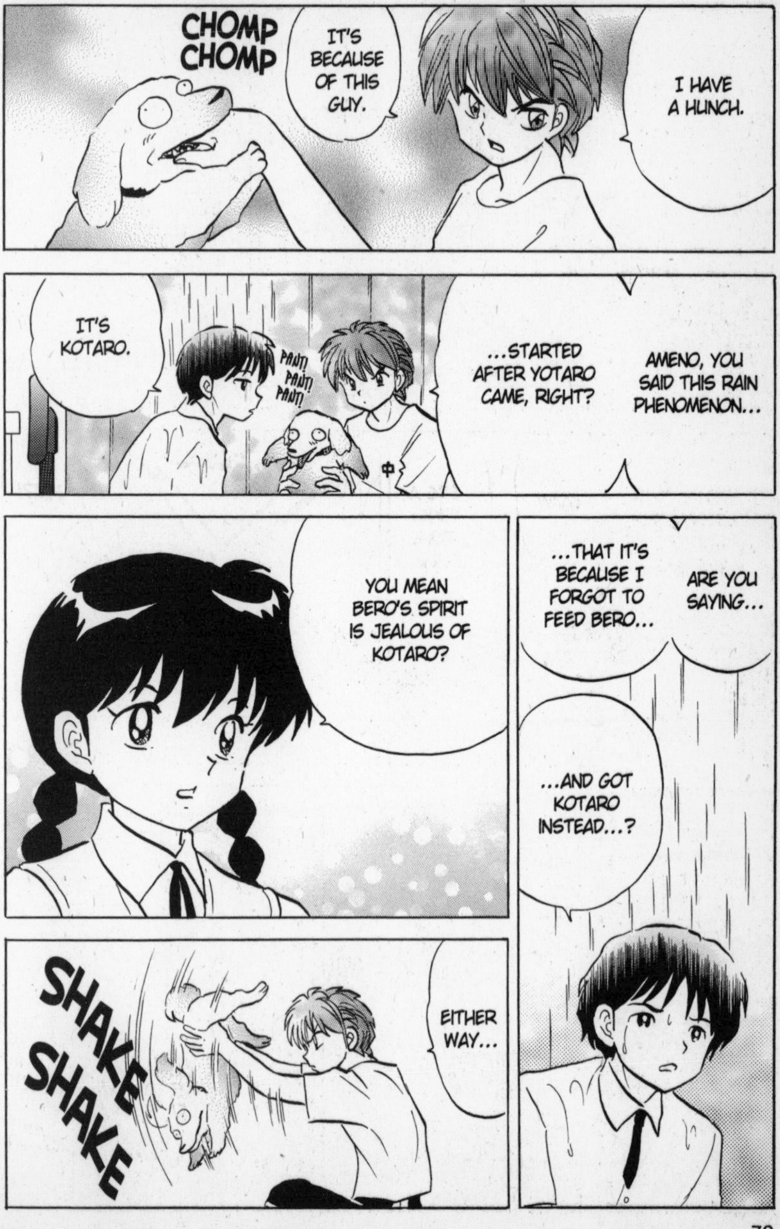
I HAVE A HUNCH.
IT'S BECAUSE OF THIS GUY.
CHOMP CHOMP
AMENO, YOU SAID THIS RAIN PHENOMENON...
...STARTED AFTER YOTARO CAME, RIGHT?
PANT! PANT! PANT!
IT'S KOTARO.
ARE YOU SAYING...
...THAT IT'S BECAUSE I FORGOT TO FEED BERO...
...AND GOT KOTARO INSTEAD...?
YOU MEAN BERO'S SPIRIT IS JEALOUS OF KOTARO?
EITHER WAY...
SHAKE SHAKE

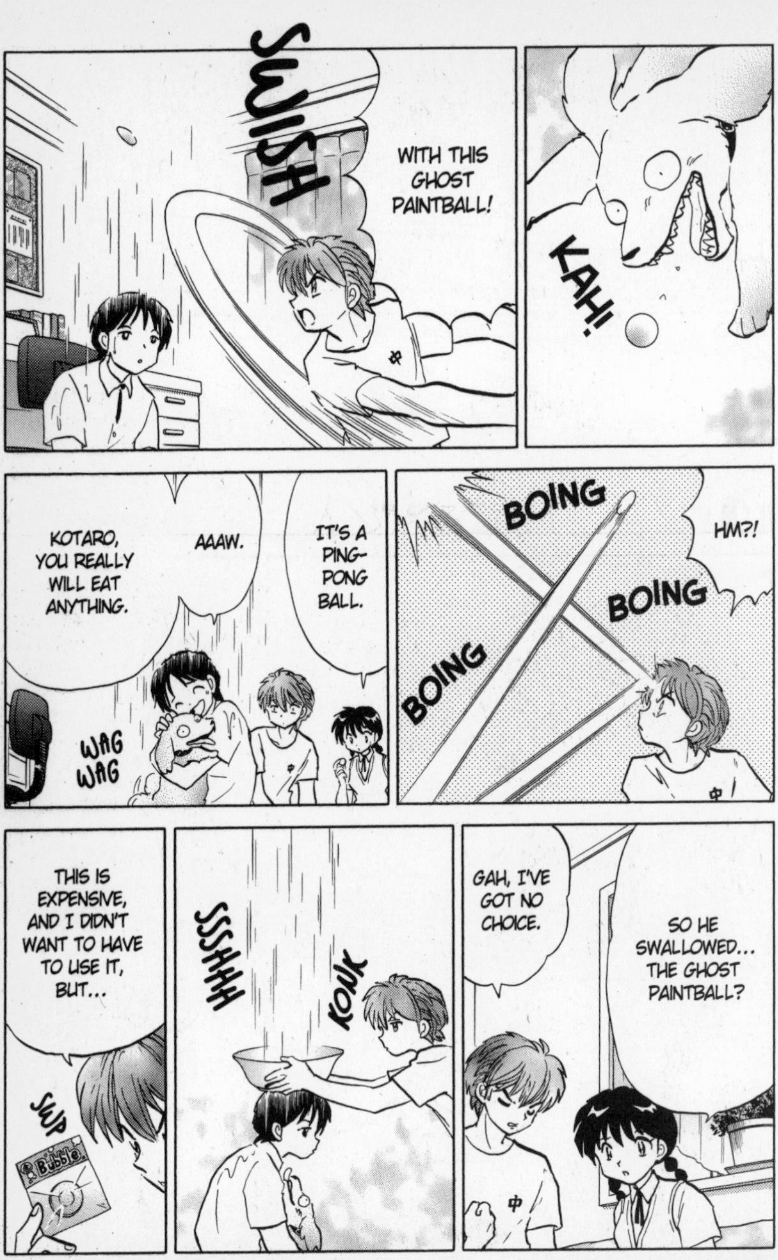
KAH!
WITH THIS GHOST PAINTBALL!
SWISH
HM?!
BOING
BOING
BOING
IT'S A PING-PONG BALL.
AAAW.
KOTARO, YOU REALLY WILL EAT ANYTHING.
WAG WAG
SO HE SWALLOWED... THE GHOST PAINTBALL?
GAH, I'VE GOT NO CHOICE.
KONK
SSSHHHH
THIS IS EXPENSIVE, AND I DIDN'T WANT TO HAVE TO USE IT, BUT...
SWIP
Bubble

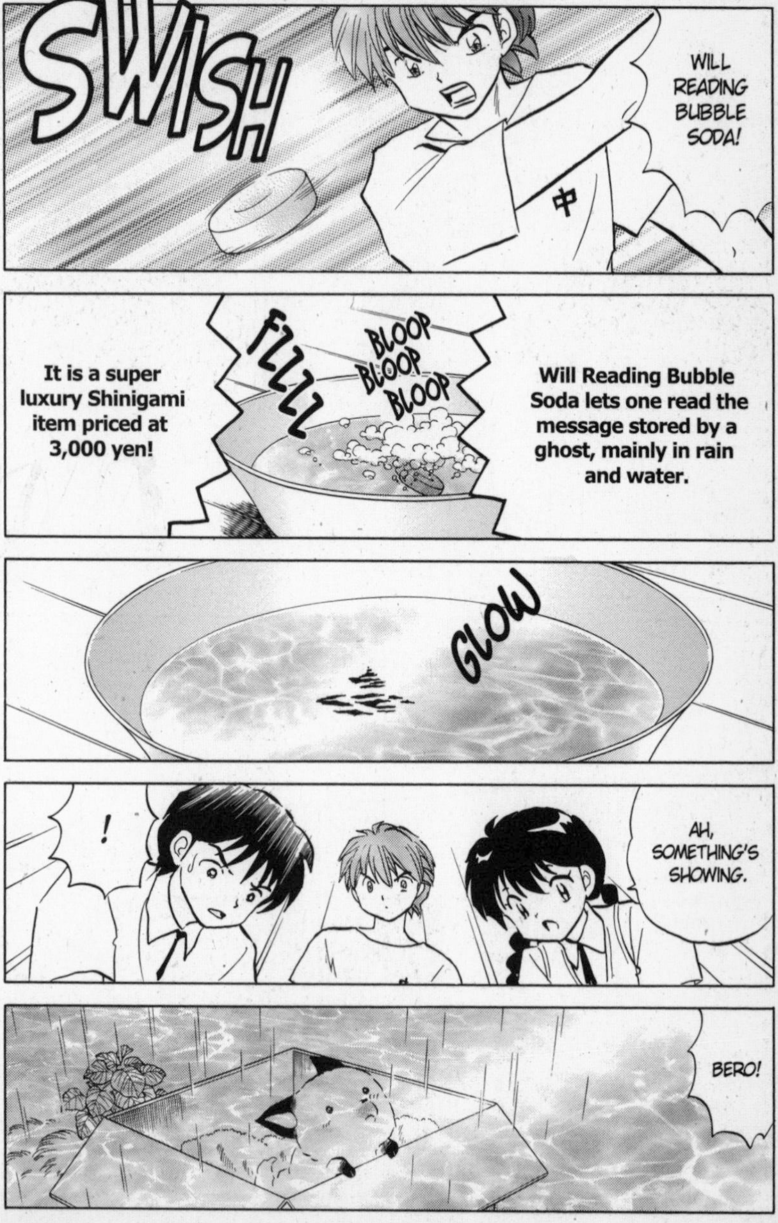
WILL READING BUBBLE SODA!
SWISH
Will Reading Bubble Soda lets one read the message stored by a ghost, mainly in rain and water.
BLOOP BLOOP BLOOP
FIZZZZ
It is a super luxury Shinigami item priced at 3,000 yen!
GLOW
AH, SOMETHING'S SHOWING.
!
BERO!

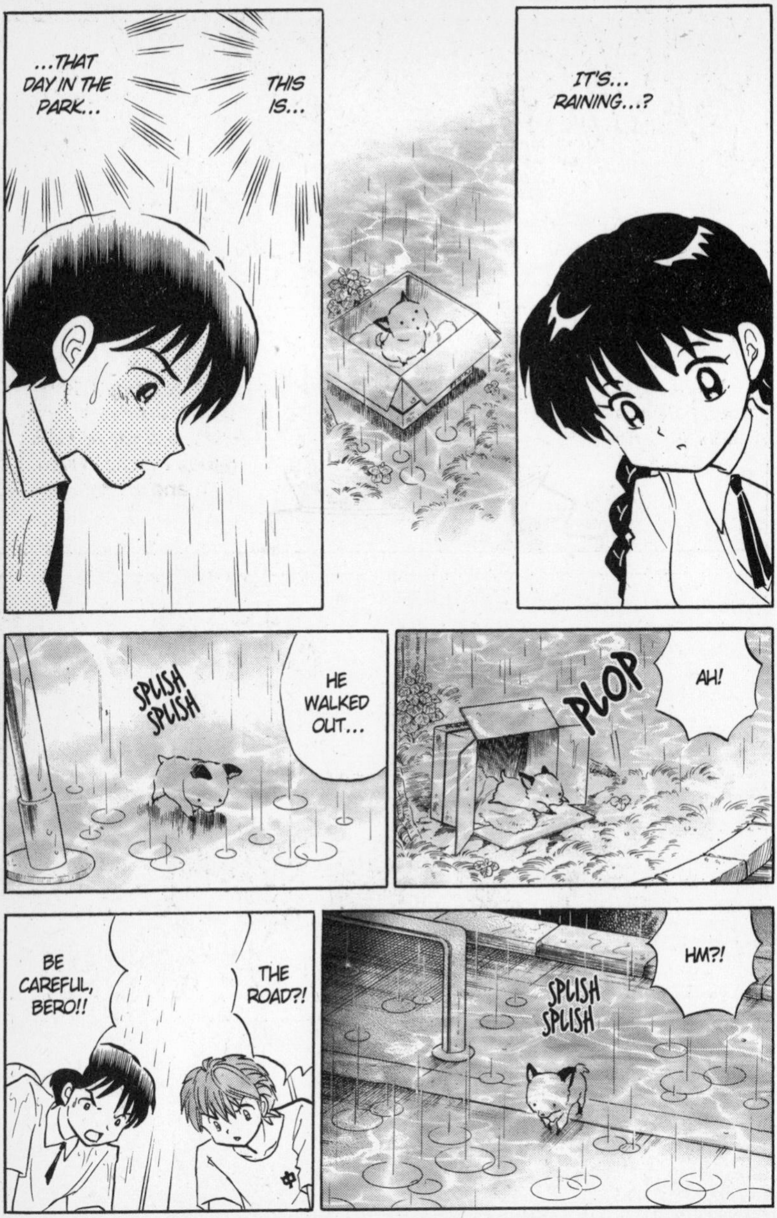
IT'S... RAINING...?
THIS IS...
...THAT DAY IN THE PARK...
AH!
PLOP
HE WALKED OUT...
SPLISH SPLISH
HM?!
SPLISH SPLISH
THE ROAD?!
BE CAREFUL, BERO!!

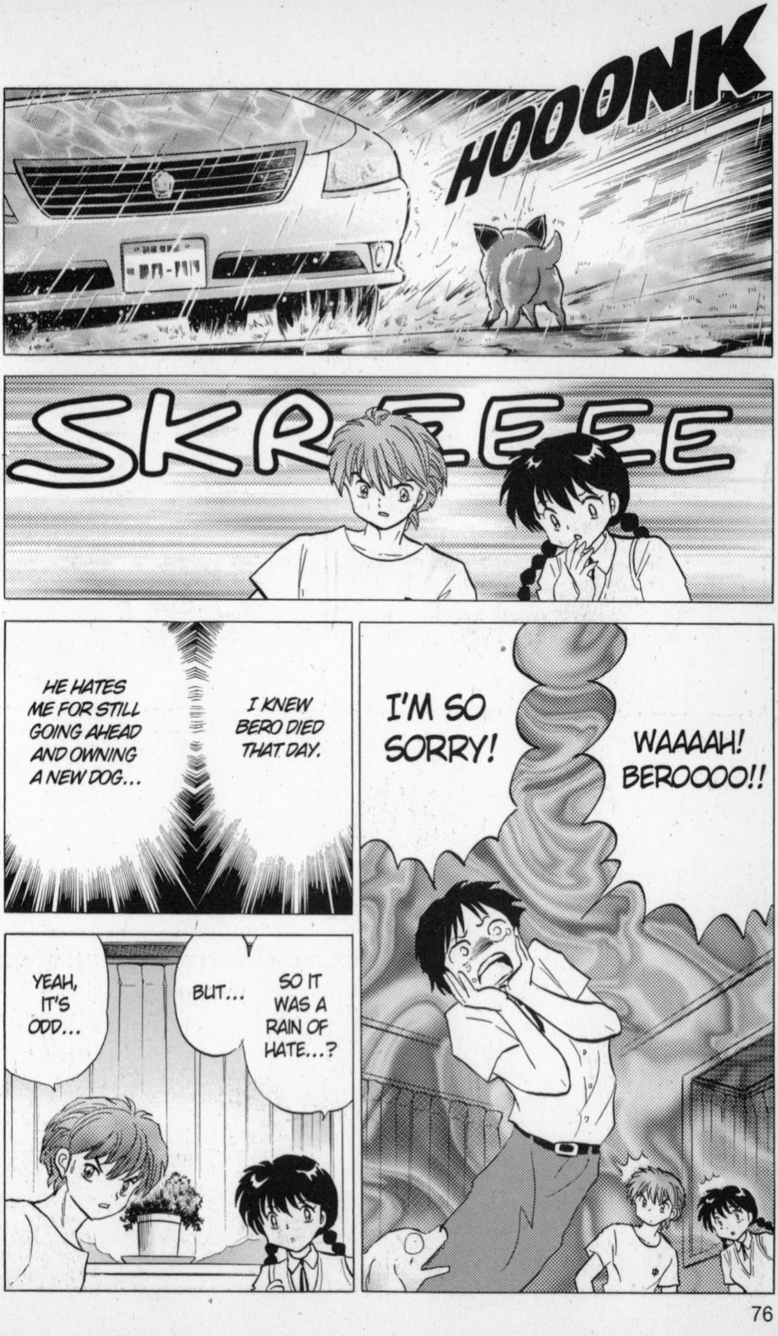
HOOONK
SKREEEE
WAAAAH! BEROOOO!!
I'M SO SORRY!
I KNEW BERO DIED THAT DAY.
HE HATES ME FOR STILL GOING AHEAD AND OWNING A NEW DOG...
SO IT WAS A RAIN OF HATE...?
BUT...
YEAH, IT'S ODD...

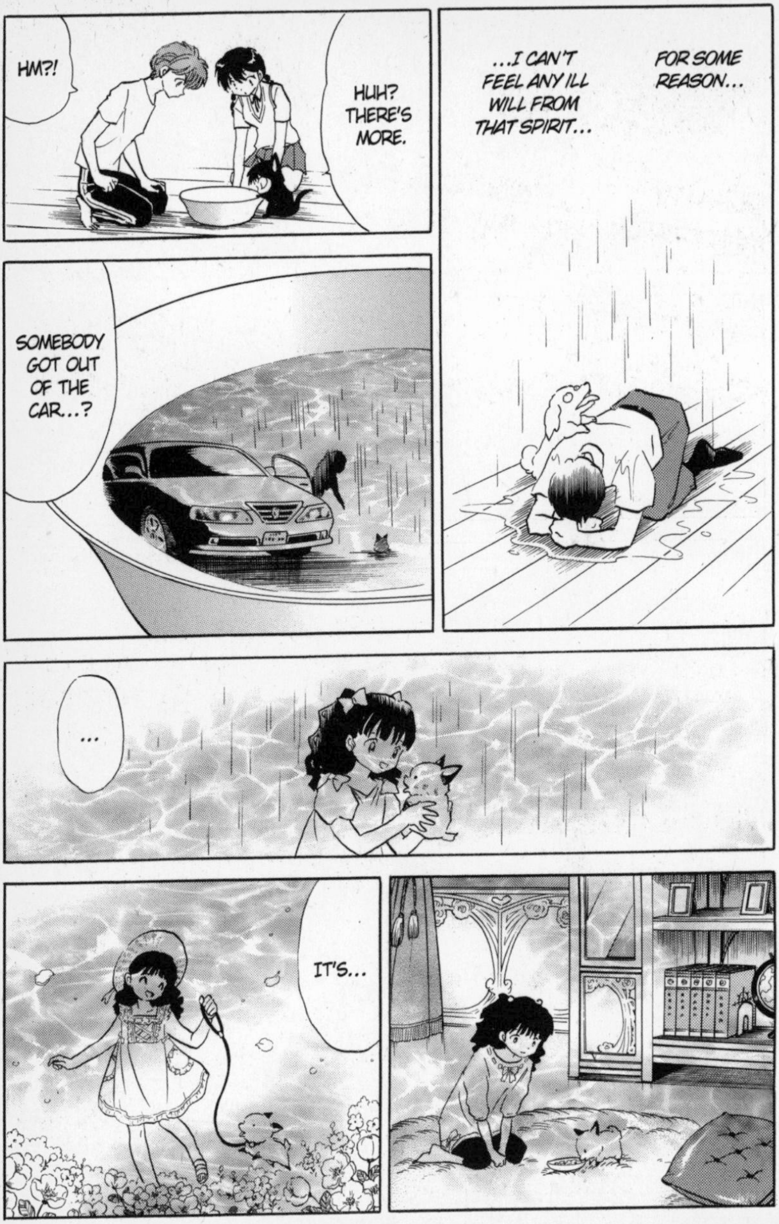
FOR SOME REASON...
...I CAN'T FEEL ANY ILL WILL FROM THAT SPIRIT...
HUH? THERE'S MORE.
HM?!
SOMEBODY GOT OUT OF THE CAR...?
...
IT'S...

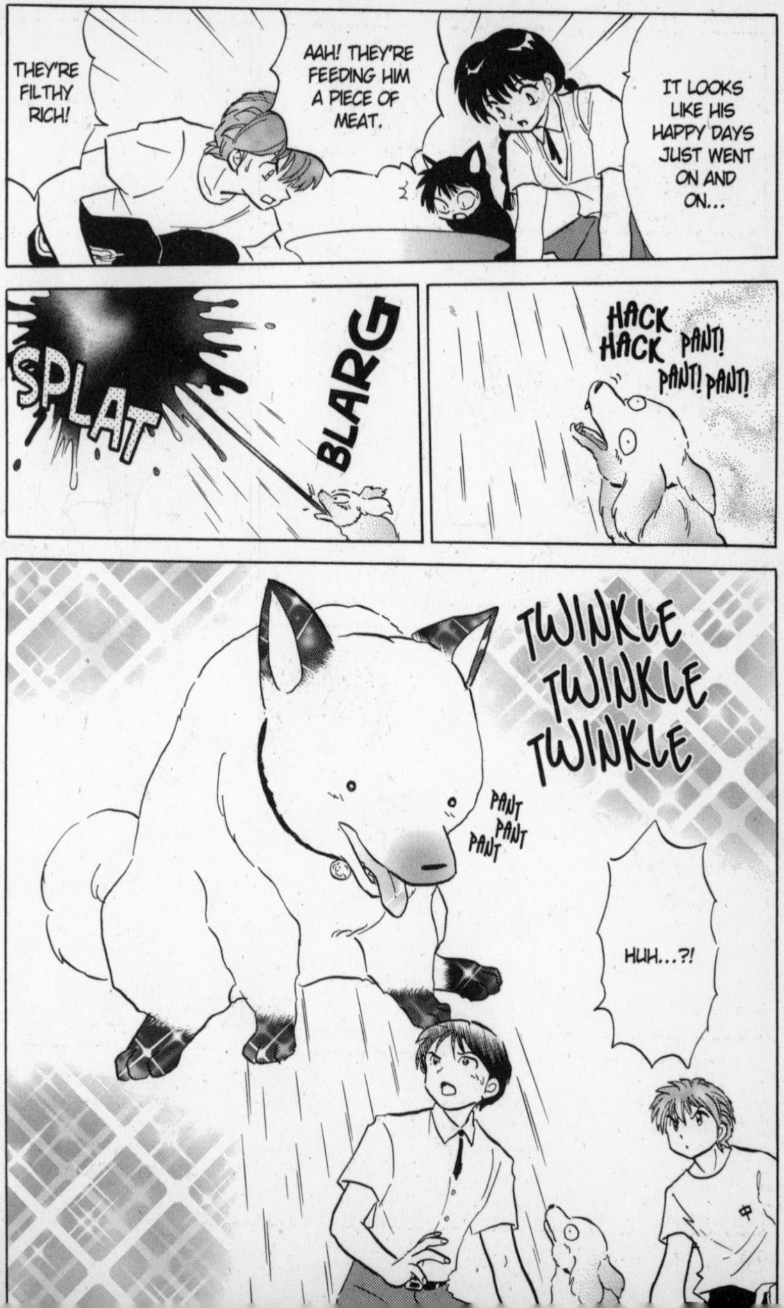
IT LOOKS LIKE HIS HAPPY DAYS JUST WENT ON AND ON...
AAH! THEY'RE FEEDING HIM A PIECE OF MEAT.
THEY'RE FILTHY RICH!
HACK HACK
PANT! PANT! PANT!
BLARG
SPLAT
TWINKLE TWINKLE TWINKLE
PANT PANT PANT
HUH...?!

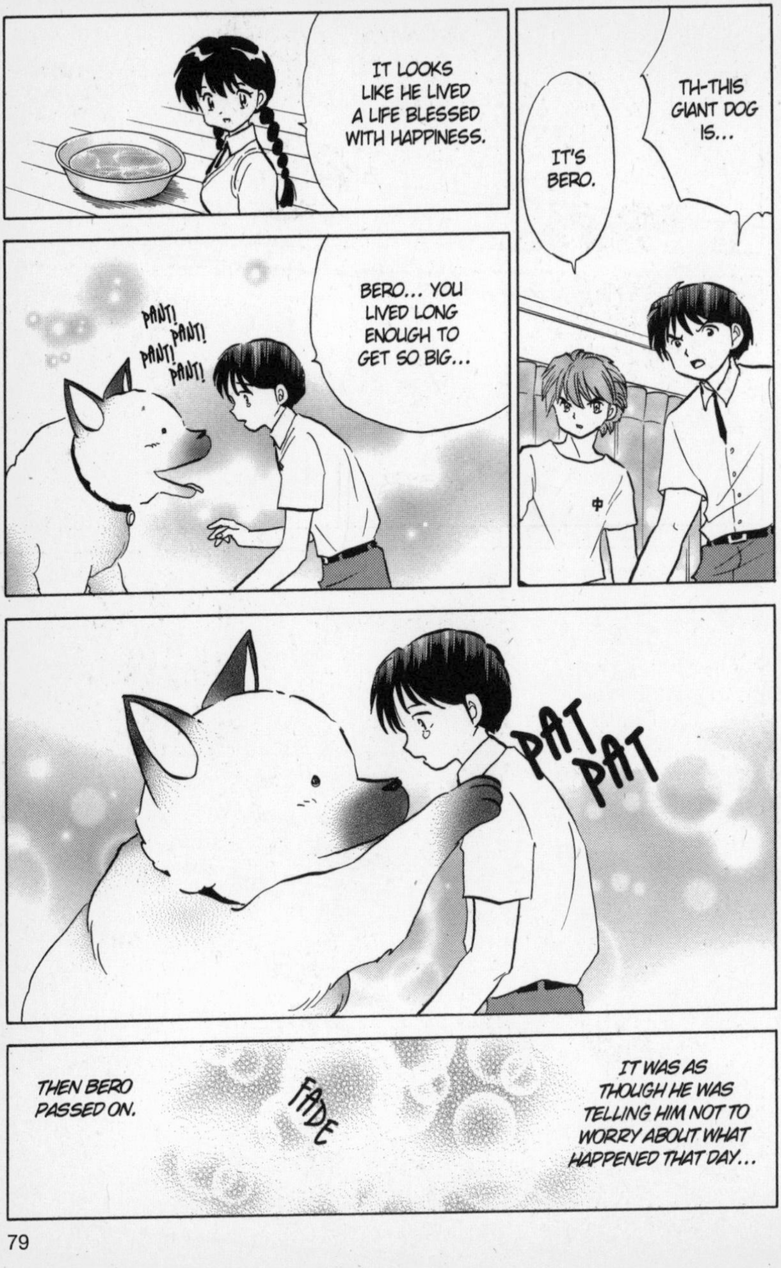

TH-THIS GIANT DOG IS...
IT'S BERO.
IT LOOKS LIKE HE LIVED A LIFE BLESSED WITH HAPPINESS.
BERO... YOU LIVED LONG ENOUGH TO GET SO BIG...
PANT! PANT! PANT! PANT!
PAT PAT
IT WAS AS THOUGH HE WAS TELLING HIM NOT TO WORRY ABOUT WHAT HAPPENED THAT DAY...
FADE
THEN BERO PASSED ON.

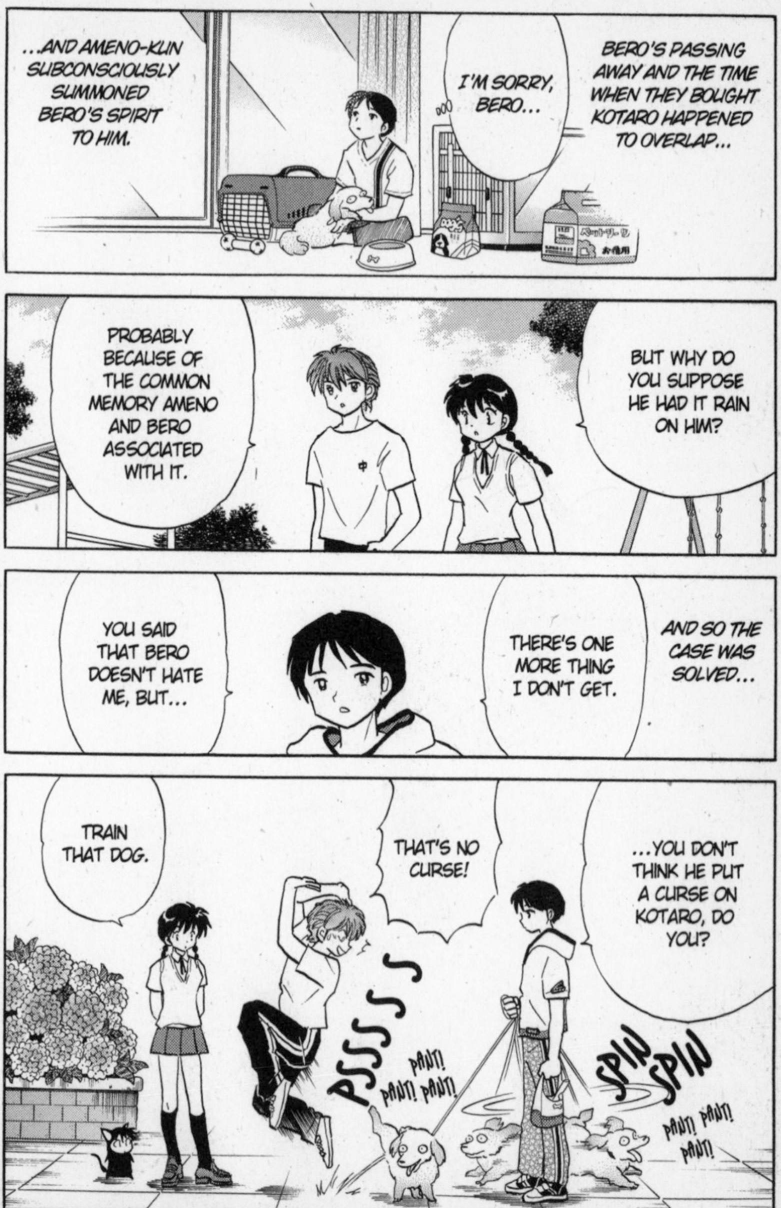
BERO'S PASSING AWAY AND THE TIME WHEN THEY BOUGHT KOTARO HAPPENED TO OVERLAP...
I'M SORRY, BERO...
...AND AMENO-KUN SUBCONSCIOUSLY SUMMONED BERO'S SPIRIT TO HIM.
BUT WHY DO YOU SUPPOSE HE HAD IT RAIN ON HIM?
PROBABLY BECAUSE OF THE COMMON MEMORY AMENO AND BERO ASSOCIATED WITH IT.
AND SO THE CASE WAS SOLVED...
THERE'S ONE MORE THING I DON'T GET.
YOU SAID THAT BERO DOESN'T HATE ME, BUT...
...YOU DON'T THINK HE PUT A CURSE ON KOTARO, DO YOU?
SPIN SPIN
PANT! PANT! PANT!
THAT'S NO CURSE!
PANT! PANT! PANT!
PSSSS
TRAIN THAT DOG.

# CHAPTER 103: THE POVERTY MOTH

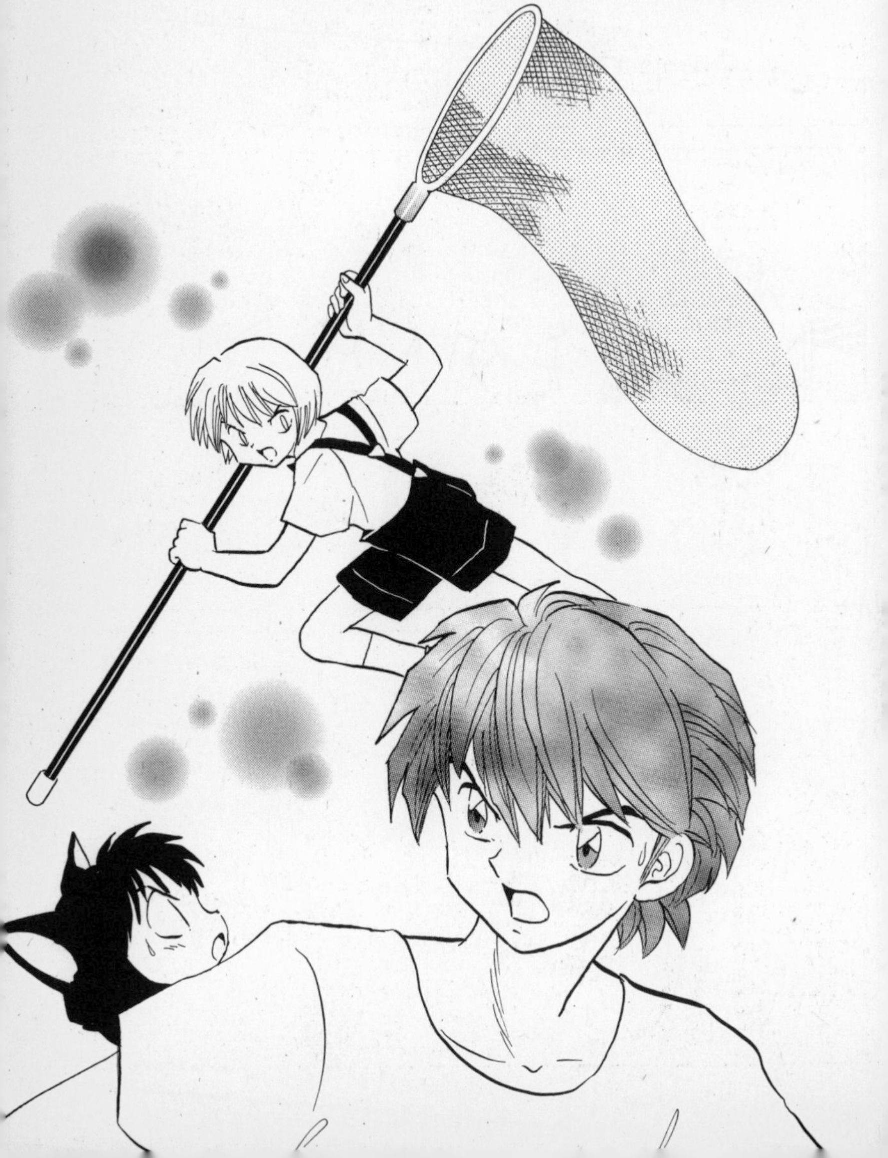

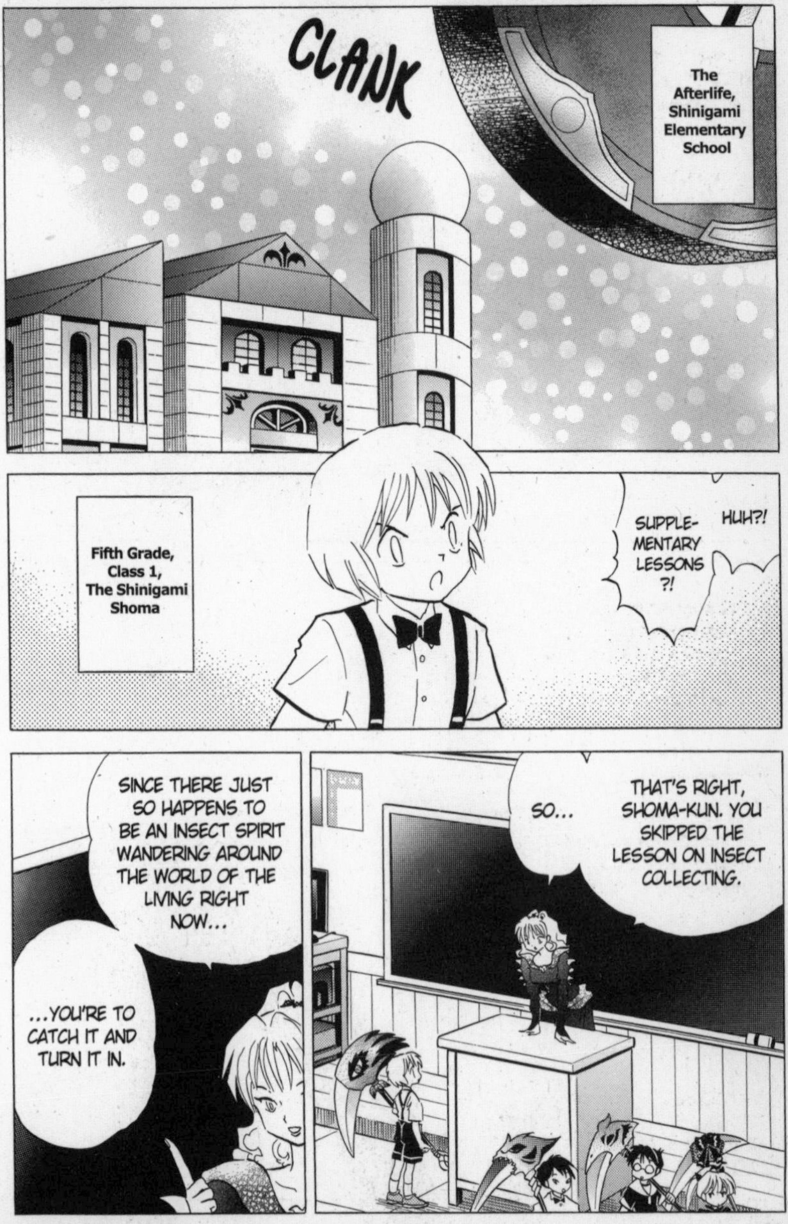
The Afterlife, Shinigami Elementary School
CLANK
HUH?!
SUPPLE-MENTARY LESSONS?!
Fifth Grade, Class 1, The Shinigami Shoma
THAT'S RIGHT, SHOMA-KUN. YOU SKIPPED THE LESSON ON INSECT COLLECTING.
SO...
SINCE THERE JUST SO HAPPENS TO BE AN INSECT SPIRIT WANDERING AROUND THE WORLD OF THE LIVING RIGHT NOW...
...YOU'RE TO CATCH IT AND TURN IT IN.

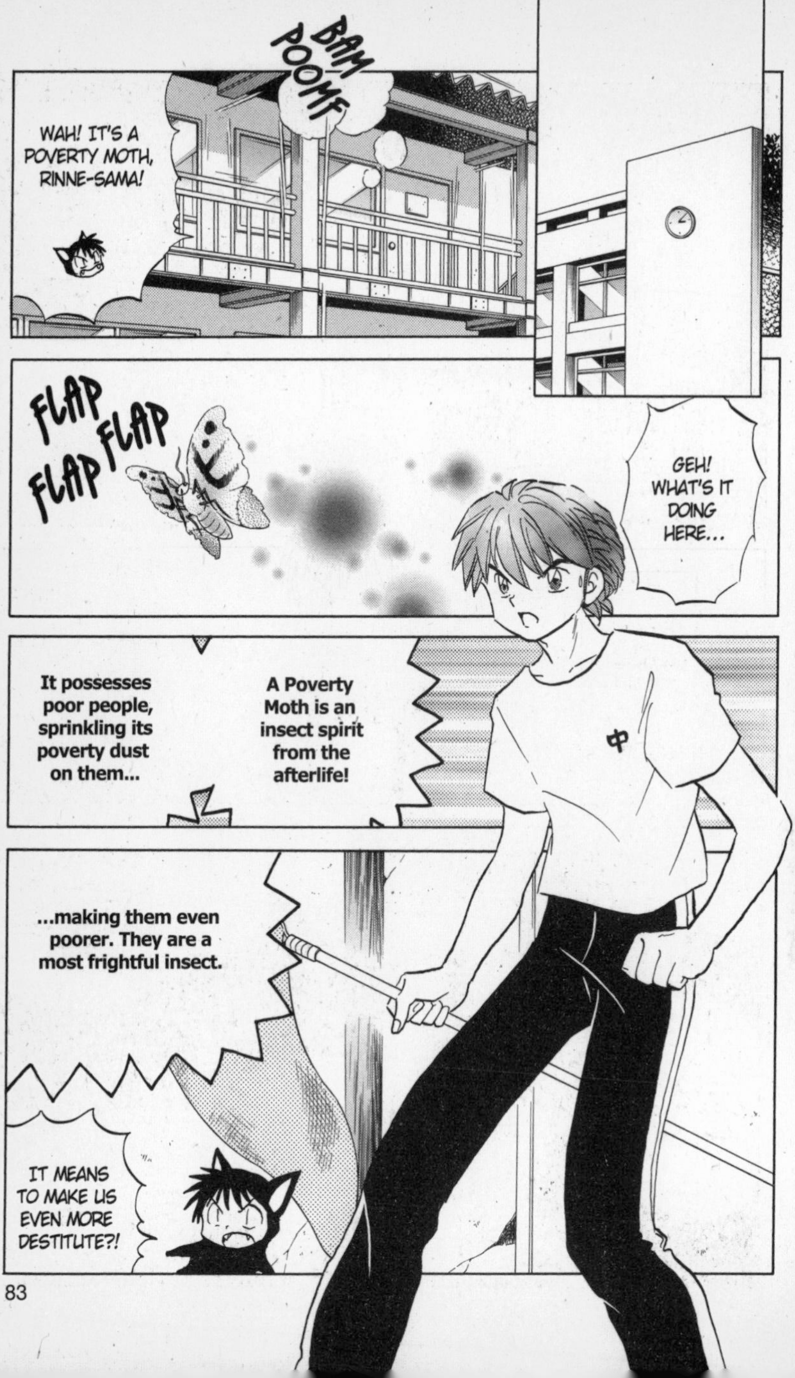
BAM
POOMF
WAH! IT'S A POVERTY MOTH, RINNE-SAMA!
GEH! WHAT'S IT DOING HERE...
FLAP FLAP FLAP
A Poverty Moth is an insect spirit from the afterlife!
It possesses poor people, sprinkling its poverty dust on them...
...making them even poorer. They are a most frightful insect.
IT MEANS TO MAKE US EVEN MORE DESTITUTE?!

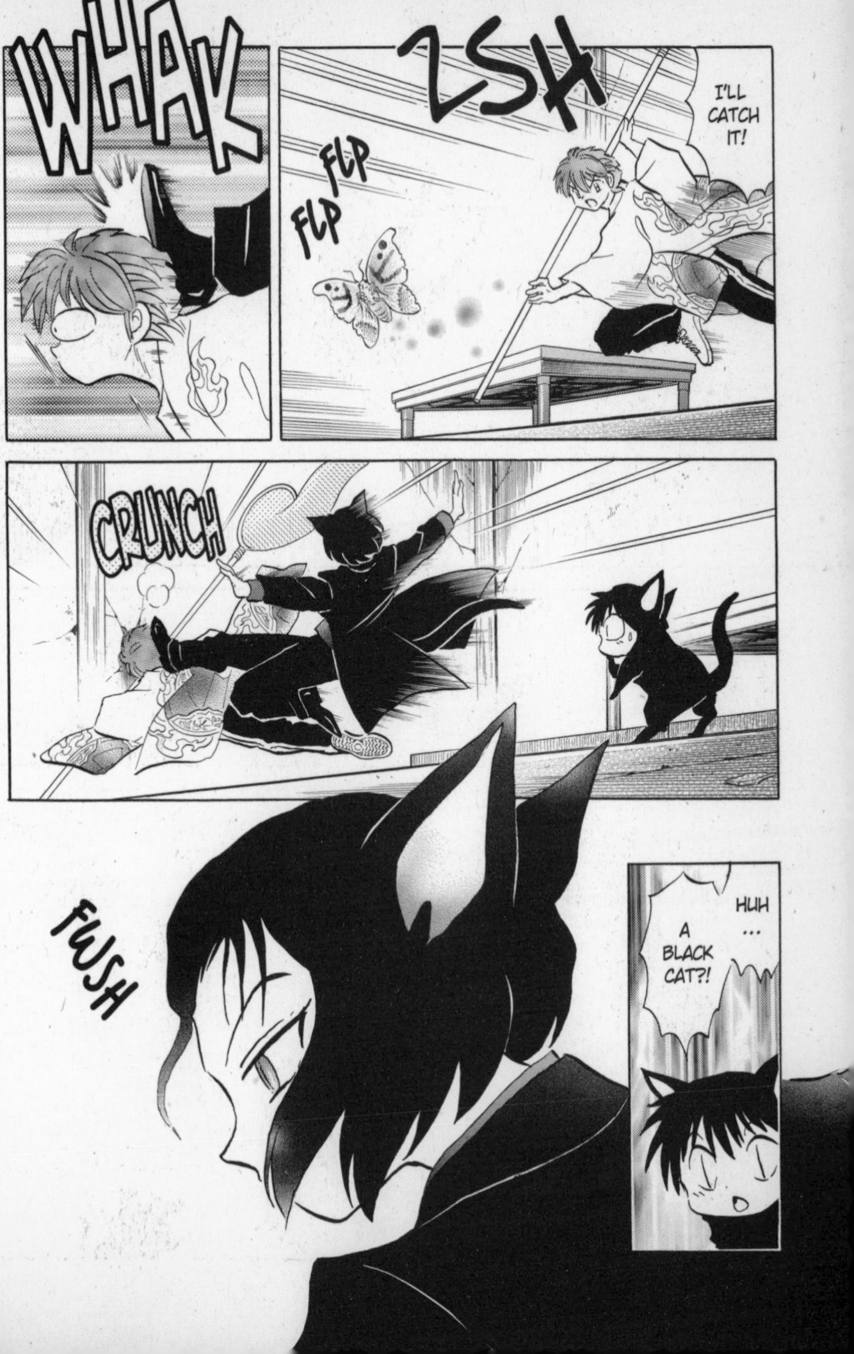
ZSH
I'LL CATCH IT!
FLP FLP
WHAK
CRUNCH
HUH ...
A BLACK CAT?!
FWSH

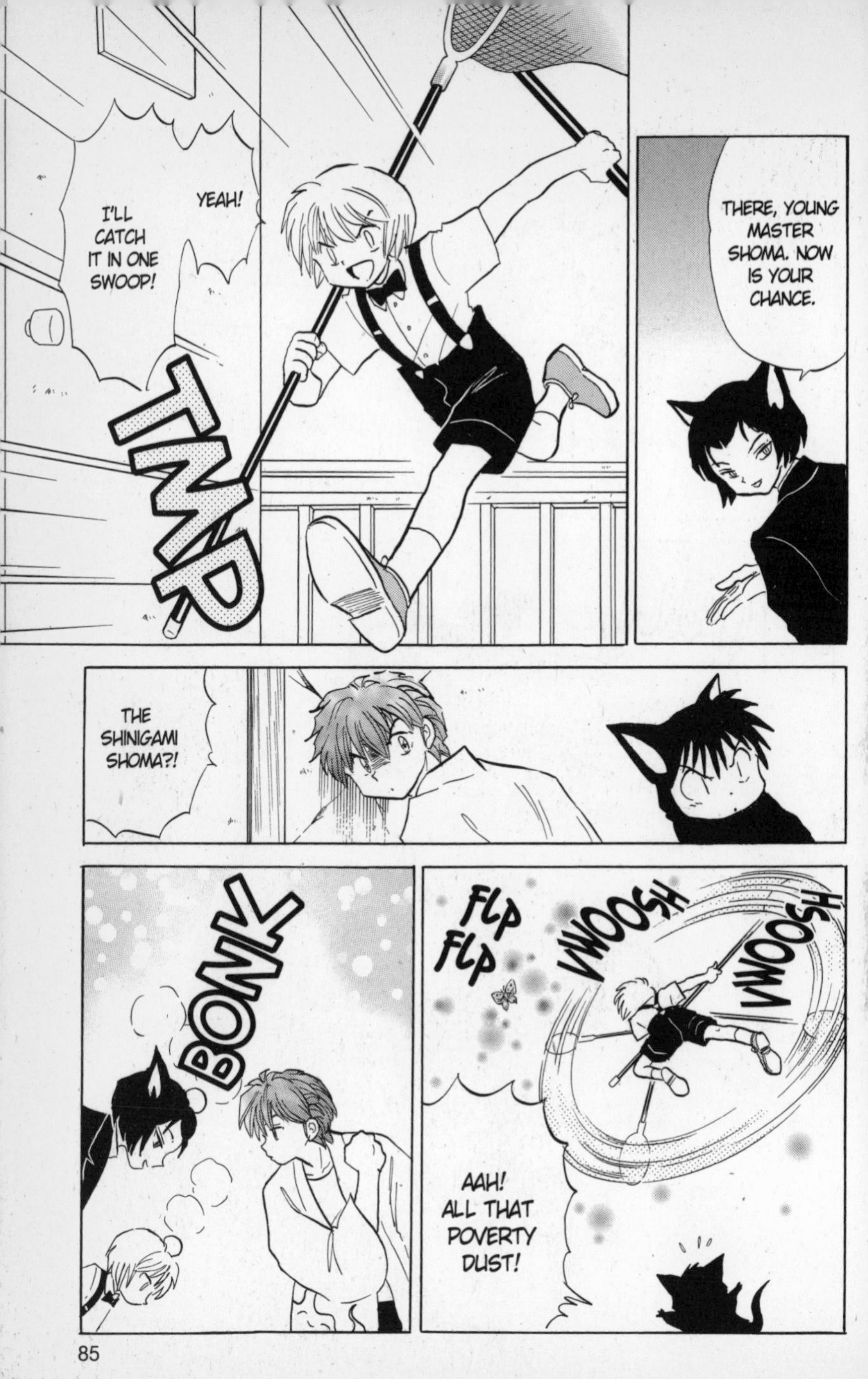
THERE, YOUNG MASTER SHOMA. NOW IS YOUR CHANCE.
YEAH!
I'LL CATCH IT IN ONE SWOOP!
TMP
THE SHINIGAMI SHOMA?!
VWOOSH
VWOOSH
FLP FLP
AAH! ALL THAT POVERTY DUST!
BONK

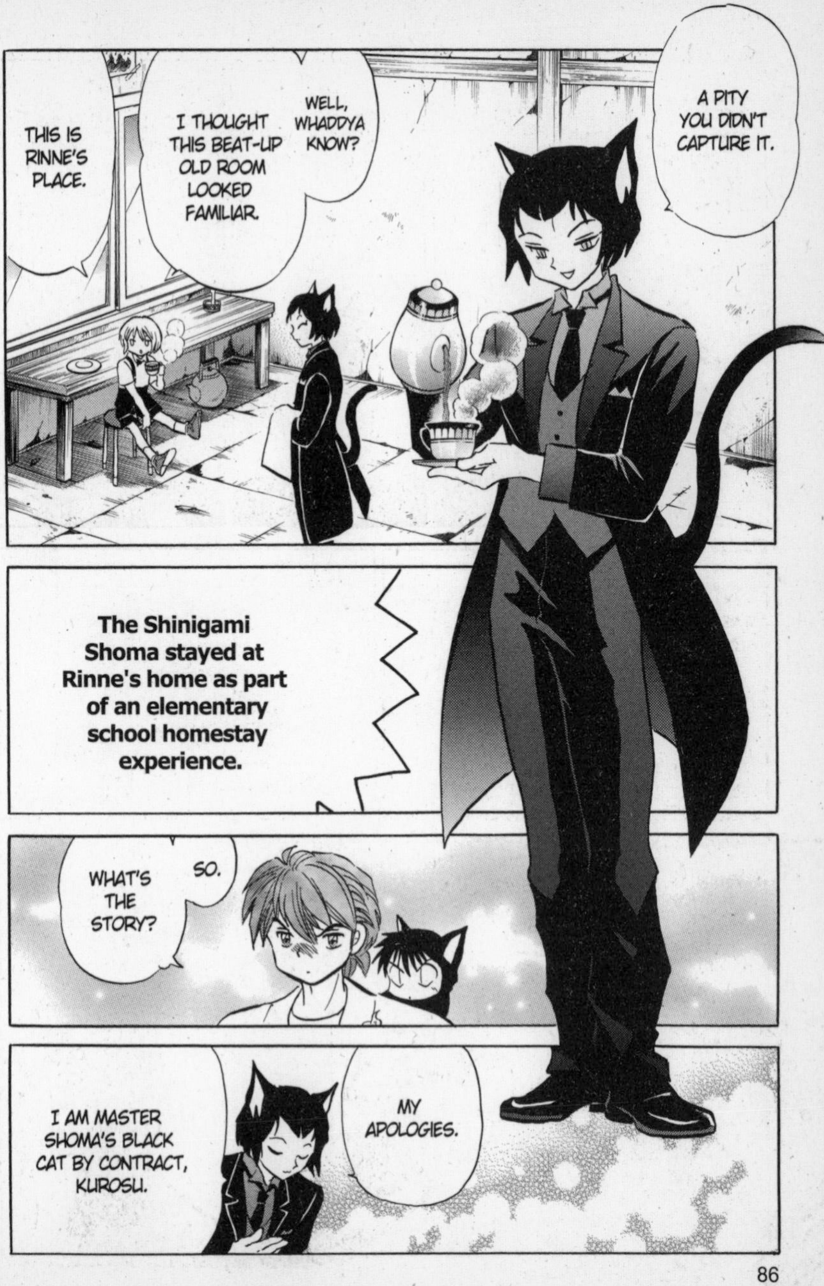
A PITY YOU DIDN'T CAPTURE IT.
WELL, WHADDYA KNOW?
I THOUGHT THIS BEAT-UP OLD ROOM LOOKED FAMILIAR.
THIS IS RINNE'S PLACE.
The Shinigami Shoma stayed at Rinne's home as part of an elementary school homestay experience.
SO.
WHAT'S THE STORY?
MY APOLOGIES.
I AM MASTER SHOMA'S BLACK CAT BY CONTRACT, KUROSU.

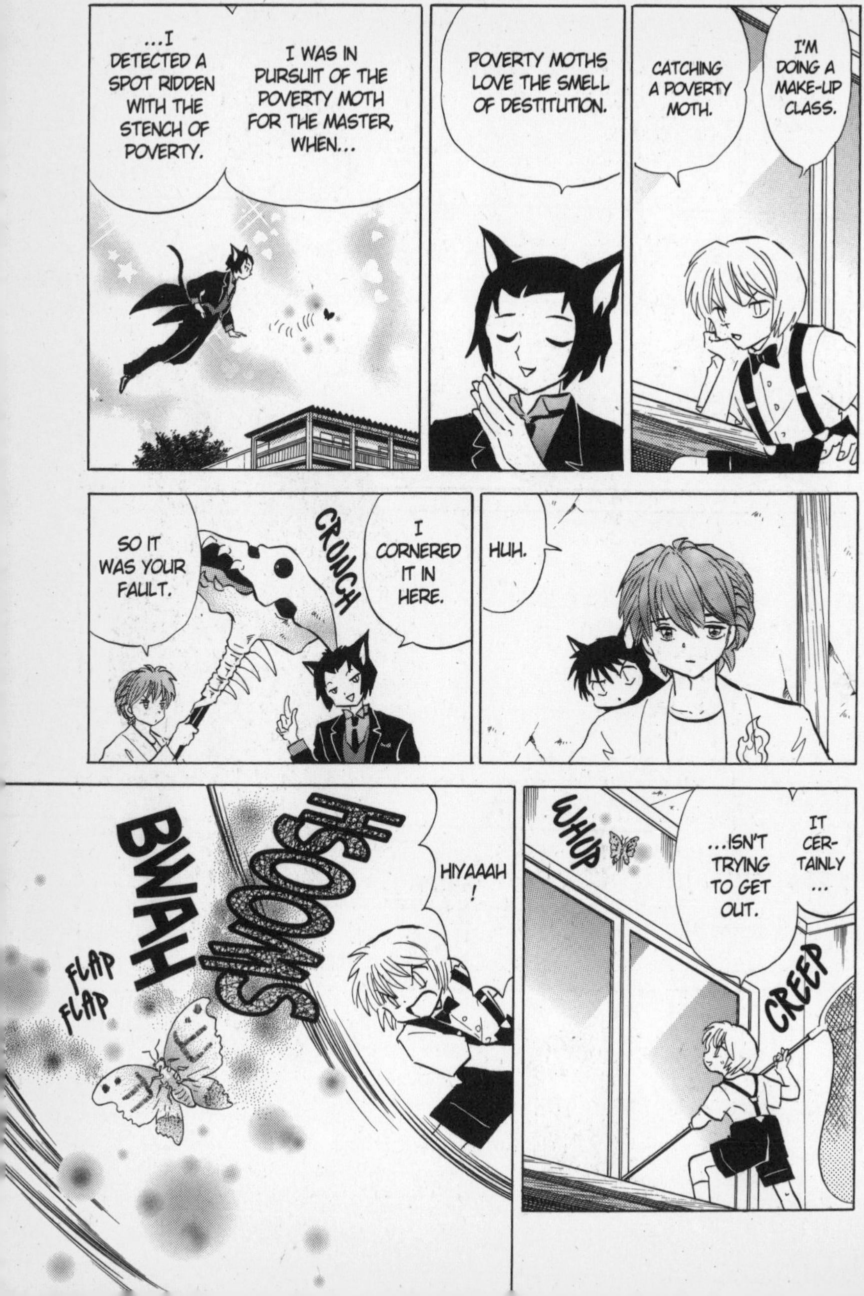
I'M DOING A MAKE-UP CLASS.
CATCHING A POVERTY MOTH.
POVERTY MOTHS LOVE THE SMELL OF DESTITUTION.
I WAS IN PURSUIT OF THE POVERTY MOTH FOR THE MASTER, WHEN...
...I DETECTED A SPOT RIDDEN WITH THE STENCH OF POVERTY.
HUH.
I CORNERED IT IN HERE.
CRUNCH
SO IT WAS YOUR FAULT.
IT CER-TAINLY...
...ISN'T TRYING TO GET OUT.
WHUP
CREEP
HIYAAAH!
SWOOSH
BWAH
FLAP FLAP

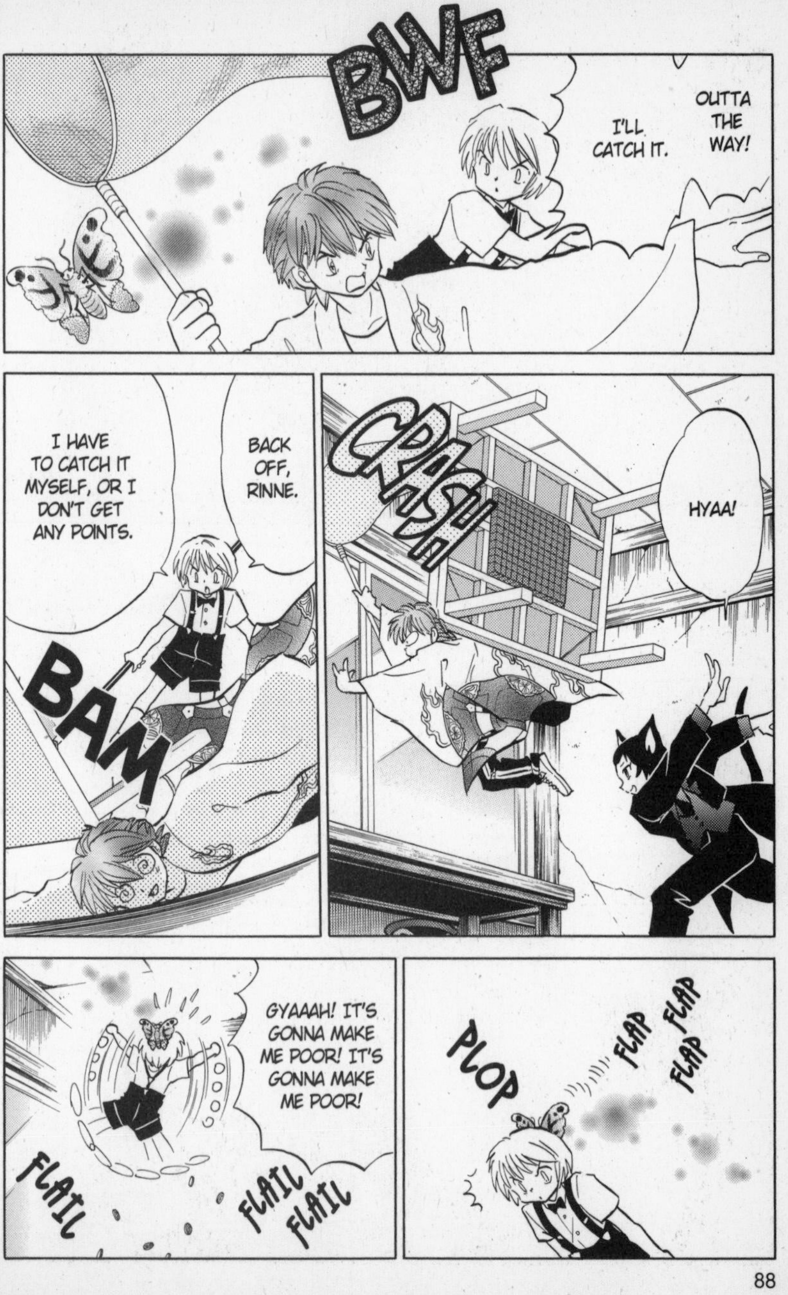
BWF
OUTTA THE WAY!
I'LL CATCH IT.
HYAA!
CRASH
BACK OFF, RINNE.
I HAVE TO CATCH IT MYSELF, OR I DON'T GET ANY POINTS.
BAM
FLAP FLAP FLAP
PLOP
GYAAAH! IT'S GONNA MAKE ME POOR! IT'S GONNA MAKE ME POOR!
FLAIL FLAIL FLAIL

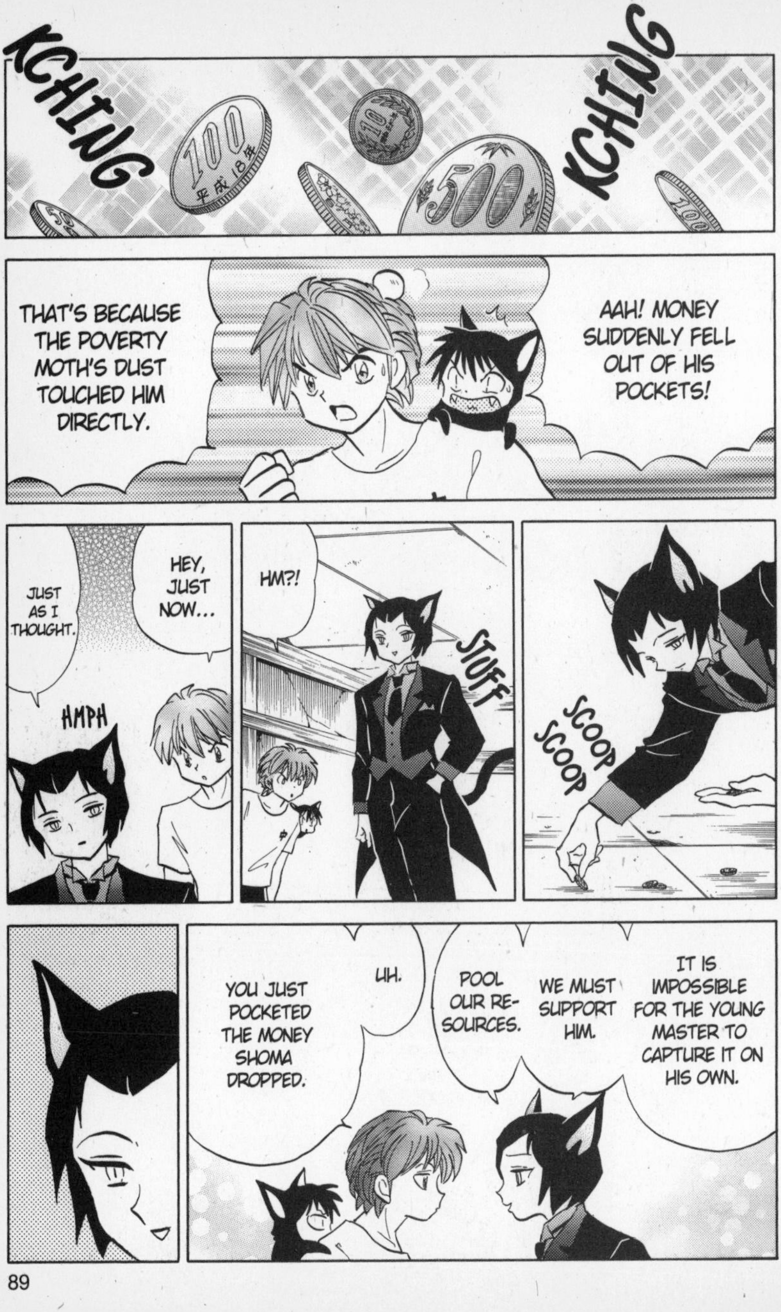
KCHING
KCHING
AAH! MONEY SUDDENLY FELL OUT OF HIS POCKETS!
THAT'S BECAUSE THE POVERTY MOTH'S DUST TOUCHED HIM DIRECTLY.
SCOOP SCOOP
HM?!
STUFF
HEY, JUST NOW...
JUST AS I THOUGHT.
HMPH
IT IS IMPOSSIBLE FOR THE YOUNG MASTER TO CAPTURE IT ON HIS OWN.
WE MUST SUPPORT HIM.
POOL OUR RE-SOURCES.
UH.
YOU JUST POCKETED THE MONEY SHOMA DROPPED.

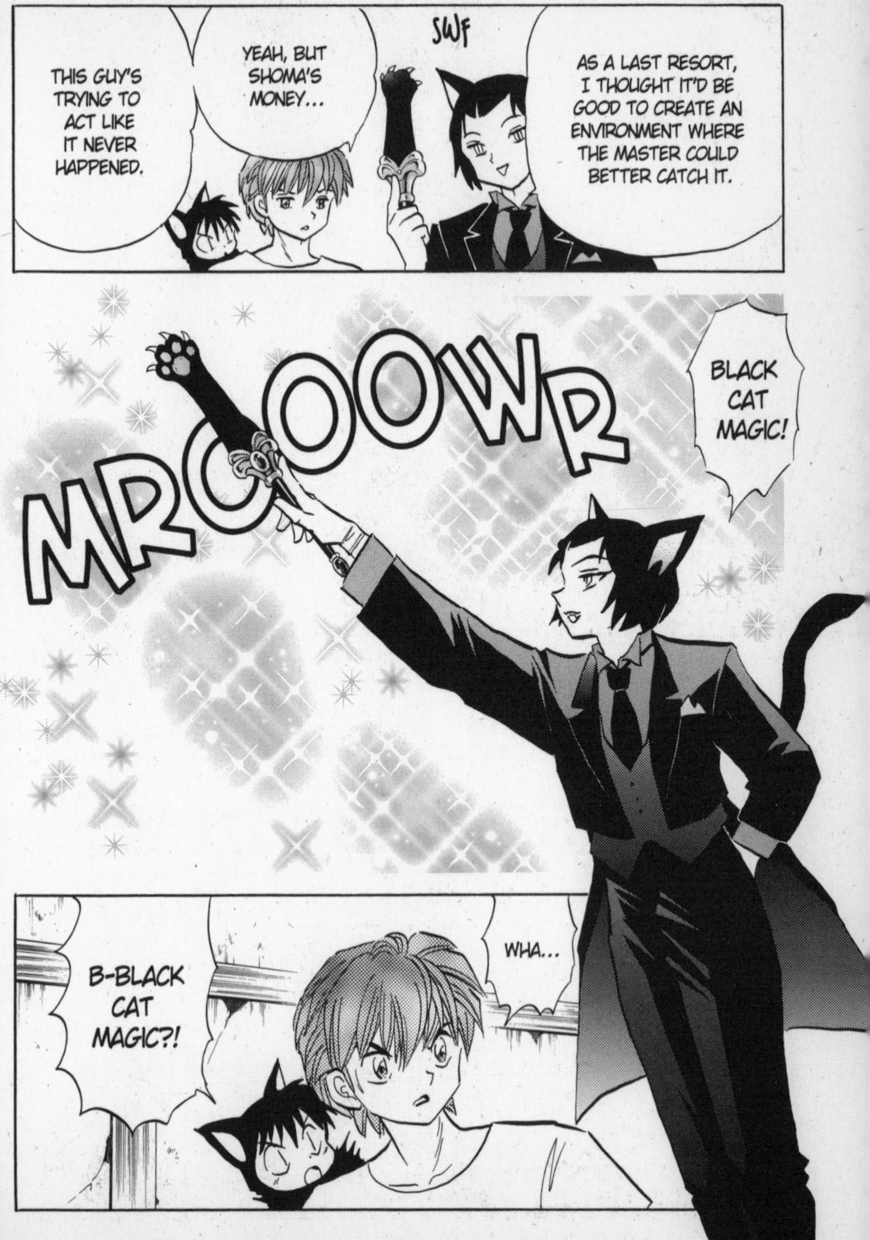
SWF
AS A LAST RESORT, I THOUGHT IT'D BE GOOD TO CREATE AN ENVIRONMENT WHERE THE MASTER COULD BETTER CATCH IT.
YEAH, BUT SHOMA'S MONEY...
THIS GUY'S TRYING TO ACT LIKE IT NEVER HAPPENED.
BLACK CAT MAGIC!
MROOOWR
WHA...
B-BLACK CAT MAGIC?!

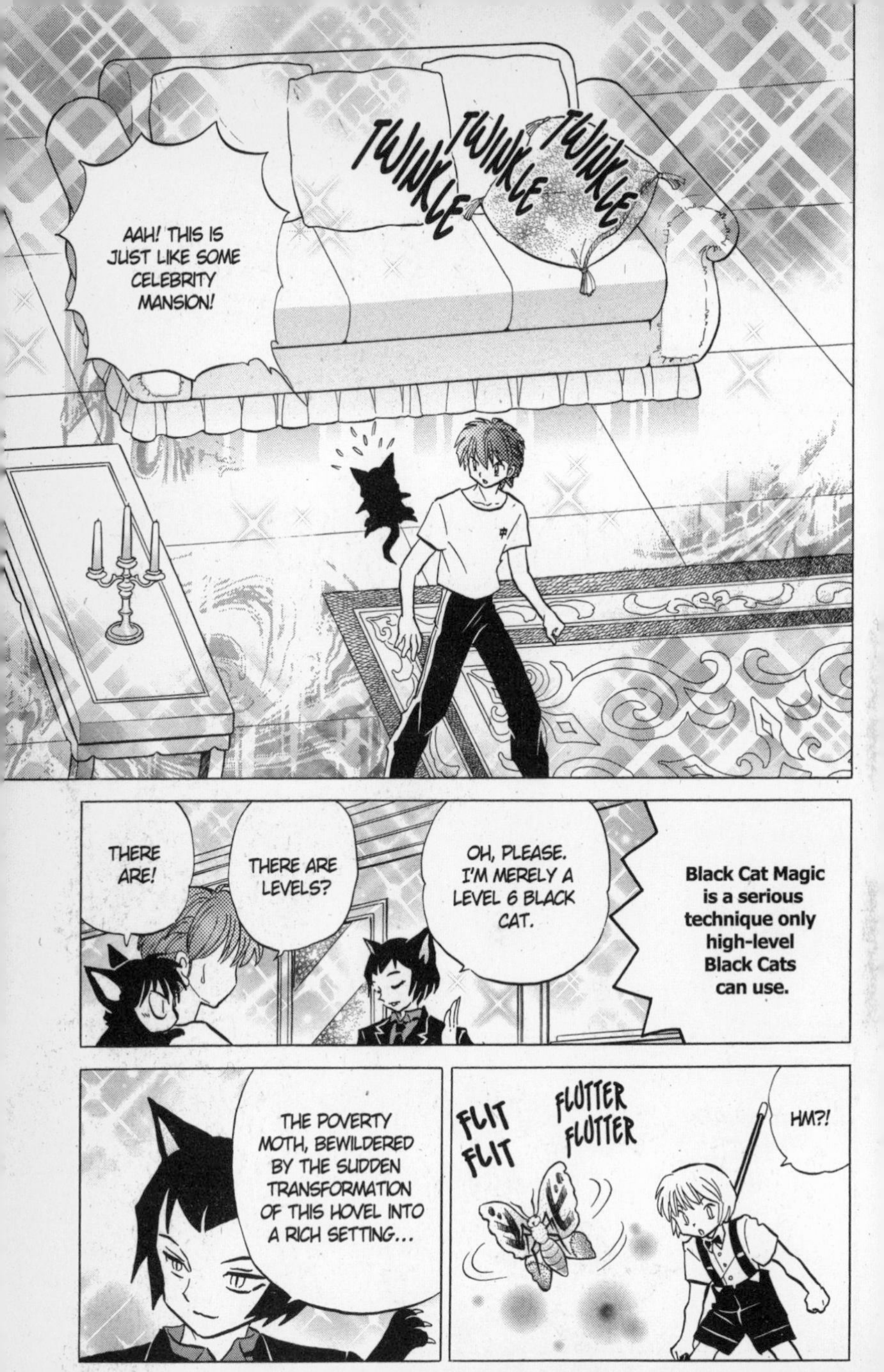
TWINKLE
TWINKLE
TWINKLE
AAH! THIS IS JUST LIKE SOME CELEBRITY MANSION!
Black Cat Magic is a serious technique only high-level Black Cats can use.
OH, PLEASE. I'M MERELY A LEVEL 6 BLACK CAT.
THERE ARE LEVELS?
THERE ARE!
HM?!
FLUTTER FLUTTER
FLIT FLIT
THE POVERTY MOTH, BEWILDERED BY THE SUDDEN TRANSFORMATION OF THIS HOVEL INTO A RICH SETTING...

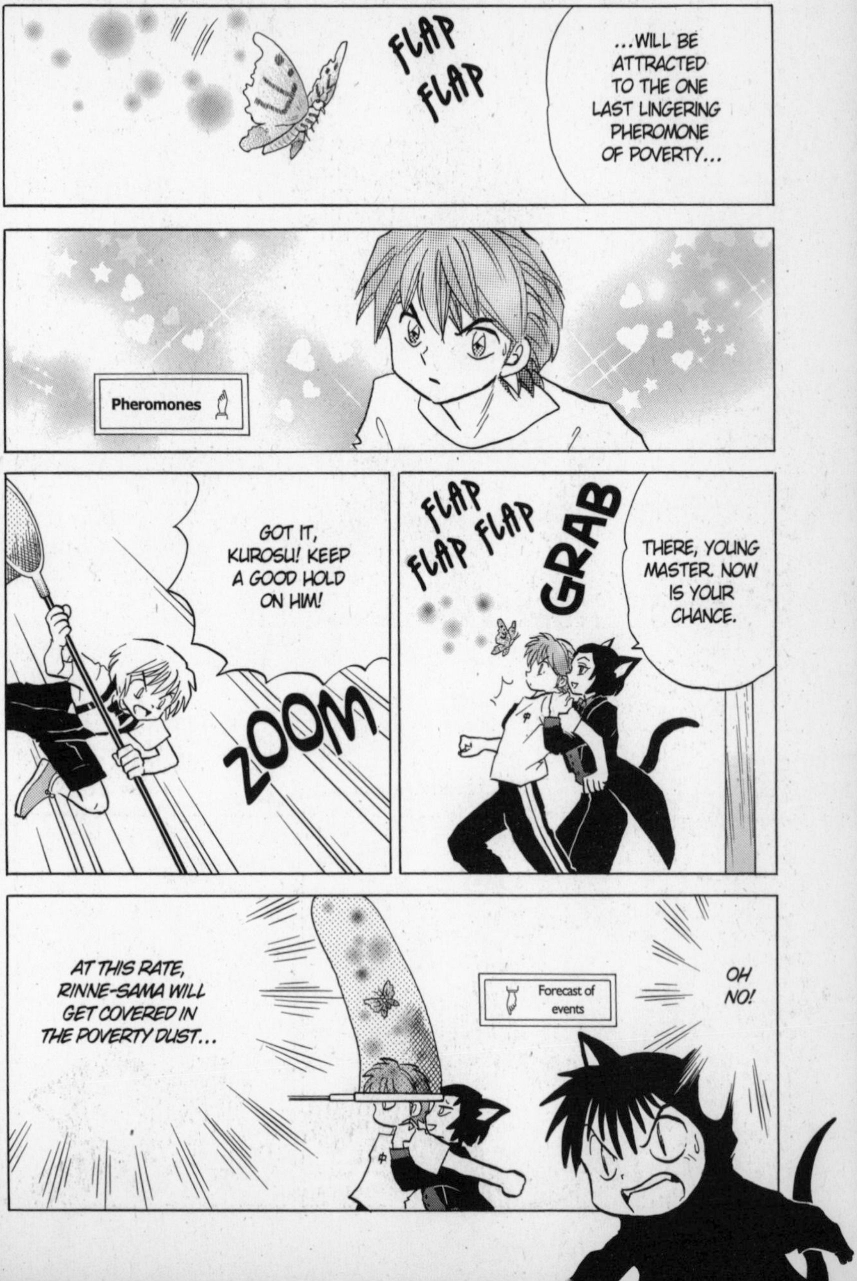

...WILL BE ATTRACTED TO THE ONE LAST LINGERING PHEROMONE OF POVERTY...
FLAP FLAP
Pheromones
THERE, YOUNG MASTER. NOW IS YOUR CHANCE.
GRAB
FLAP FLAP FLAP FLAP
GOT IT, KUROSU! KEEP A GOOD HOLD ON HIM!
ZOOM
OH NO!
Forecast of events
AT THIS RATE, RINNE-SAMA WILL GET COVERED IN THE POVERTY DUST...

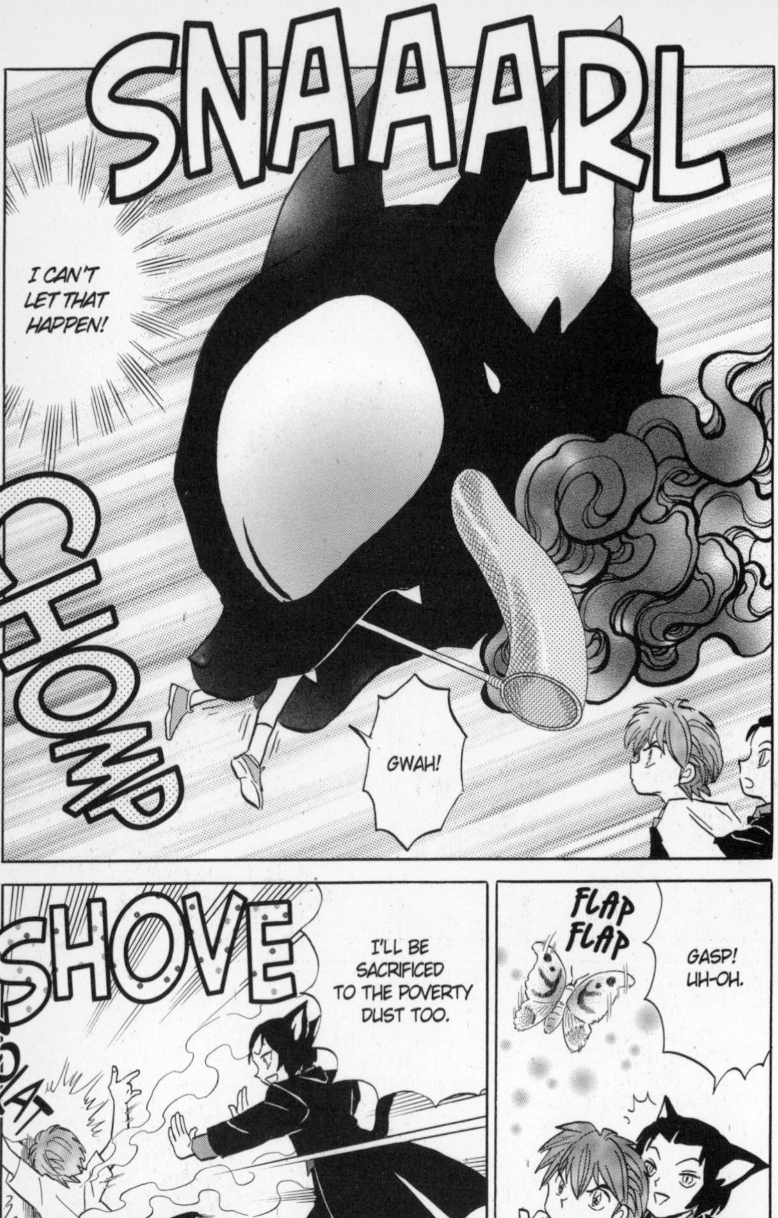
SNAAARL
I CAN'T LET THAT HAPPEN!
CHOMP
GWAH!
FLAP FLAP
GASP! UH-OH.
SHOVE
I'LL BE SACRIFICED TO THE POVERTY DUST TOO.
SPLAT

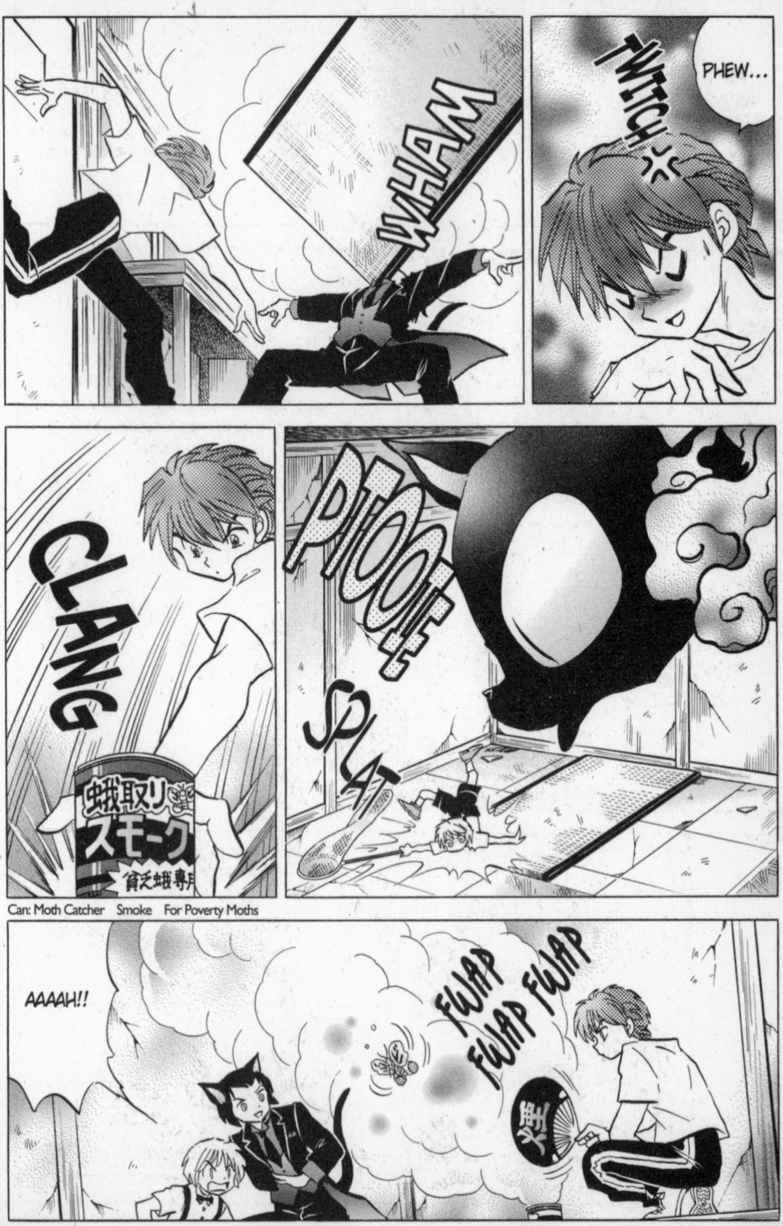
PHEW...
TWITCH
WHAM
PTOOIE!
SPLAT
CLANG
蛾取り
スモーク
Can: Moth Catcher Smoke For Poverty Moths
AAAAH!!
FWAP
FWAP FWAP

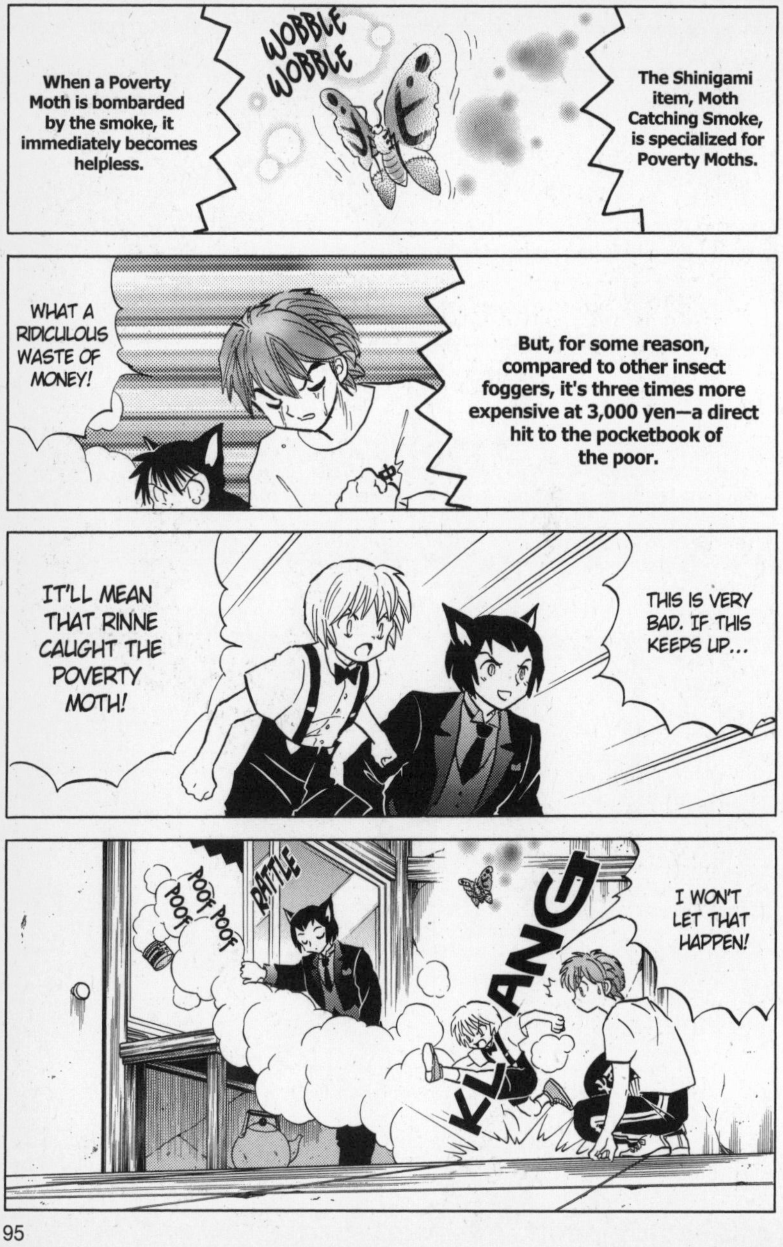
The Shinigami item, Moth Catching Smoke, is specialized for Poverty Moths.
WOBBLE WOBBLE
When a Poverty Moth is bombarded by the smoke, it immediately becomes helpless.
But, for some reason, compared to other insect foggers, it's three times more expensive at 3,000 yen—a direct hit to the pocketbook of the poor.
WHAT A RIDICULOUS WASTE OF MONEY!
THIS IS VERY BAD. IF THIS KEEPS UP...
IT'LL MEAN THAT RINNE CAUGHT THE POVERTY MOTH!
I WON'T LET THAT HAPPEN!
KLANG
RATTLE
POOF POOF POOF

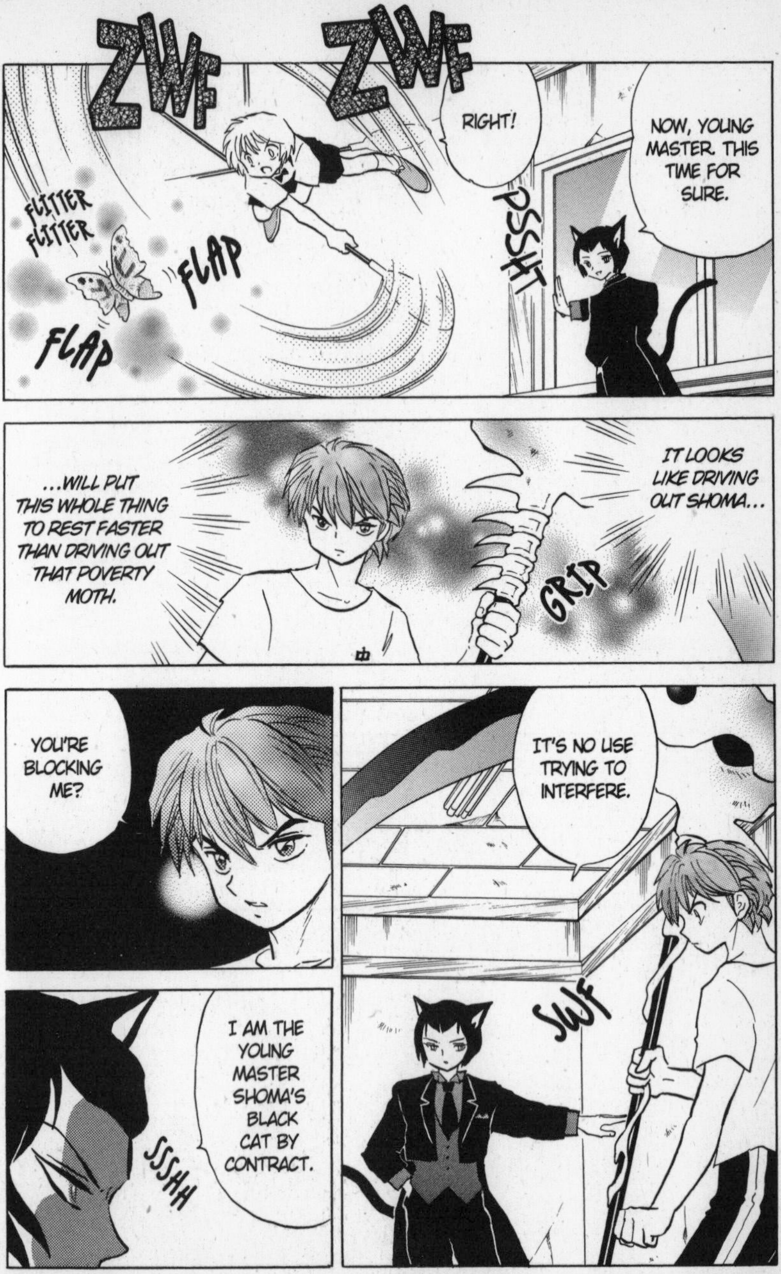
ZWF
ZWF
NOW, YOUNG MASTER. THIS TIME FOR SURE.
RIGHT!
PSSHT
FLAP
FLAP
FLITTER FLITTER
IT LOOKS LIKE DRIVING OUT SHOMA...
...WILL PUT THIS WHOLE THING TO REST FASTER THAN DRIVING OUT THAT POVERTY MOTH.
GRIP
IT'S NO USE TRYING TO INTERFERE.
SWF
YOU'RE BLOCKING ME?
I AM THE YOUNG MASTER SHOMA'S BLACK CAT BY CONTRACT.
SSSHH

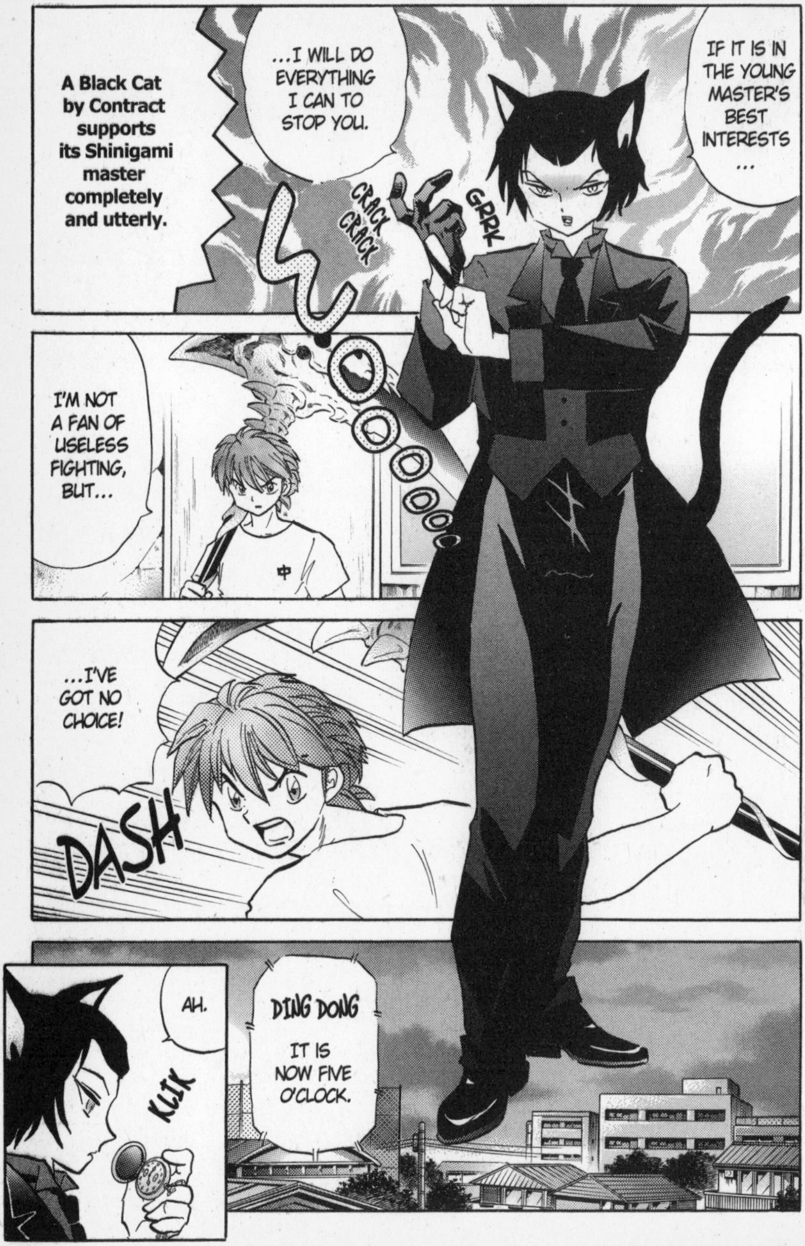
IF IT IS IN THE YOUNG MASTER'S BEST INTERESTS ...
...I WILL DO EVERYTHING I CAN TO STOP YOU.
GRRK
CRACK CRACK
A Black Cat by Contract supports its Shinigami master completely and utterly.
I'M NOT A FAN OF USELESS FIGHTING, BUT...
...I'VE GOT NO CHOICE!
DASH
DING DONG
IT IS NOW FIVE O'CLOCK.
AH.
KLIK

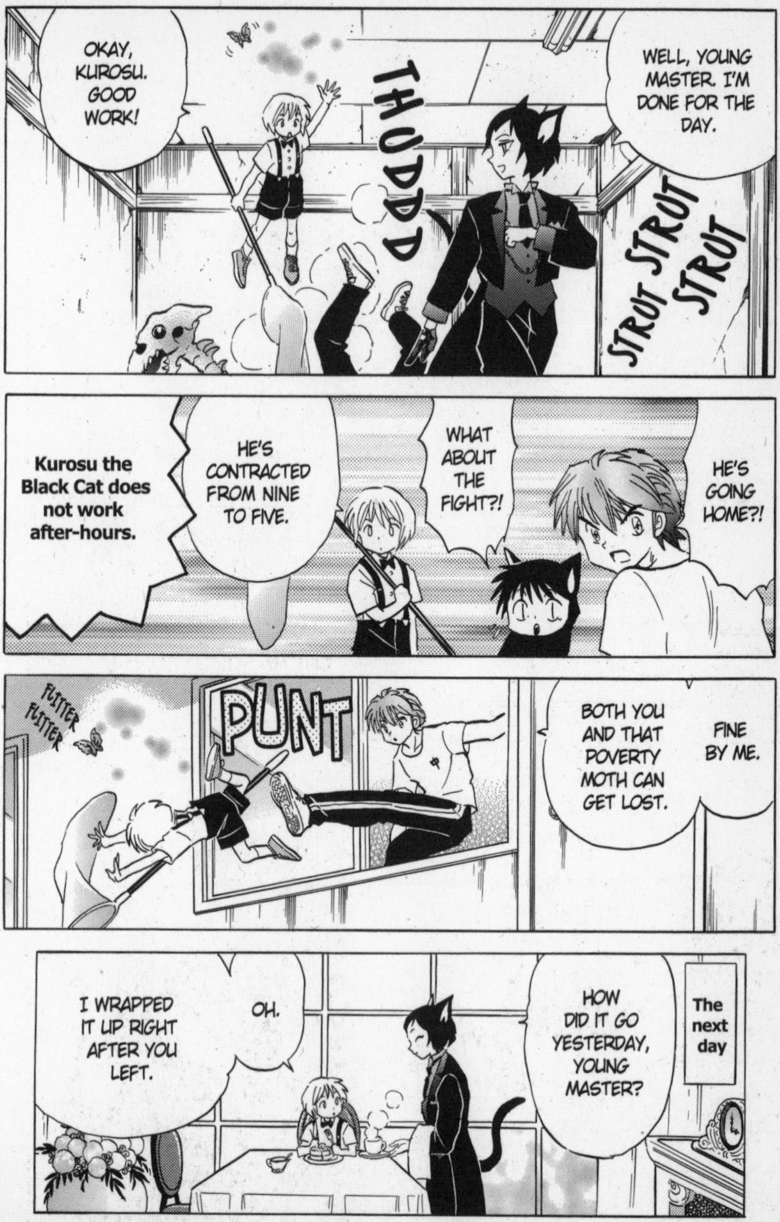
WELL, YOUNG MASTER. I'M DONE FOR THE DAY.
STRUT STRUT STRUT
THUDDD
OKAY, KUROSU. GOOD WORK!
HE'S GOING HOME?!
WHAT ABOUT THE FIGHT?!
HE'S CONTRACTED FROM NINE TO FIVE.
Kurosu the Black Cat does not work after-hours.
FINE BY ME.
BOTH YOU AND THAT POVERTY MOTH CAN GET LOST.
PUNT
FLITTER FLITTER
The next day
HOW DID IT GO YESTERDAY, YOUNG MASTER?
OH.
I WRAPPED IT UP RIGHT AFTER YOU LEFT.

# CHAPTER 104: THE ENVIOUS CAT

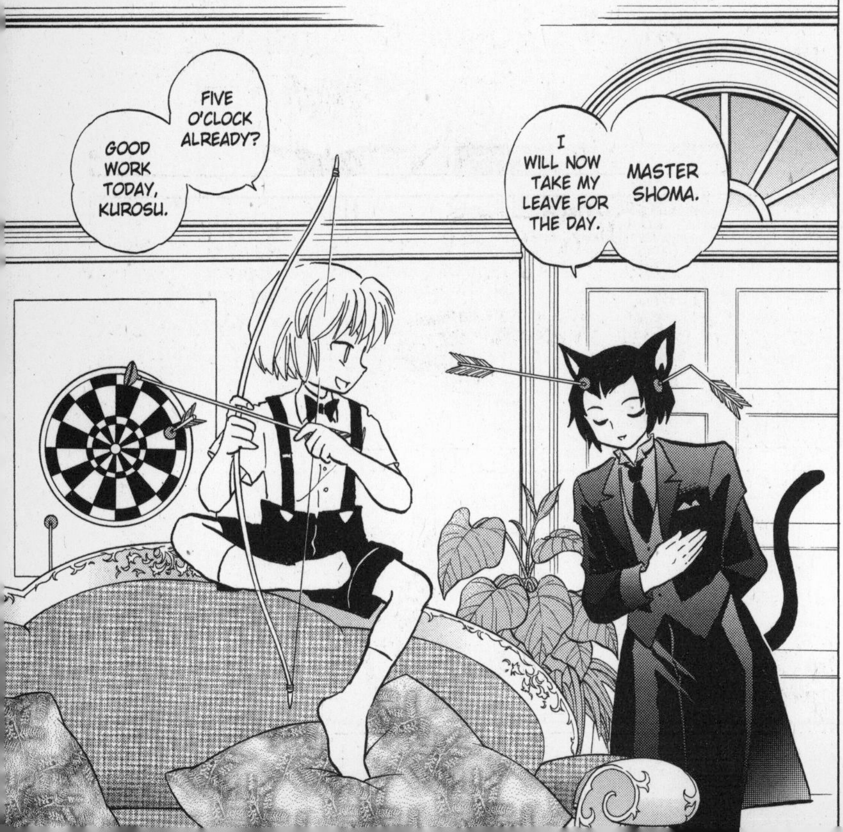
I WILL NOW TAKE MY LEAVE FOR THE DAY. MASTER SHOMA.
FIVE O'CLOCK ALREADY?
GOOD WORK TODAY, KUROSU.

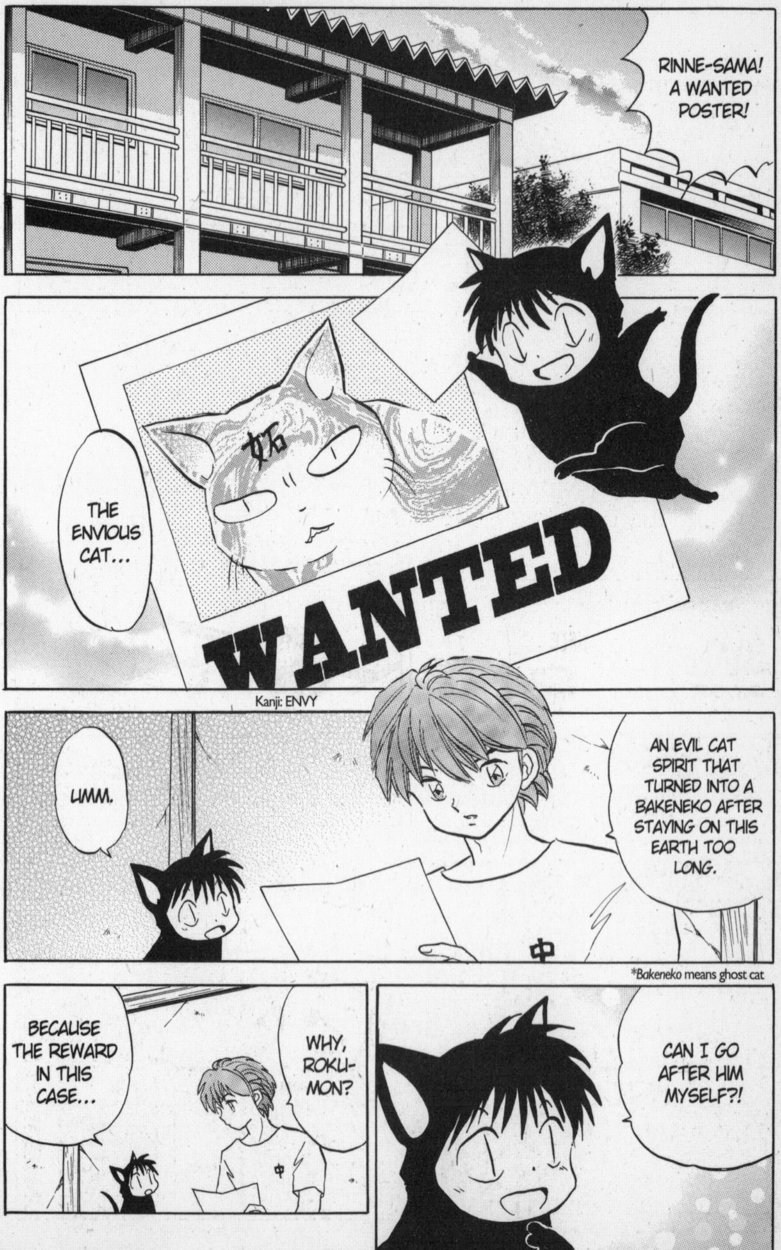
RINNE-SAMA! A WANTED POSTER!
妬
WANTED
THE ENVIOUS CAT...
AN EVIL CAT SPIRIT THAT TURNED INTO A BAKENEKO AFTER STAYING ON THIS EARTH TOO LONG.
UMM.
中
CAN I GO AFTER HIM MYSELF?!
WHY, ROKU-MON?
BECAUSE THE REWARD IN THIS CASE...
Kanji: ENVY

**Bakeneko means ghost cat*

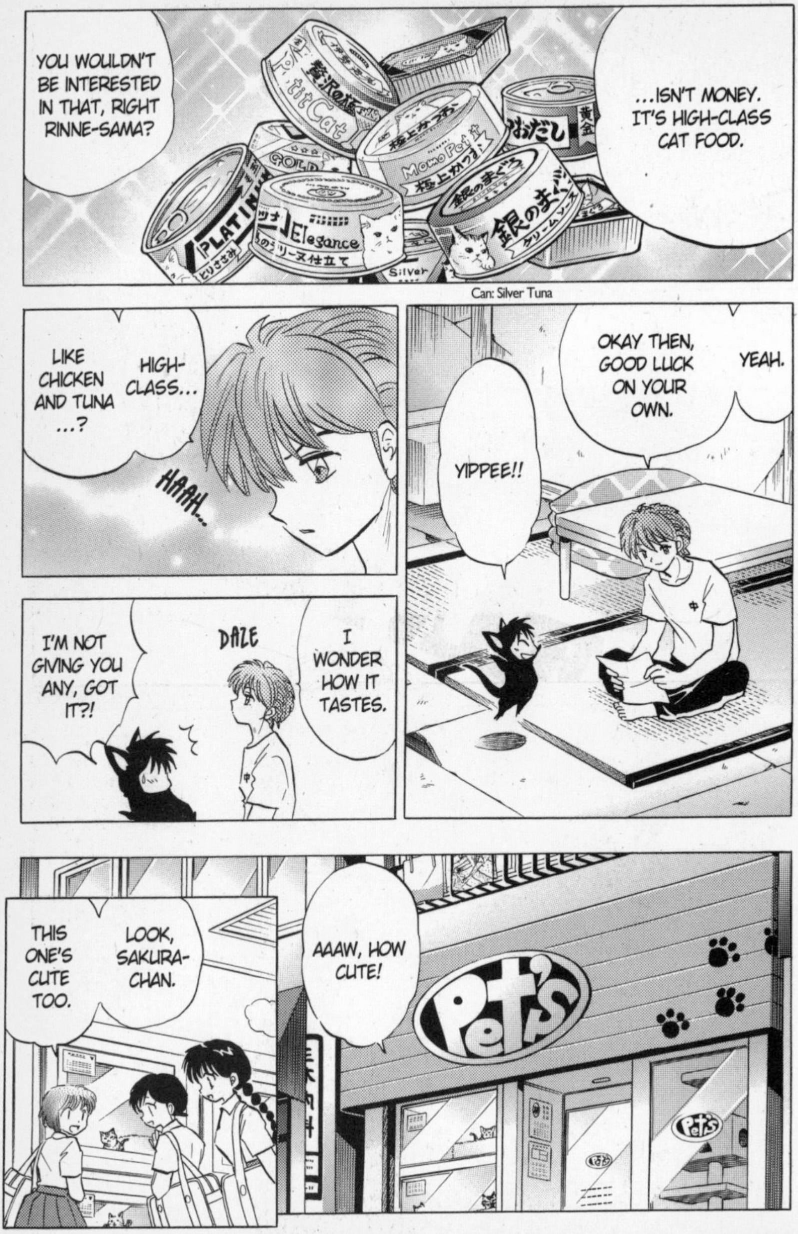
...ISN'T MONEY. IT'S HIGH-CLASS CAT FOOD.
YOU WOULDN'T BE INTERESTED IN THAT, RIGHT RINNE-SAMA?
YEAH.
OKAY THEN, GOOD LUCK ON YOUR OWN.
YIPPEE!!
HIGH-CLASS...
LIKE CHICKEN AND TUNA ...?
HAAAH...
I WONDER HOW IT TASTES.
DAZE
I'M NOT GIVING YOU ANY, GOT IT?!
AAAW, HOW CUTE!
LOOK, SAKURA-CHAN.
THIS ONE'S CUTE TOO.
Pet's
Can: Silver Tuna

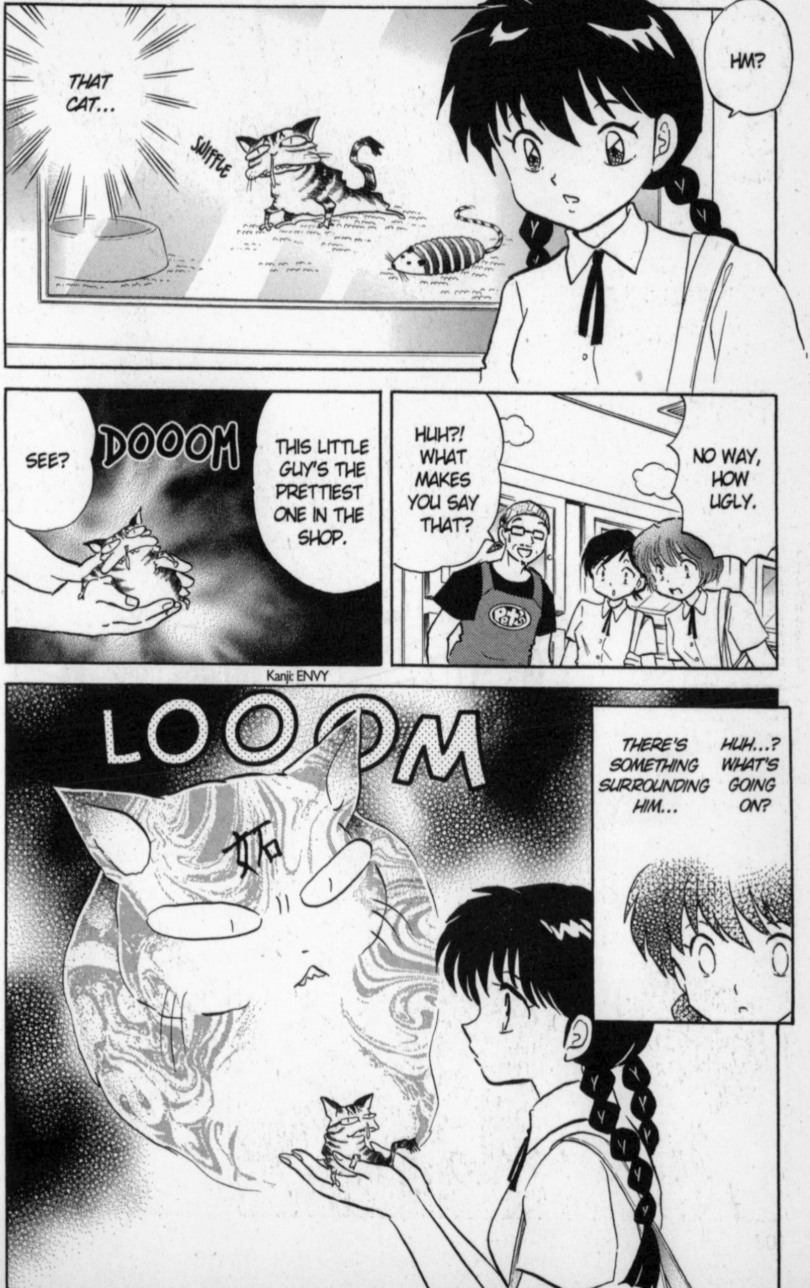
HM?
THAT CAT...
SWIFFLE
NO WAY, HOW UGLY.
HUH?! WHAT MAKES YOU SAY THAT?
THIS LITTLE GUY'S THE PRETTIEST ONE IN THE SHOP.
DOOOM
SEE?
Kanji: ENVY
HUH...? WHAT'S GOING ON?
THERE'S SOMETHING SURROUNDING HIM...
LOOOM

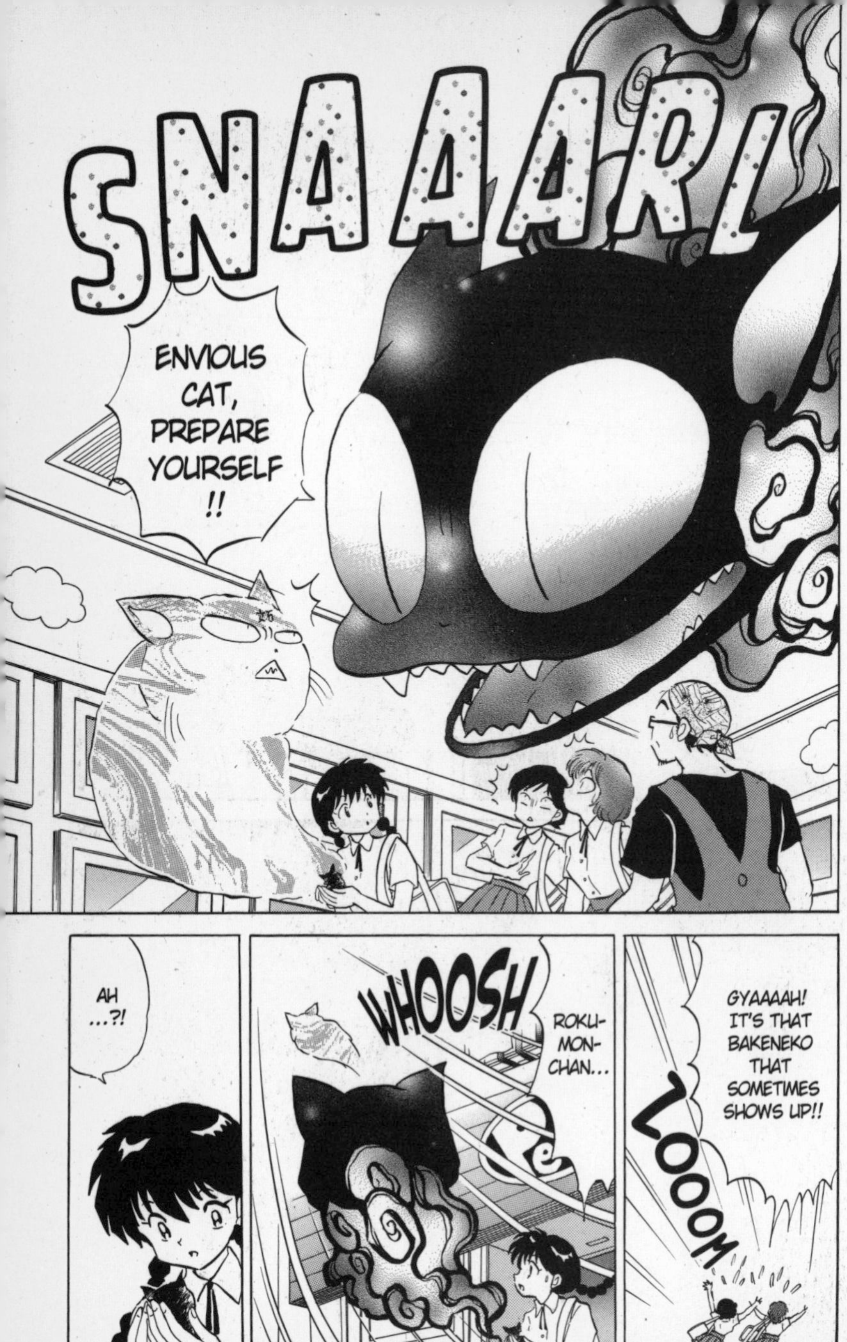
SNAAARL
ENVIOUS CAT, PREPARE YOURSELF !!
GYAAAAH! IT'S THAT BAKENEKO THAT SOMETIMES SHOWS UP!!
ZOOOOM
ROKU-MON-CHAN...
WHOOSH
AH ...?!

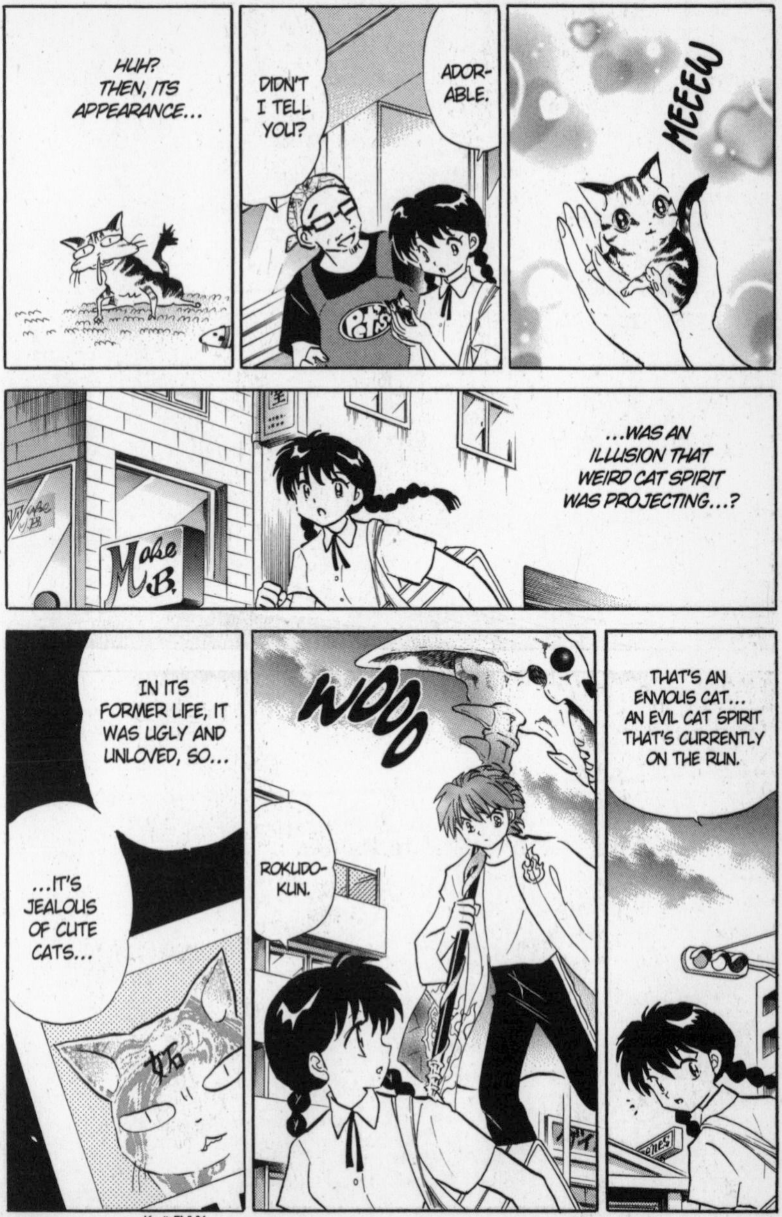
MEEEW
ADOR-ABLE.
DIDN'T I TELL YOU?
HUH? THEN, ITS APPEARANCE...
...WAS AN ILLUSION THAT WEIRD CAT SPIRIT WAS PROJECTING...?
THAT'S AN ENVIOUS CAT... AN EVIL CAT SPIRIT THAT'S CURRENTLY ON THE RUN.
WOOO
ROKUDO-KUN.
IN ITS FORMER LIFE, IT WAS UGLY AND UNLOVED, SO...
...IT'S JEALOUS OF CUTE CATS...
妬
Kanji: ENVY

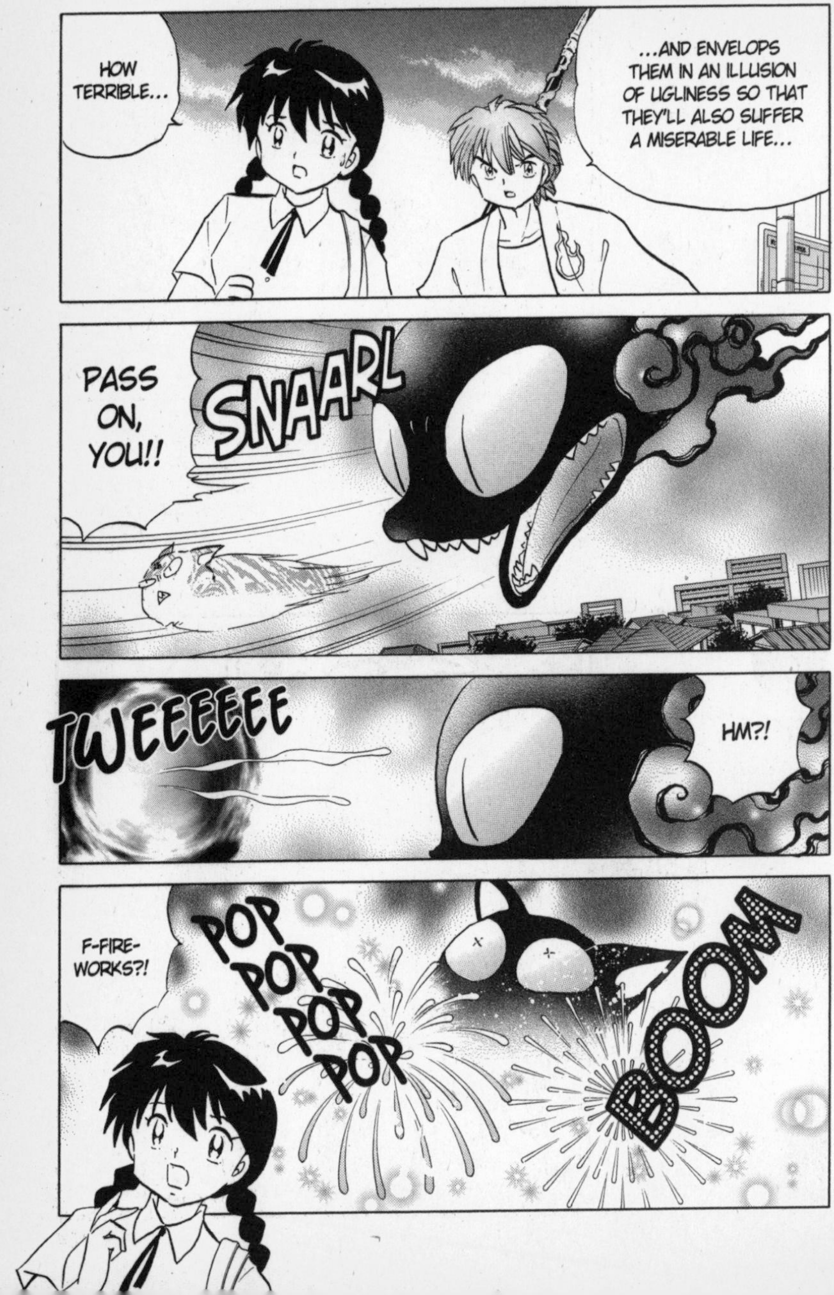
...AND ENVELOPS THEM IN AN ILLUSION OF UGLINESS SO THAT THEY'LL ALSO SUFFER A MISERABLE LIFE...
HOW TERRIBLE...
SNAARL
PASS ON, YOU!!
HM?!
TWEEEEEE
BOOOM
POP POP POP POP POP
F-FIRE-WORKS?!

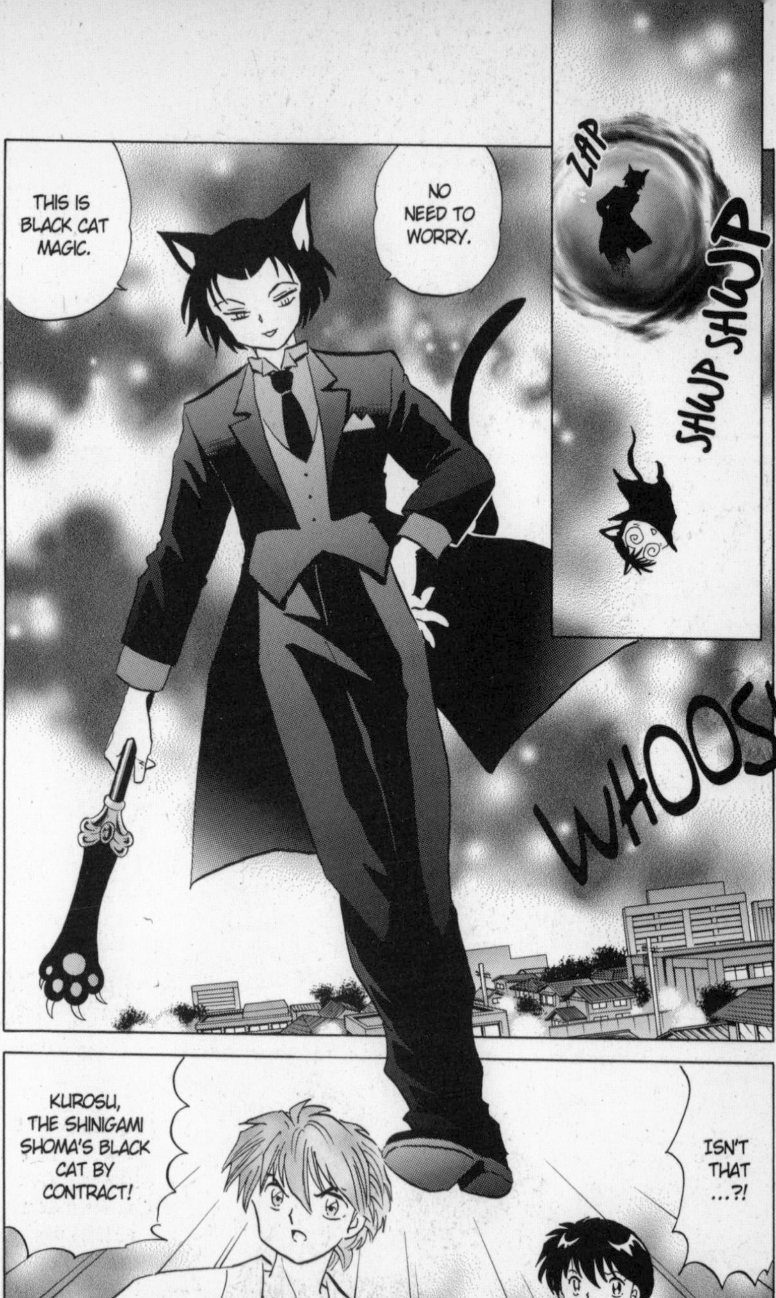
ZAP
SHWP SHWP
NO NEED TO WORRY.
THIS IS BLACK CAT MAGIC.
WHOOSH
ISN'T THAT ...?!
KUROSU, THE SHINIGAMI SHOMA'S BLACK CAT BY CONTRACT!

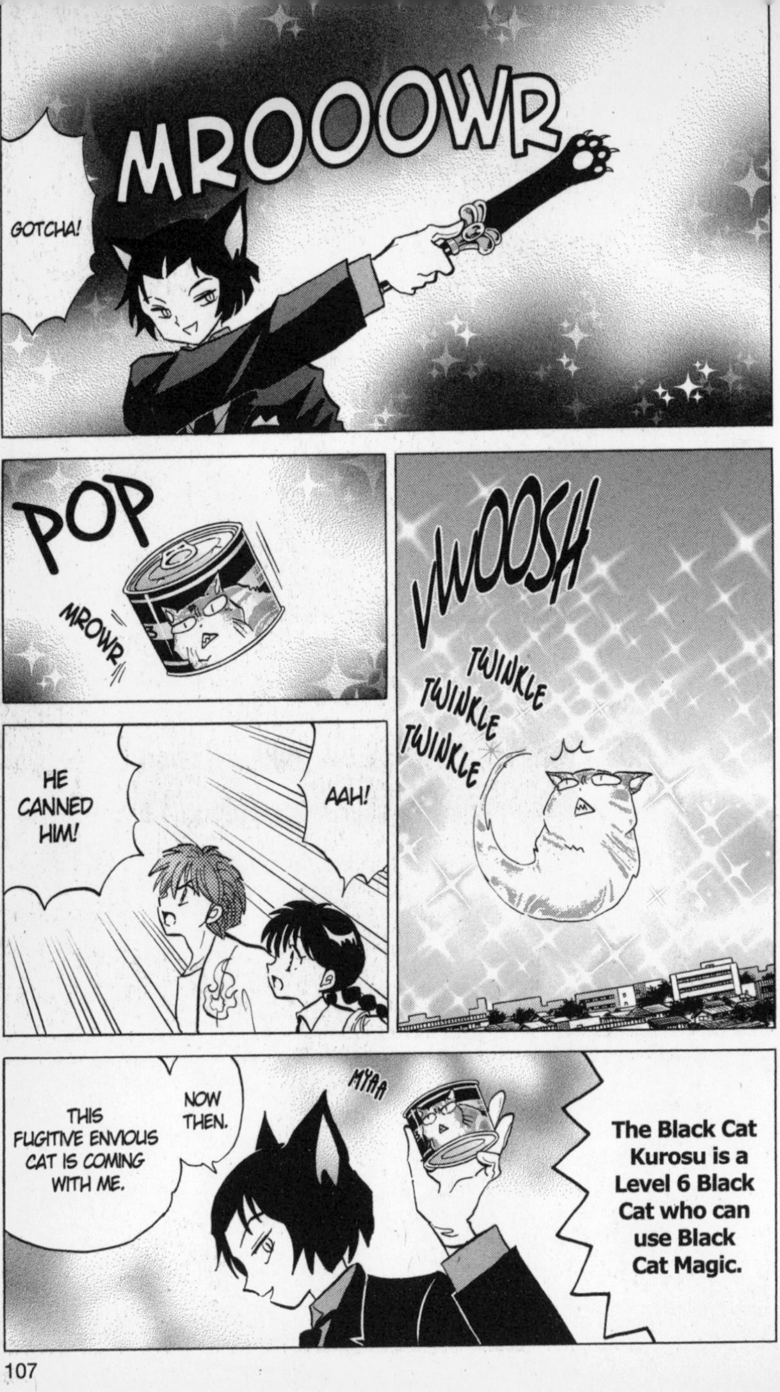
MROOOWR
GOTCHA!
VWOOSH
TWINKLE
TWINKLE
TWINKLE
POP
MROWR
AAH!
HE CANNED HIM!
MYAA
The Black Cat Kurosu is a Level 6 Black Cat who can use Black Cat Magic.
NOW THEN.
THIS FUGITIVE ENVIOUS CAT IS COMING WITH ME.

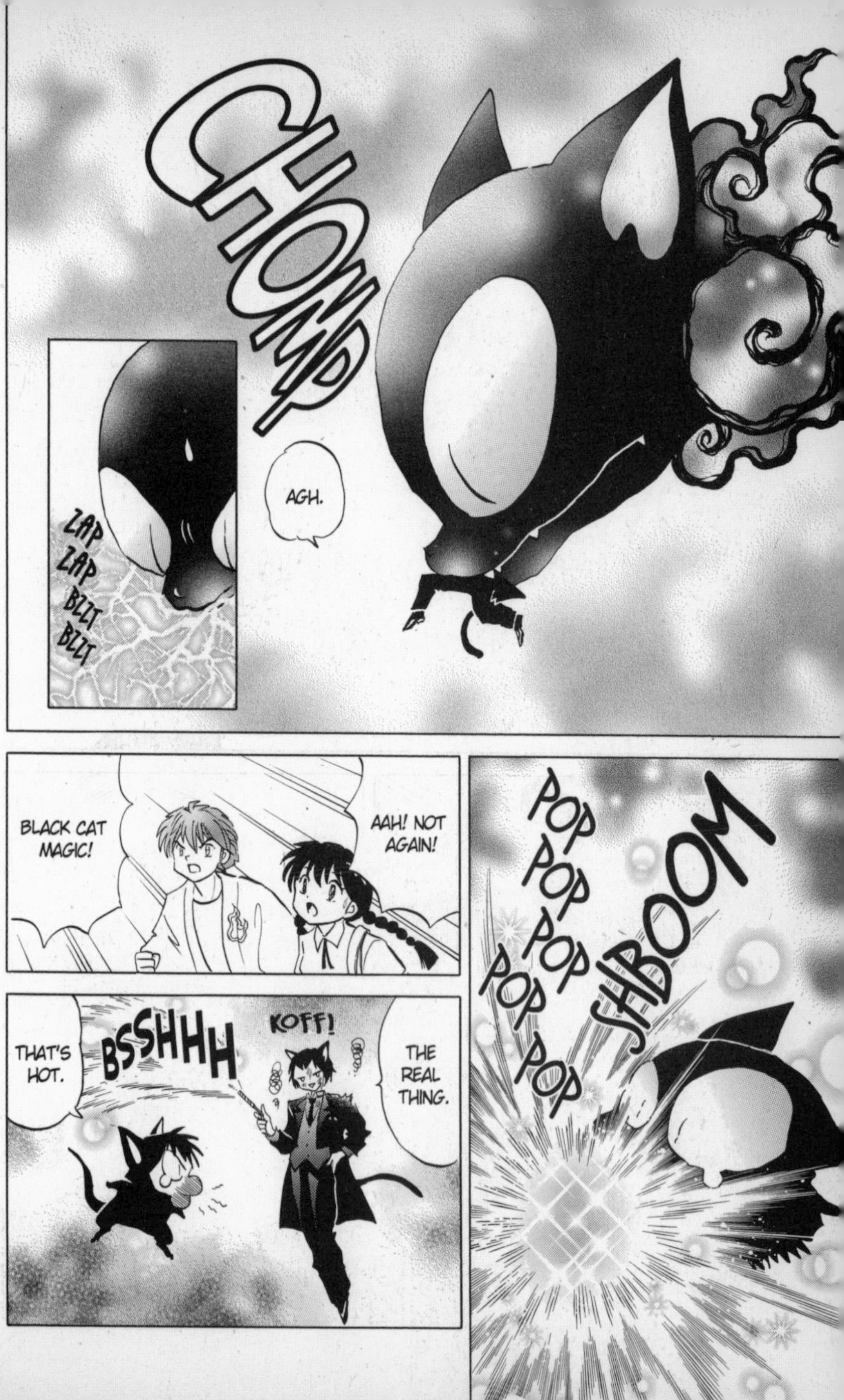
CHOMP
AGH.
ZAP ZAP BZZT BZZT
POP POP POP POP
SHBOOM
AAH! NOT AGAIN!
BLACK CAT MAGIC!
THE REAL THING.
KOFF!
BSSHHH
THAT'S HOT.

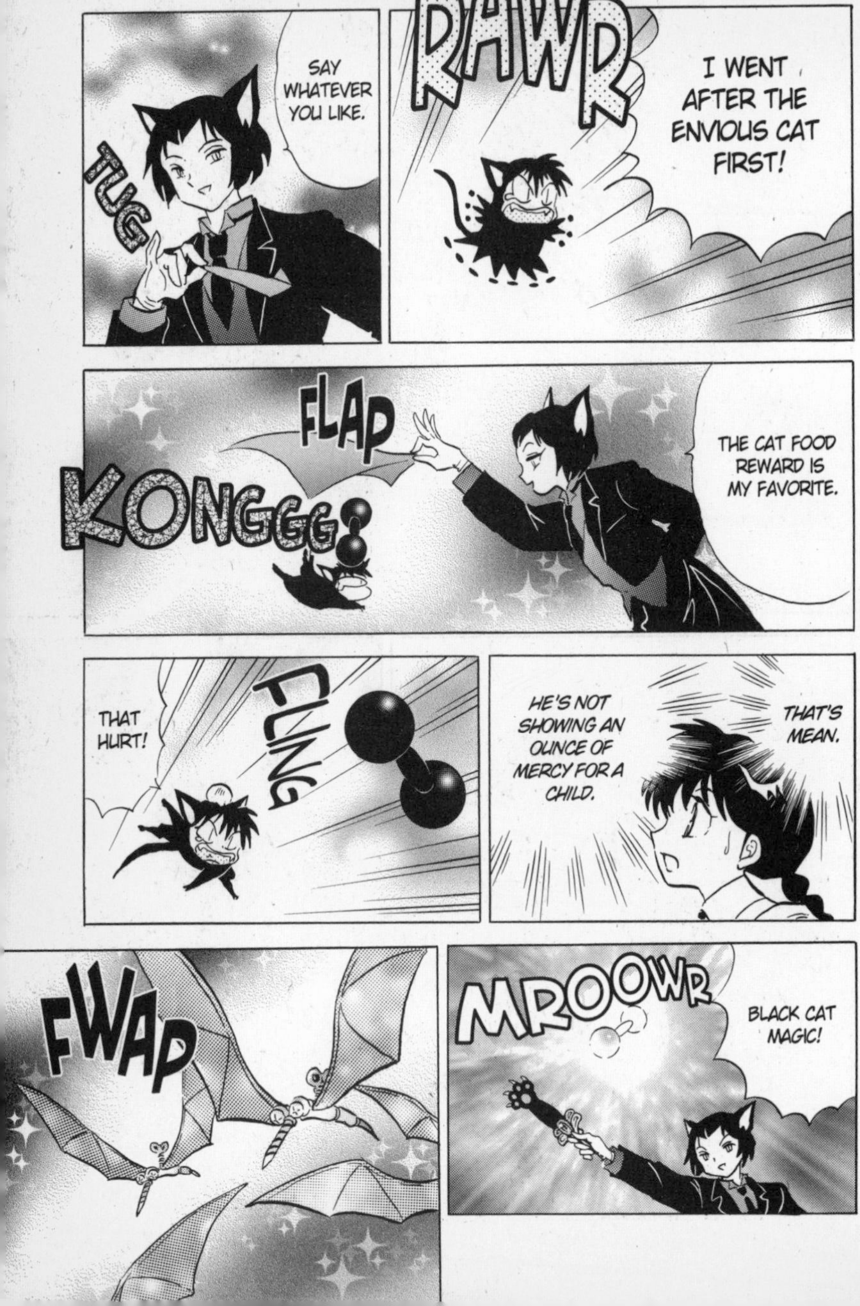
RAWR
I WENT AFTER THE ENVIOUS CAT FIRST!
SAY WHATEVER YOU LIKE.
TUG
THE CAT FOOD REWARD IS MY FAVORITE.
FLAP
KONGGG
THAT'S MEAN.
HE'S NOT SHOWING AN OUNCE OF MERCY FOR A CHILD.
FLING
THAT HURT!
MROOWR
BLACK CAT MAGIC!
FWAP

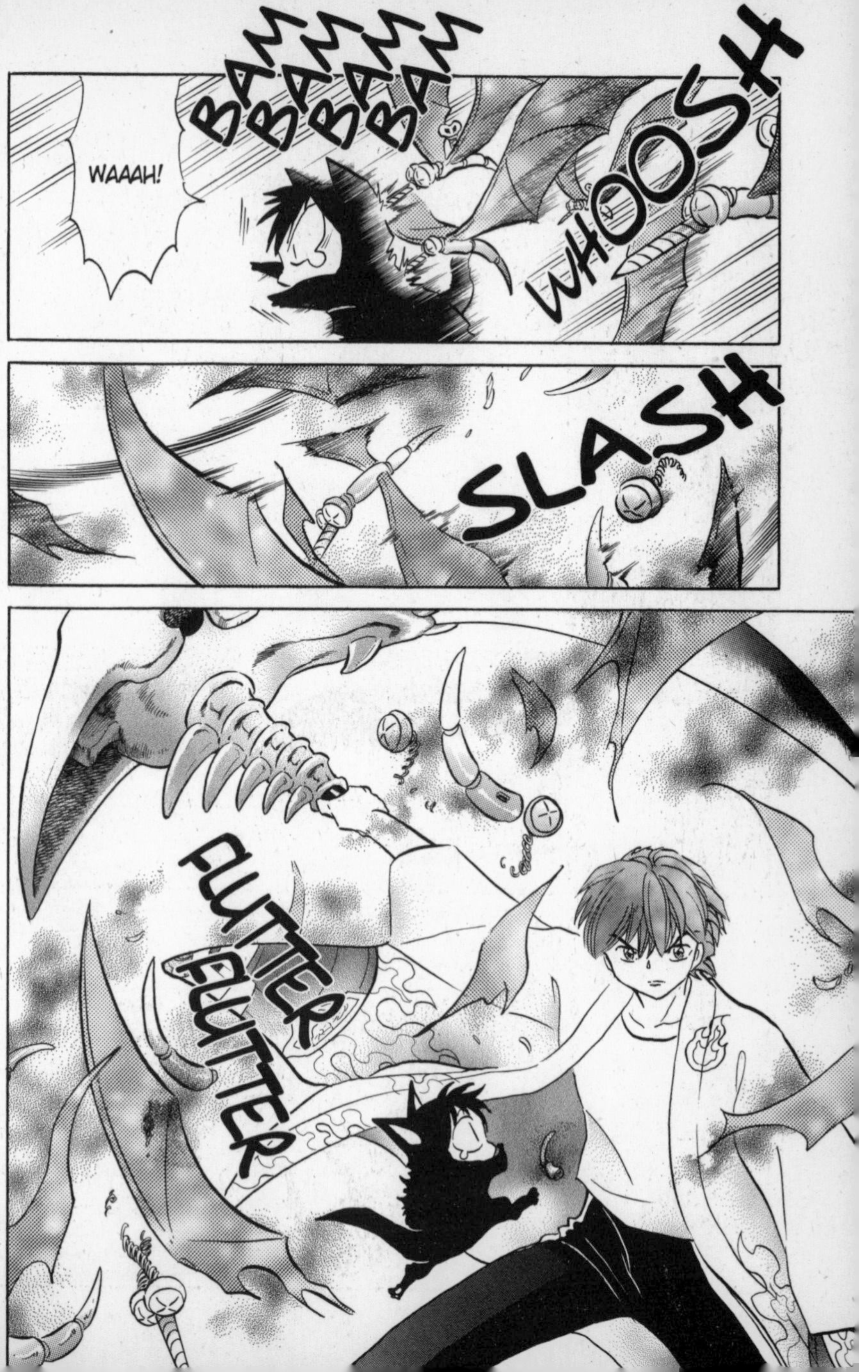
WHOOSH
BAM BAM BAM BAM
WAAAH!
SLASH
FLUTTER FLUTTER

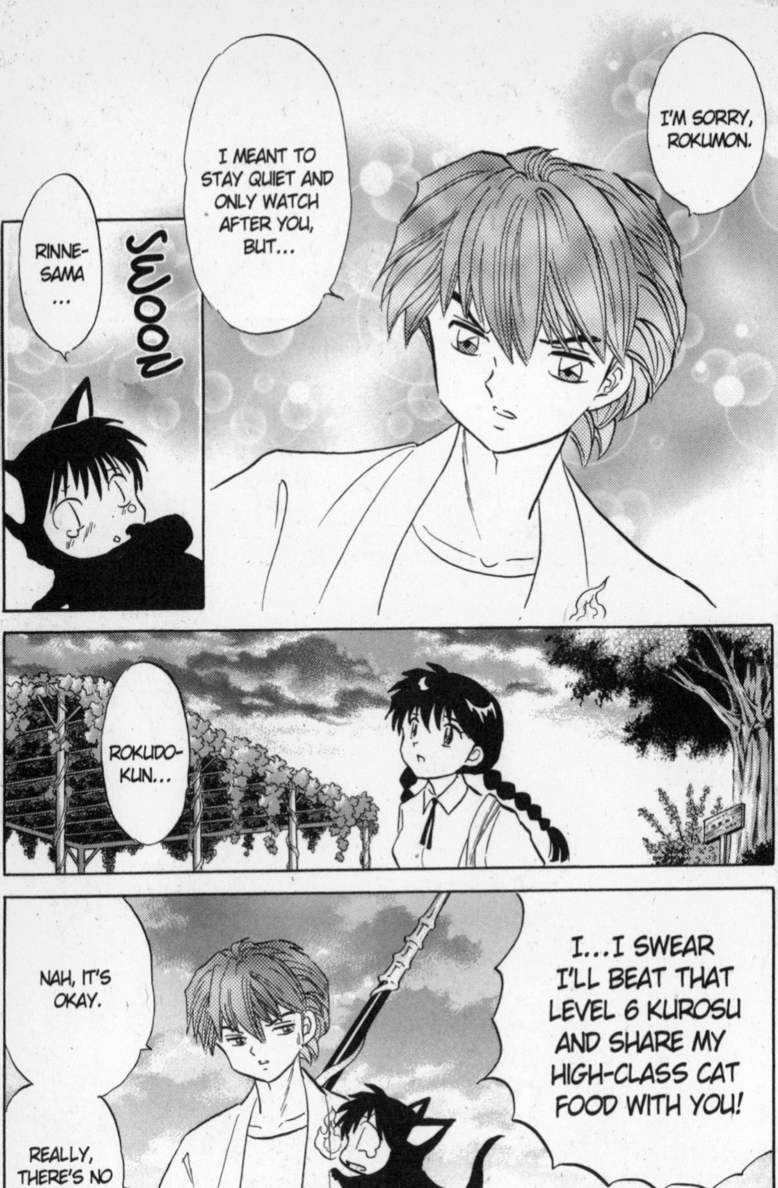
I'M SORRY, ROKUMON.
I MEANT TO STAY QUIET AND ONLY WATCH AFTER YOU, BUT...
RINNE-SAMA...
SWOON
ROKUDO-KUN...
I...I SWEAR I'LL BEAT THAT LEVEL 6 KUROSU AND SHARE MY HIGH-CLASS CAT FOOD WITH YOU!
NAH, IT'S OKAY.
REALLY, THERE'S NO NEED.

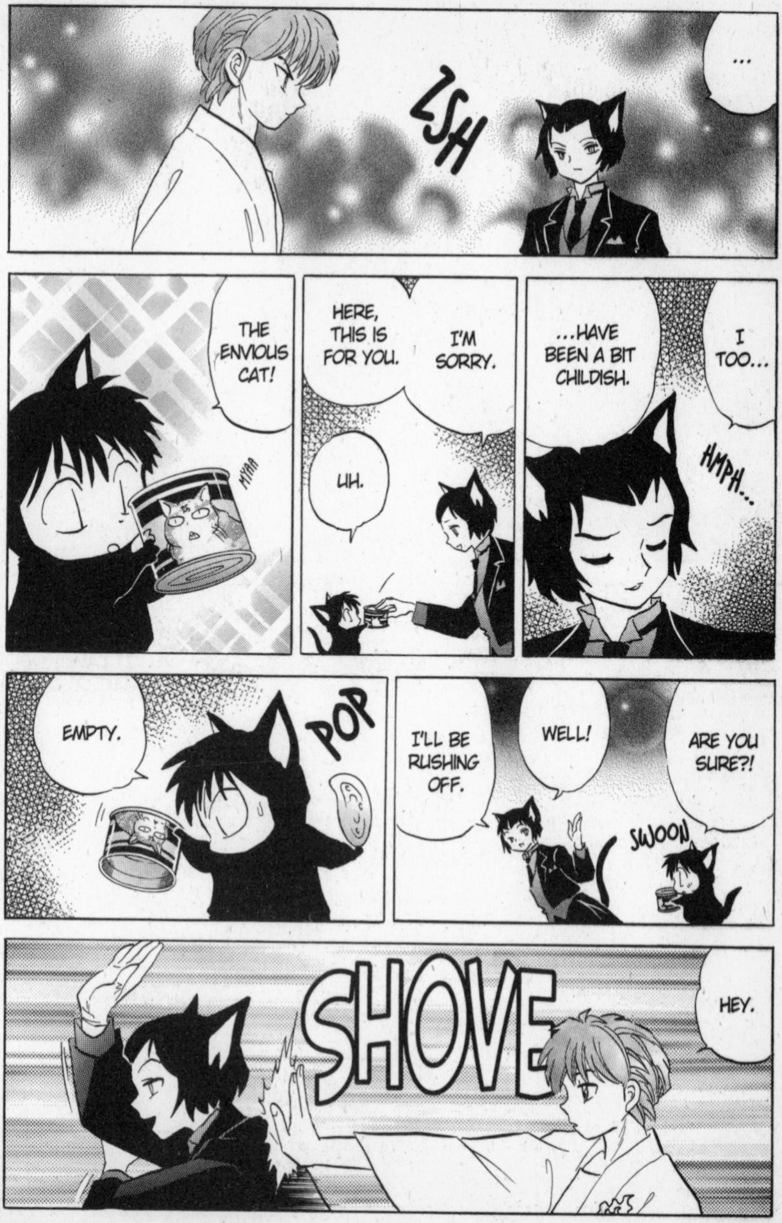
...
ZSH
I TOO...
...HAVE BEEN A BIT CHILDISH.
HMPH...
I'M SORRY.
HERE, THIS IS FOR YOU.
UH.
THE ENVIOUS CAT!
MYAA
ARE YOU SURE?!
WELL!
I'LL BE RUSHING OFF.
SWOON
POP
EMPTY.
HEY.
SHOVE

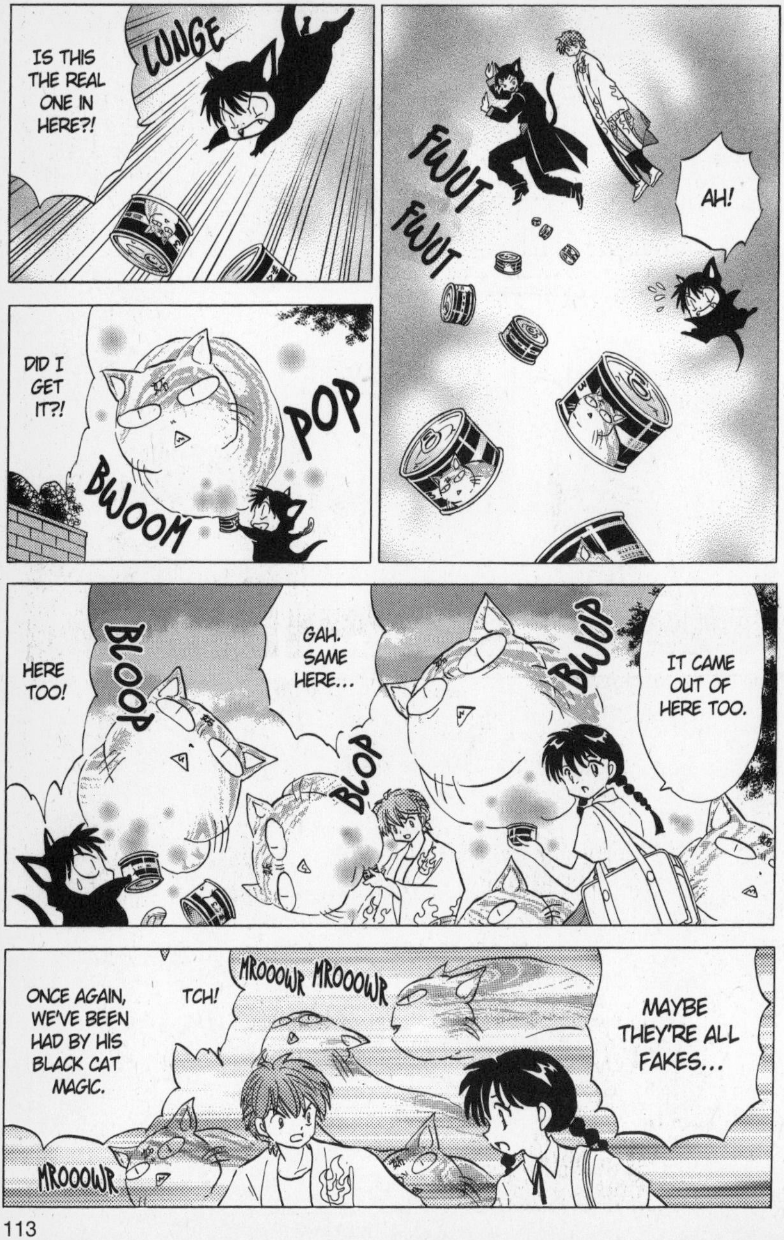
FWUUT
FWUUT
AH!
LUNGE
IS THIS THE REAL ONE IN HERE?!
POP
DID I GET IT?!
BWOOM
IT CAME OUT OF HERE TOO.
BWUP
GAH. SAME HERE...
BLOP
BLOOP
HERE TOO!
MAYBE THEY'RE ALL FAKES...
MROOOWR MROOOWR
TCH!
ONCE AGAIN, WE'VE BEEN HAD BY HIS BLACK CAT MAGIC.
MROOOWR

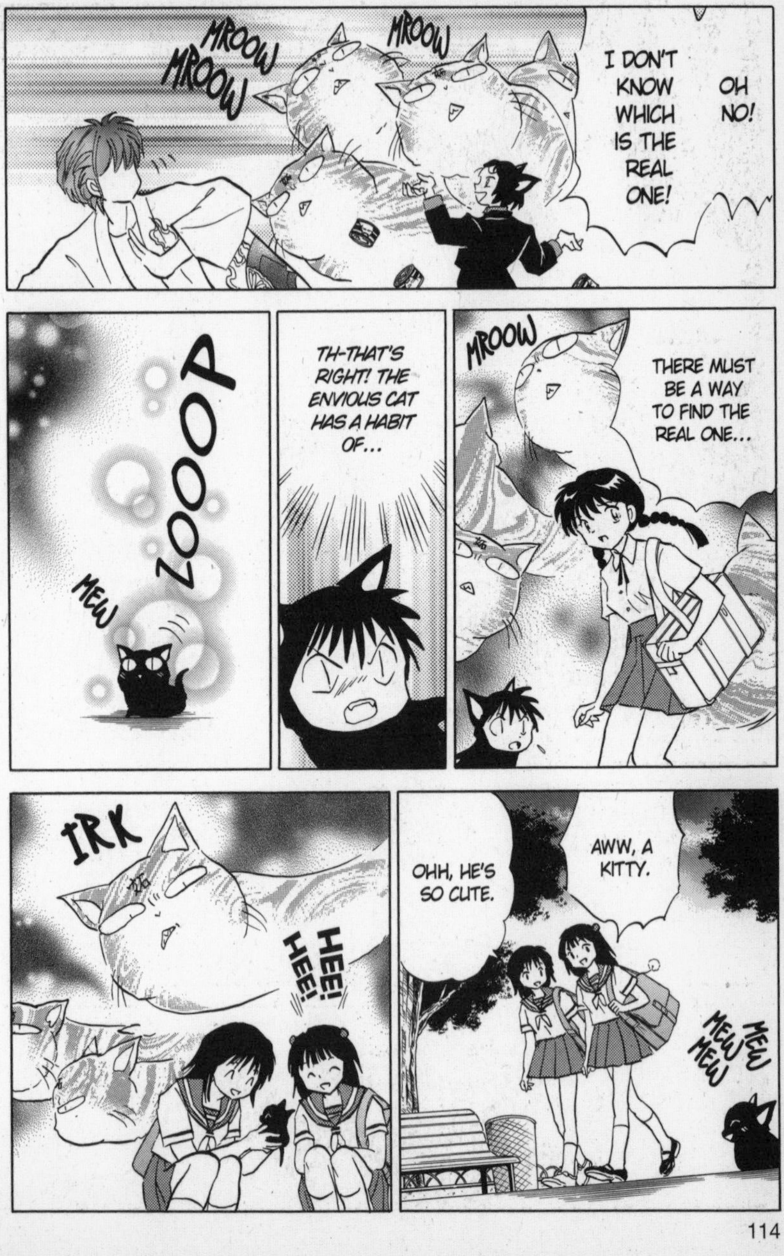
OH NO!
I DON'T KNOW WHICH IS THE REAL ONE!
MROOW
MROOW
MROOW
THERE MUST BE A WAY TO FIND THE REAL ONE...
MROOW
TH-THAT'S RIGHT! THE ENVIOUS CAT HAS A HABIT OF...
ZOOOP
MEW
AWW, A KITTY.
OHH, HE'S SO CUTE.
MEW MEW MEW
IRK
HEE! HEE!

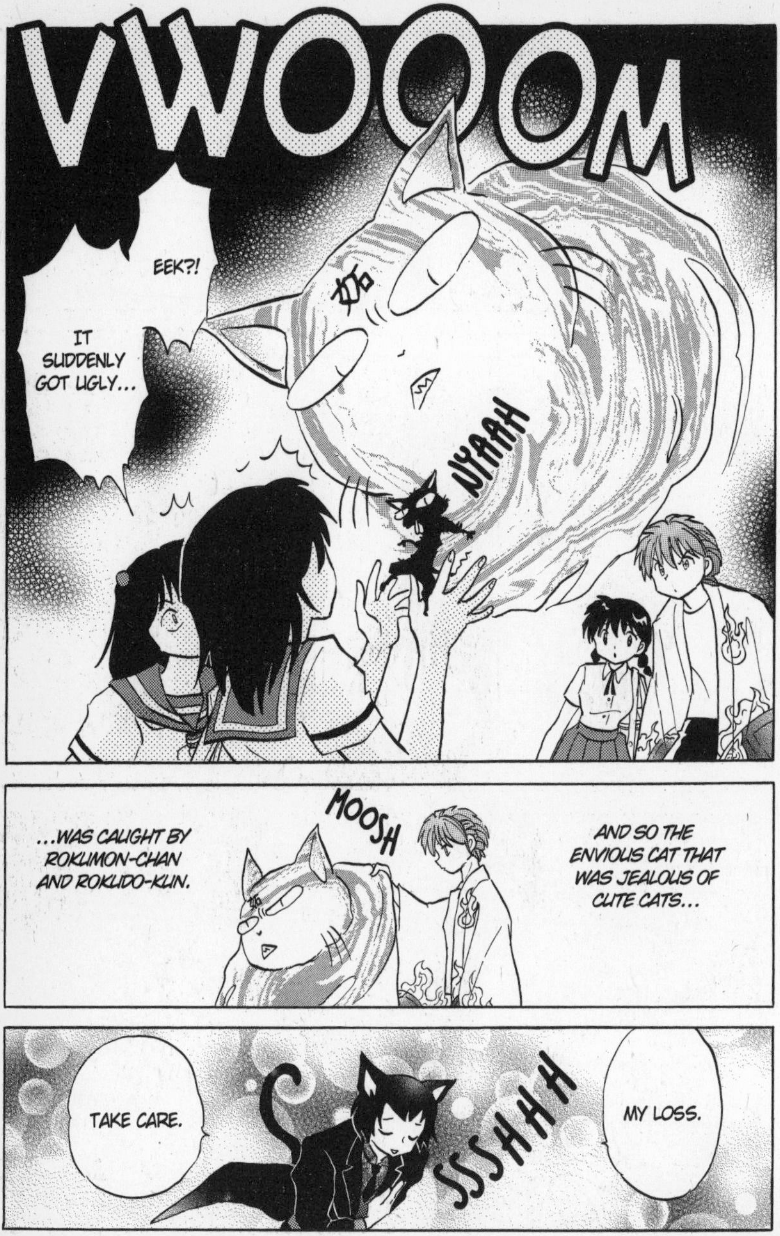
VWOOOM
EEK?!
IT SUDDENLY GOT UGLY...
NYAAH
AND SO THE ENVIOUS CAT THAT WAS JEALOUS OF CUTE CATS...
MOOSH
...WAS CAUGHT BY ROKUMON-CHAN AND ROKUDO-KUN.
MY LOSS.
SSSHHH
TAKE CARE.

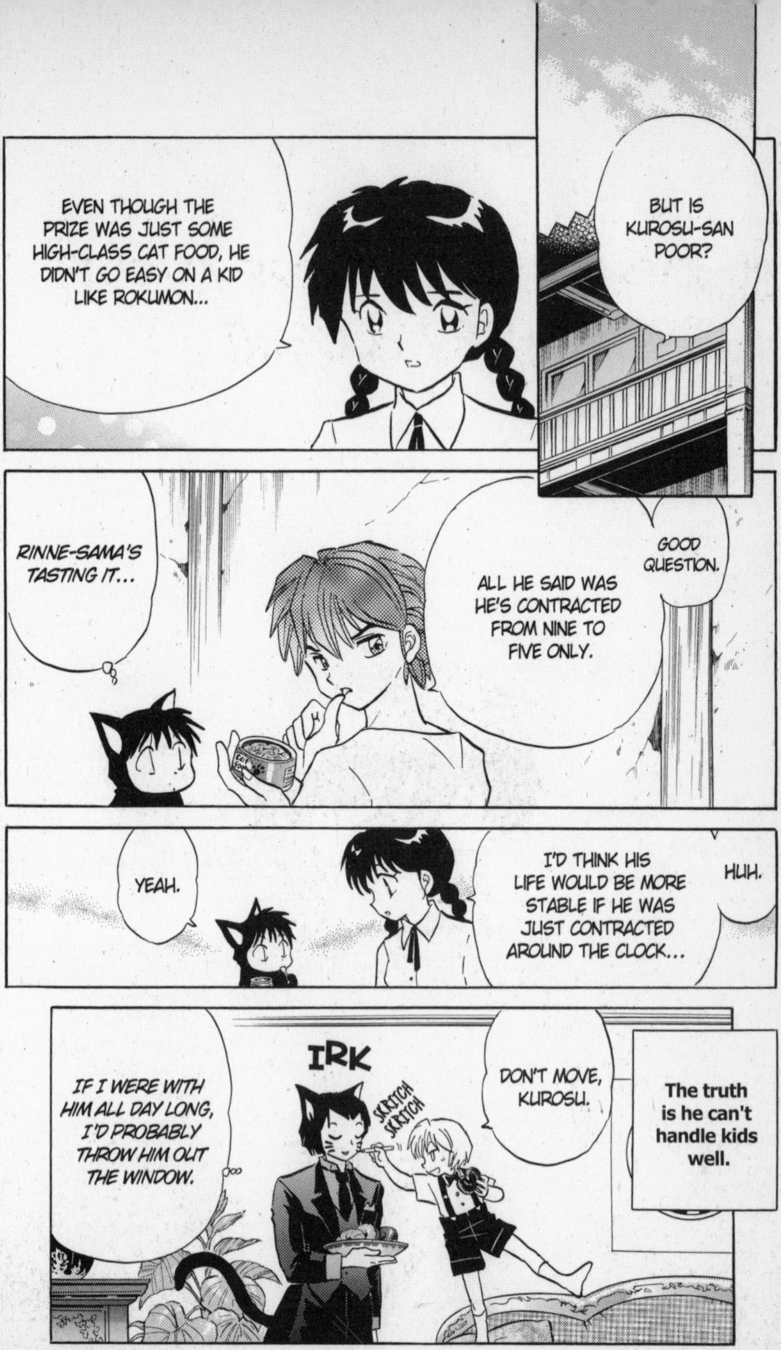
BUT IS KUROSU-SAN POOR?
EVEN THOUGH THE PRIZE WAS JUST SOME HIGH-CLASS CAT FOOD, HE DIDN'T GO EASY ON A KID LIKE ROKUMON...
GOOD QUESTION.
ALL HE SAID WAS HE'S CONTRACTED FROM NINE TO FIVE ONLY.
RINNE-SAMA'S TASTING IT...
HUH.
I'D THINK HIS LIFE WOULD BE MORE STABLE IF HE WAS JUST CONTRACTED AROUND THE CLOCK...
YEAH.
The truth is he can't handle kids well.
DON'T MOVE, KUROSU.
SKRITCH SKRITCH
IRK
IF I WERE WITH HIM ALL DAY LONG, I'D PROBABLY THROW HIM OUT THE WINDOW.

# CHAPTER 105: HALF-OFF AT THE HAUNTED HOUSE!!

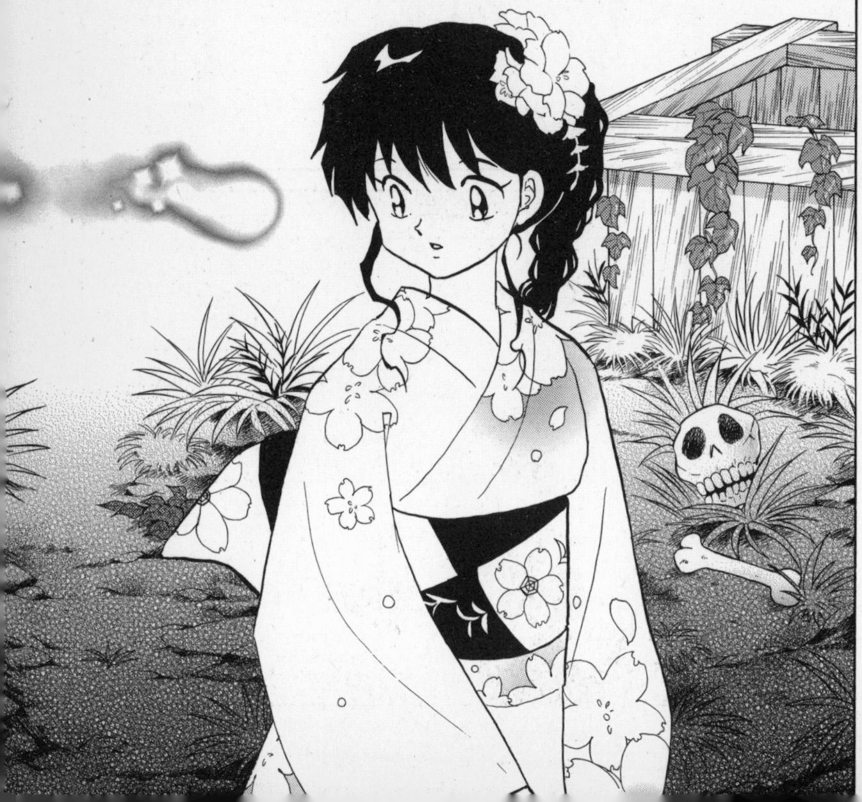

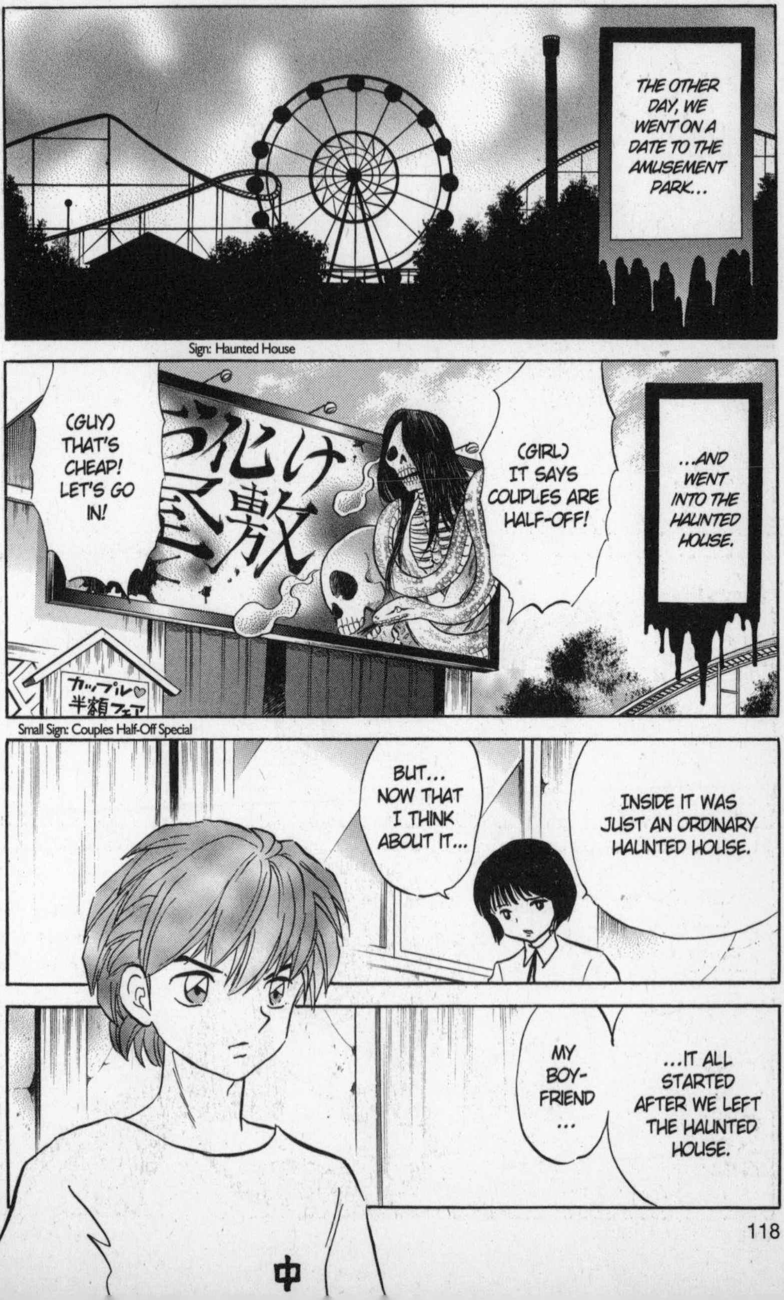
THE OTHER DAY, WE WENT ON A DATE TO THE AMUSEMENT PARK...
Sign: Haunted House
...AND WENT INTO THE HAUNTED HOUSE.
(GIRL) IT SAYS COUPLES ARE HALF-OFF!
(GUY) THAT'S CHEAP! LET'S GO IN!
カップル♡
半額フェア
Small Sign: Couples Half-Off Special
INSIDE IT WAS JUST AN ORDINARY HAUNTED HOUSE.
BUT... NOW THAT I THINK ABOUT IT...
...IT ALL STARTED AFTER WE LEFT THE HAUNTED HOUSE.
MY BOY-FRIEND...

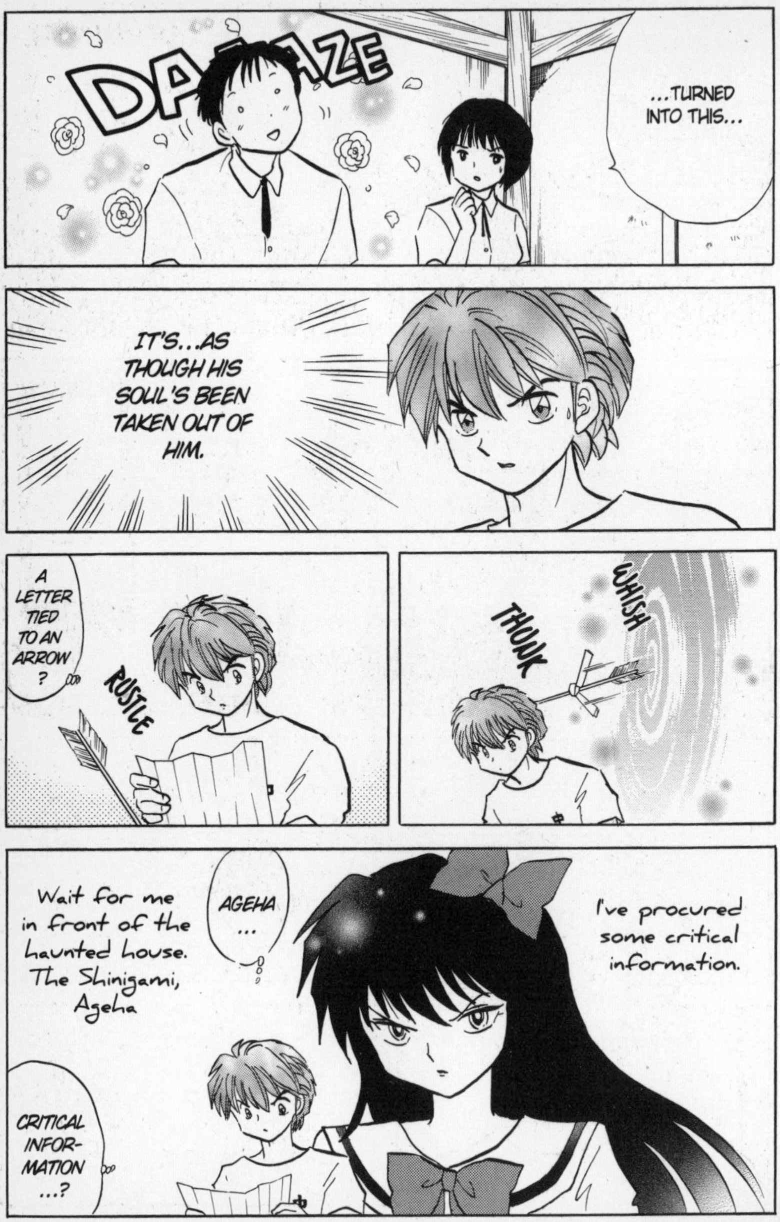
...TURNED INTO THIS...
DA AZE
IT'S...AS THOUGH HIS SOUL'S BEEN TAKEN OUT OF HIM.
WHISH
THUNK
A LETTER TIED TO AN ARROW?
RUSTLE
I've procured some critical information.
AGEHA...
Wait for me in front of the haunted house. The Shinigami, Ageha
CRITICAL INFORMATION...?

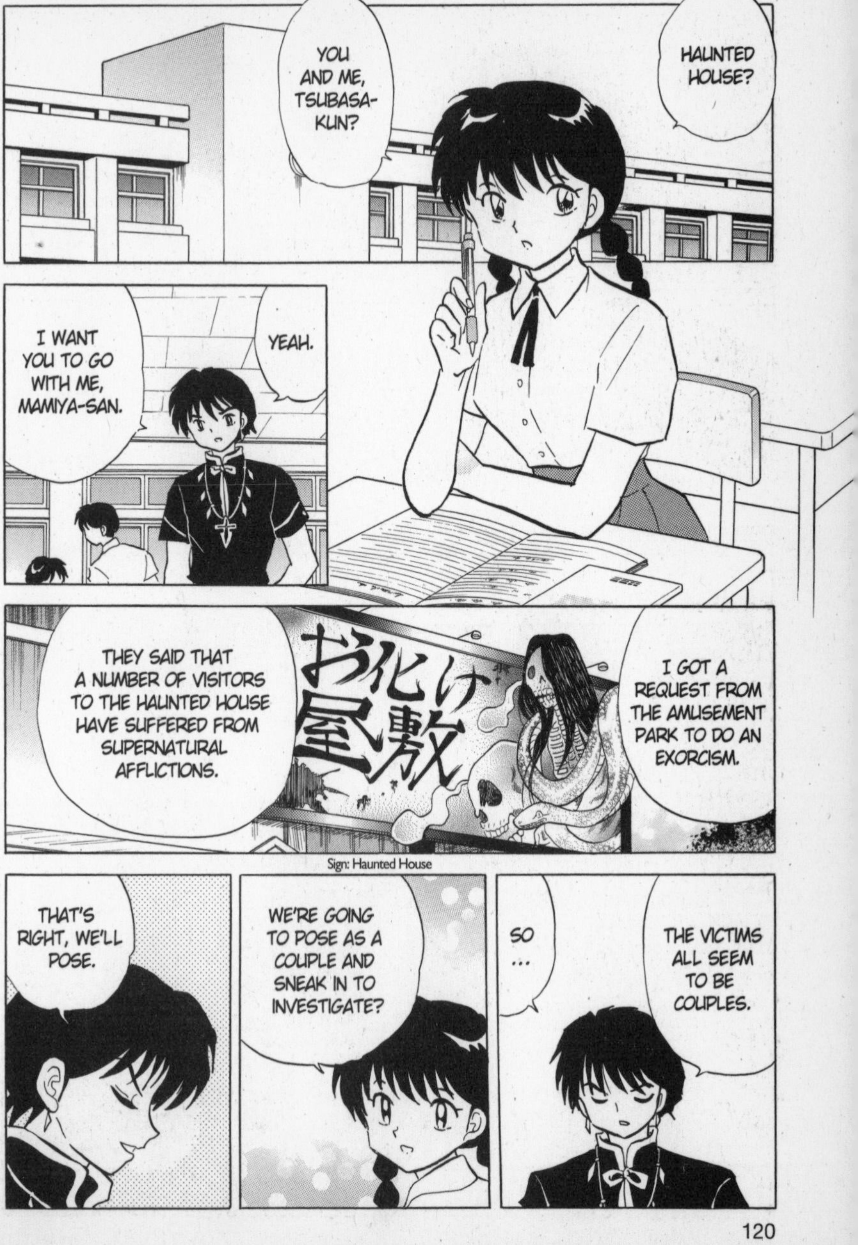
HAUNTED HOUSE?
YOU AND ME, TSUBASA-KUN?
YEAH.
I WANT YOU TO GO WITH ME, MAMIYA-SAN.
I GOT A REQUEST FROM THE AMUSEMENT PARK TO DO AN EXORCISM.
お化け屋敷
THEY SAID THAT A NUMBER OF VISITORS TO THE HAUNTED HOUSE HAVE SUFFERED FROM SUPERNATURAL AFFLICTIONS.
Sign: Haunted House
THE VICTIMS ALL SEEM TO BE COUPLES.
SO ...
WE'RE GOING TO POSE AS A COUPLE AND SNEAK IN TO INVESTIGATE?
THAT'S RIGHT, WE'LL POSE.

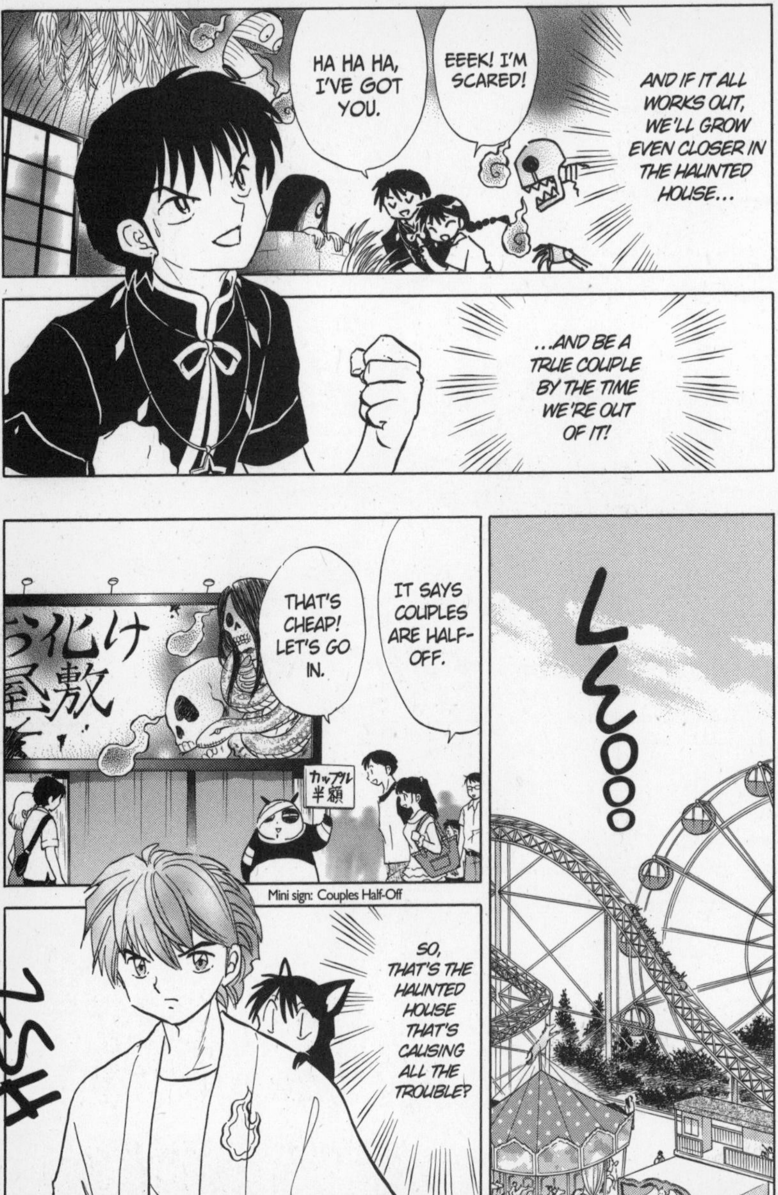
AND IF IT ALL WORKS OUT, WE'LL GROW EVEN CLOSER IN THE HAUNTED HOUSE...
EEEK! I'M SCARED!
HA HA HA, I'VE GOT YOU.
...AND BE A TRUE COUPLE BY THE TIME WE'RE OUT OF IT!
IT SAYS COUPLES ARE HALF-OFF.
THAT'S CHEAP! LET'S GO IN.
カップル半額
SO, THAT'S THE HAUNTED HOUSE THAT'S CAUSING ALL THE TROUBLE?
Mini sign: Couples Half-Off

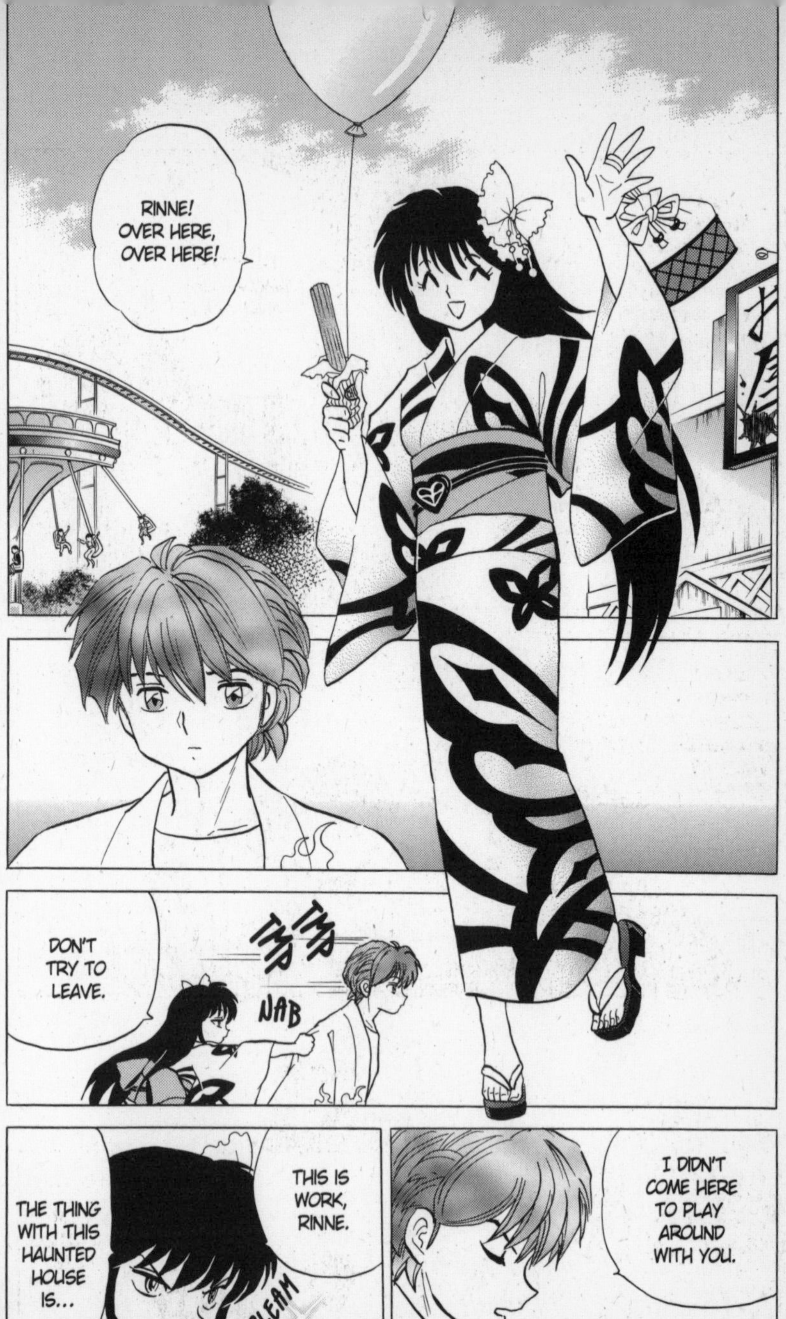
RINNE! OVER HERE, OVER HERE!
TMP TMP
NAB
DON'T TRY TO LEAVE.
I DIDN'T COME HERE TO PLAY AROUND WITH YOU.
THIS IS WORK, RINNE.
THE THING WITH THIS HAUNTED HOUSE IS...
GLEAM

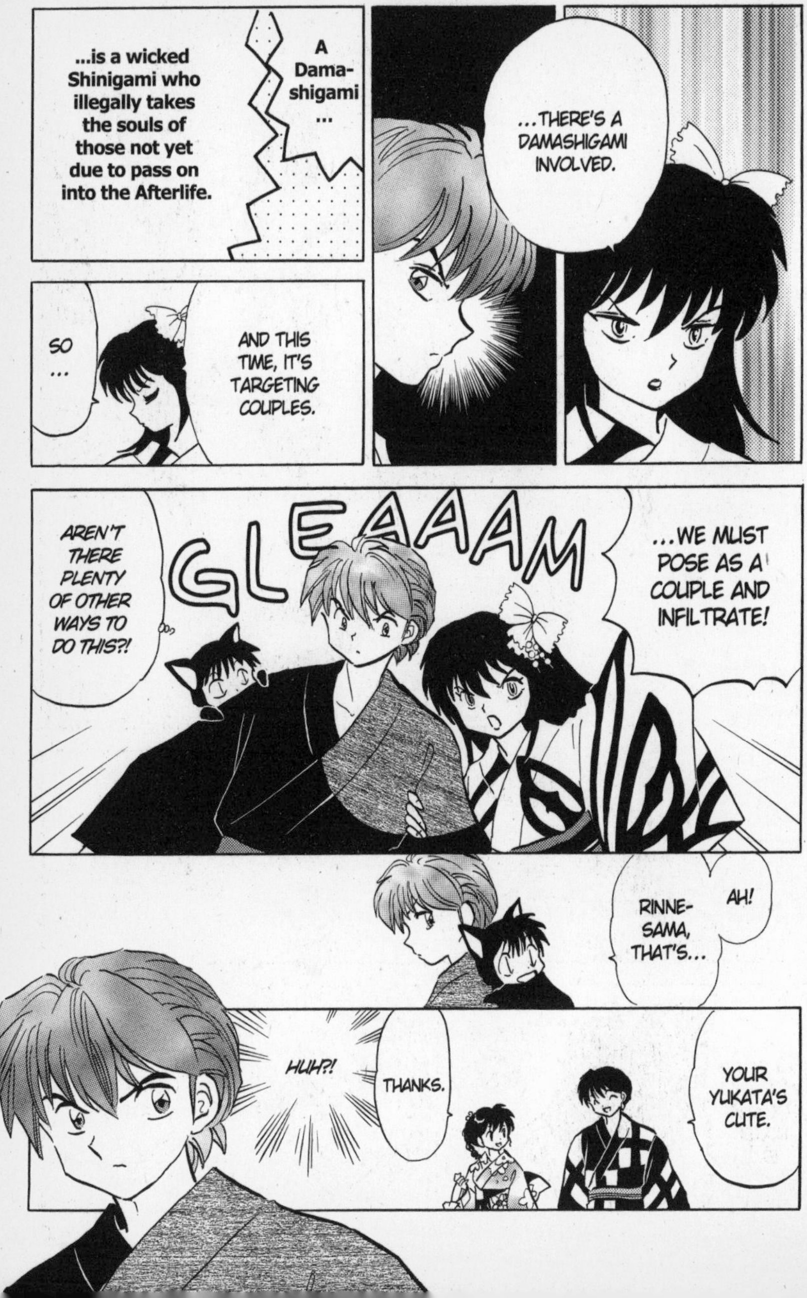

...THERE'S A DAMASHIGAMI INVOLVED.
A Damashigami...
...is a wicked Shinigami who illegally takes the souls of those not yet due to pass on into the Afterlife.
AND THIS TIME, IT'S TARGETING COUPLES.
SO...
...WE MUST POSE AS A COUPLE AND INFILTRATE!
GLEAAAM
AREN'T THERE PLENTY OF OTHER WAYS TO DO THIS?!
AH!
RINNE-SAMA, THAT'S...
YOUR YUKATA'S CUTE.
THANKS.
HUH?!

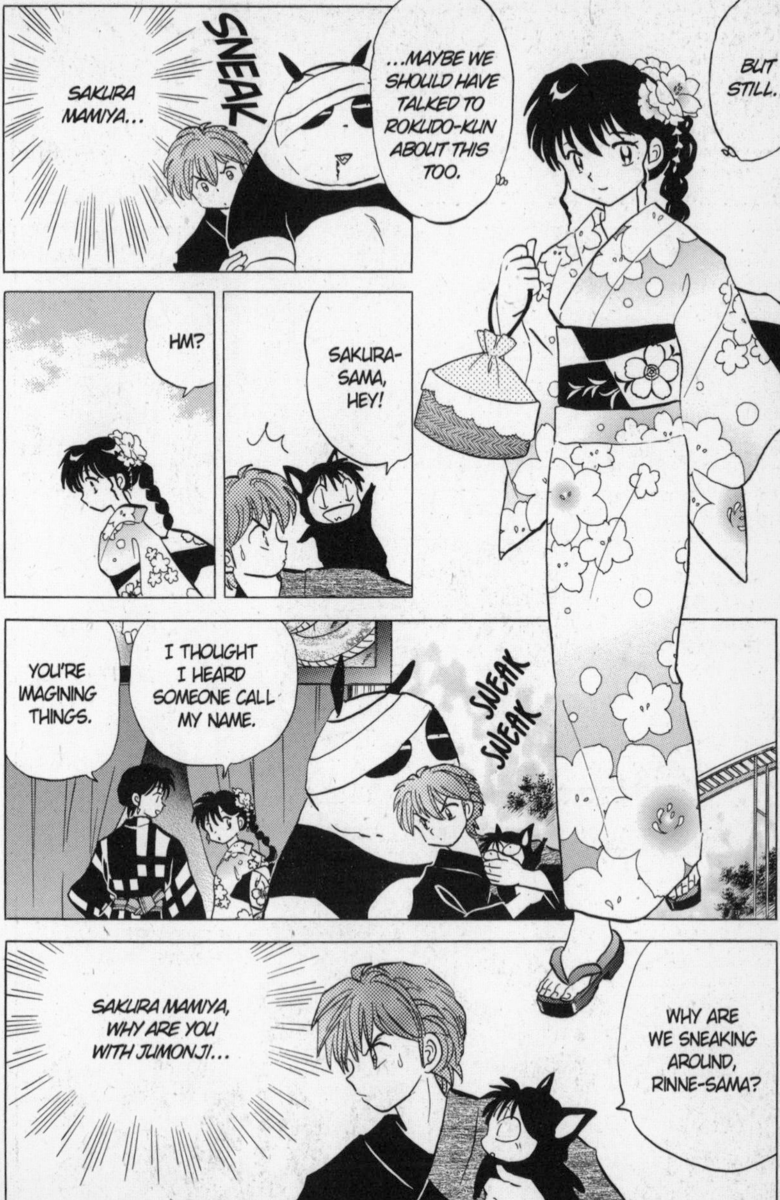
BUT STILL...
...MAYBE WE SHOULD HAVE TALKED TO ROKUDO-KUN ABOUT THIS TOO.
SNEAK
SAKURA MAMIYA...
SAKURA-SAMA, HEY!
HM?
SNEAK SNEAK
I THOUGHT I HEARD SOMEONE CALL MY NAME.
YOU'RE IMAGINING THINGS.
WHY ARE WE SNEAKING AROUND, RINNE-SAMA?
SAKURA MAMIYA, WHY ARE YOU WITH JUMONJI...

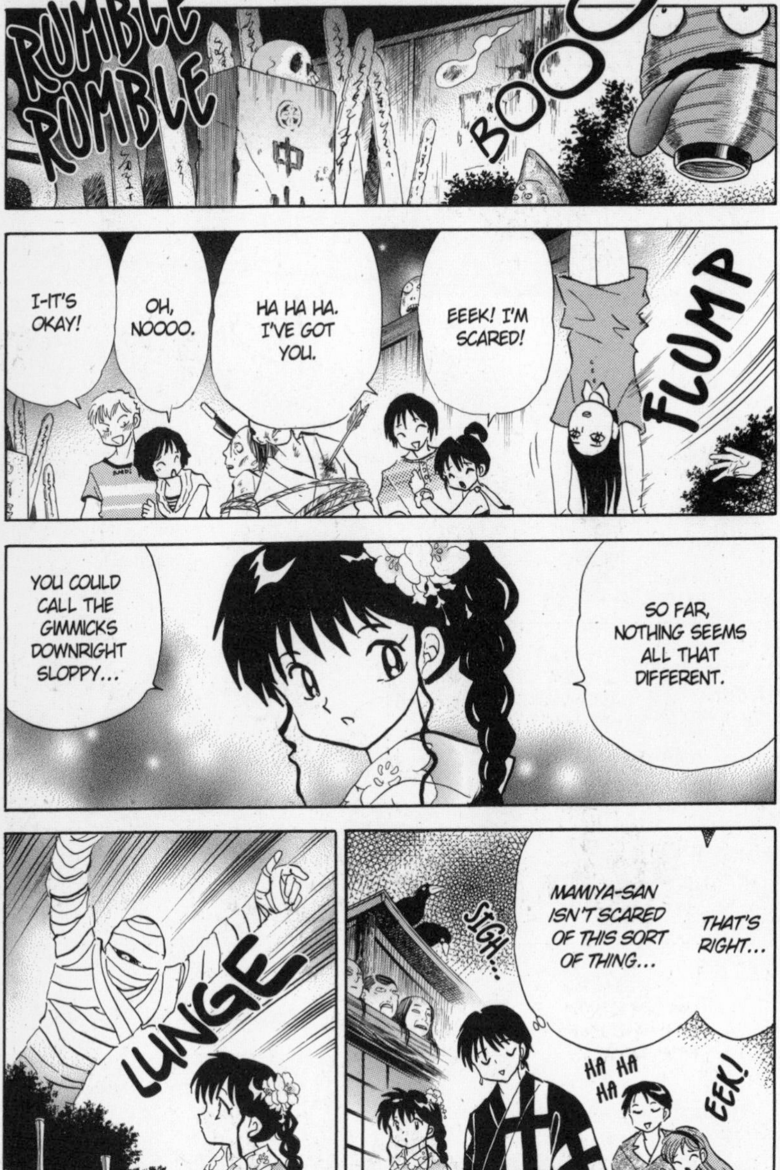
BOOO
RUMBLE RUMBLE
FLUMP
EEEK! I'M SCARED!
HA HA HA. I'VE GOT YOU.
OH, NOOOO.
I-IT'S OKAY!
SO FAR, NOTHING SEEMS ALL THAT DIFFERENT.
YOU COULD CALL THE GIMMICKS DOWNRIGHT SLOPPY...
THAT'S RIGHT...
MAMIYA-SAN ISN'T SCARED OF THIS SORT OF THING...
SIGH...
EEK!
HA HA HA
LUNGE

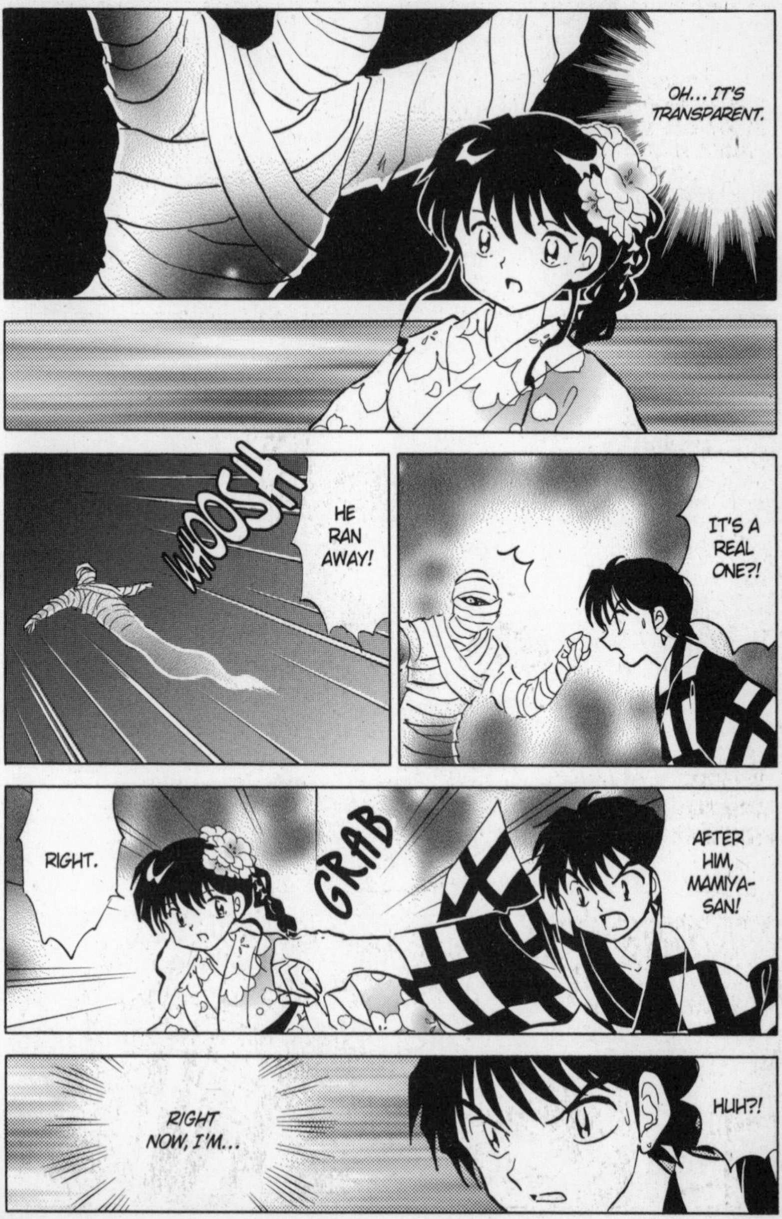
OH... IT'S TRANSPARENT.
IT'S A REAL ONE?!
HE RAN AWAY!
WHOOSH
AFTER HIM, MAMIYA-SAN!
GRAB
RIGHT.
HUH?!
RIGHT NOW, I'M...

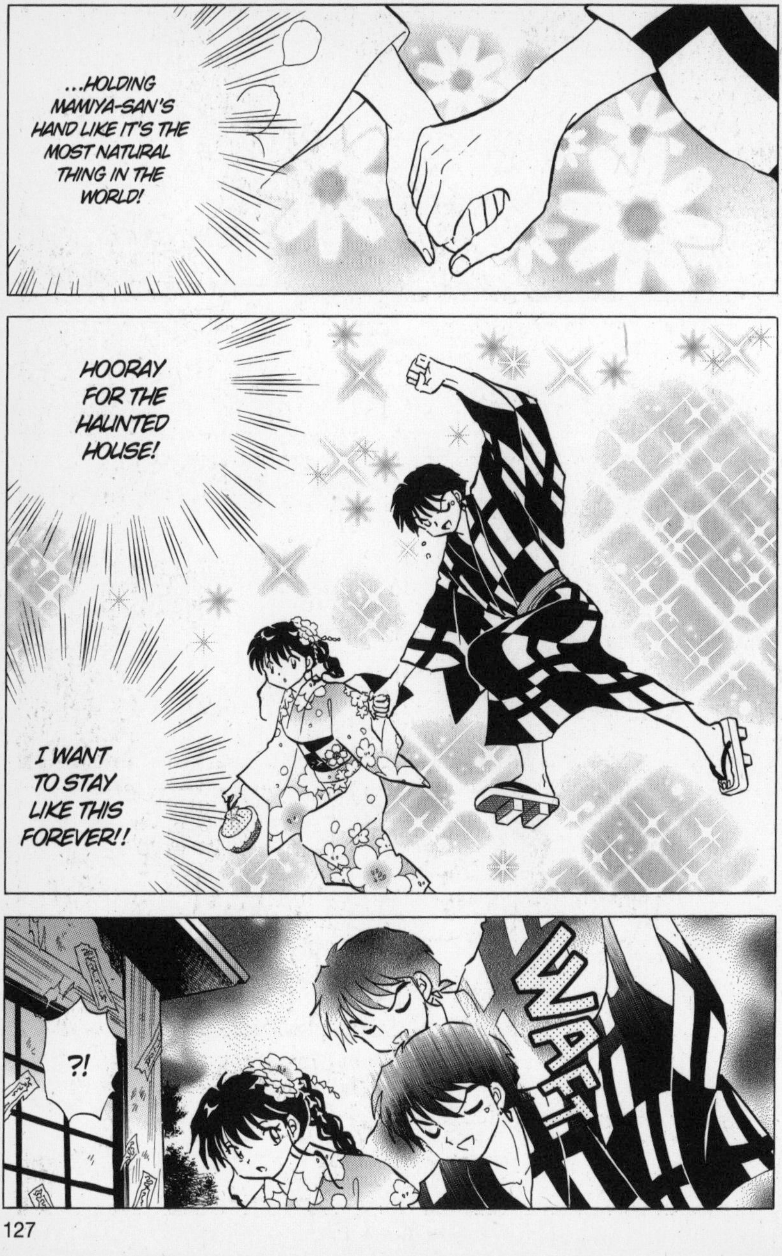
...HOLDING MAMIYA-SAN'S HAND LIKE IT'S THE MOST NATURAL THING IN THE WORLD!
HOORAY FOR THE HAUNTED HOUSE!
I WANT TO STAY LIKE THIS FOREVER!!
WAFT
?!

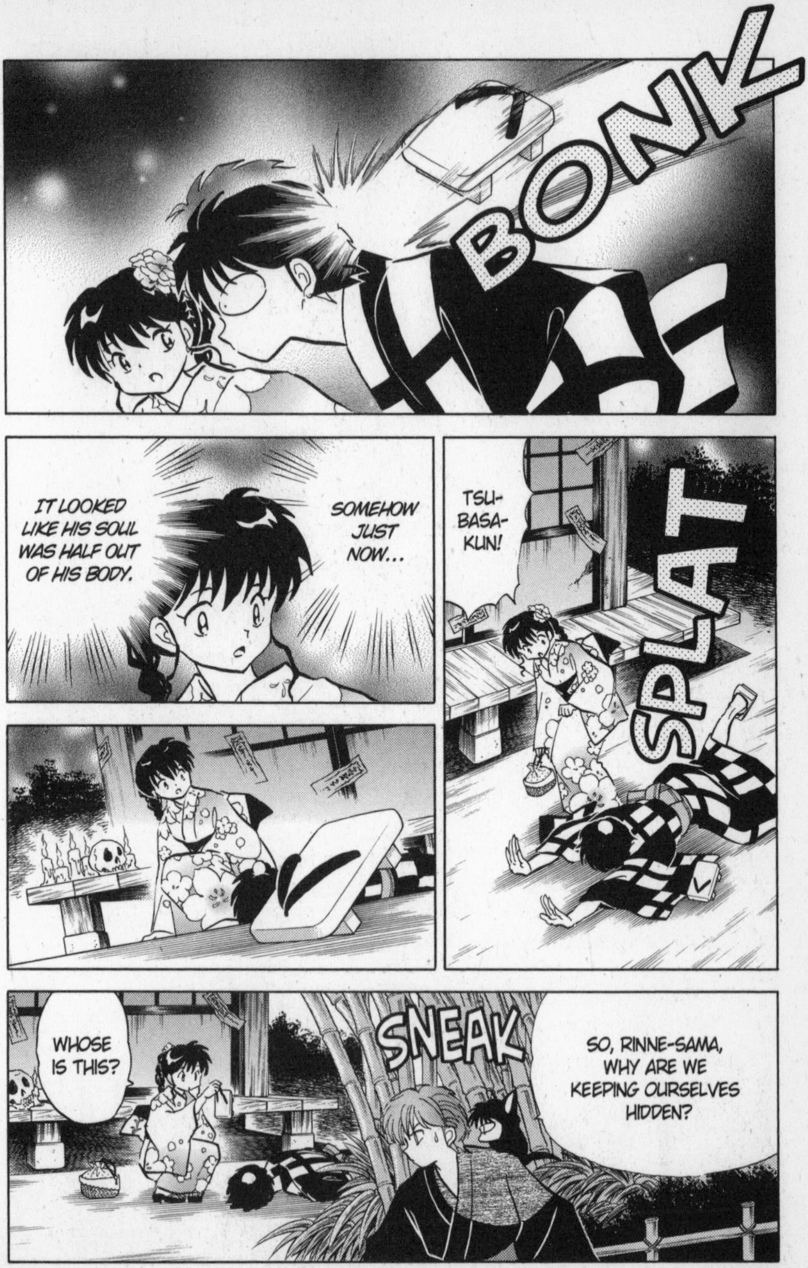
BONK
TSU-BASA-KUN!
SPLAT
SOMEHOW JUST NOW...
IT LOOKED LIKE HIS SOUL WAS HALF OUT OF HIS BODY.
SO, RINNE-SAMA, WHY ARE WE KEEPING OURSELVES HIDDEN?
SNEAK
WHOSE IS THIS?

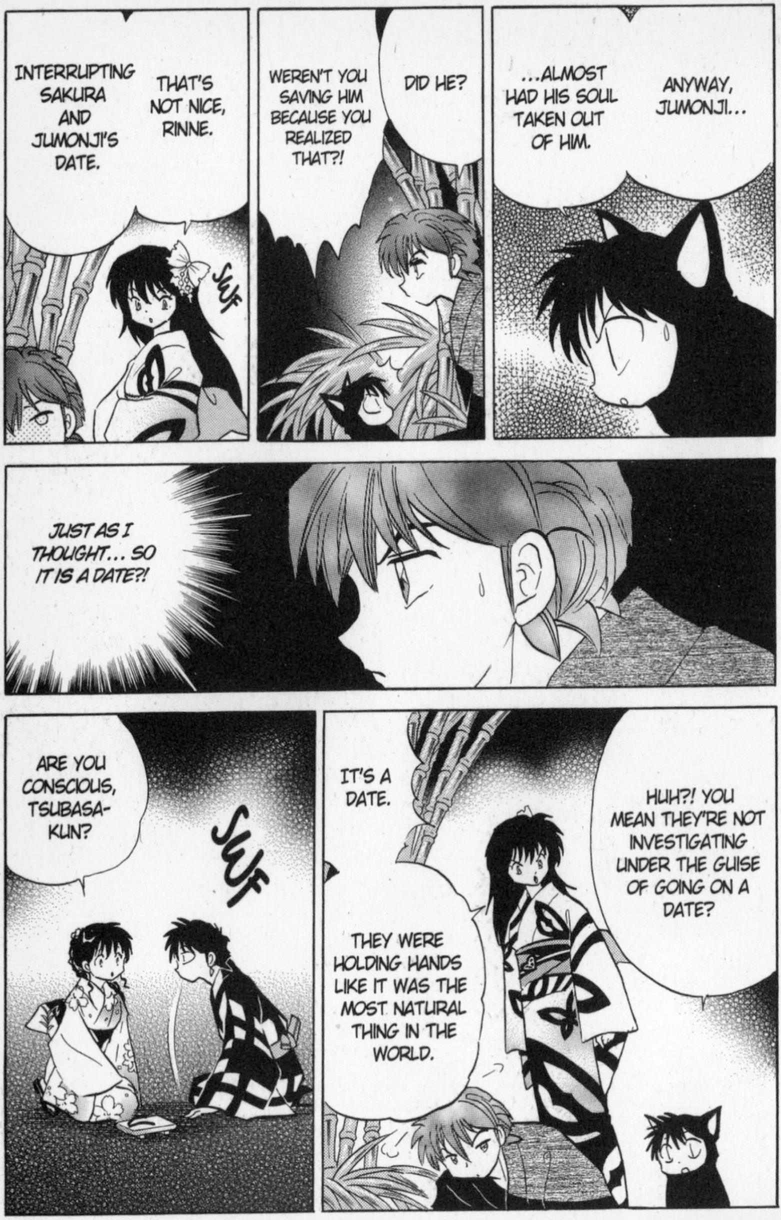
ANYWAY, JUMONJI...
...ALMOST HAD HIS SOUL TAKEN OUT OF HIM.
DID HE?
WEREN'T YOU SAVING HIM BECAUSE YOU REALIZED THAT?!
THAT'S NOT NICE, RINNE.
INTERRUPTING SAKURA AND JUMONJI'S DATE.
SWF
JUST AS I THOUGHT... SO IT IS A DATE?!
HUH?! YOU MEAN THEY'RE NOT INVESTIGATING UNDER THE GUISE OF GOING ON A DATE?
IT'S A DATE.
THEY WERE HOLDING HANDS LIKE IT WAS THE MOST NATURAL THING IN THE WORLD.
ARE YOU CONSCIOUS, TSUBASA-KUN?
SWF

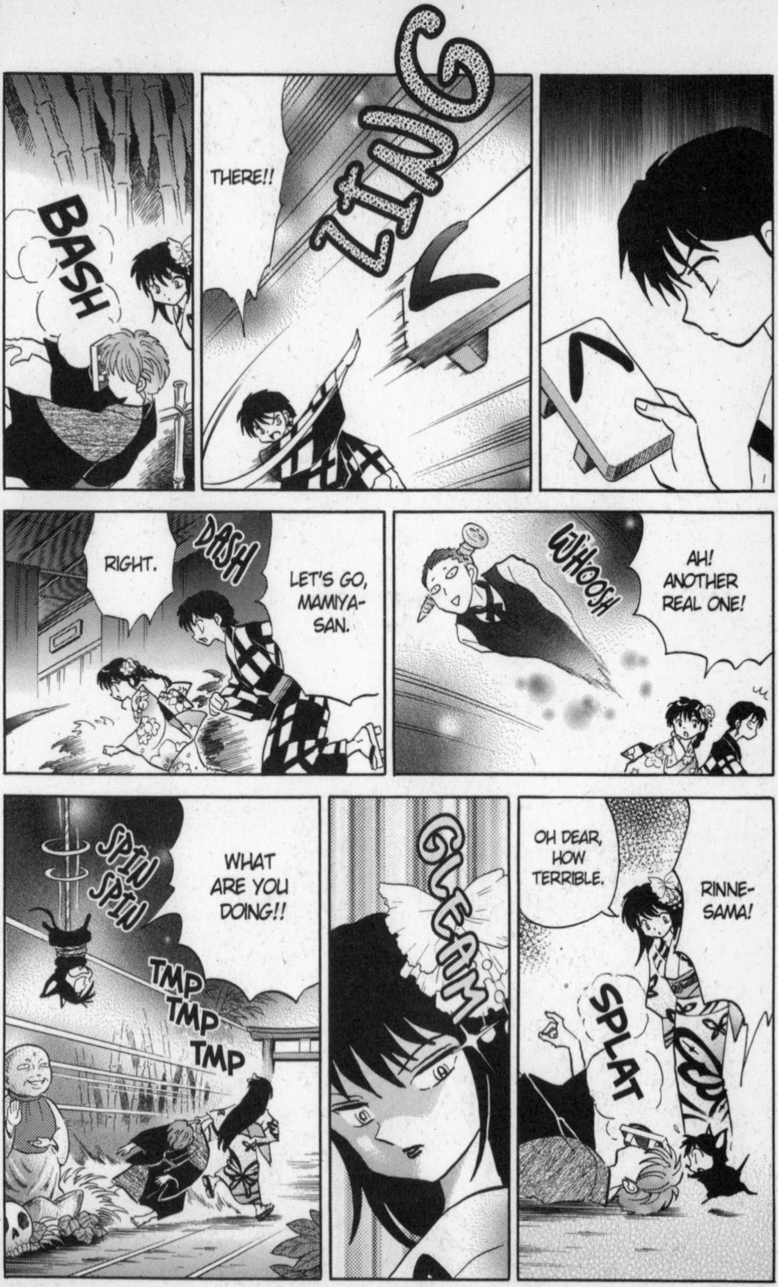
ZING
THERE!!
BASH
WHOOSH
AH! ANOTHER REAL ONE!
LET'S GO, MAMIYA-SAN.
DASH
RIGHT.
RINNE-SAMA!
OH DEAR, HOW TERRIBLE.
SPLAT
GLEAM
WHAT ARE YOU DOING!!
SPIN SPIN
TMP TMP TMP

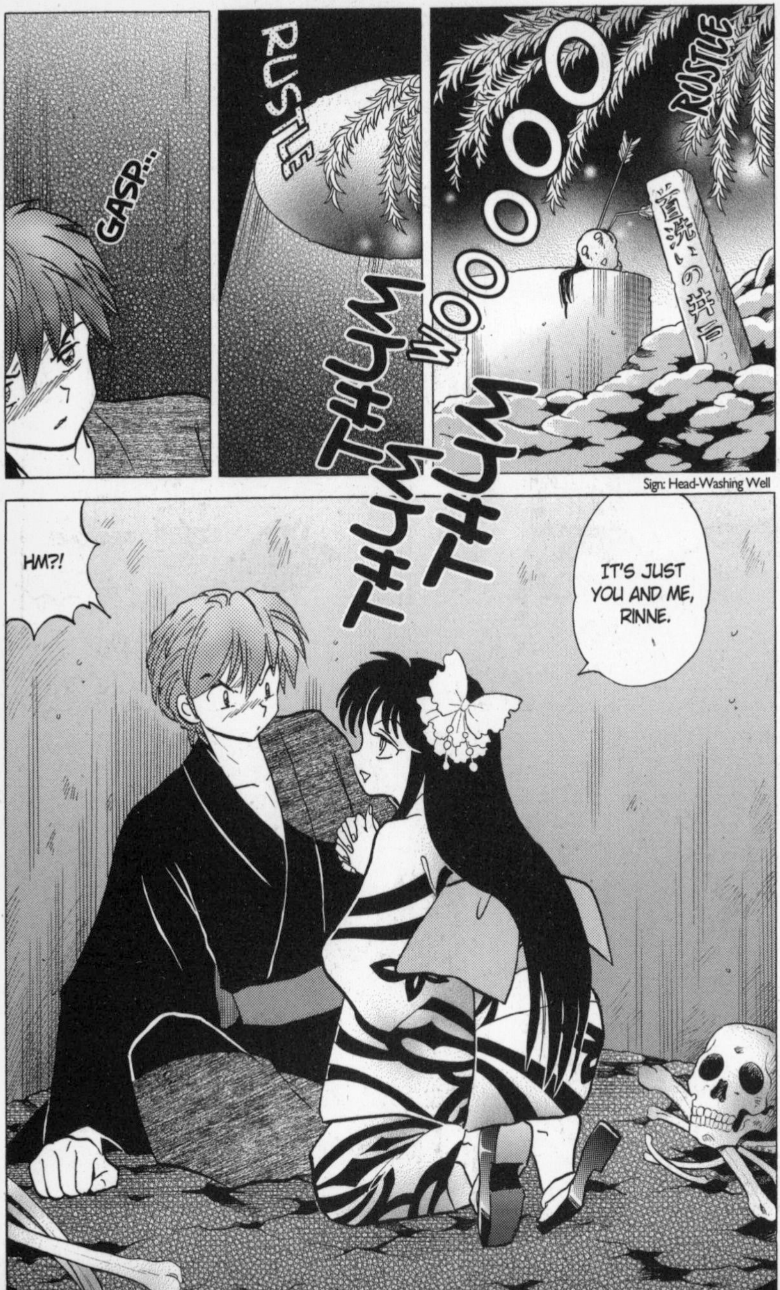
RUSTLE
WOOOOOO
首洗いの井戸
Sign: Head-Washing Well
THUMP THUMP
RUSTLE
THUMP THUMP
GASP...
IT'S JUST YOU AND ME, RINNE.
HM?!

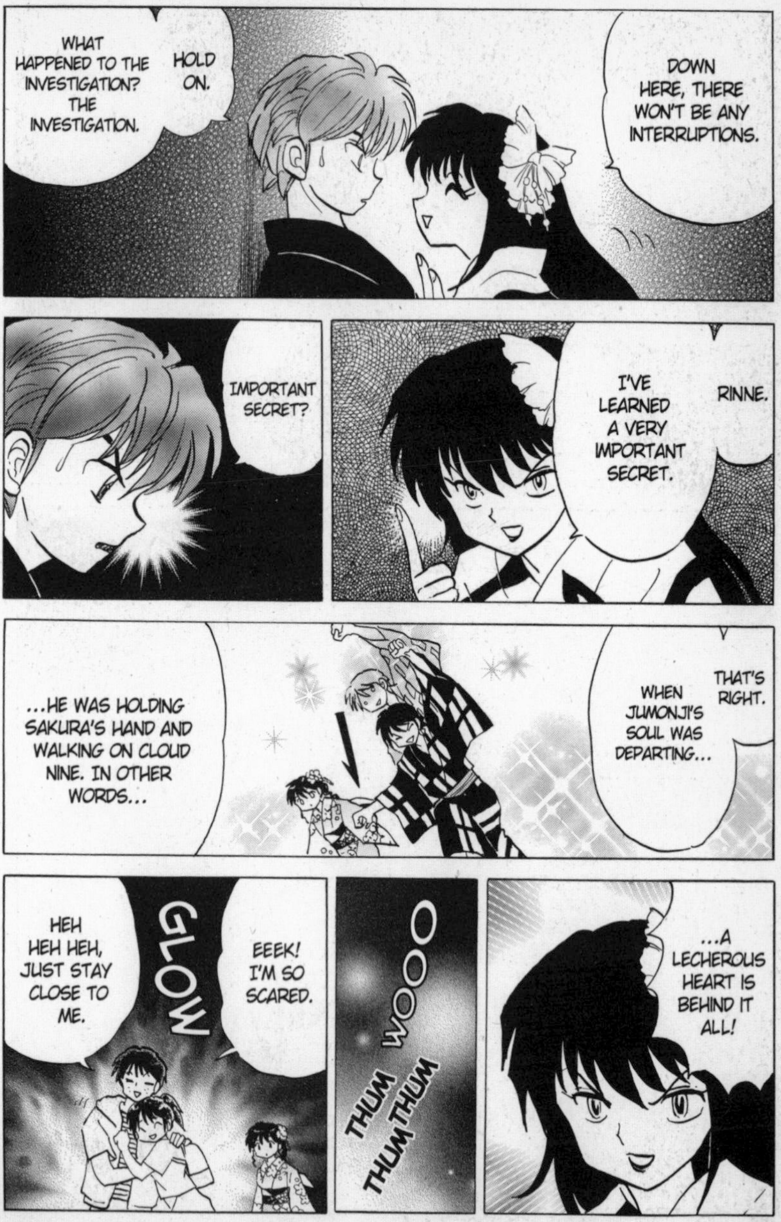
DOWN HERE, THERE WON'T BE ANY INTERRUPTIONS.
HOLD ON.
WHAT HAPPENED TO THE INVESTIGATION? THE INVESTIGATION.
RINNE.
I'VE LEARNED A VERY IMPORTANT SECRET.
IMPORTANT SECRET?
THAT'S RIGHT.
WHEN JUMONJI'S SOUL WAS DEPARTING...
...HE WAS HOLDING SAKURA'S HAND AND WALKING ON CLOUD NINE. IN OTHER WORDS...
...A LECHEROUS HEART IS BEHIND IT ALL!
WOOO
THUM THUM THUM
EEEK! I'M SO SCARED.
GLOW
HEH HEH HEH, JUST STAY CLOSE TO ME.

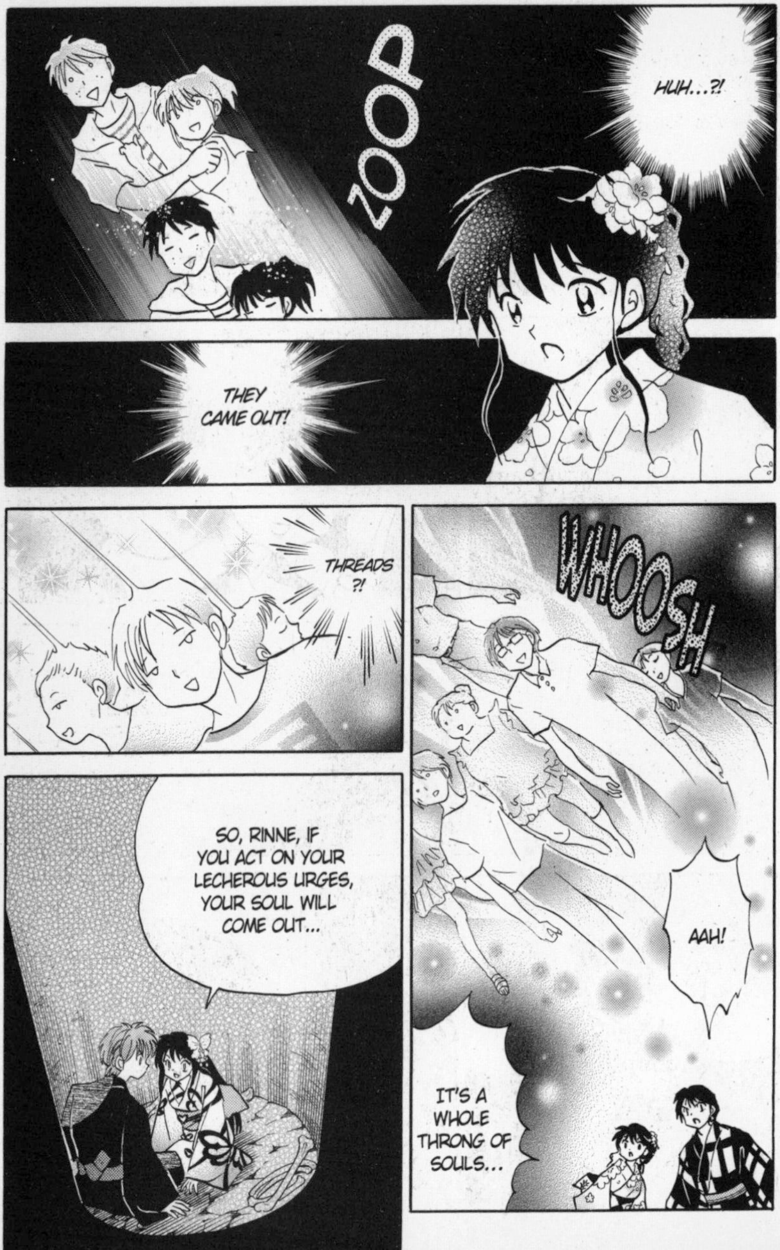
HUH...?!
ZOOP
THEY CAME OUT!
WHOOSH
AAH!
IT'S A WHOLE THRONG OF SOULS...
THREADS ?!
SO, RINNE, IF YOU ACT ON YOUR LECHEROUS URGES, YOUR SOUL WILL COME OUT...

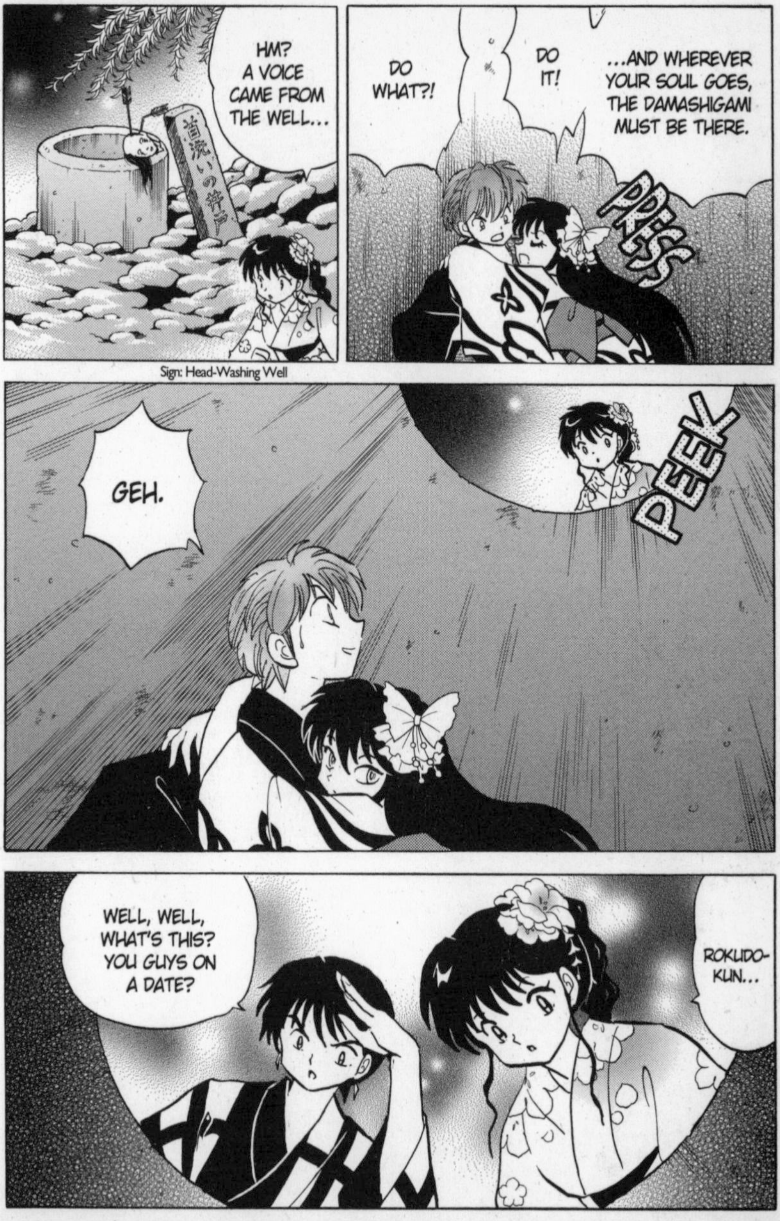
...AND WHEREVER YOUR SOUL GOES, THE DAMASHIGAMI MUST BE THERE.
DO IT!
DO WHAT?!
PRESS
HM? A VOICE CAME FROM THE WELL...
Sign: Head-Washing Well
PEEK
GEH.
ROKUDO-KUN...
WELL, WELL, WHAT'S THIS? YOU GUYS ON A DATE?

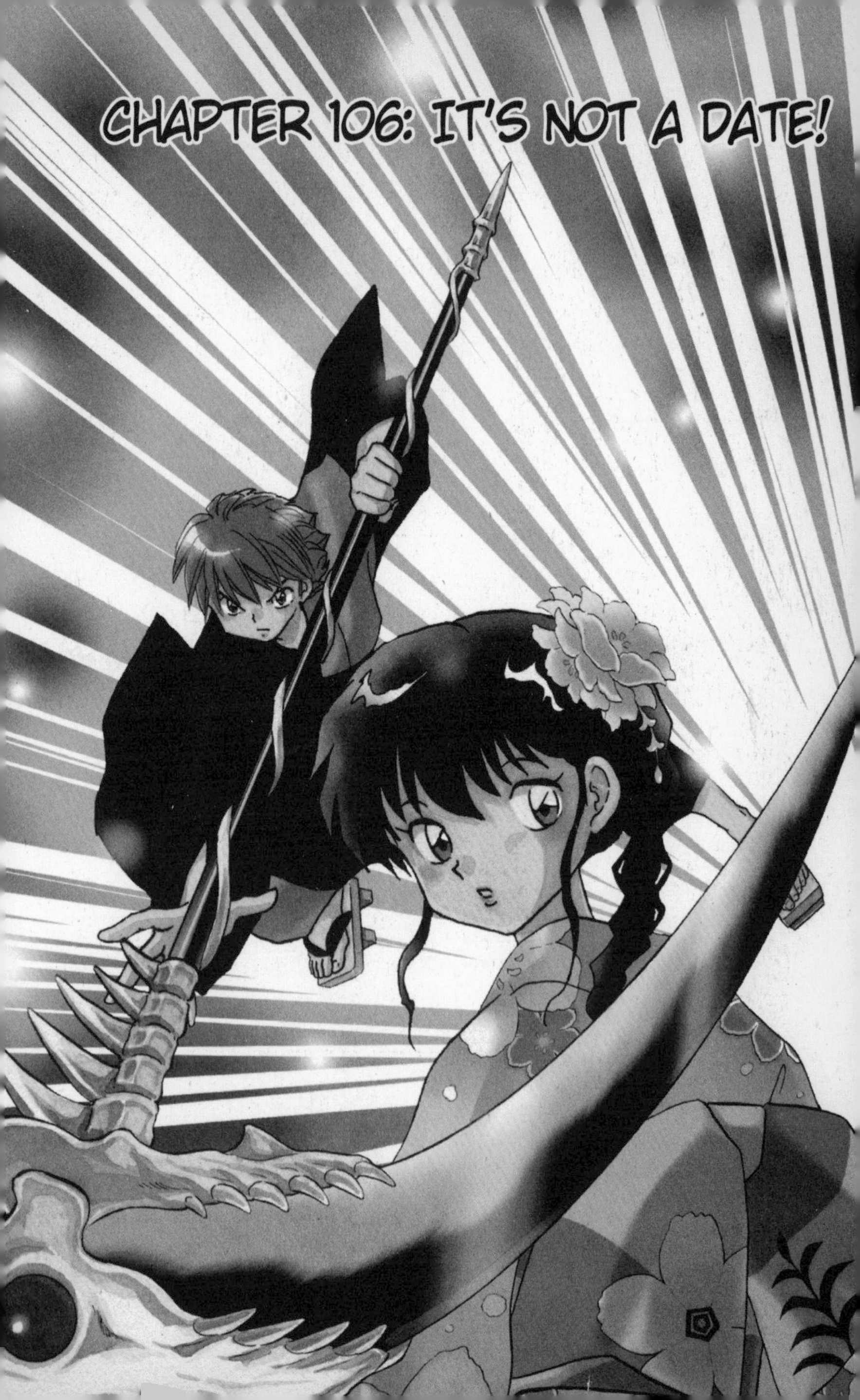
CHAPTER 106: IT'S NOT A DATE!

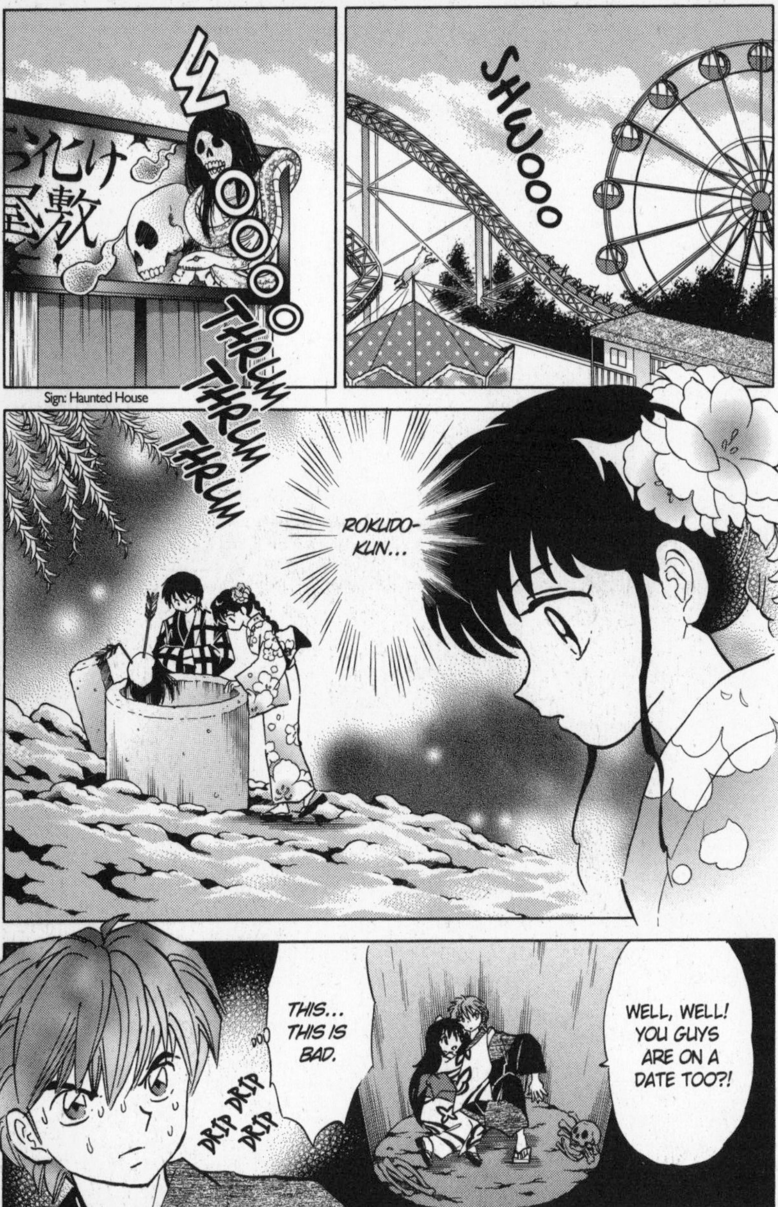
SHWOOO
WOOOOOO
THRUM THRUM THRUM
ROKUDO-KUN...
WELL, WELL! YOU GUYS ARE ON A DATE TOO?!
THIS... THIS IS BAD.
DRIP DRIP DRIP
Sign: Haunted House

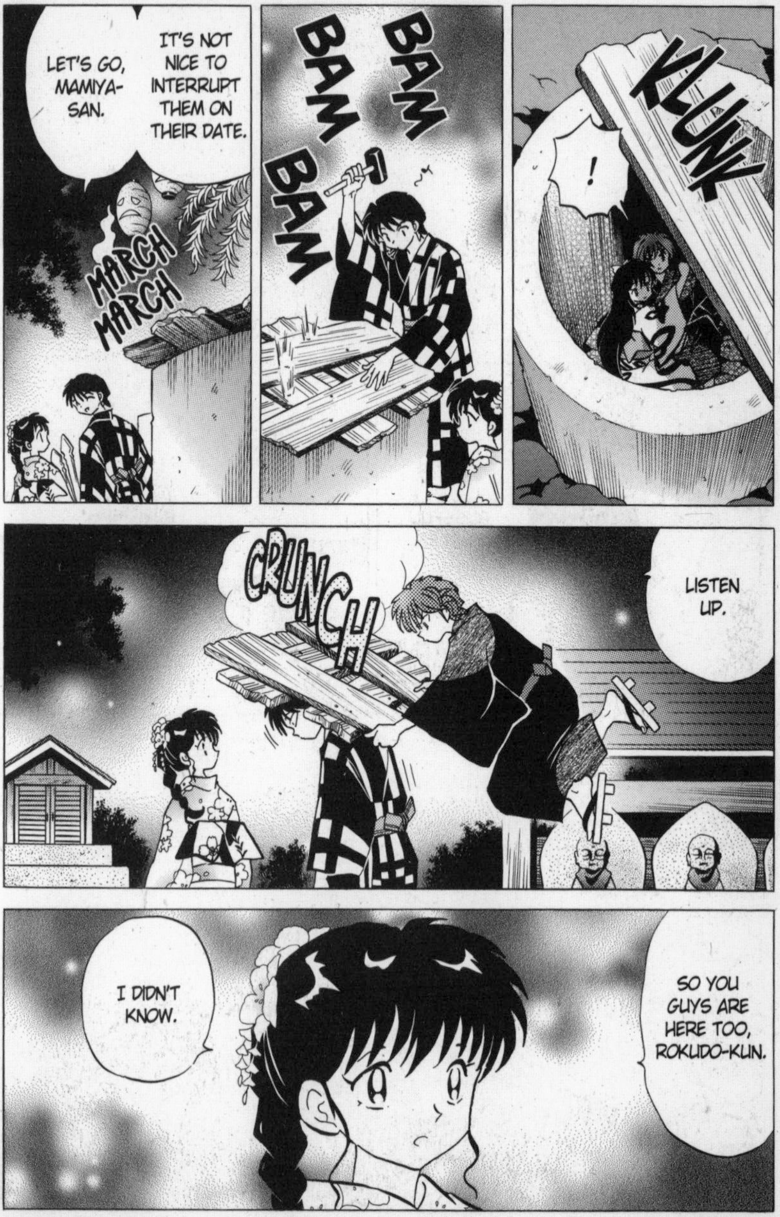
KLUNK
!
BAM
BAM
BAM
BAM
IT'S NOT NICE TO INTERRUPT THEM ON THEIR DATE.
LET'S GO, MAMIYA-SAN.
MARCH MARCH
LISTEN UP.
CRUNCH
SO YOU GUYS ARE HERE TOO, ROKUDO-KUN.
I DIDN'T KNOW.

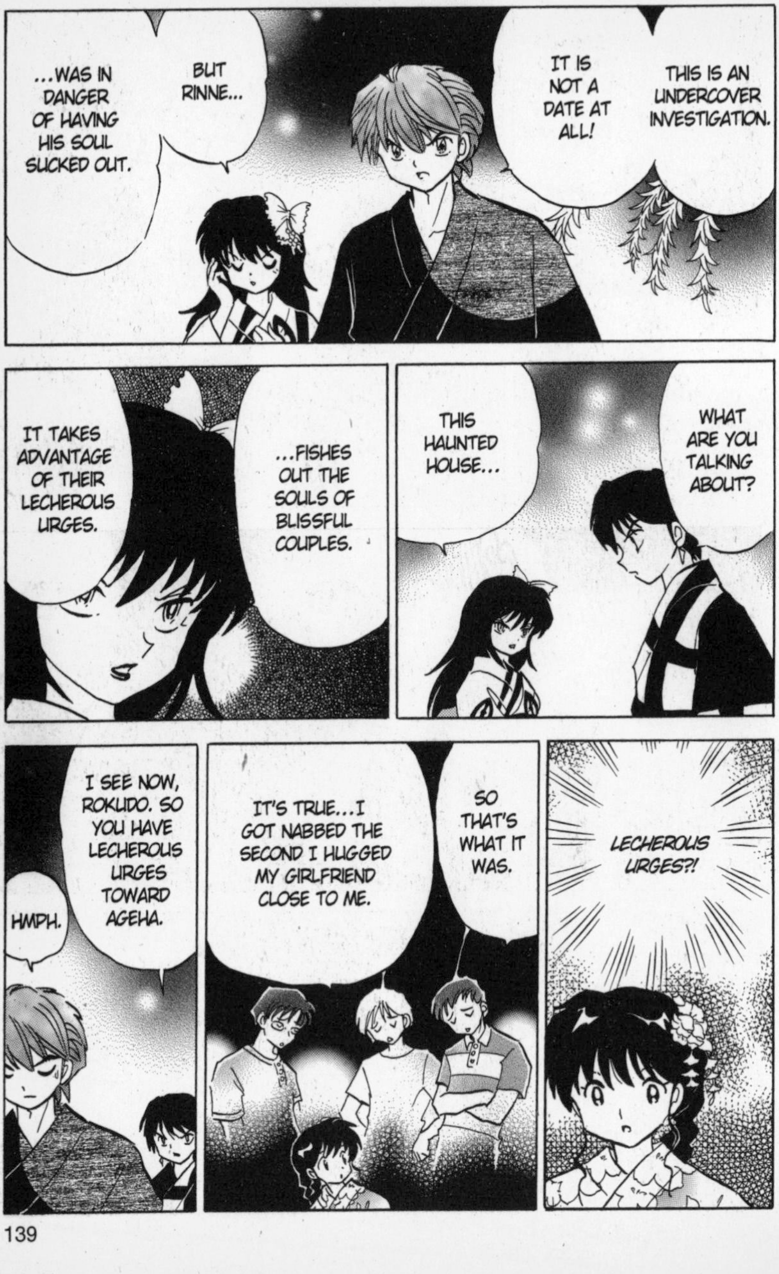
THIS IS AN UNDERCOVER INVESTIGATION.
IT IS NOT A DATE AT ALL!
BUT RINNE...
...WAS IN DANGER OF HAVING HIS SOUL SUCKED OUT.
WHAT ARE YOU TALKING ABOUT?
THIS HAUNTED HOUSE...
...FISHES OUT THE SOULS OF BLISSFUL COUPLES.
IT TAKES ADVANTAGE OF THEIR LECHEROUS URGES.
LECHEROUS URGES?!
SO THAT'S WHAT IT WAS.
IT'S TRUE...I GOT NABBED THE SECOND I HUGGED MY GIRLFRIEND CLOSE TO ME.
I SEE NOW, ROKUDO. SO YOU HAVE LECHEROUS URGES TOWARD AGEHA.
HMPH.

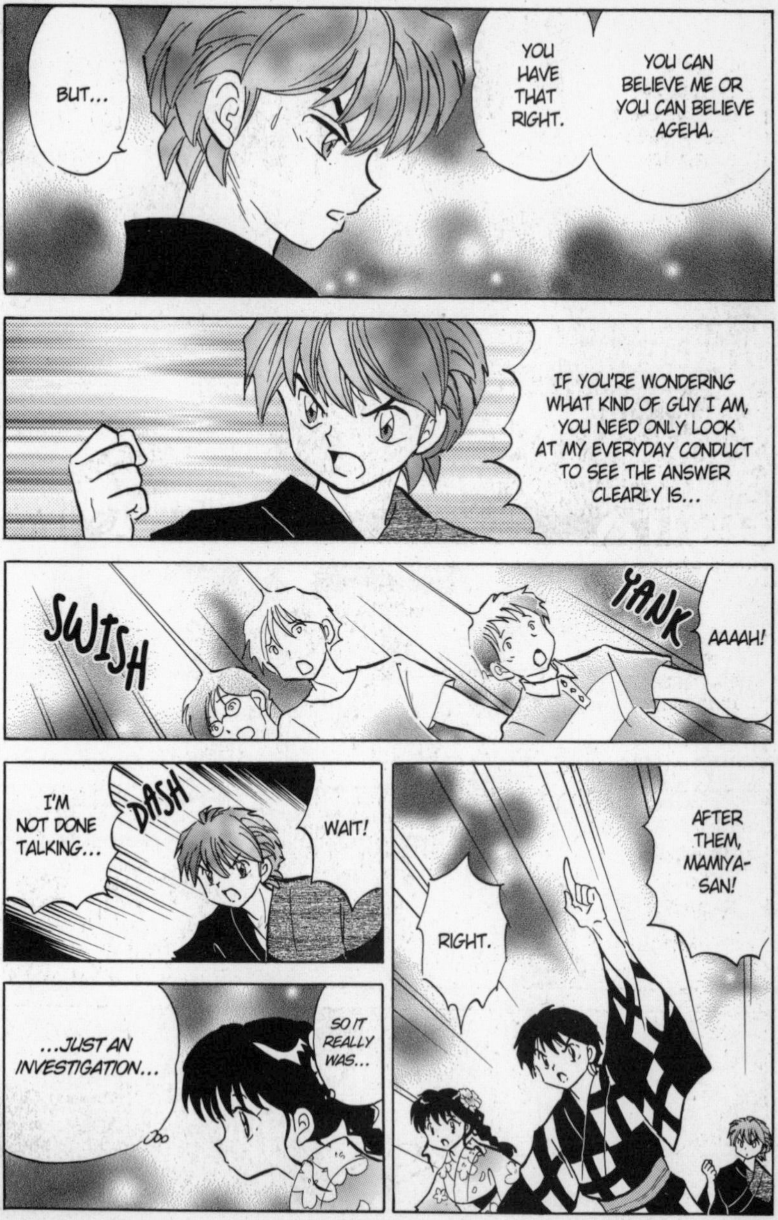
YOU CAN BELIEVE ME OR YOU CAN BELIEVE AGEHA.
YOU HAVE THAT RIGHT.
BUT...
IF YOU'RE WONDERING WHAT KIND OF GUY I AM, YOU NEED ONLY LOOK AT MY EVERYDAY CONDUCT TO SEE THE ANSWER CLEARLY IS...
YANK
AAAAH!
SWISH
AFTER THEM, MAMIYA-SAN!
RIGHT.
WAIT!
DASH
I'M NOT DONE TALKING...
SO IT REALLY WAS...
...JUST AN INVESTIGATION...

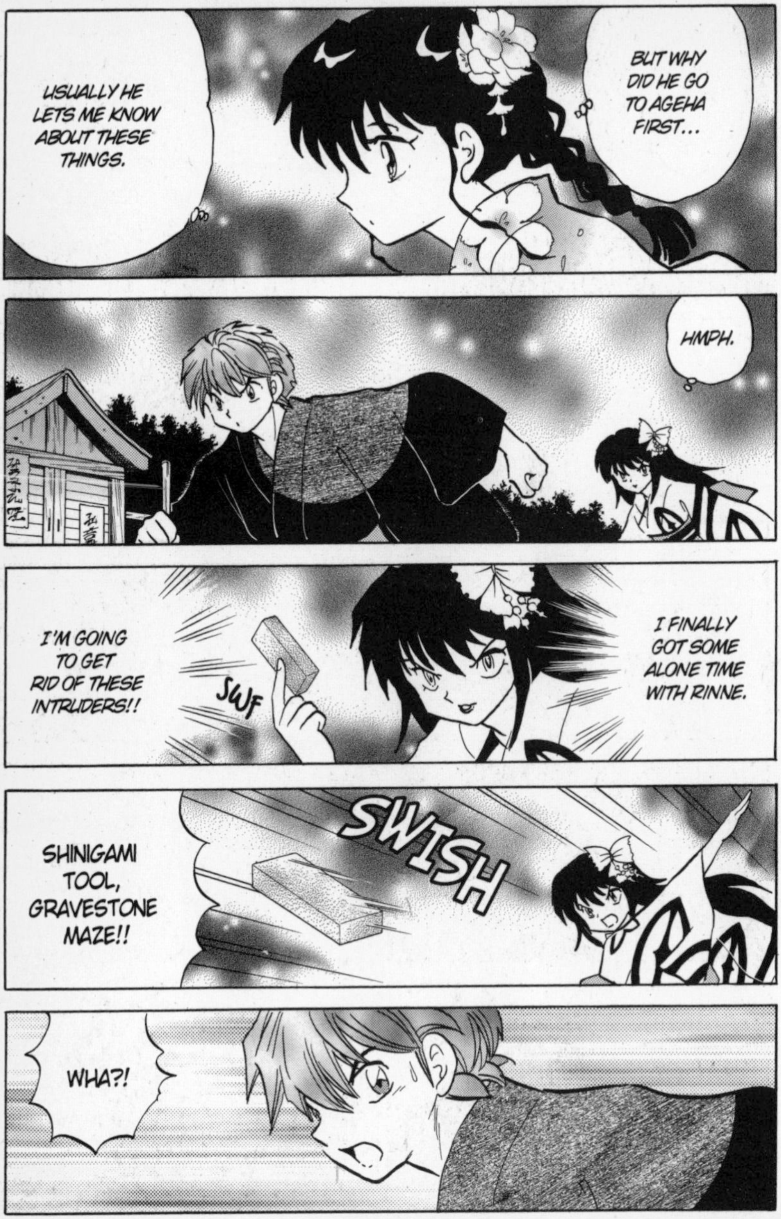
BUT WHY DID HE GO TO AGEHA FIRST...
USUALLY HE LETS ME KNOW ABOUT THESE THINGS.
HMPH.
I FINALLY GOT SOME ALONE TIME WITH RINNE.
I'M GOING TO GET RID OF THESE INTRUDERS!!
SWF
SWISH
SHINIGAMI TOOL, GRAVESTONE MAZE!!
WHA?!

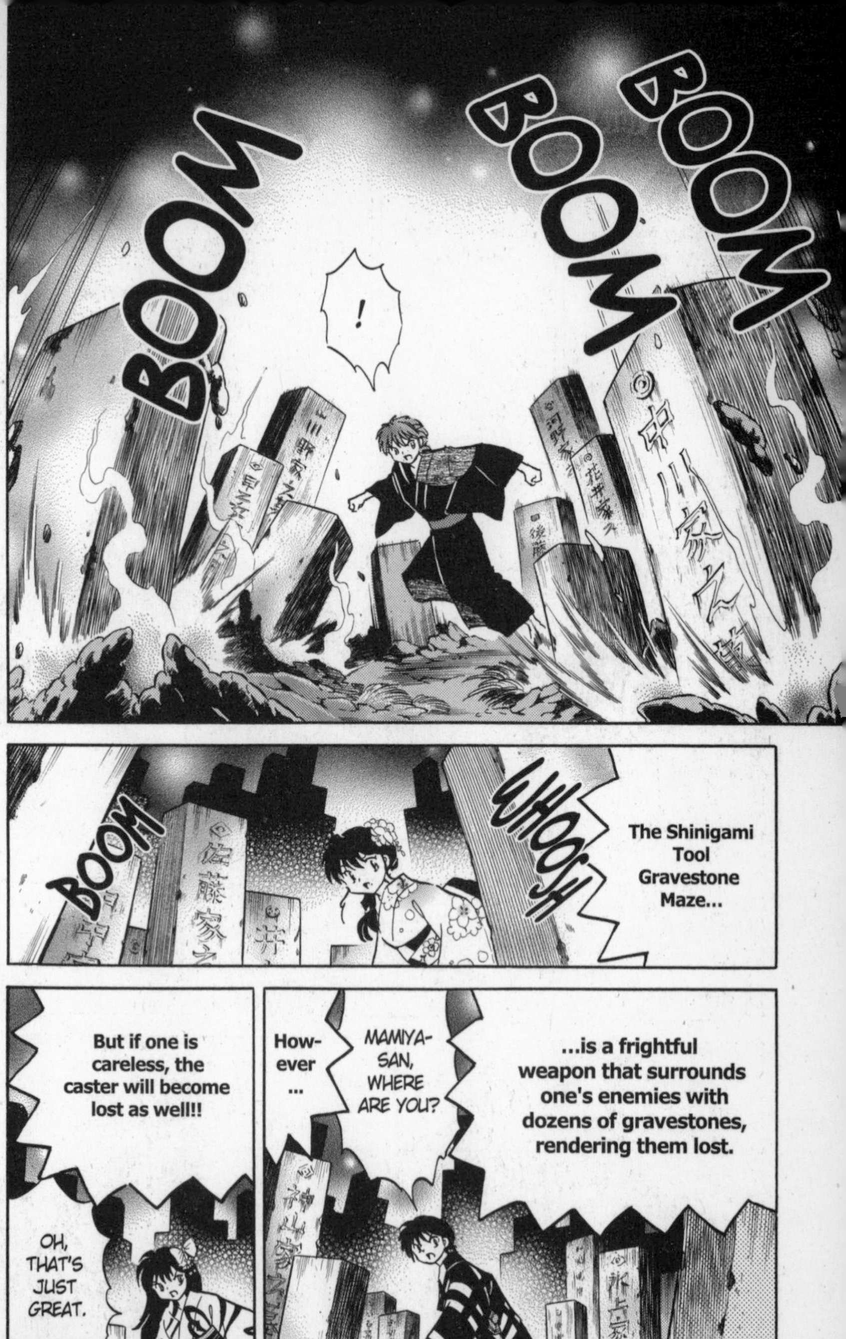
BOOM
BOOM
BOOM
!
The Shinigami Tool Gravestone Maze...
WHOOSH
BOOM
...is a frightful weapon that surrounds one's enemies with dozens of gravestones, rendering them lost.
MAMIYA-SAN, WHERE ARE YOU?
How-ever ...
But if one is careless, the caster will become lost as well!!
OH, THAT'S JUST GREAT.

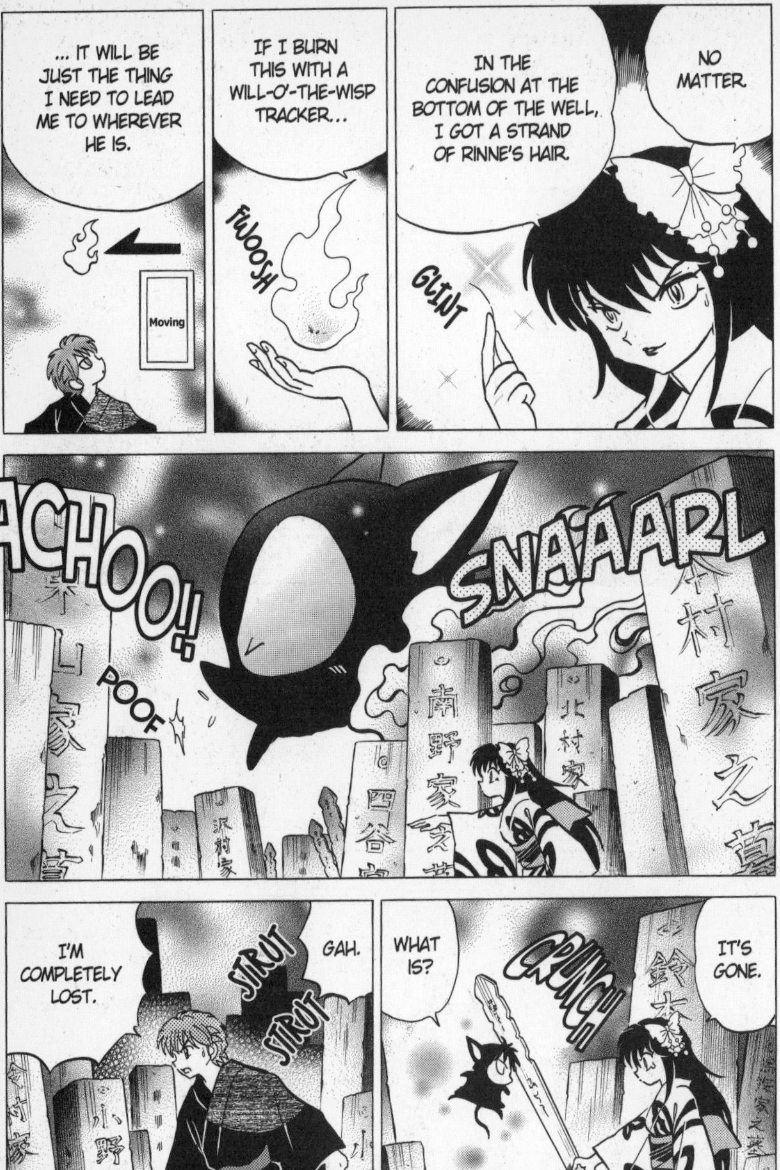
NO MATTER.
IN THE CONFUSION AT THE BOTTOM OF THE WELL, I GOT A STRAND OF RINNE'S HAIR.
GLINT
IF I BURN THIS WITH A WILL-O'-THE-WISP TRACKER...
FWOOSH
... IT WILL BE JUST THE THING I NEED TO LEAD ME TO WHEREVER HE IS.
Moving
SNAAARL
ACHOO!!
POOF
IT'S GONE.
CRUNCH
WHAT IS?
GAH.
STRUT
STRUT
I'M COMPLETELY LOST.

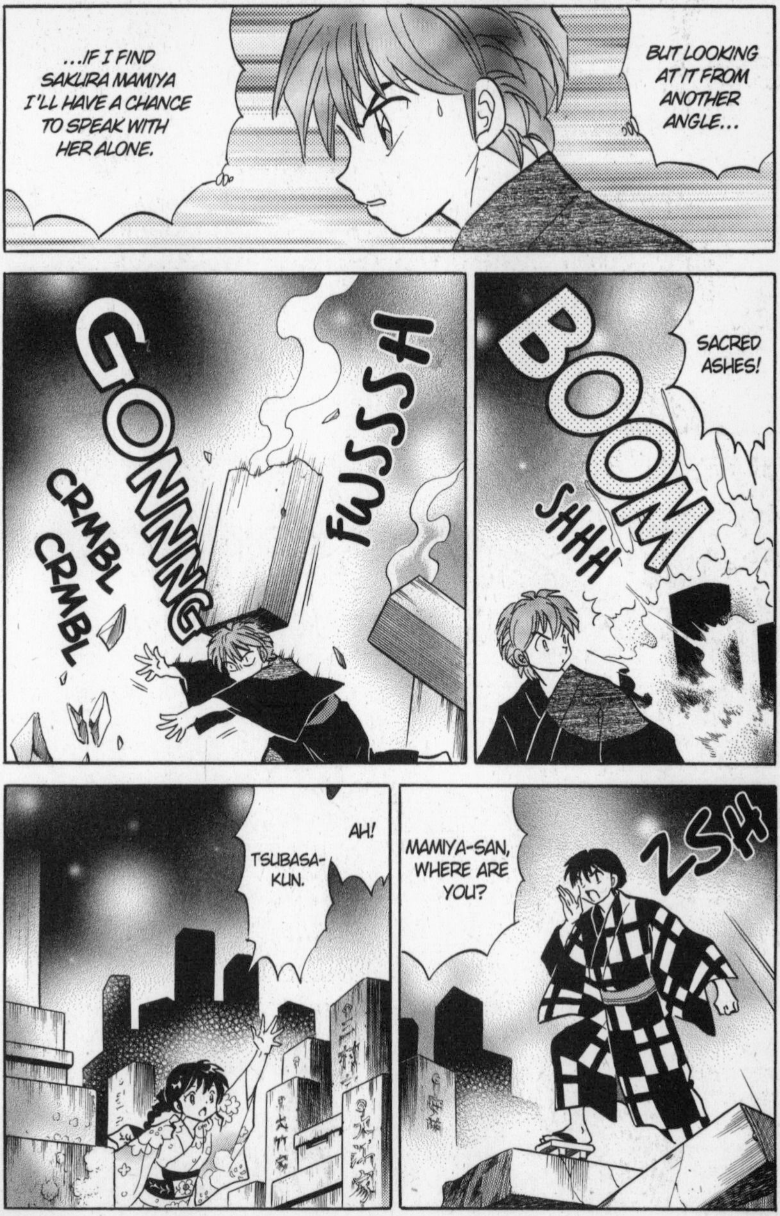
BUT LOOKING AT IT FROM ANOTHER ANGLE...
...IF I FIND SAKURA MAMIYA I'LL HAVE A CHANCE TO SPEAK WITH HER ALONE.
SACRED ASHES!
BOOM
SHHH
FWSSSH
GONNNNG
CRMBL CRMBL
ZSH
MAMIYA-SAN, WHERE ARE YOU?
AH!
TSUBASA-KUN.

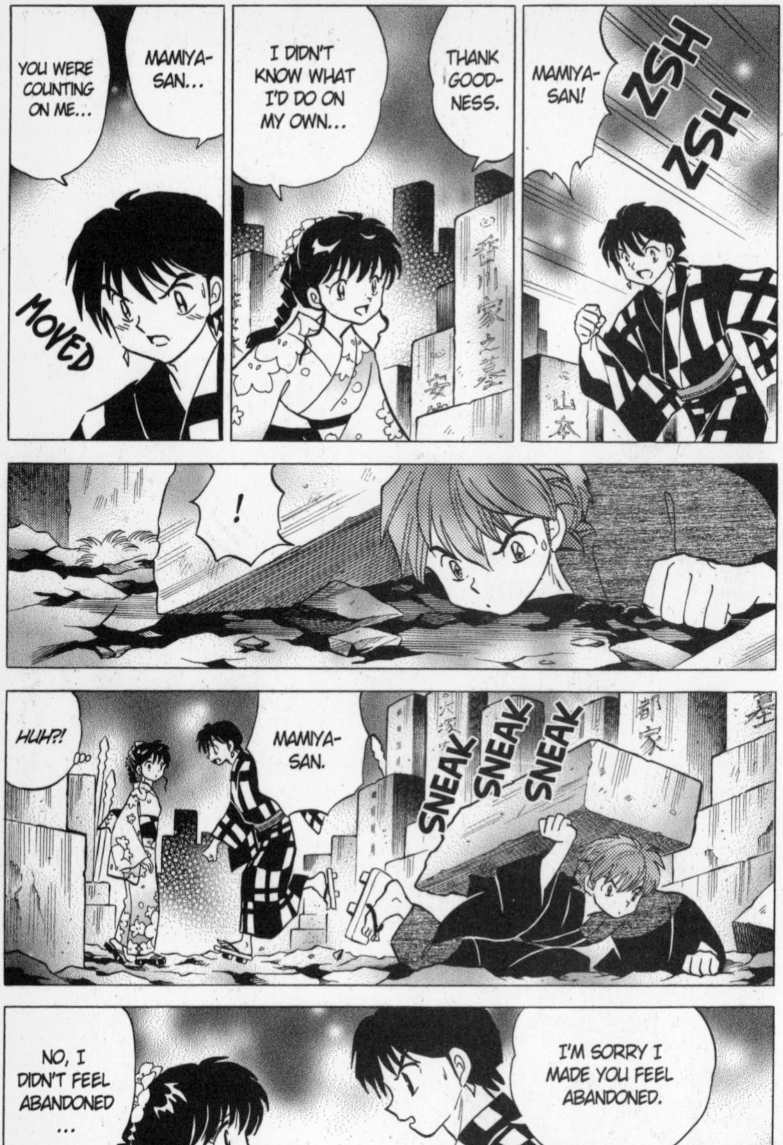
ZSH
ZSH
MAMIYA-SAN!
THANK GOODNESS.
I DIDN'T KNOW WHAT I'D DO ON MY OWN...
MAMIYA-SAN...
YOU WERE COUNTING ON ME...
MOVED
!
SNEAK
SNEAK
SNEAK
MAMIYA-SAN.
HUH?!
I'M SORRY I MADE YOU FEEL ABANDONED.
NO, I DIDN'T FEEL ABANDONED ...

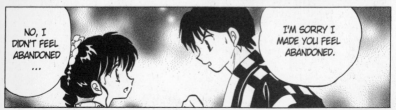

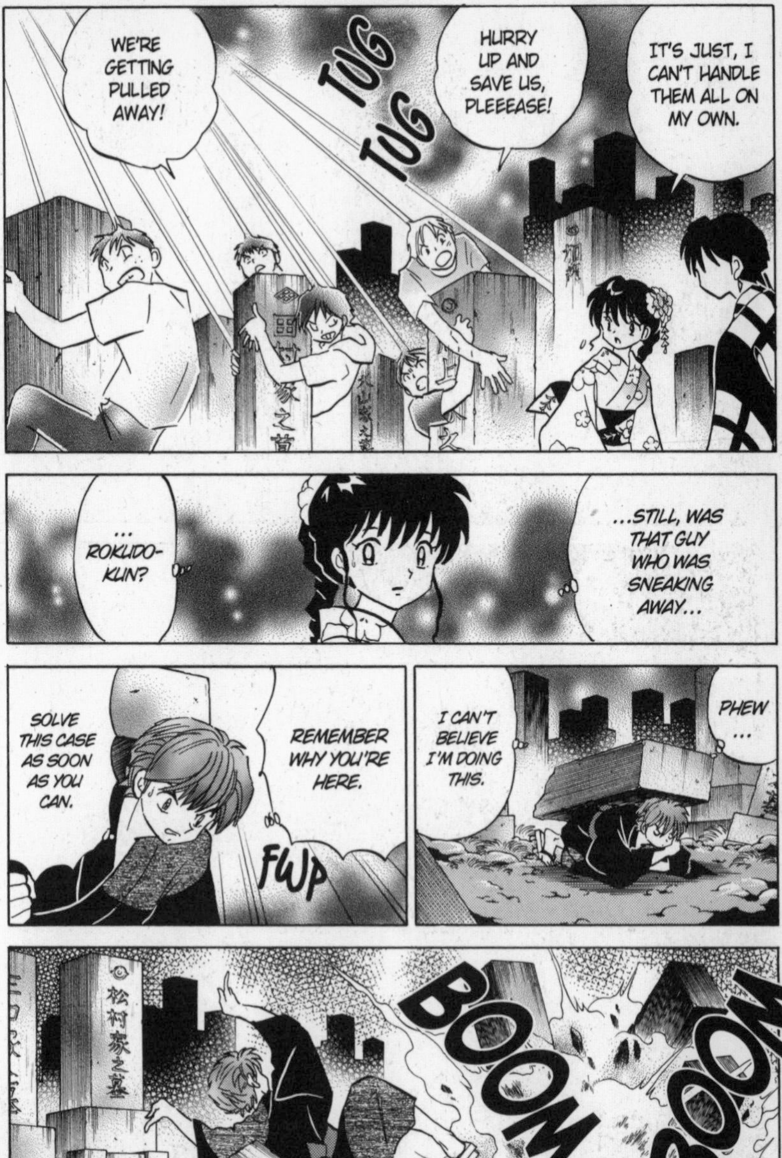
IT'S JUST, I CAN'T HANDLE THEM ALL ON MY OWN.
HURRY UP AND SAVE US, PLEEEASE!
TUG TUG
WE'RE GETTING PULLED AWAY!
...STILL, WAS THAT GUY WHO WAS SNEAKING AWAY...
... ROKUDO-KUN?
PHEW ...
I CAN'T BELIEVE I'M DOING THIS.
REMEMBER WHY YOU'RE HERE.
SOLVE THIS CASE AS SOON AS YOU CAN.
FWP
BOOM
BOOM
松村家之墓

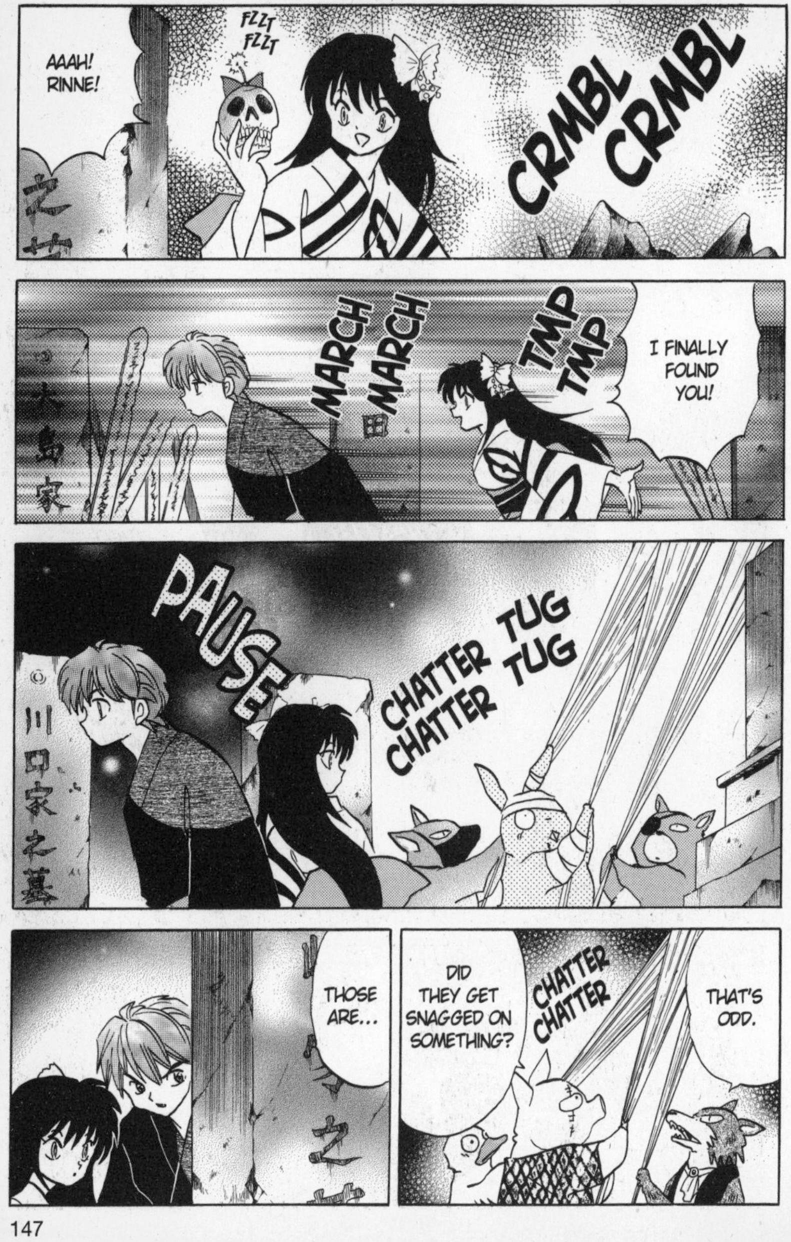
CRMBL CRMBL
FZZT FZZT
AAAH! RINNE!
I FINALLY FOUND YOU!
TMP TMP
MARCH MARCH
CHATTER TUG
CHATTER TUG
PAUSE
THAT'S ODD.
CHATTER CHATTER
DID THEY GET SNAGGED ON SOMETHING?
THOSE ARE...

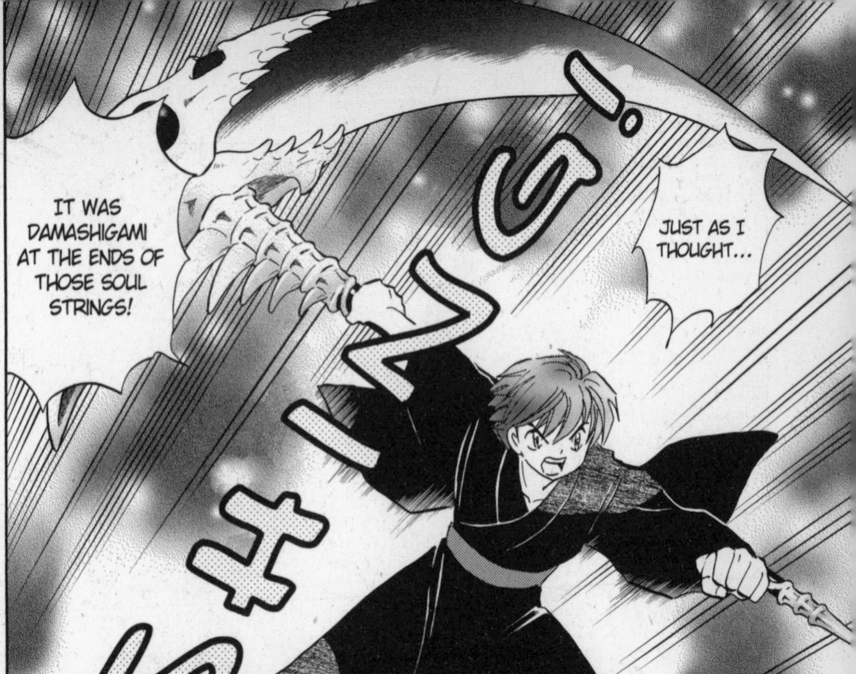
JUST AS I THOUGHT...
SHING!
IT WAS DAMASHIGAMI AT THE ENDS OF THOSE SOUL STRINGS!

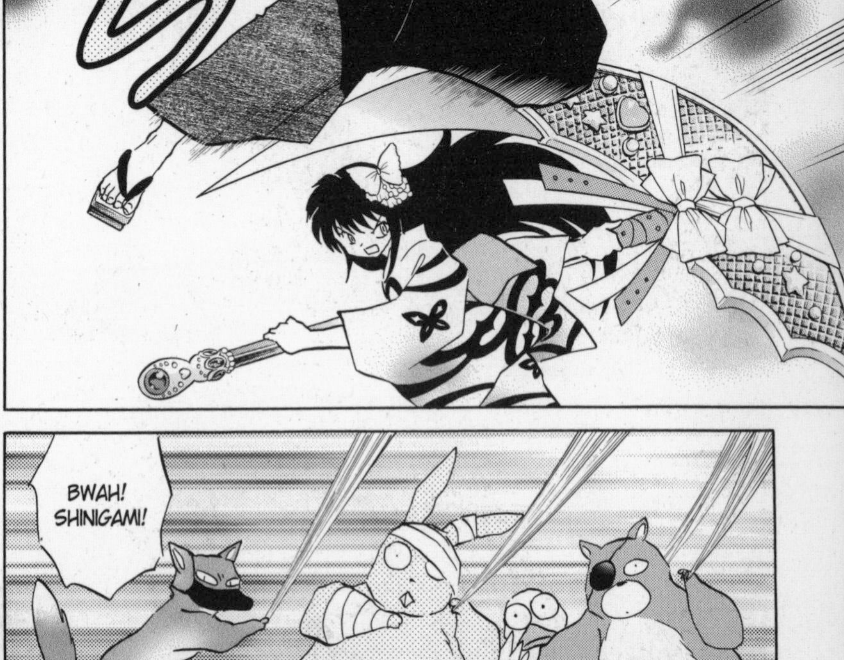
BWAH! SHINIGAMI!

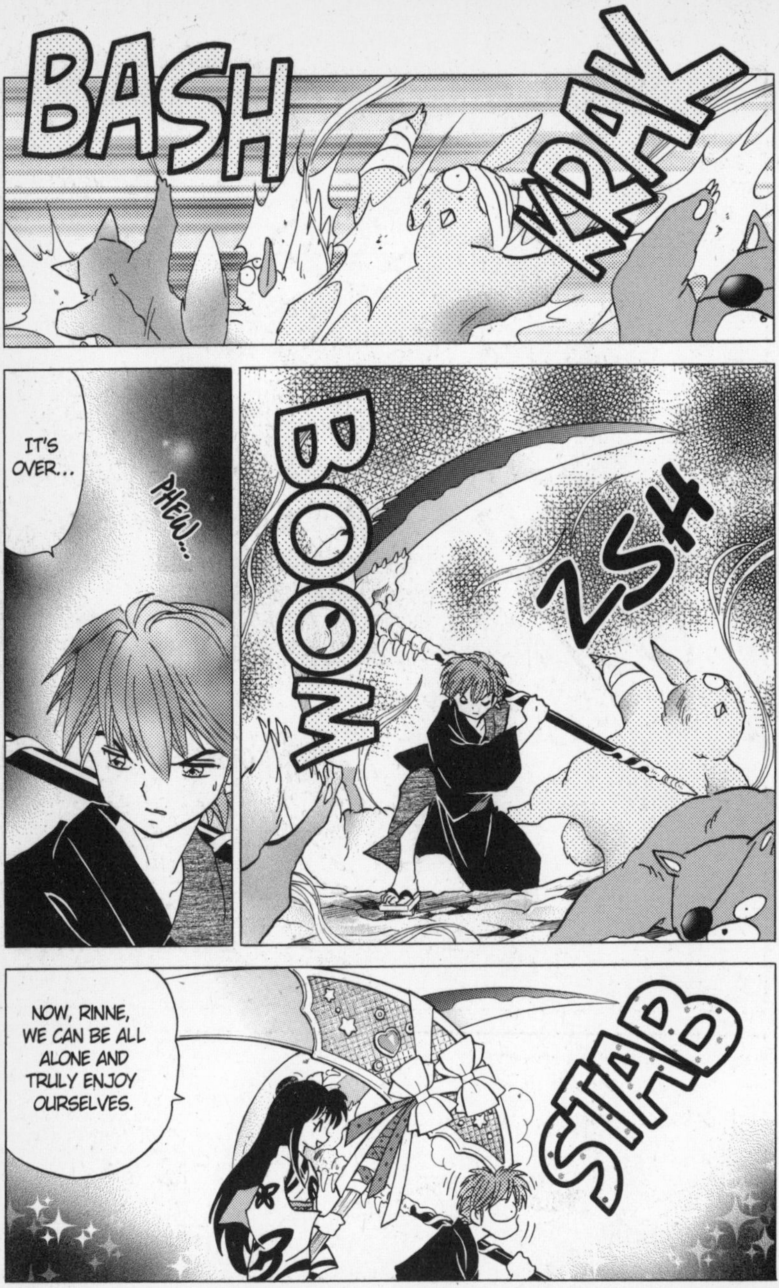
KRAK
BASH
BOOM
ZSH
IT'S OVER...
PHEW...
STAB
NOW, RINNE, WE CAN BE ALL ALONE AND TRULY ENJOY OURSELVES.

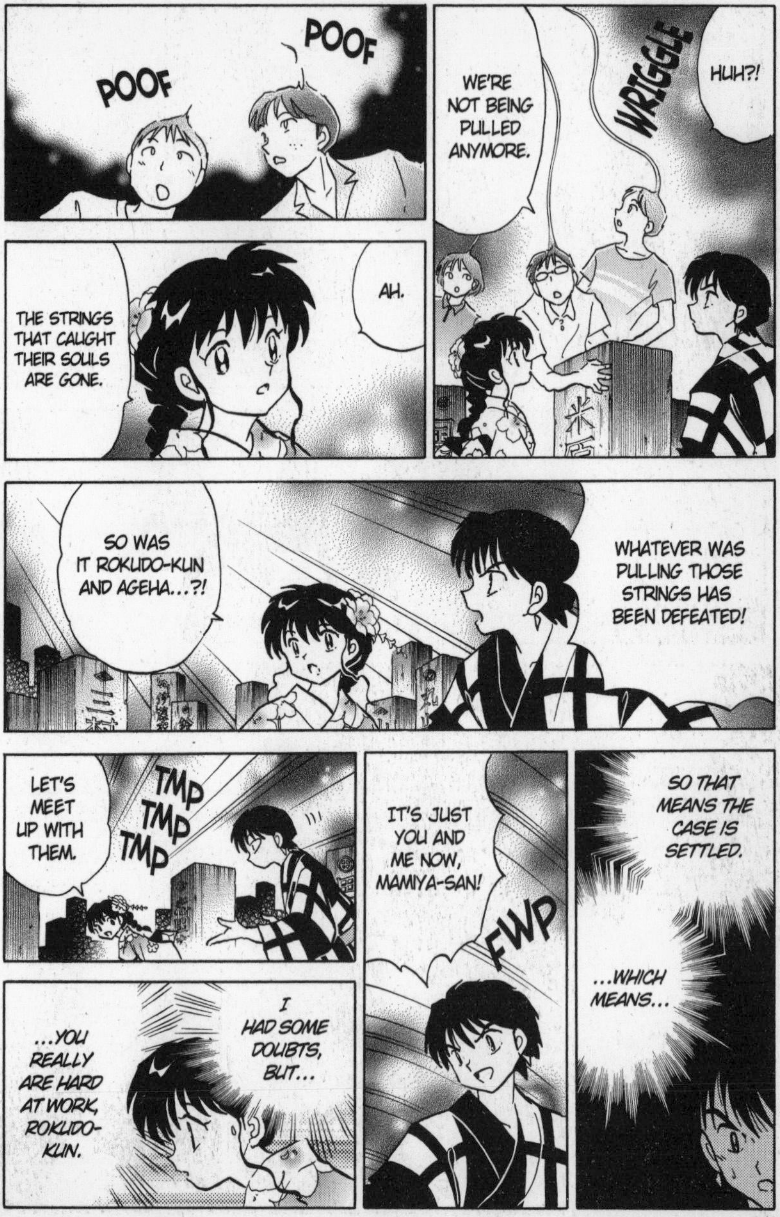
HUH?!
WRIGGLE
WE'RE NOT BEING PULLED ANYMORE.
POOF
POOF
AH.
THE STRINGS THAT CAUGHT THEIR SOULS ARE GONE.
WHATEVER WAS PULLING THOSE STRINGS HAS BEEN DEFEATED!
SO WAS IT ROKUDO-KUN AND AGEHA...?!
SO THAT MEANS THE CASE IS SETTLED.
...WHICH MEANS...
IT'S JUST YOU AND ME NOW, MAMIYA-SAN!
FWP
LET'S MEET UP WITH THEM.
TMP TMP TMP
I HAD SOME DOUBTS, BUT...
...YOU REALLY ARE HARD AT WORK, ROKUDO-KUN.

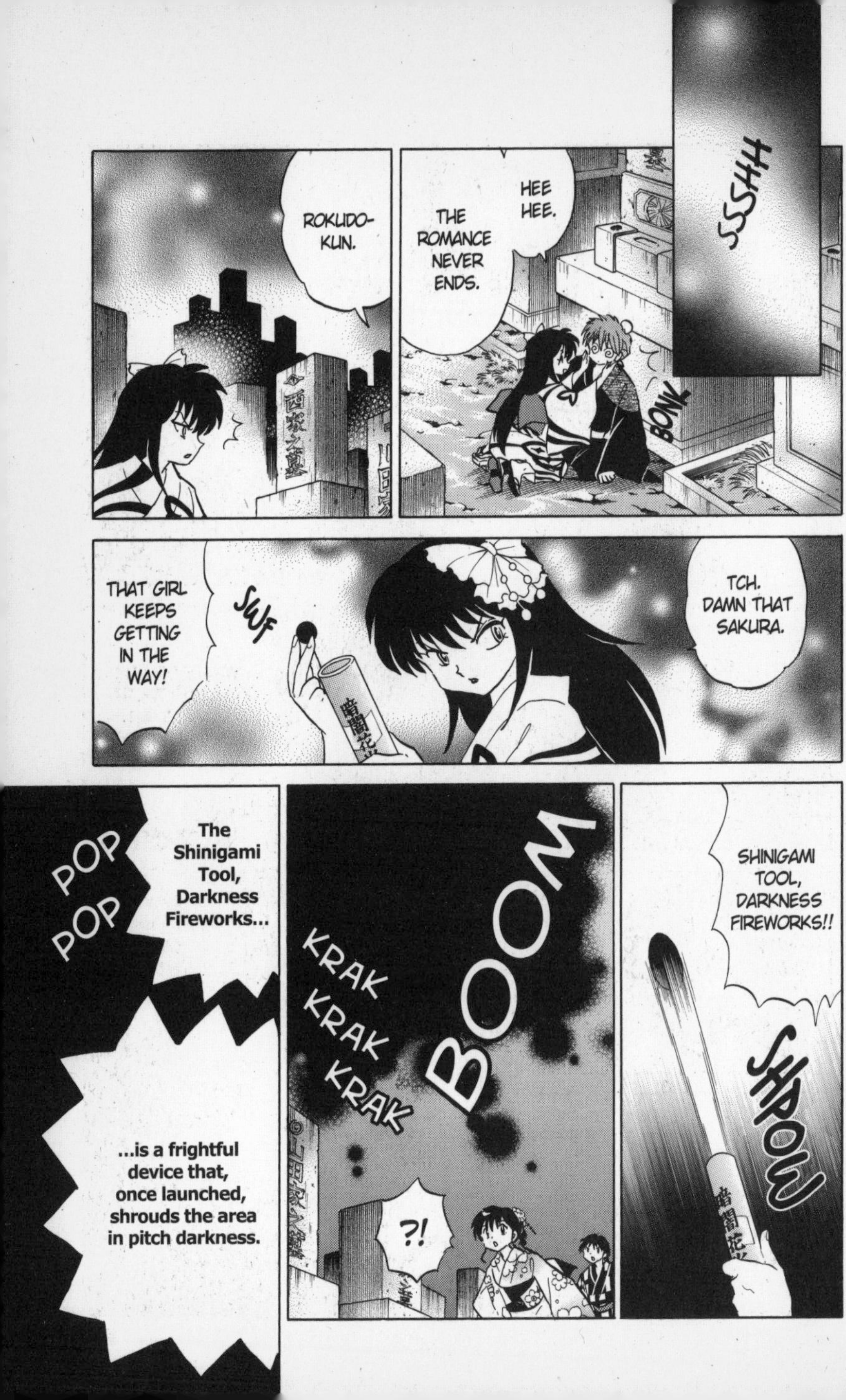
SSSHHH
HEE HEE.
THE ROMANCE NEVER ENDS.
BONK
ROKUDO-KUN.
TCH. DAMN THAT SAKURA.
SWF
THAT GIRL KEEPS GETTING IN THE WAY!
SHINIGAMI TOOL, DARKNESS FIREWORKS!!
SHPOW
BOOM
KRAK KRAK KRAK
?!
POP POP
The Shinigami Tool, Darkness Fireworks...
...is a frightful device that, once launched, shrouds the area in pitch darkness.

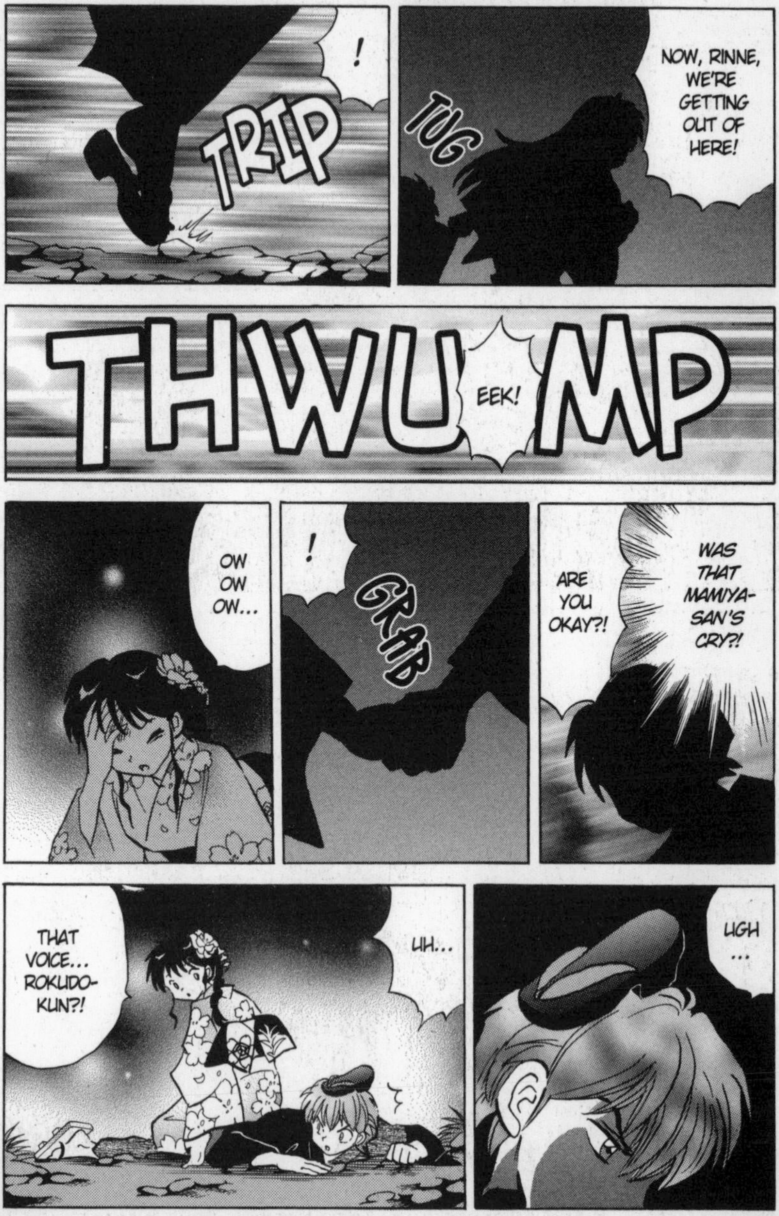
NOW, RINNE, WE'RE GETTING OUT OF HERE!
TUG
!
TRIP
THWUMP
EEK!
WAS THAT MAMIYA-SAN'S CRY?!
ARE YOU OKAY?!
!
GRAB
OW OW OW...
UGH ...
UH...
THAT VOICE... ROKUDO-KUN?!

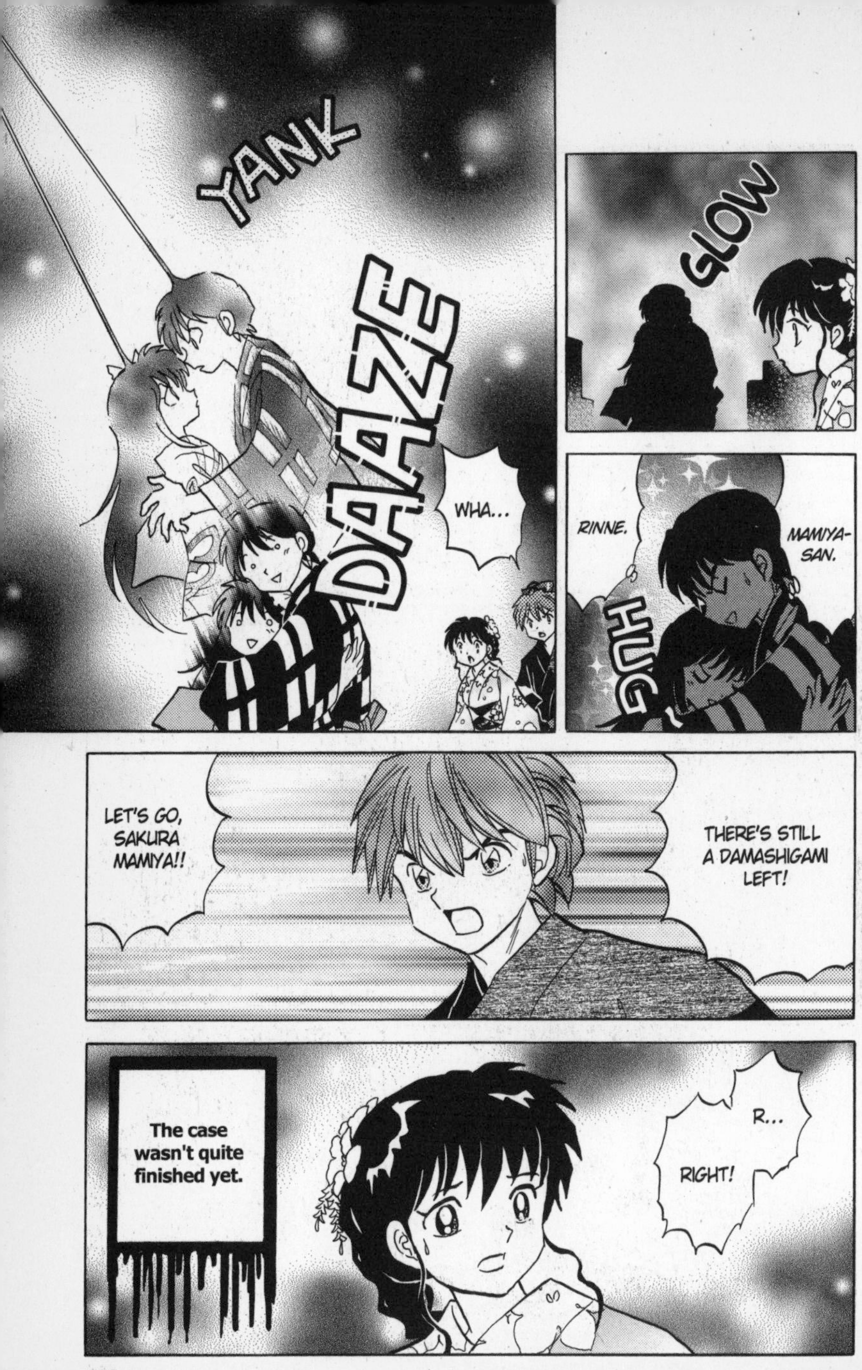
GLOW
MAMIYA-SAN.
RINNE.
HUG
YANK
DAZE
WHA...
THERE'S STILL A DAMASHIGAMI LEFT!
LET'S GO, SAKURA MAMIYA!!
R...
RIGHT!
The case wasn't quite finished yet.

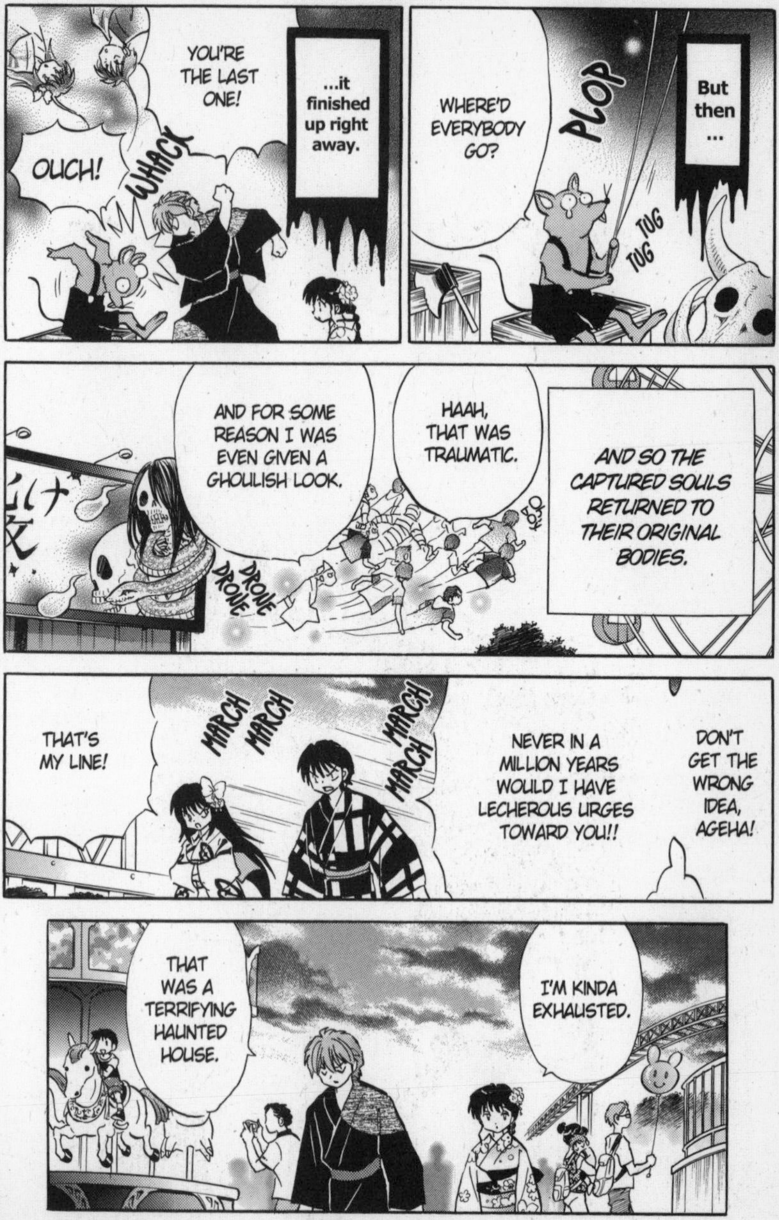

But then ...
PLOP
WHERE'D EVERYBODY GO?
TOG TOG
...it finished up right away.
YOU'RE THE LAST ONE!
WHACK
OUCH!
AND SO THE CAPTURED SOULS RETURNED TO THEIR ORIGINAL BODIES.
HAAH, THAT WAS TRAUMATIC.
AND FOR SOME REASON I WAS EVEN GIVEN A GHOULISH LOOK.
DRONE DRONE
DON'T GET THE WRONG IDEA, AGEHA!
NEVER IN A MILLION YEARS WOULD I HAVE LECHEROUS URGES TOWARD YOU!!
MARCH MARCH
MARCH MARCH
THAT'S MY LINE!
I'M KINDA EXHAUSTED.
THAT WAS A TERRIFYING HAUNTED HOUSE.

# CHAPTER 107: PIPING HOT

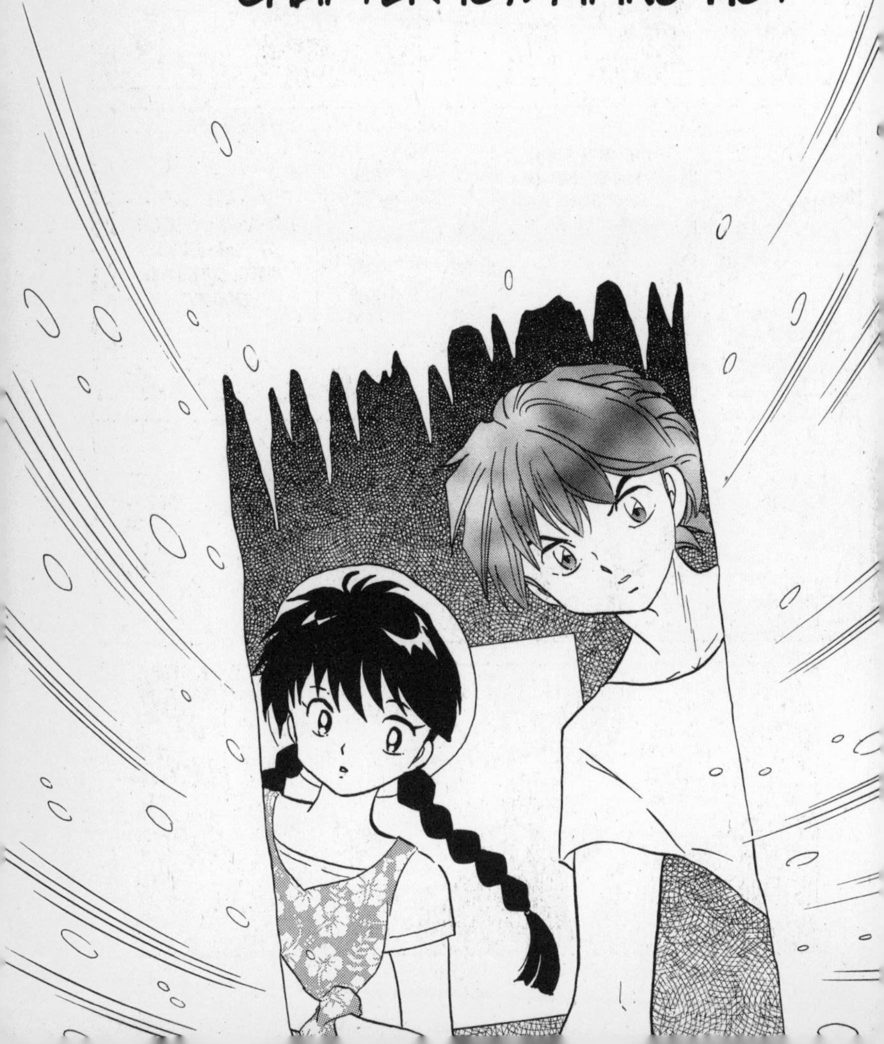

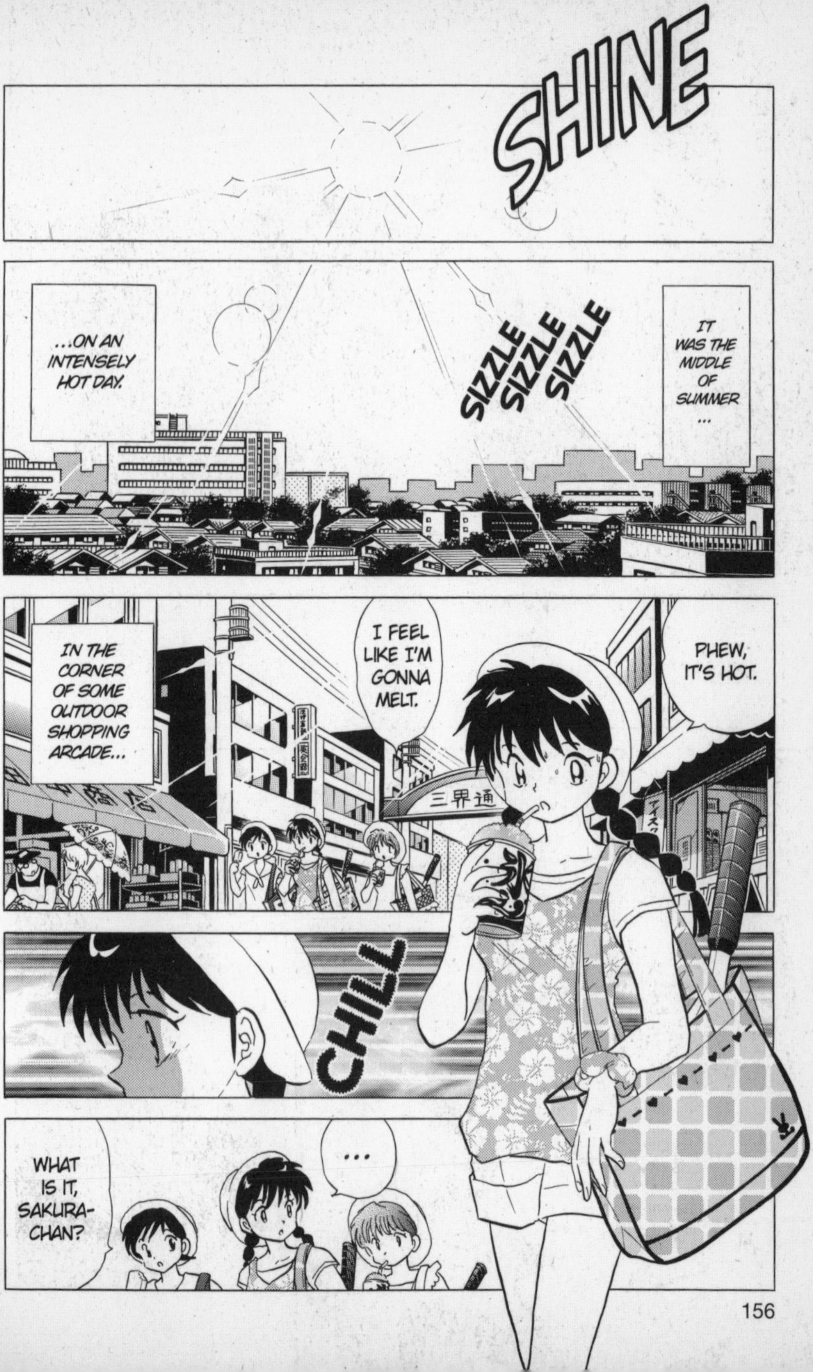
SHINE
IT WAS THE MIDDLE OF SUMMER ...
SIZZLE SIZZLE SIZZLE
...ON AN INTENSELY HOT DAY.
PHEW, IT'S HOT.
I FEEL LIKE I'M GONNA MELT.
三界通
IN THE CORNER OF SOME OUTDOOR SHOPPING ARCADE...
CHILL
...
WHAT IS IT, SAKURA-CHAN?

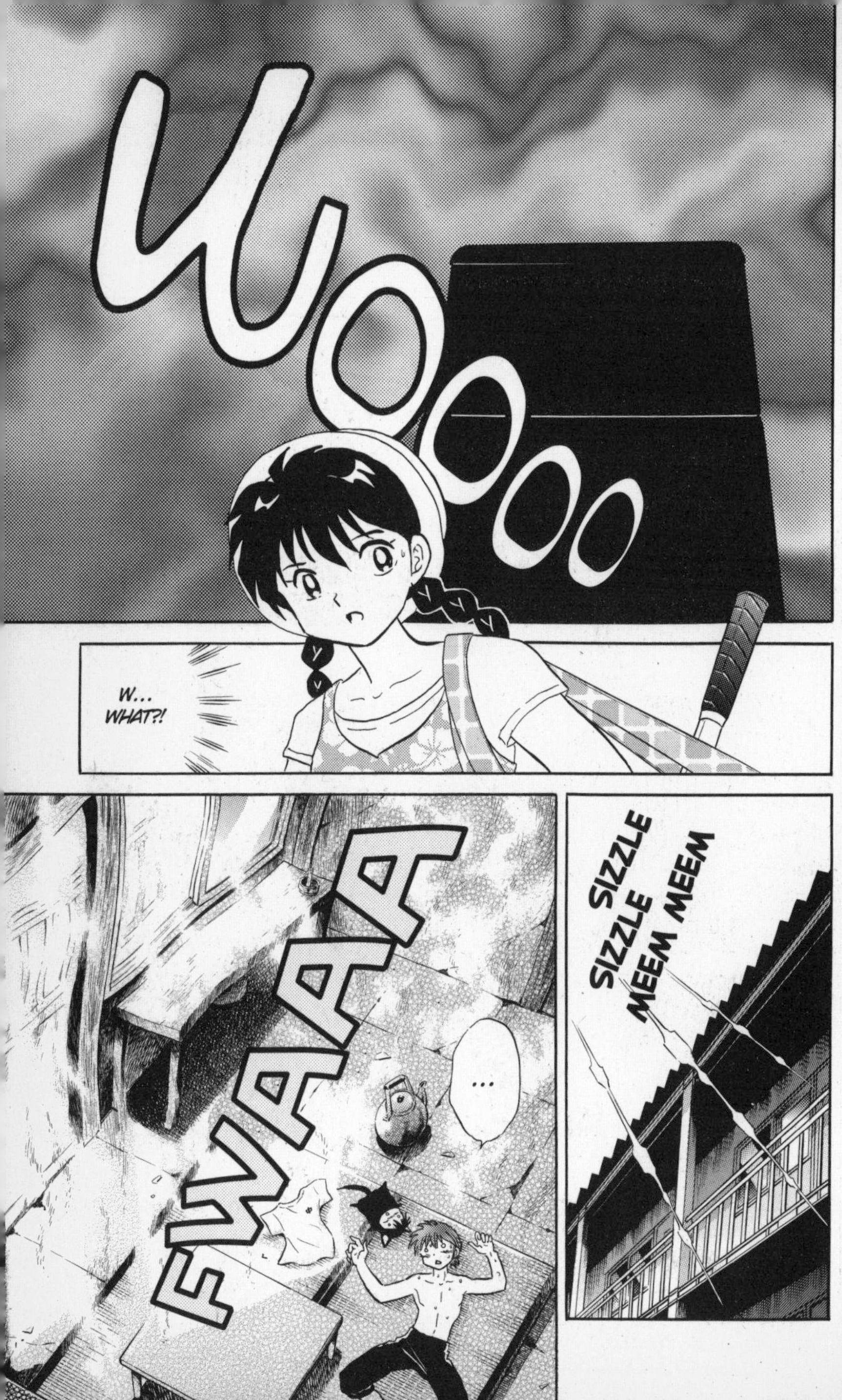
WOOOO
W... WHAT?!
SIZZLE SIZZLE
MEEM MEEM
FWAAA
...

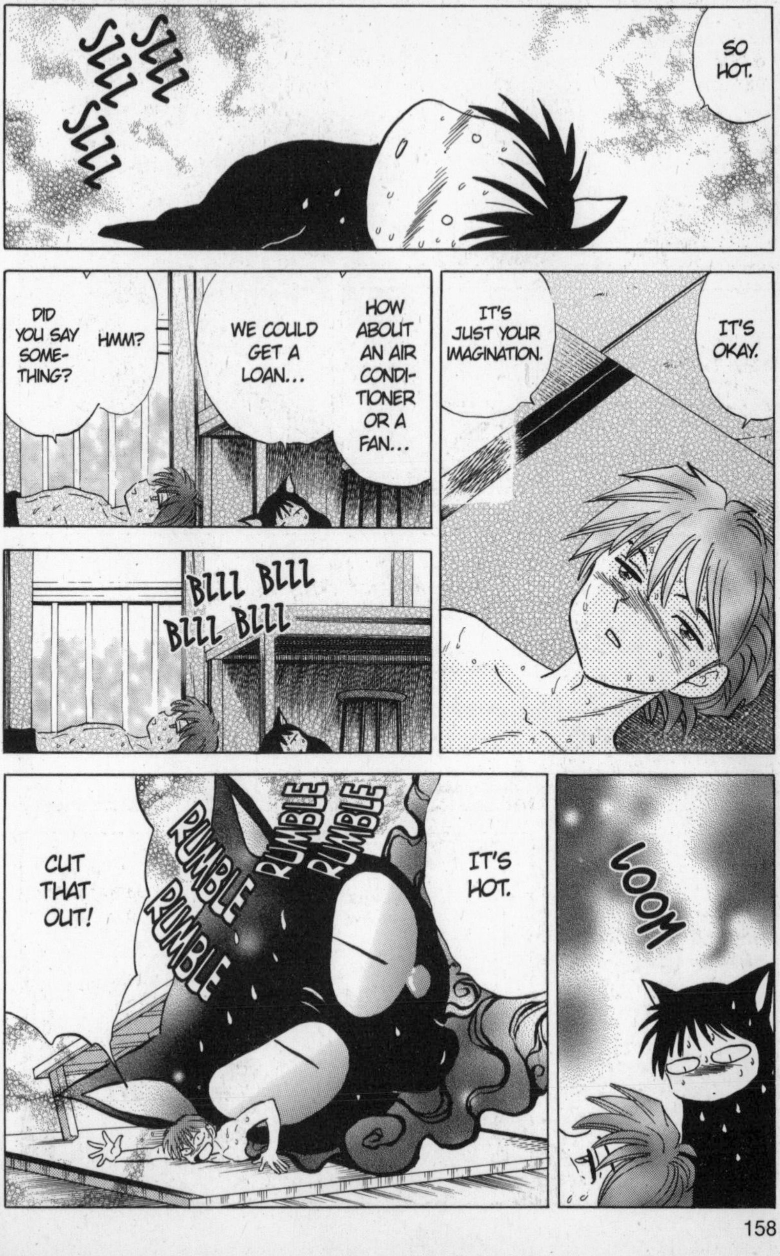
SO HOT.
SZZZ SZZZ SZZZ
IT'S OKAY.
IT'S JUST YOUR IMAGINATION.
HOW ABOUT AN AIR CONDI-TIONER OR A FAN...
WE COULD GET A LOAN...
HMM?
DID YOU SAY SOME-THING?
BZZZ BZZZ BZZZ BZZZ
LOOM
IT'S HOT.
RUMBLE RUMBLE
RUMBLE RUMBLE
CUT THAT OUT!

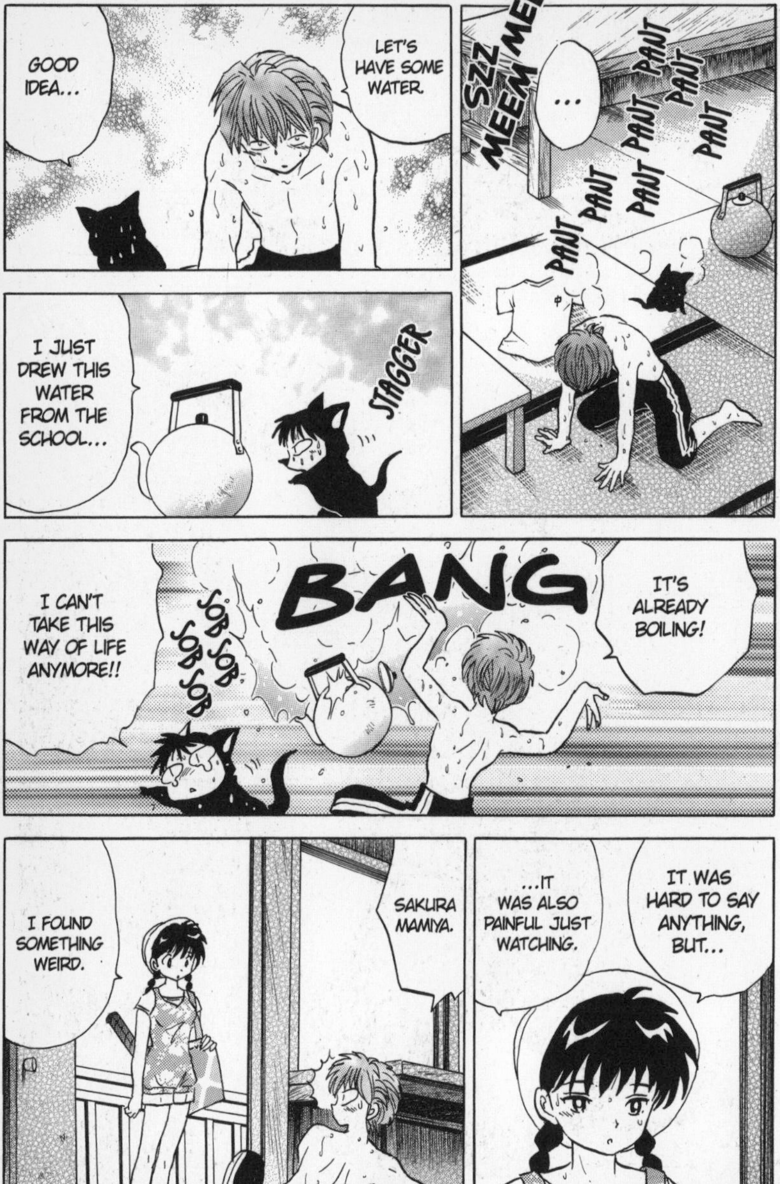
SZZ MEEM MEEM MEEM
...
PANT PANT PANT PANT PANT PANT PANT PANT
LET'S HAVE SOME WATER.
GOOD IDEA...
STAGGER
I JUST DREW THIS WATER FROM THE SCHOOL...
IT'S ALREADY BOILING!
BANG
SOB SOB SOB SOB
I CAN'T TAKE THIS WAY OF LIFE ANYMORE!!
IT WAS HARD TO SAY ANYTHING, BUT...
...IT WAS ALSO PAINFUL JUST WATCHING.
SAKURA MAMIYA.
I FOUND SOMETHING WEIRD.

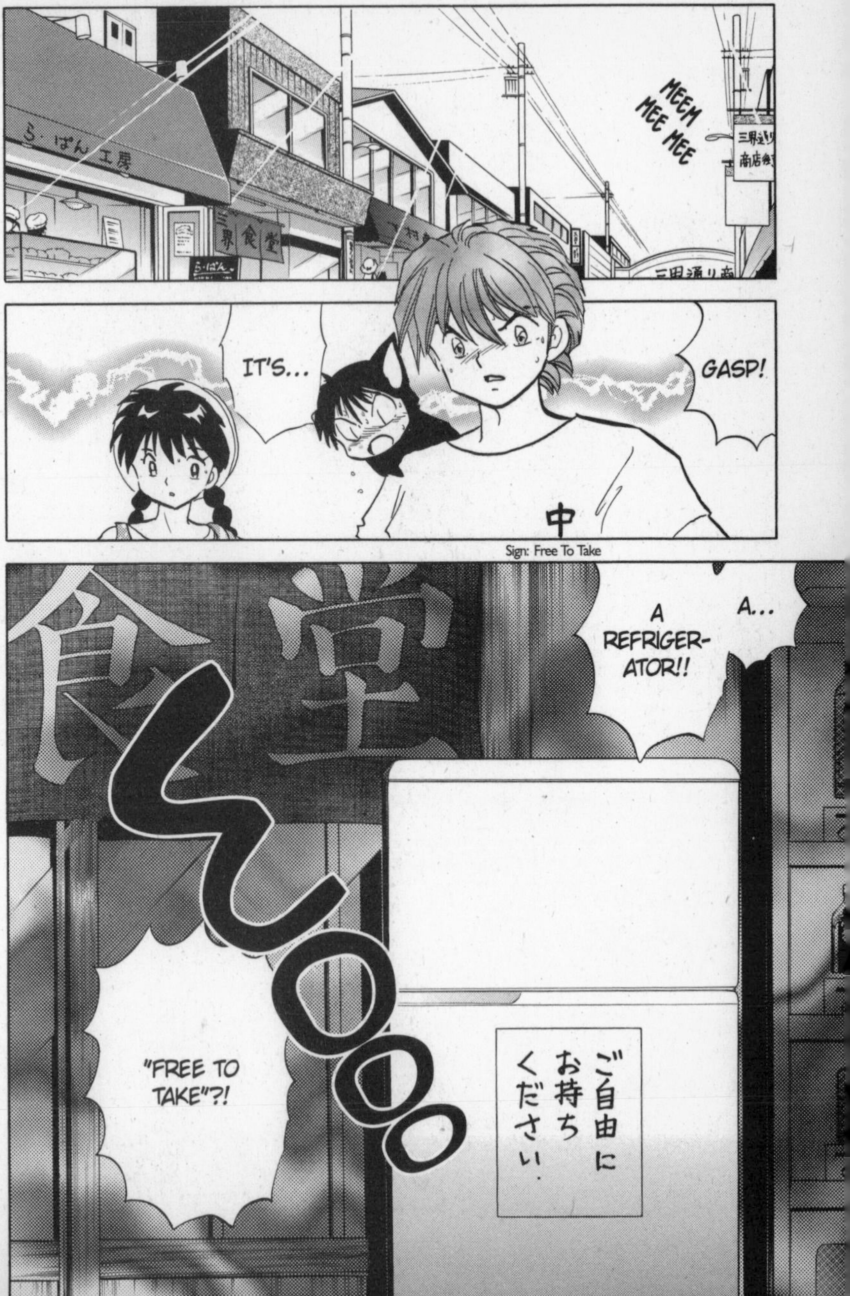
MEEM MEE MEE
GASP!
IT'S...
A...
A REFRIGER-ATOR!!
"FREE TO TAKE"?!
ご自由にお持ちください.
Sign: Free To Take

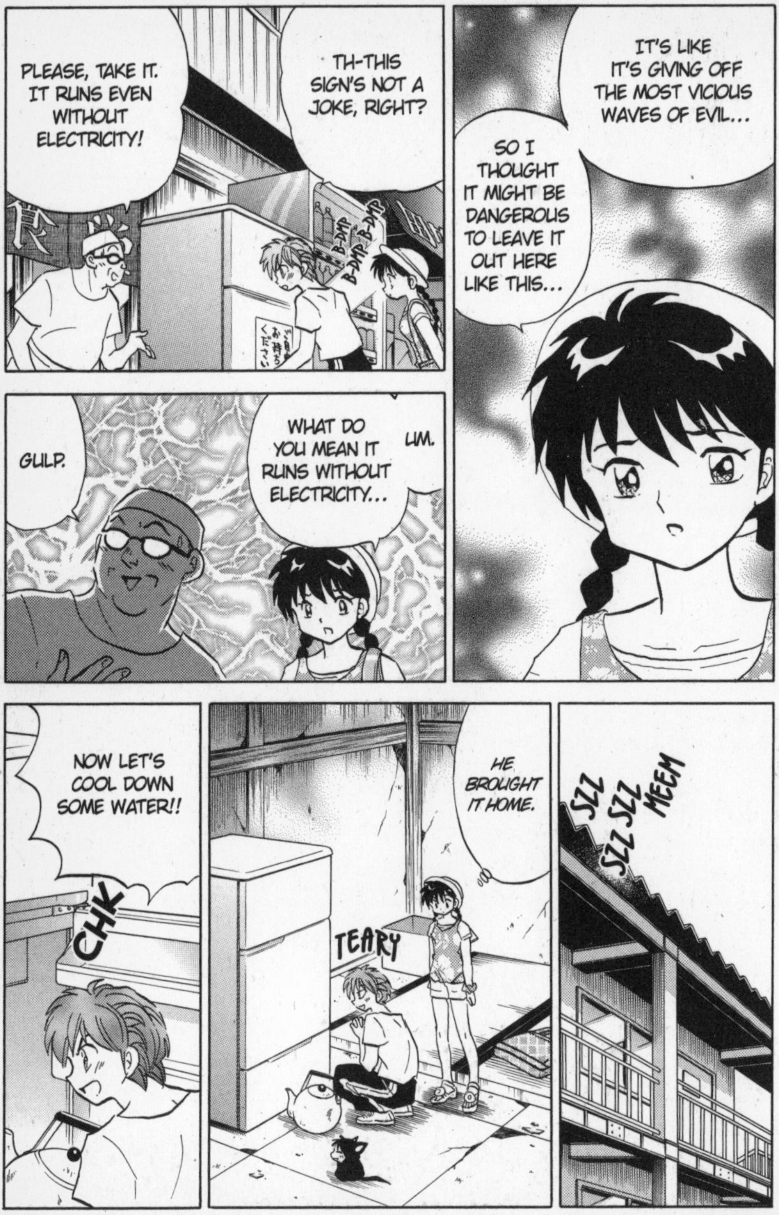
IT'S LIKE IT'S GIVING OFF THE MOST VICIOUS WAVES OF EVIL...
SO I THOUGHT IT MIGHT BE DANGEROUS TO LEAVE IT OUT HERE LIKE THIS...
TH-THIS SIGN'S NOT A JOKE, RIGHT?
B-DMP B-DMP B-DMP
PLEASE, TAKE IT. IT RUNS EVEN WITHOUT ELECTRICITY!
UM.
WHAT DO YOU MEAN IT RUNS WITHOUT ELECTRICITY...
GULP.
SZZ SZZ SZZ MEEM
HE BROUGHT IT HOME.
TEARY
NOW LET'S COOL DOWN SOME WATER!!
CHK

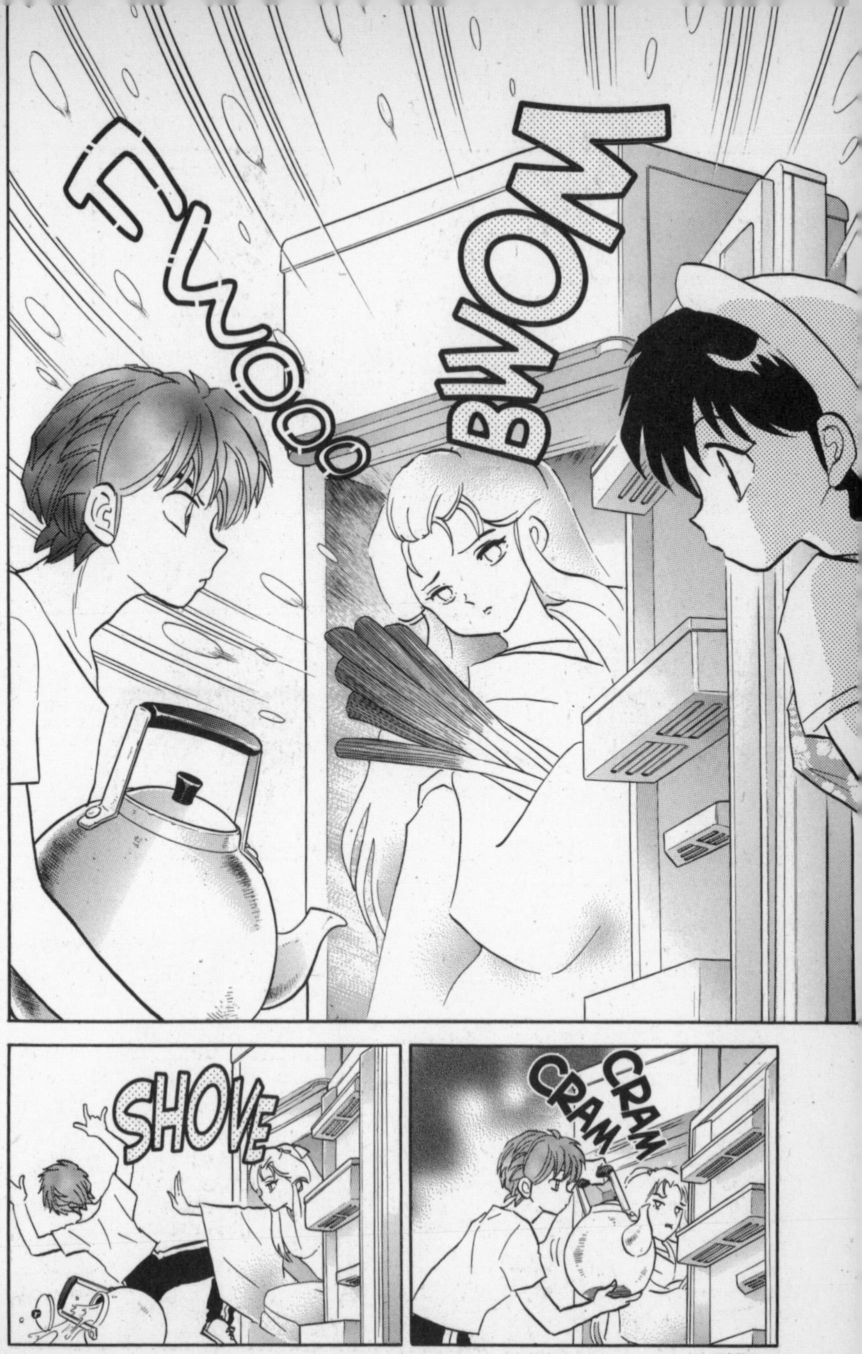
BWOM
FWOOOO
CRAM
CRAM
SHOVE

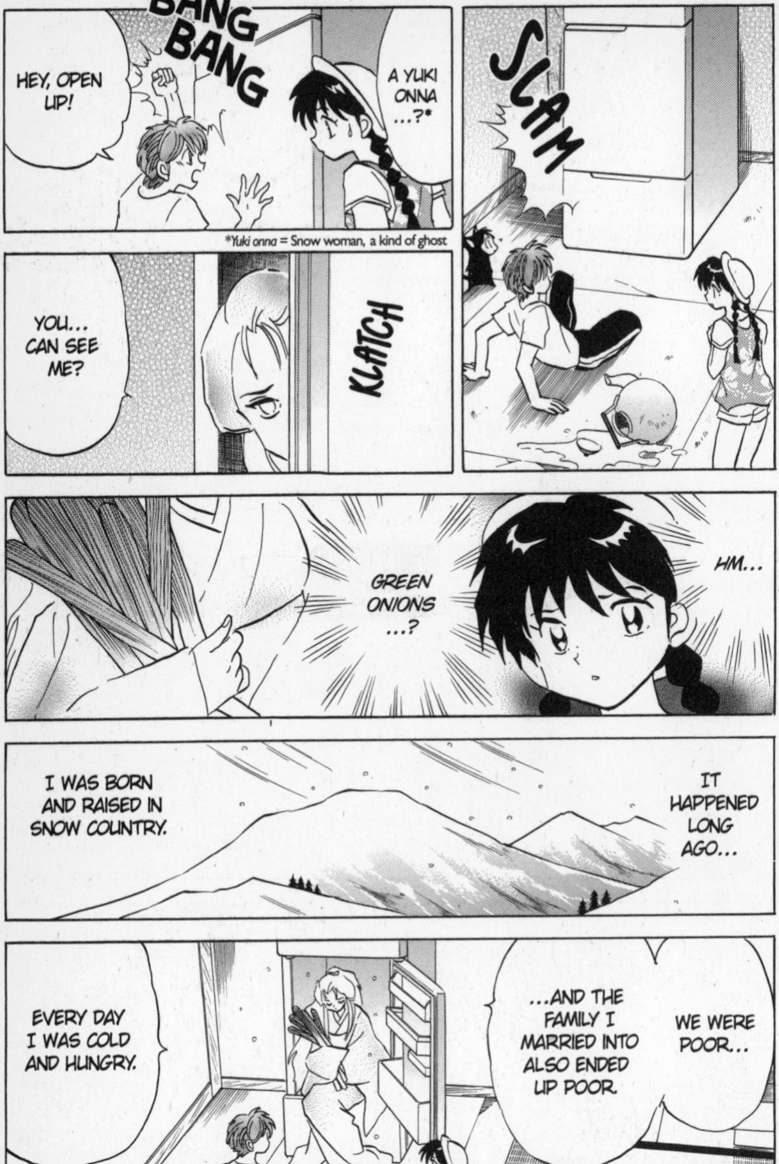
SLAM
HEY, OPEN UP!
BANG BANG
A YUKI ONNA ...?*
KLATCH
YOU... CAN SEE ME?
HM...
GREEN ONIONS ...?
IT HAPPENED LONG AGO...
I WAS BORN AND RAISED IN SNOW COUNTRY.
WE WERE POOR...
...AND THE FAMILY I MARRIED INTO ALSO ENDED UP POOR.
EVERY DAY I WAS COLD AND HUNGRY.

*Yuki onna = Snow woman, a kind of ghost

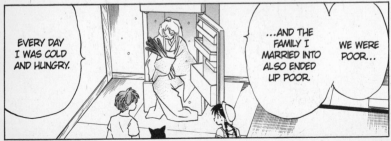

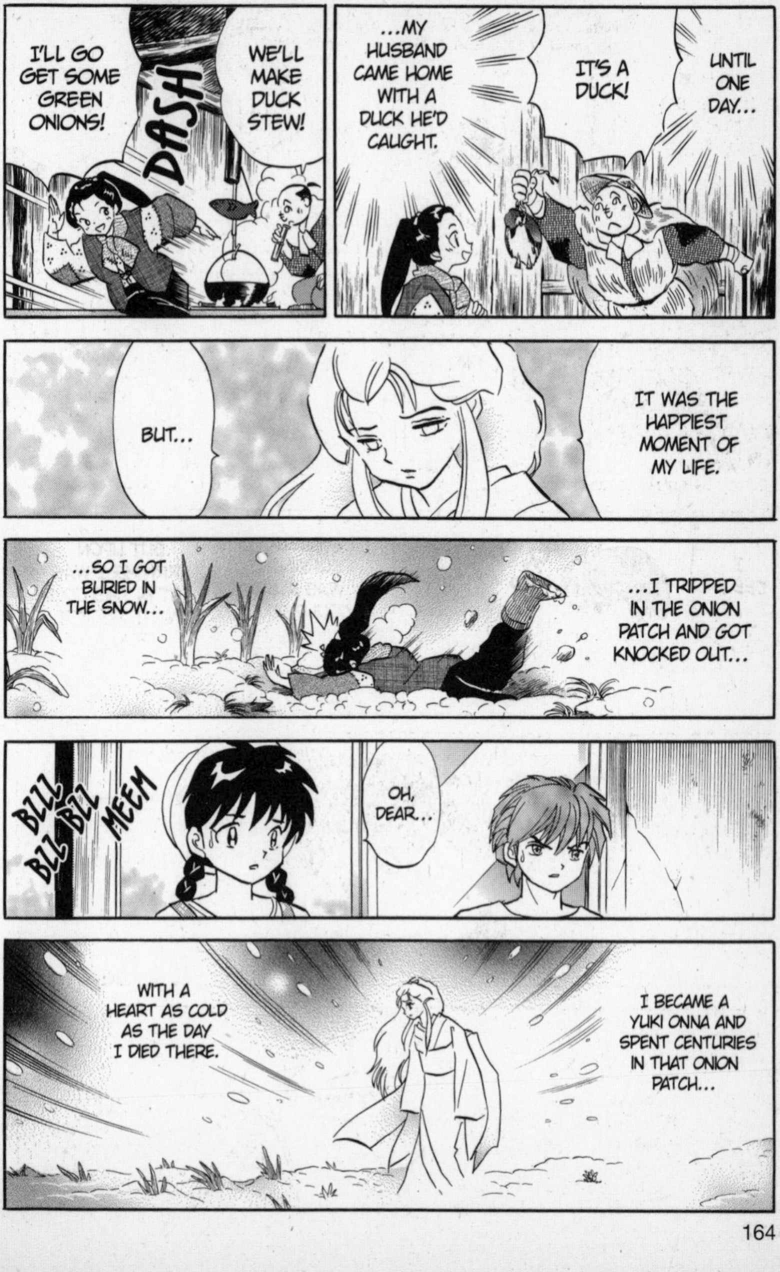
UNTIL ONE DAY...
IT'S A DUCK!
...MY HUSBAND CAME HOME WITH A DUCK HE'D CAUGHT.
WE'LL MAKE DUCK STEW!
DASH
I'LL GO GET SOME GREEN ONIONS!
IT WAS THE HAPPIEST MOMENT OF MY LIFE.
BUT...
...I TRIPPED IN THE ONION PATCH AND GOT KNOCKED OUT...
...SO I GOT BURIED IN THE SNOW...
OH, DEAR...
MEEM
BZZZ BZZ BZZ
I BECAME A YUKI ONNA AND SPENT CENTURIES IN THAT ONION PATCH...
WITH A HEART AS COLD AS THE DAY I DIED THERE.

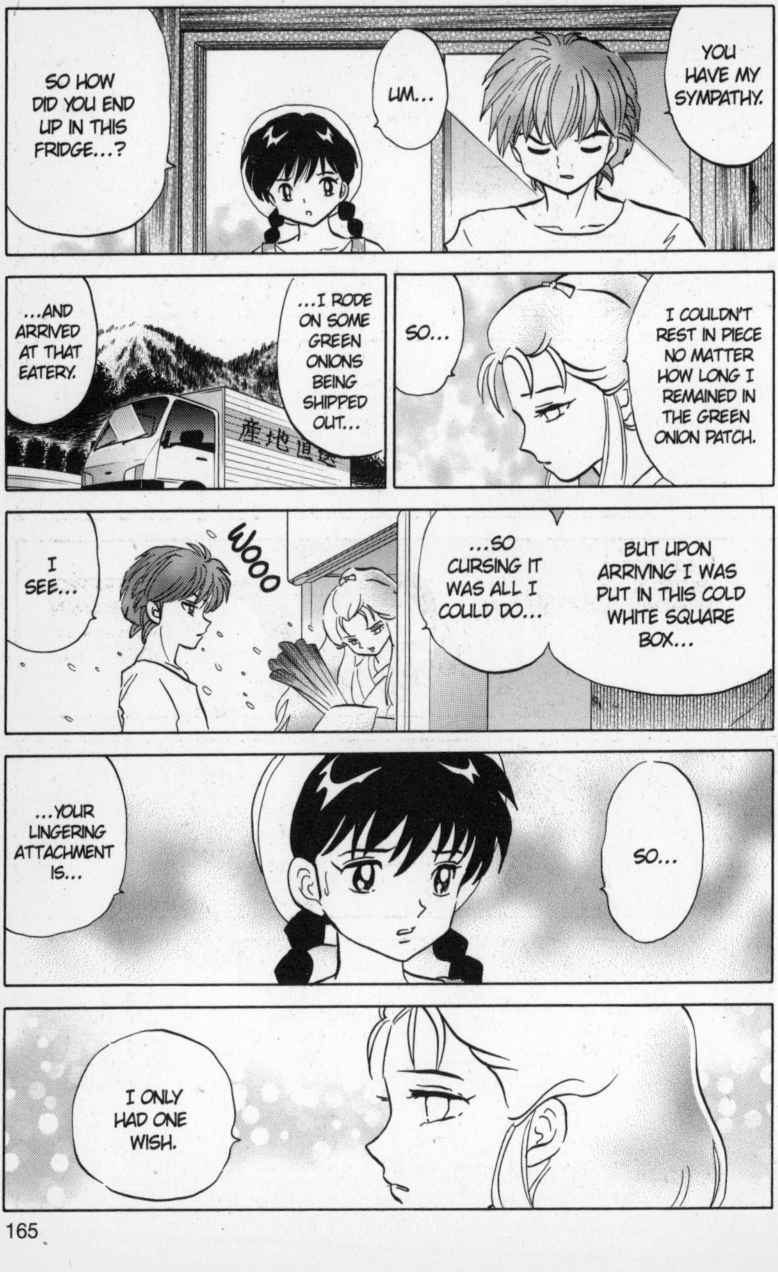
YOU HAVE MY SYMPATHY.
UM...
SO HOW DID YOU END UP IN THIS FRIDGE...?
I COULDN'T REST IN PIECE NO MATTER HOW LONG I REMAINED IN THE GREEN ONION PATCH.
SO...
...I RODE ON SOME GREEN ONIONS BEING SHIPPED OUT...
...AND ARRIVED AT THAT EATERY.
BUT UPON ARRIVING I WAS PUT IN THIS COLD WHITE SQUARE BOX...
...SO CURSING IT WAS ALL I COULD DO...
WOOO
I SEE...
SO...
...YOUR LINGERING ATTACHMENT IS...
I ONLY HAD ONE WISH.

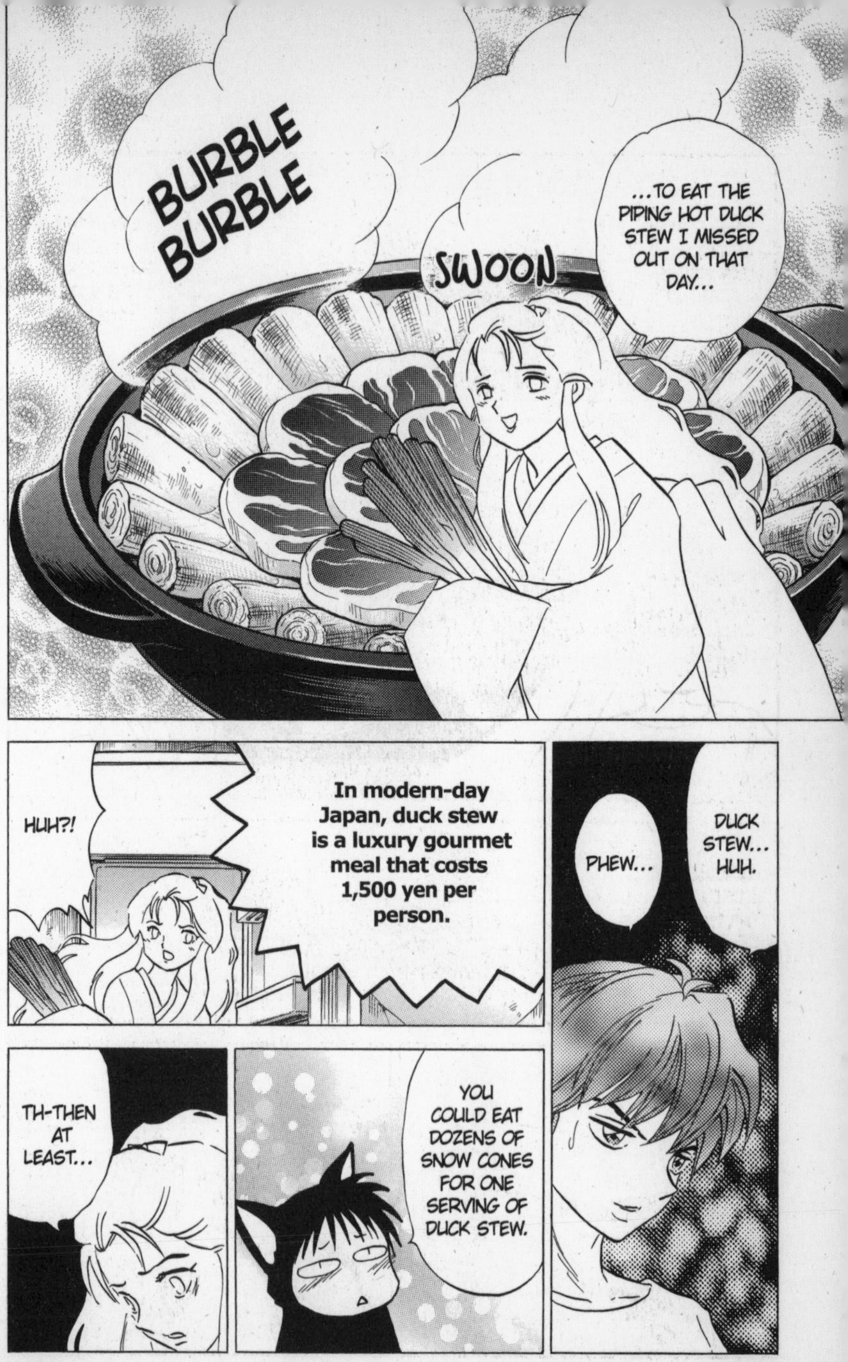
...TO EAT THE PIPING HOT DUCK STEW I MISSED OUT ON THAT DAY...
SWOON
BURBLE BURBLE
DUCK STEW... HUH.
PHEW...
In modern-day Japan, duck stew is a luxury gourmet meal that costs 1,500 yen per person.
HUH?!
YOU COULD EAT DOZENS OF SNOW CONES FOR ONE SERVING OF DUCK STEW.
TH-THEN AT LEAST...

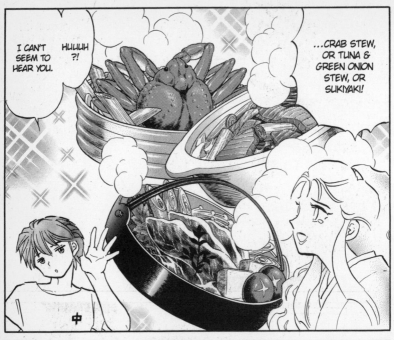

...CRAB STEW, OR TUNA & GREEN ONION STEW, OR SUKIYAKI!
HUUUH ?!
I CAN'T SEEM TO HEAR YOU.
ALL OF THOSE ARE EXPENSIVE!
FRET FRET
WELL ...
HOW ABOUT SOME PIPING HOT GREEN ONION RAMEN AT LEAST...
PFFT
SHE SNORTED AT ME!
SLAM

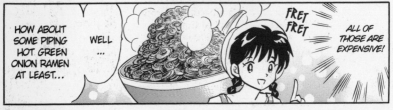

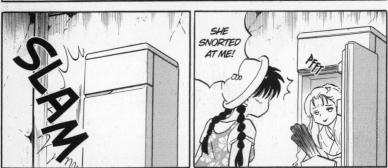

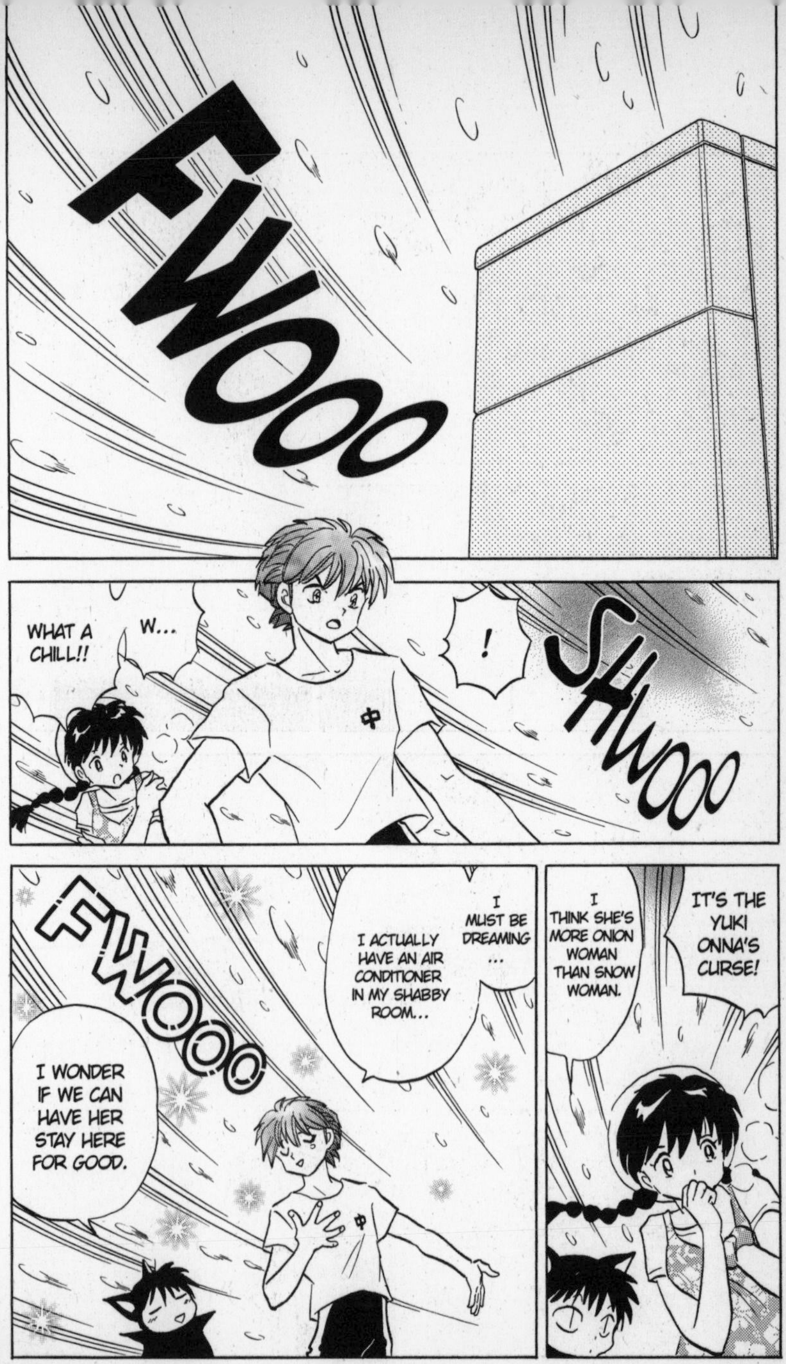
FWOOO
SHWOOO
!
W...
WHAT A CHILL!!
IT'S THE YUKI ONNA'S CURSE!
I THINK SHE'S MORE ONION WOMAN THAN SNOW WOMAN.
I MUST BE DREAMING...
I ACTUALLY HAVE AN AIR CONDITIONER IN MY SHABBY ROOM...
FWOOO
I WONDER IF WE CAN HAVE HER STAY HERE FOR GOOD.

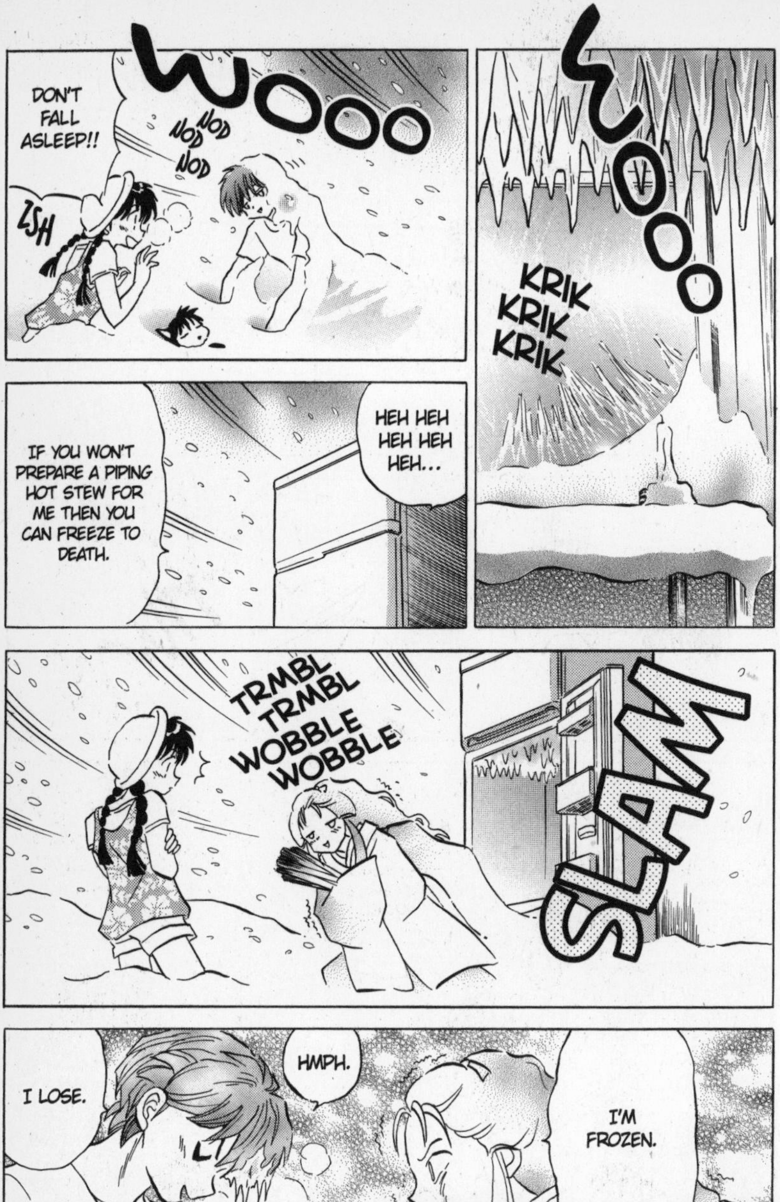
WOOOO
KRIK KRIK KRIK
WOOO
DON'T FALL ASLEEP!!
NOD NOD NOD
ZSH
HEH HEH HEH HEH HEH...
IF YOU WON'T PREPARE A PIPING HOT STEW FOR ME THEN YOU CAN FREEZE TO DEATH.
SLAM
TRMBL TRMBL WOBBLE WOBBLE
I'M FROZEN.
HMPH.
I LOSE.

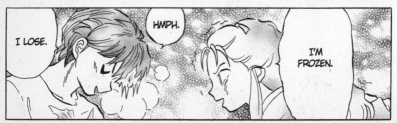

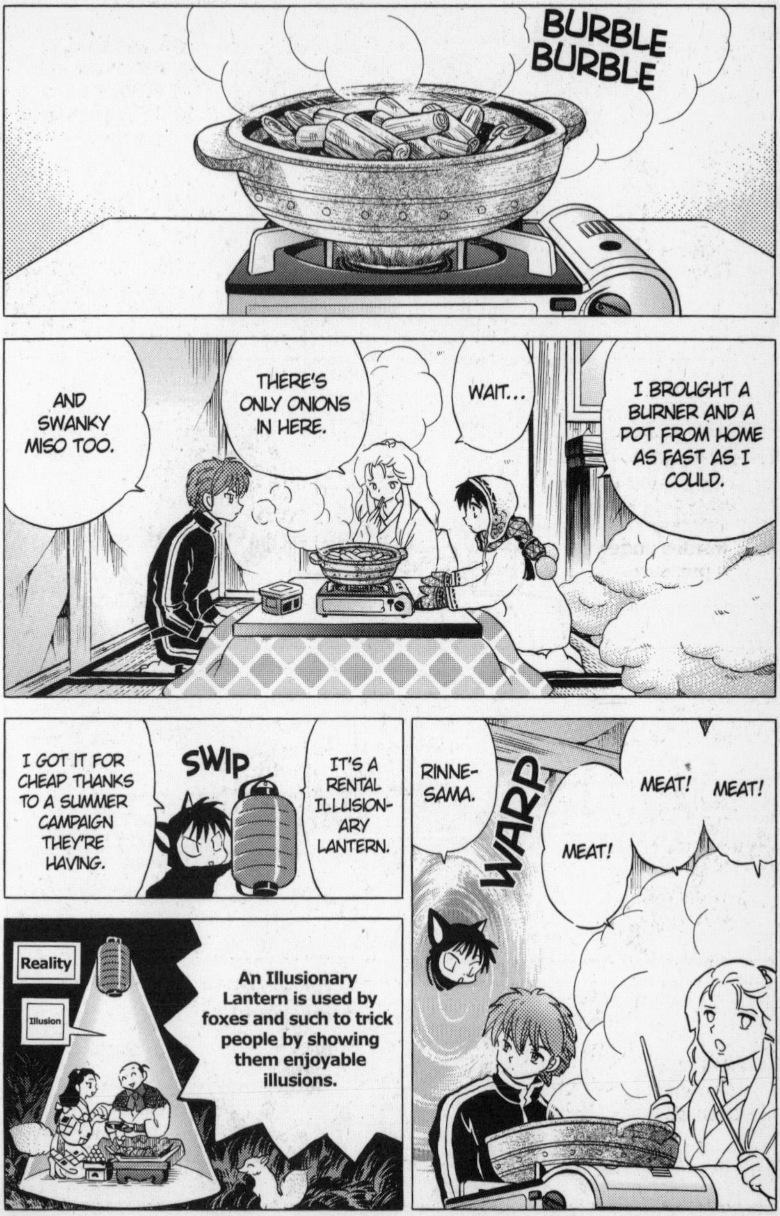
BURBLE BURBLE
I BROUGHT A BURNER AND A POT FROM HOME AS FAST AS I COULD.
WAIT...
THERE'S ONLY ONIONS IN HERE.
AND SWANKY MISO TOO.
MEAT!
MEAT!
RINNE-SAMA.
WARP
MEAT!
IT'S A RENTAL ILLUSION-ARY LANTERN.
SWIP
I GOT IT FOR CHEAP THANKS TO A SUMMER CAMPAIGN THEY'RE HAVING.
An Illusionary Lantern is used by foxes and such to trick people by showing them enjoyable illusions.
Reality
Illusion

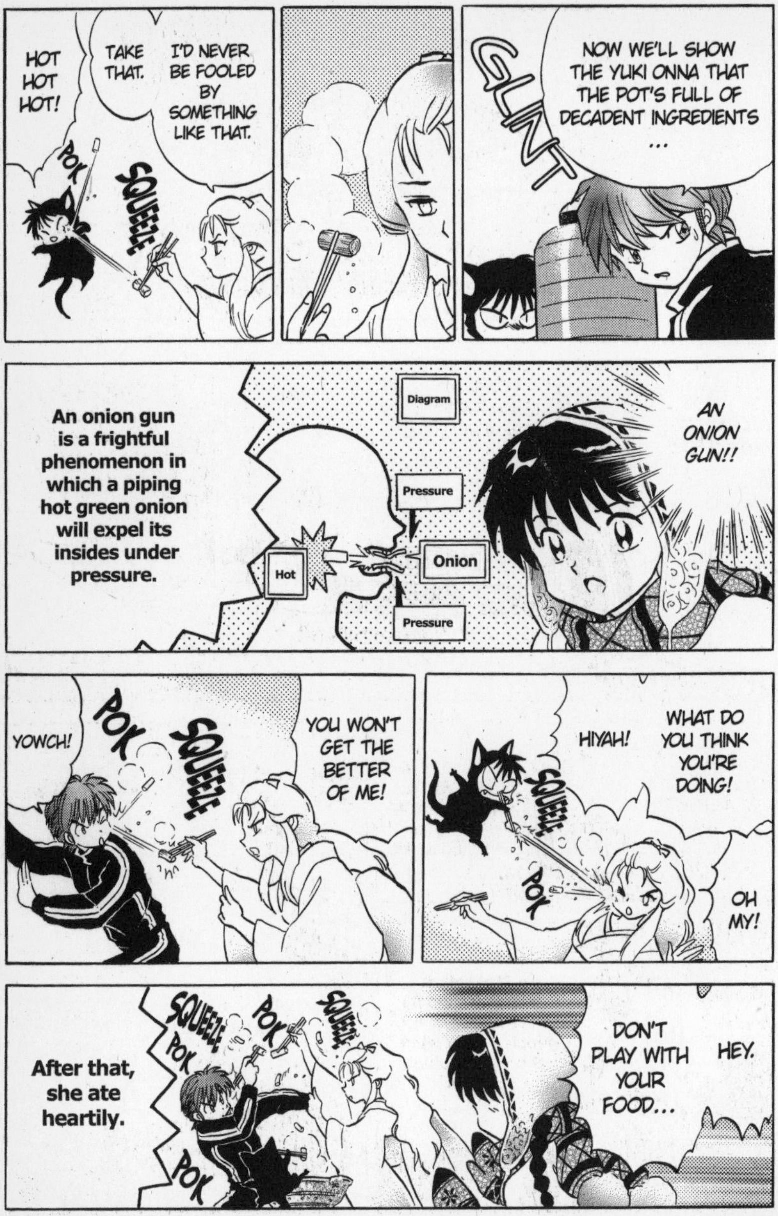
NOW WE'LL SHOW THE YUKI ONNA THAT THE POT'S FULL OF DECADENT INGREDIENTS ...
GLINT
I'D NEVER BE FOOLED BY SOMETHING LIKE THAT.
TAKE THAT.
HOT HOT HOT!
SQUEEZE
POK
AN ONION GUN!!
Diagram
Pressure
Onion
Hot
Pressure
An onion gun is a frightful phenomenon in which a piping hot green onion will expel its insides under pressure.
WHAT DO YOU THINK YOU'RE DOING!
HIYAH!
SQUEEZE
POK
OH MY!
YOU WON'T GET THE BETTER OF ME!
SQUEEZE
POK
YOWCH!
HEY.
DON'T PLAY WITH YOUR FOOD...
SQUEEZE
POK
SQUEEZE
POK
POK
After that, she ate heartily.

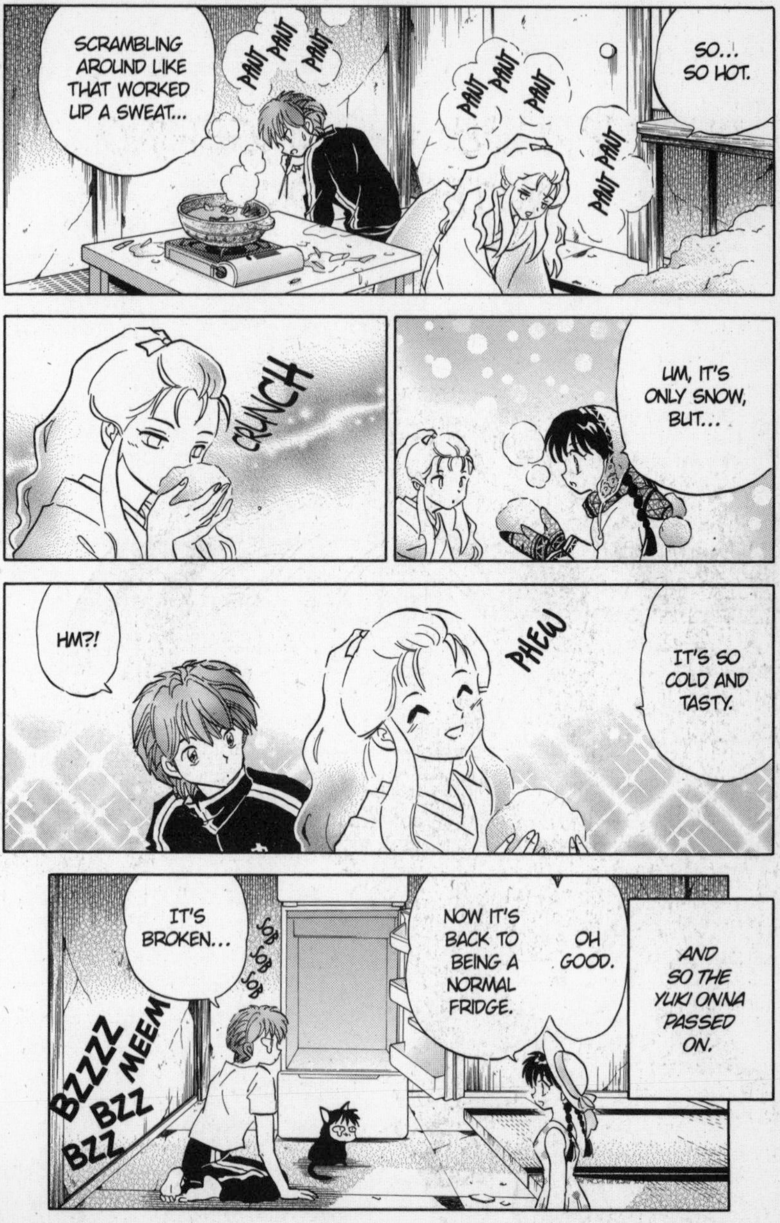
SO... SO HOT.
PANT PANT
PANT PANT PANT
PANT PANT PANT
SCRAMBLING AROUND LIKE THAT WORKED UP A SWEAT...
UM, IT'S ONLY SNOW, BUT...
CRUNCH
IT'S SO COLD AND TASTY.
PHEW
HM?!
AND SO THE YUKI ONNA PASSED ON.
OH GOOD.
NOW IT'S BACK TO BEING A NORMAL FRIDGE.
SOB SOB SOB
IT'S BROKEN...
BZZZZ BZZ BZZ MEEM

# CHAPTER 108: THE LINGERING WATERMELON

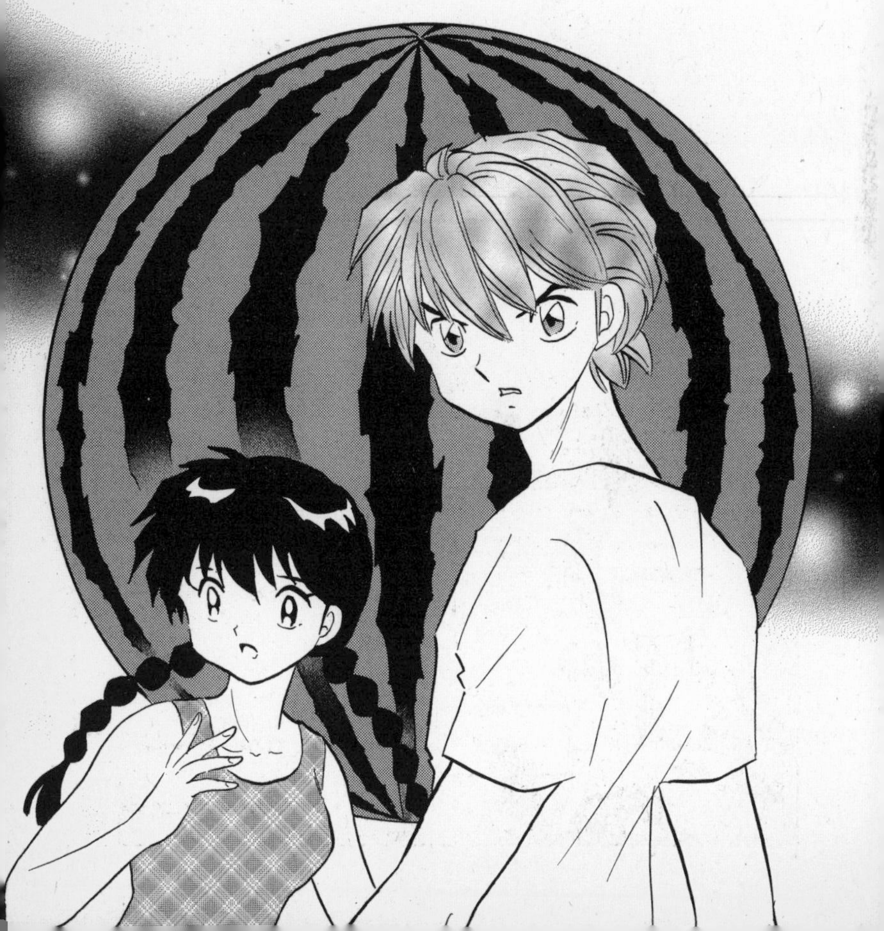

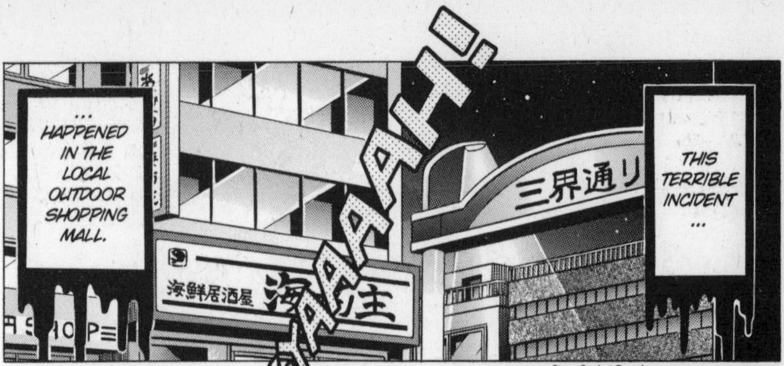
THIS TERRIBLE INCIDENT ...
三界通り
GRAAAH!
... HAPPENED IN THE LOCAL OUTDOOR SHOPPING MALL.

Sign: Sankai Road

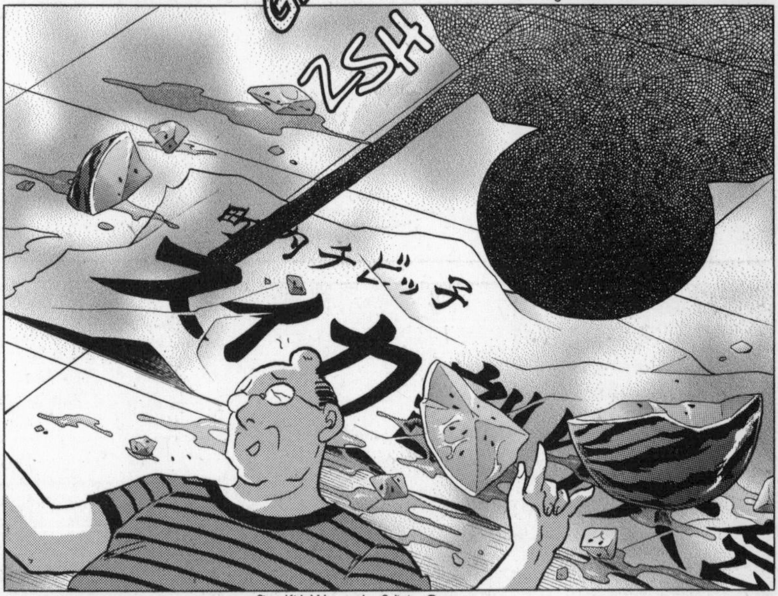
ZSH

Sign: Kids Watermelon Splitting Contest

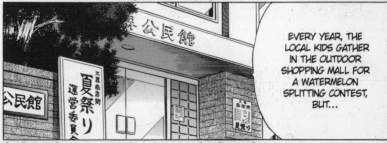

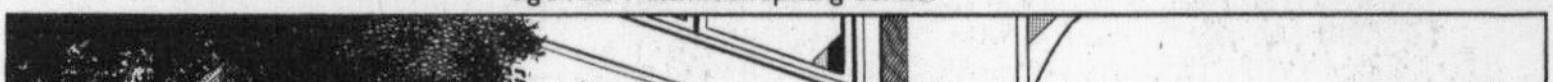
EVERY YEAR, THE LOCAL KIDS GATHER IN THE OUTDOOR SHOPPING MALL FOR A WATERMELON SPLITTING CONTEST, BUT...
公民館
三界商店街 夏祭り 運営委員会

Signs: Community Center Summer Festival Steering Committee Sankai Community Center

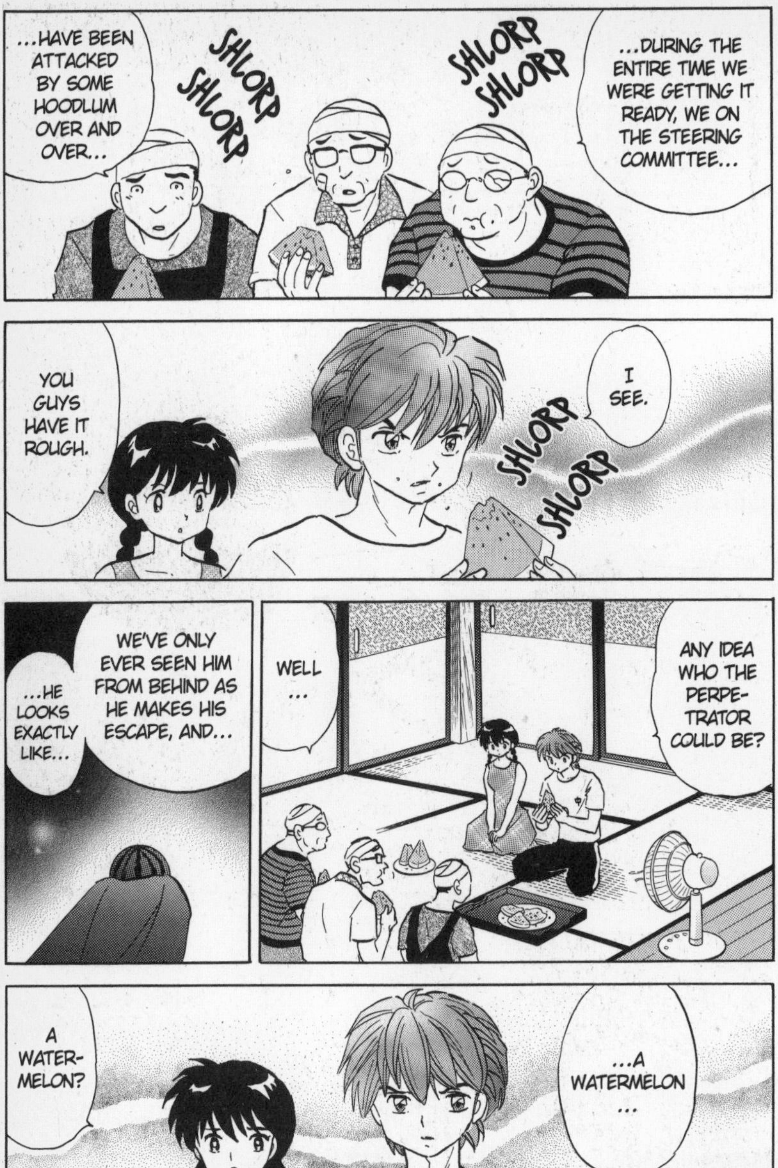
...DURING THE ENTIRE TIME WE WERE GETTING IT READY, WE ON THE STEERING COMMITTEE...
SHLORP SHLORP
SHLORP SHLORP
...HAVE BEEN ATTACKED BY SOME HOODLUM OVER AND OVER...
I SEE.
SHLORP SHLORP
YOU GUYS HAVE IT ROUGH.
ANY IDEA WHO THE PERPETRATOR COULD BE?
WELL...
WE'VE ONLY EVER SEEN HIM FROM BEHIND AS HE MAKES HIS ESCAPE, AND...
...HE LOOKS EXACTLY LIKE...
...A WATERMELON...
A WATERMELON?

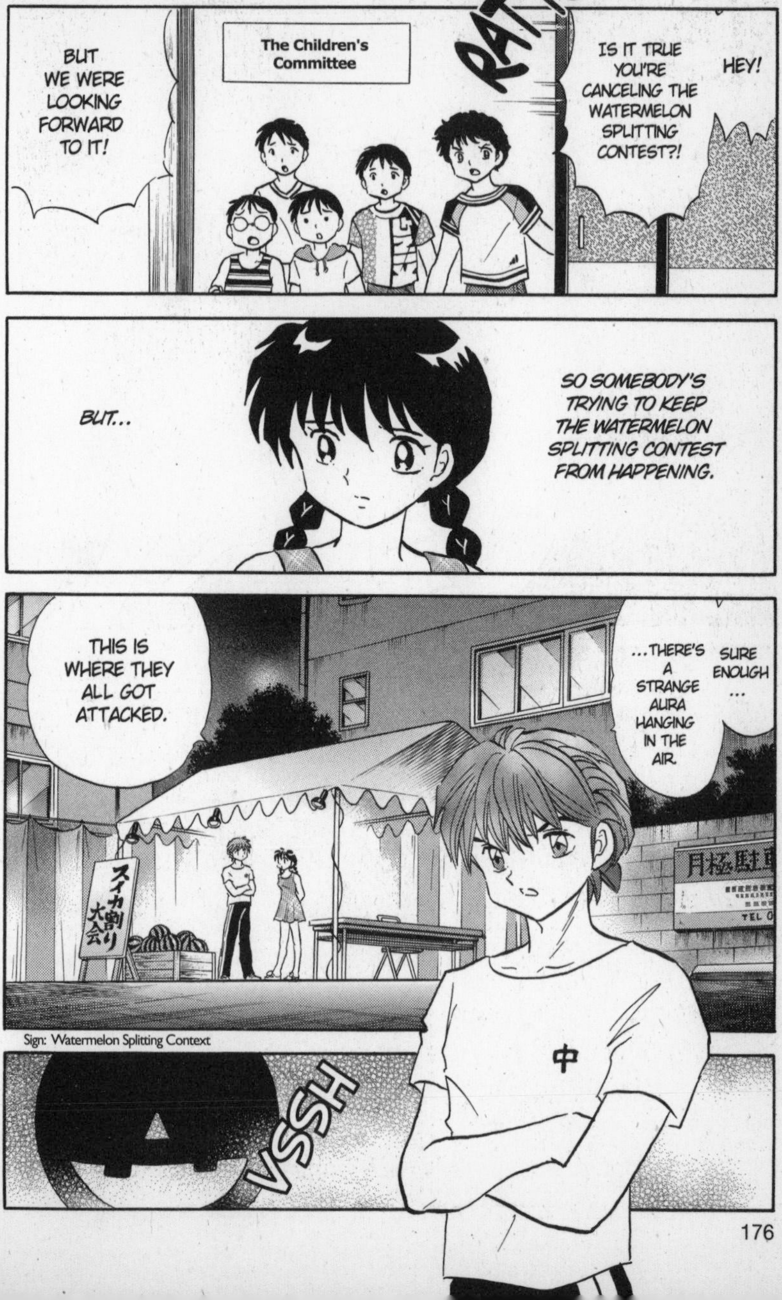
HEY!
IS IT TRUE YOU'RE CANCELING THE WATERMELON SPLITTING CONTEST?!
RATTLE
The Children's Committee
BUT WE WERE LOOKING FORWARD TO IT!
SO SOMEBODY'S TRYING TO KEEP THE WATERMELON SPLITTING CONTEST FROM HAPPENING.
BUT...
SURE ENOUGH...
...THERE'S A STRANGE AURA HANGING IN THE AIR.
THIS IS WHERE THEY ALL GOT ATTACKED.
スイカ割り大会
中
VSSH
Sign: Watermelon Splitting Context

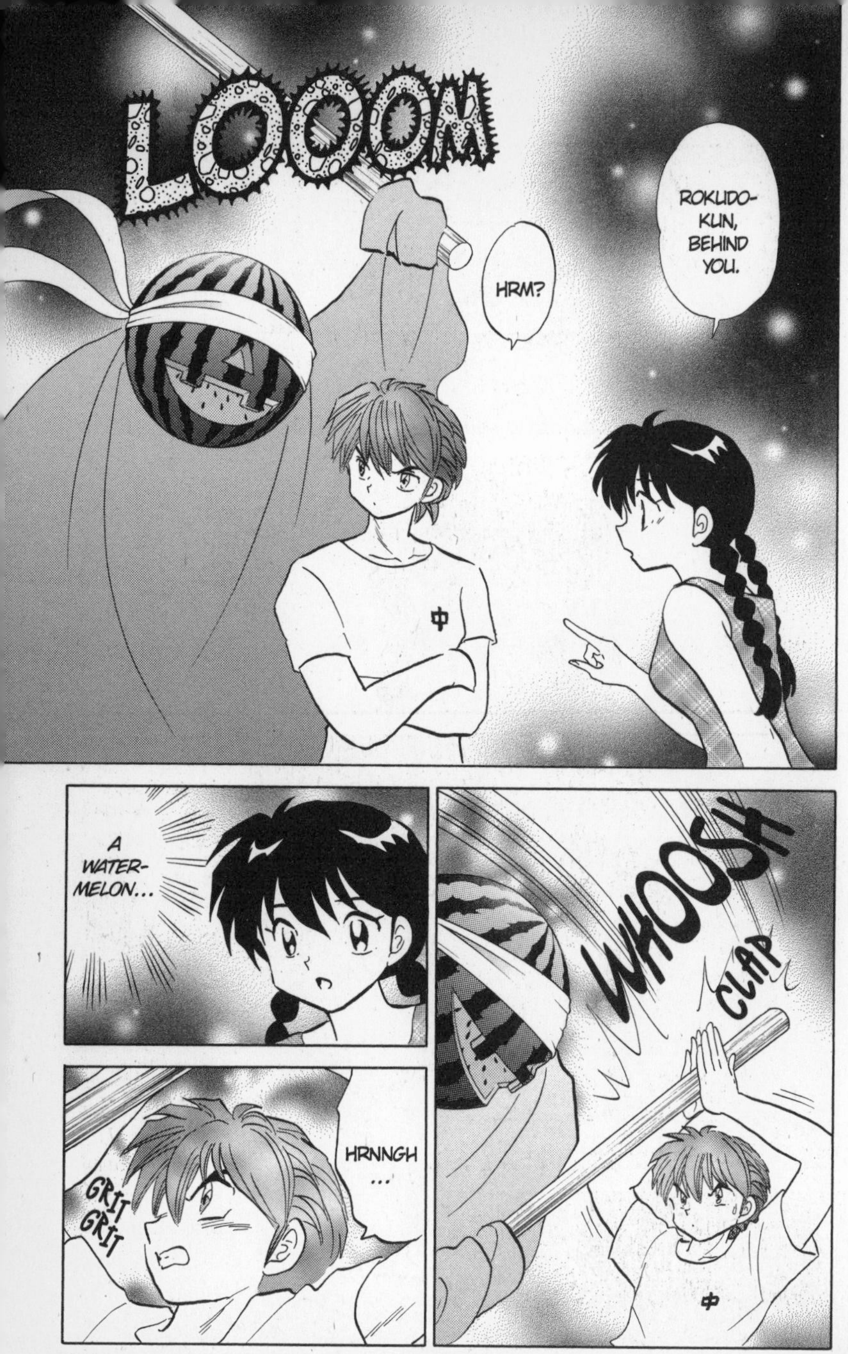
ROKUDO-KUN, BEHIND YOU.
HRM?
LOOOM
WHOOSH
CLAP
A WATER-MELON...
HRNNGH...
GRIT GRIT

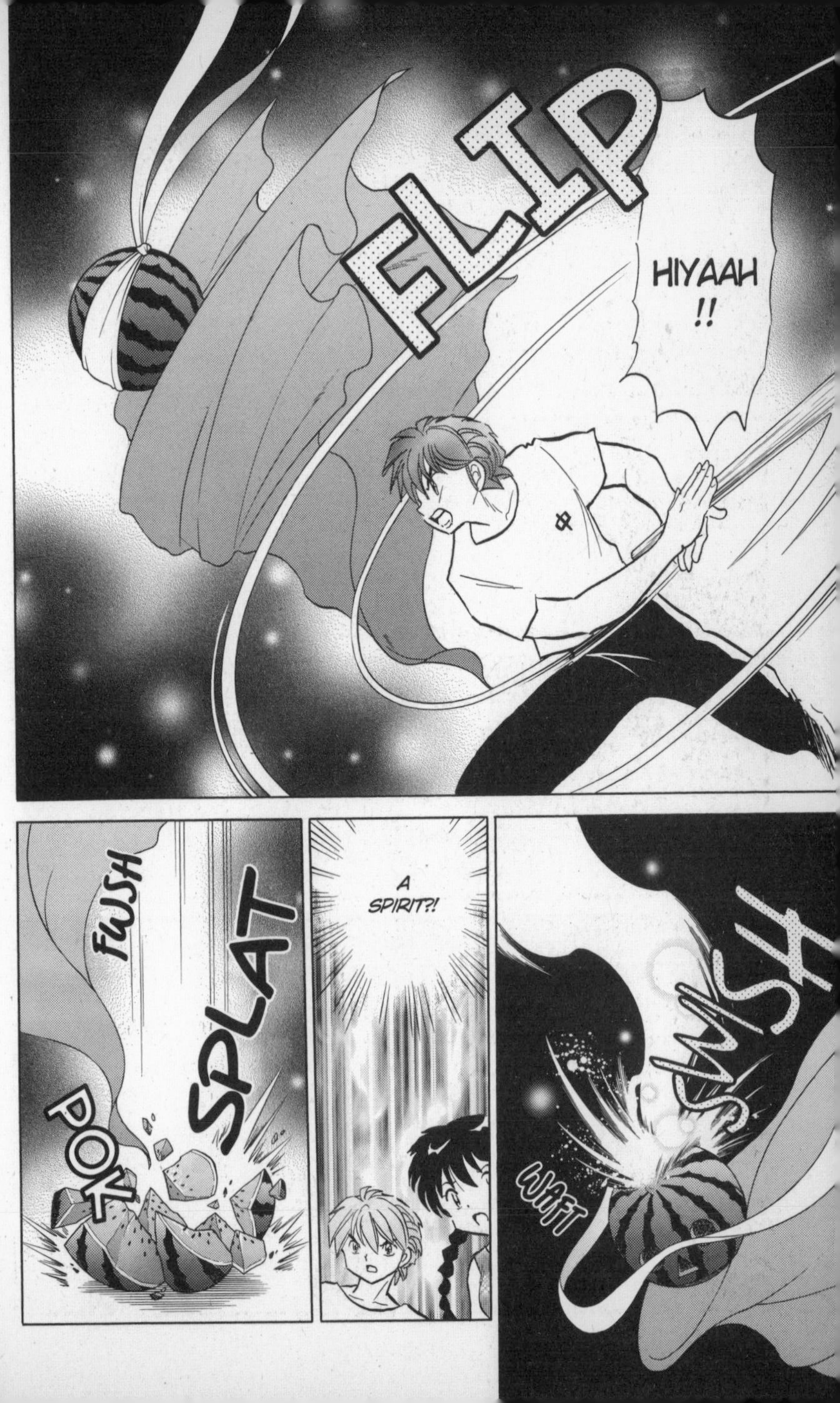
FLIP
HIYAAH !!
SWISH
WAFT
A SPIRIT?!
FWSH
SPLAT
POK

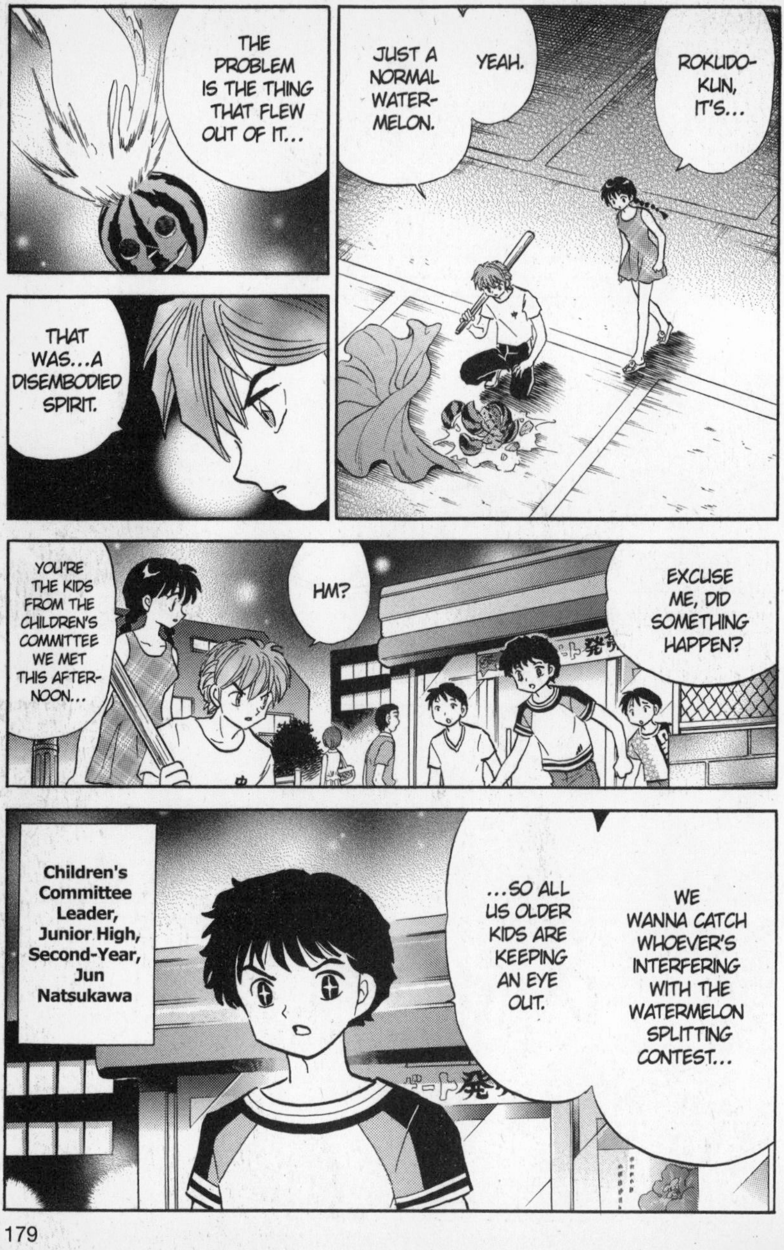
ROKUDO-KUN, IT'S...
YEAH.
JUST A NORMAL WATER-MELON.
THE PROBLEM IS THE THING THAT FLEW OUT OF IT...
THAT WAS...A DISEMBODIED SPIRIT.
EXCUSE ME, DID SOMETHING HAPPEN?
HM?
YOU'RE THE KIDS FROM THE CHILDREN'S COMMITTEE WE MET THIS AFTER-NOON...
WE WANNA CATCH WHOEVER'S INTERFERING WITH THE WATERMELON SPLITTING CONTEST...
...SO ALL US OLDER KIDS ARE KEEPING AN EYE OUT.
Children's Committee Leader, Junior High, Second-Year, Jun Natsukawa

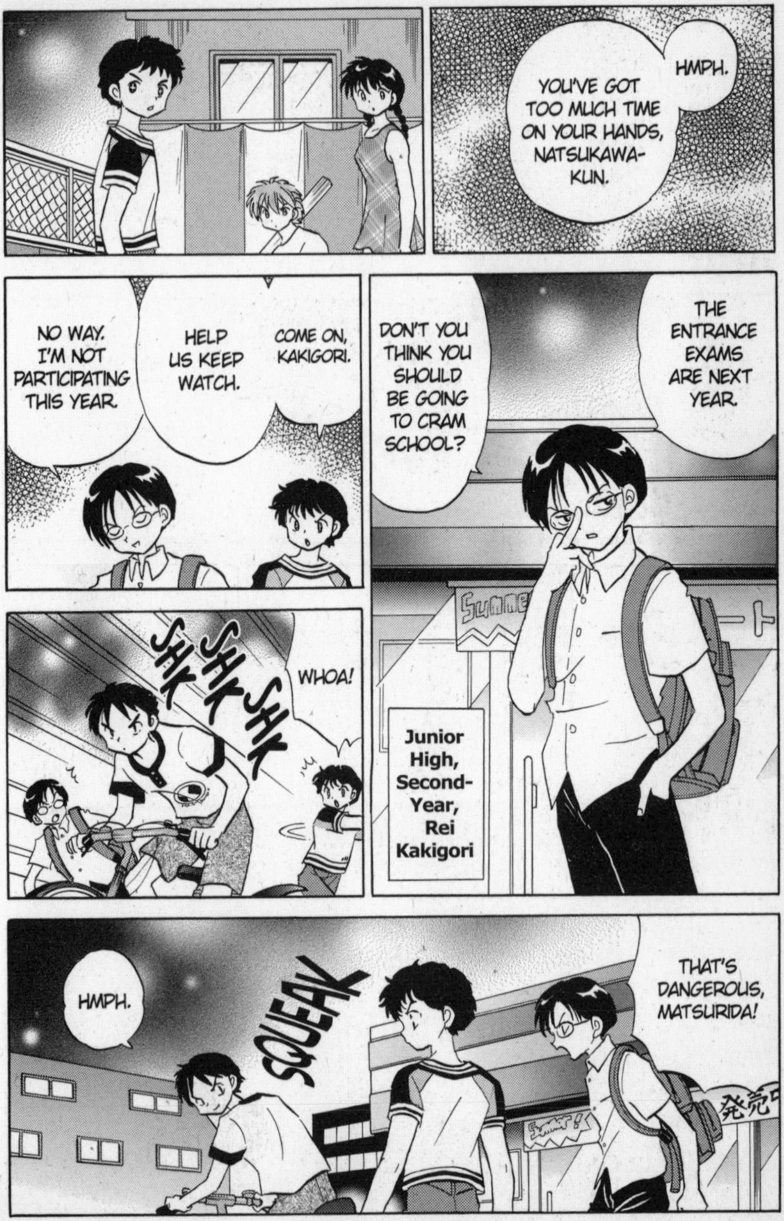
HMPH.
YOU'VE GOT TOO MUCH TIME ON YOUR HANDS, NATSUKAWA-KUN.
THE ENTRANCE EXAMS ARE NEXT YEAR.
DON'T YOU THINK YOU SHOULD BE GOING TO CRAM SCHOOL?
Junior High, Second-Year, Rei Kakigori
COME ON, KAKIGORI.
HELP US KEEP WATCH.
NO WAY. I'M NOT PARTICIPATING THIS YEAR.
WHOA!
SHAK SHAK SHAK
THAT'S DANGEROUS, MATSURIDA!
SQUEAK
HMPH.

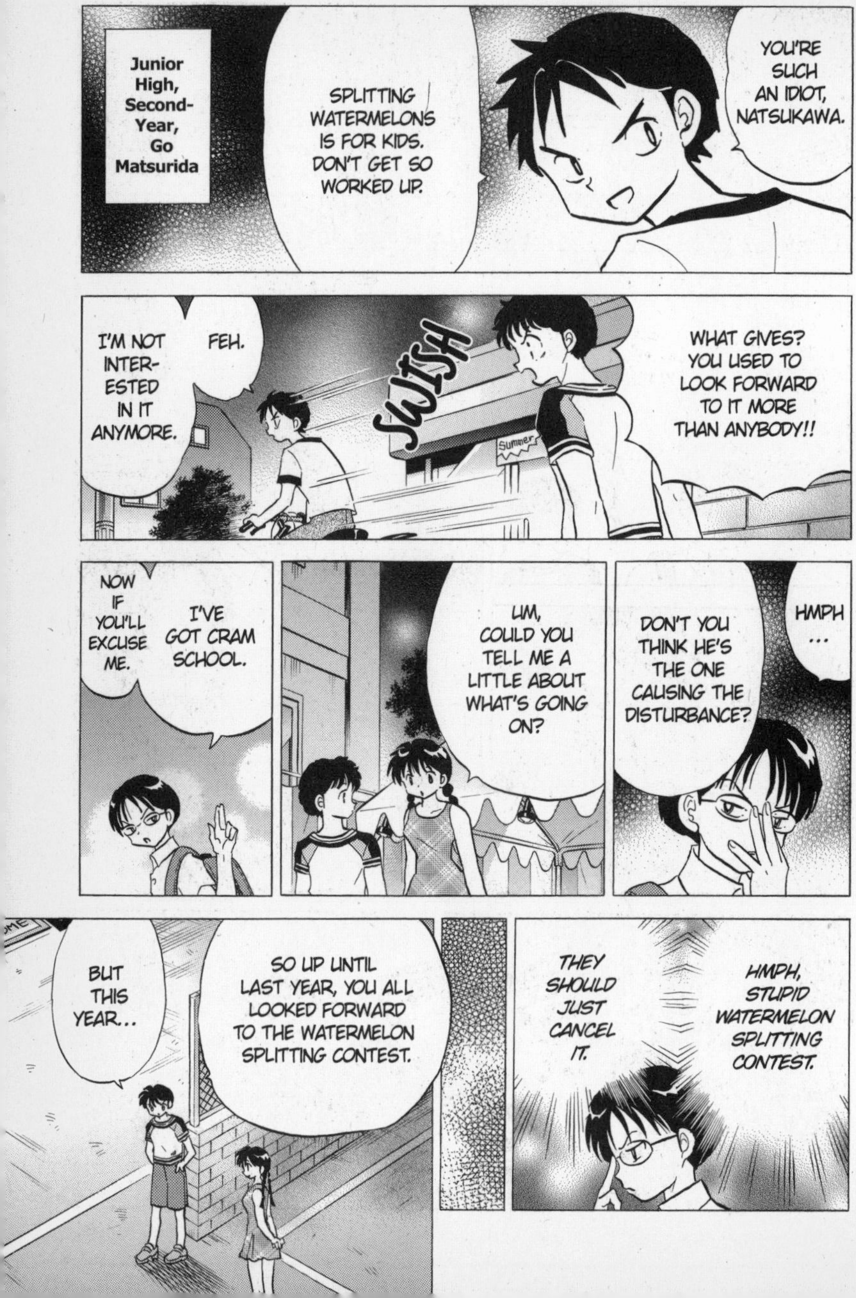
YOU'RE SUCH AN IDIOT, NATSUKAWA.
SPLITTING WATERMELONS IS FOR KIDS. DON'T GET SO WORKED UP.
Junior High, Second-Year, Go Matsurida
WHAT GIVES? YOU USED TO LOOK FORWARD TO IT MORE THAN ANYBODY!!
SWISH
FEH.
I'M NOT INTER-ESTED IN IT ANYMORE.
HMPH...
DON'T YOU THINK HE'S THE ONE CAUSING THE DISTURBANCE?
UM, COULD YOU TELL ME A LITTLE ABOUT WHAT'S GOING ON?
I'VE GOT CRAM SCHOOL.
NOW IF YOU'LL EXCUSE ME.
HMPH, STUPID WATERMELON SPLITTING CONTEST.
THEY SHOULD JUST CANCEL IT.
SO UP UNTIL LAST YEAR, YOU ALL LOOKED FORWARD TO THE WATERMELON SPLITTING CONTEST.
BUT THIS YEAR...

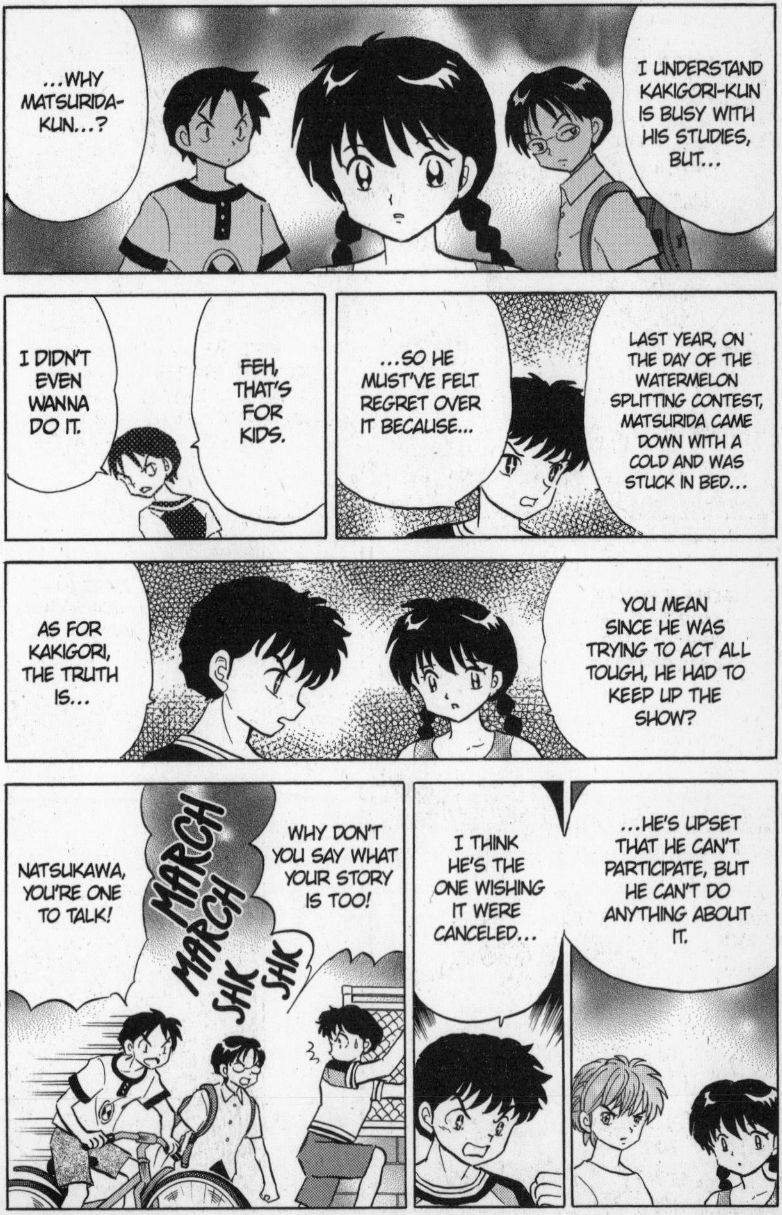
I UNDERSTAND KAKIGORI-KUN IS BUSY WITH HIS STUDIES, BUT...
...WHY MATSURIDA-KUN...?
LAST YEAR, ON THE DAY OF THE WATERMELON SPLITTING CONTEST, MATSURIDA CAME DOWN WITH A COLD AND WAS STUCK IN BED...
...SO HE MUST'VE FELT REGRET OVER IT BECAUSE...
FEH, THAT'S FOR KIDS.
I DIDN'T EVEN WANNA DO IT.
YOU MEAN SINCE HE WAS TRYING TO ACT ALL TOUGH, HE HAD TO KEEP UP THE SHOW?
AS FOR KAKIGORI, THE TRUTH IS...
...HE'S UPSET THAT HE CAN'T PARTICIPATE, BUT HE CAN'T DO ANYTHING ABOUT IT.
I THINK HE'S THE ONE WISHING IT WERE CANCELED...
WHY DON'T YOU SAY WHAT YOUR STORY IS TOO!
MARCH MARCH
SHK SHK
NATSUKAWA, YOU'RE ONE TO TALK!

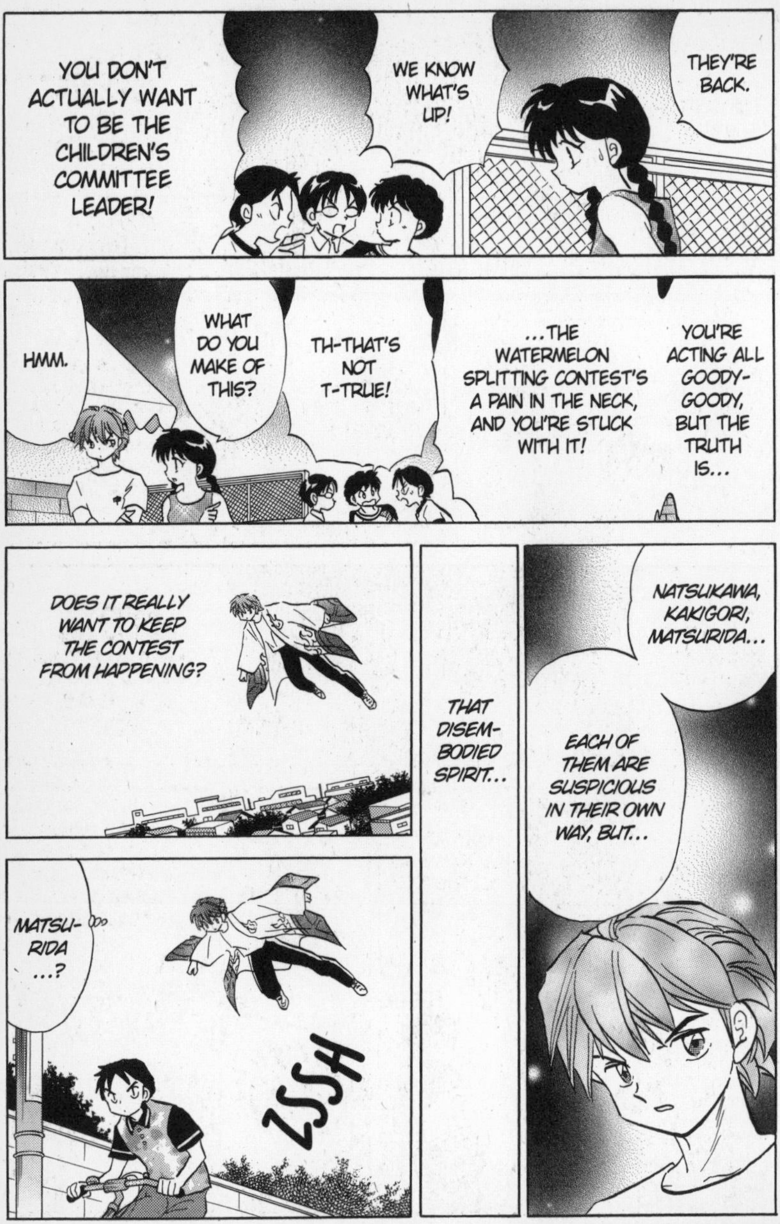
THEY'RE BACK.
WE KNOW WHAT'S UP!
YOU DON'T ACTUALLY WANT TO BE THE CHILDREN'S COMMITTEE LEADER!
YOU'RE ACTING ALL GOODY-GOODY, BUT THE TRUTH IS...
...THE WATERMELON SPLITTING CONTEST'S A PAIN IN THE NECK, AND YOU'RE STUCK WITH IT!
TH-THAT'S NOT T-TRUE!
WHAT DO YOU MAKE OF THIS?
HMM.
NATSUKAWA, KAKIGORI, MATSURIDA...
EACH OF THEM ARE SUSPICIOUS IN THEIR OWN WAY, BUT...
THAT DISEM-BODIED SPIRIT...
DOES IT REALLY WANT TO KEEP THE CONTEST FROM HAPPENING?
ZSSH
MATSU-RIDA ...?

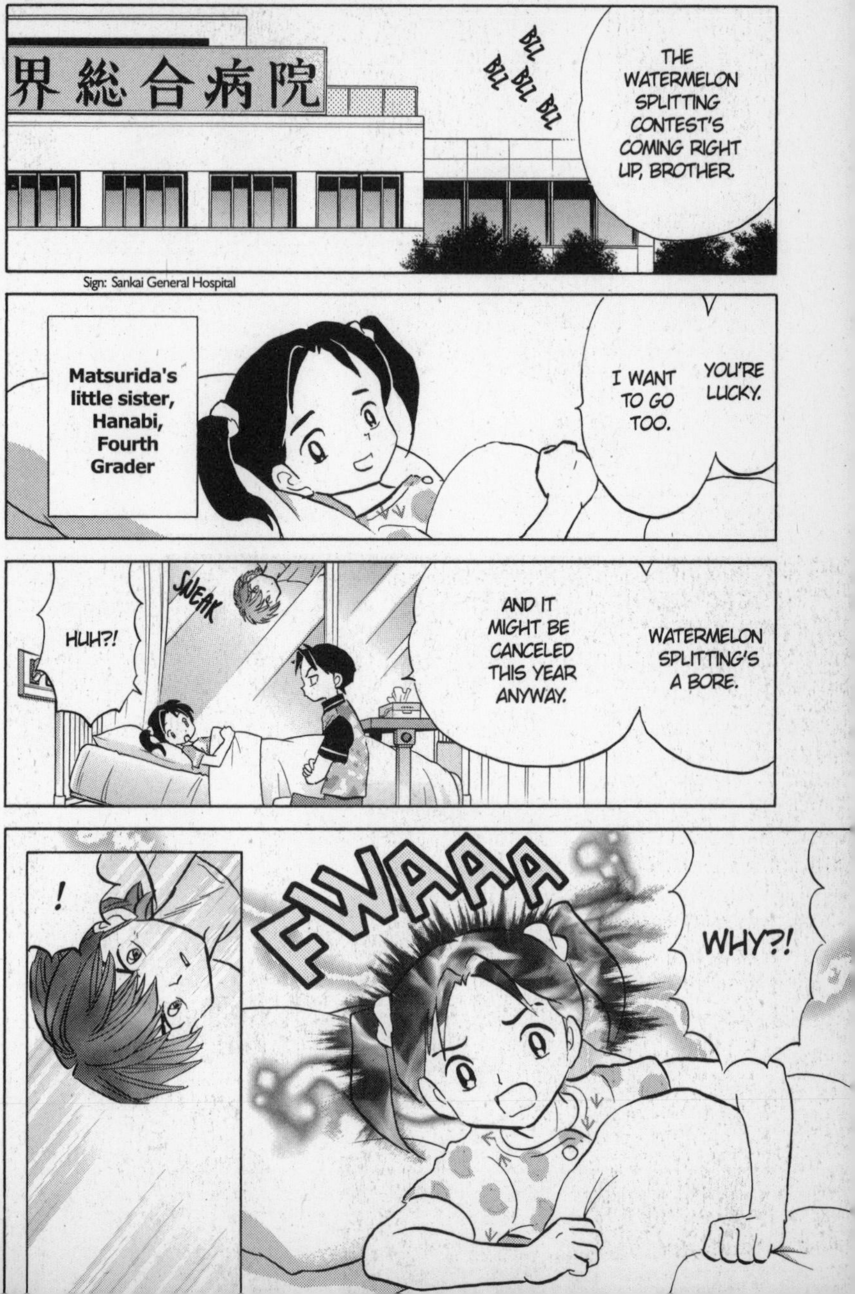
界総合病院
BZZ BZZ BZZ BZZ
THE WATERMELON SPLITTING CONTEST'S COMING RIGHT UP, BROTHER.
Sign: Sankai General Hospital
YOU'RE LUCKY.
I WANT TO GO TOO.
Matsurida's little sister, Hanabi, Fourth Grader
WATERMELON SPLITTING'S A BORE.
AND IT MIGHT BE CANCELED THIS YEAR ANYWAY.
SWEAK
HUH?!
WHY?!
FWAAA
!

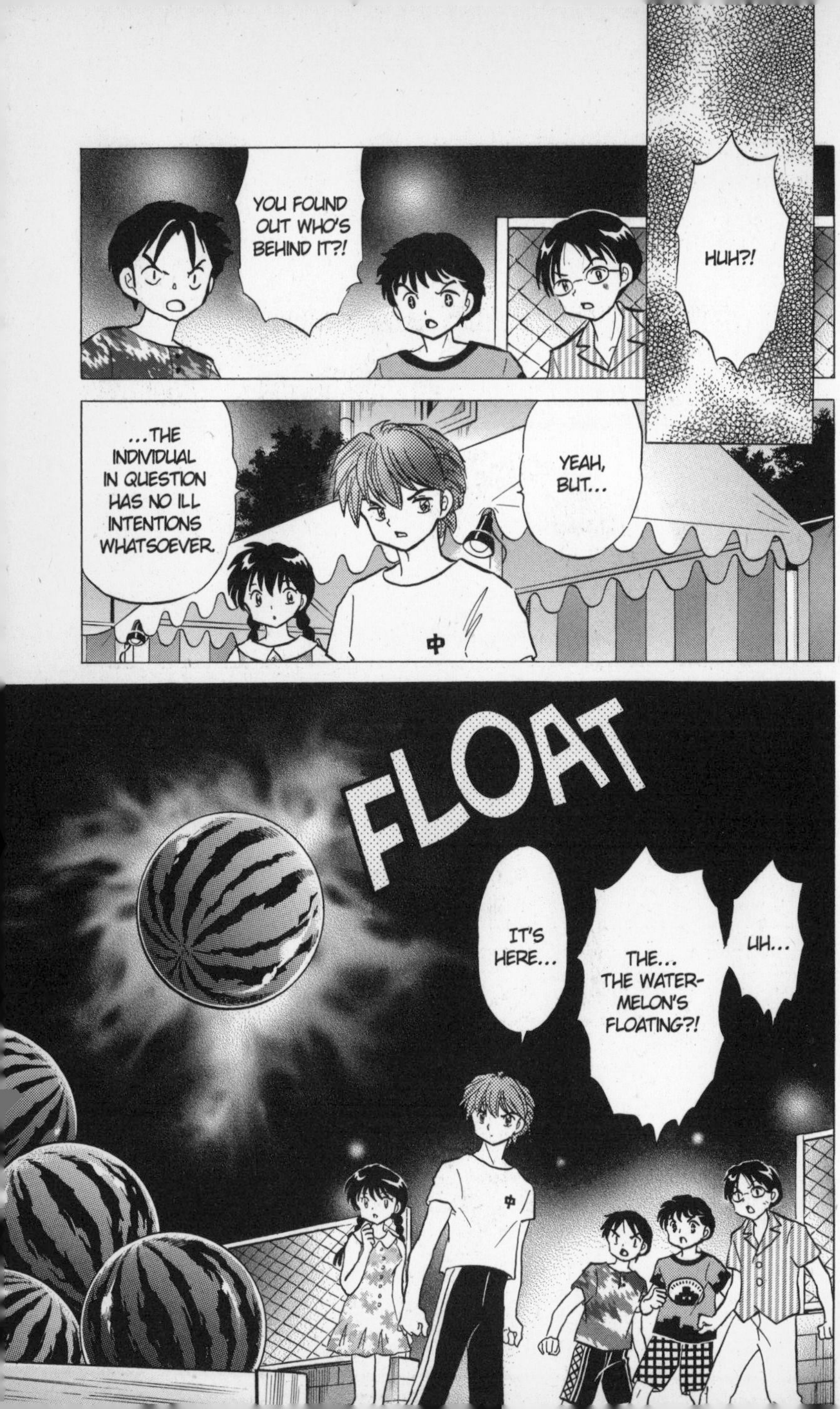
HUH?!
YOU FOUND OUT WHO'S BEHIND IT?!
YEAH, BUT...
...THE INDIVIDUAL IN QUESTION HAS NO ILL INTENTIONS WHATSOEVER.
FLOAT
UH...
THE... THE WATER-MELON'S FLOATING?!
IT'S HERE...

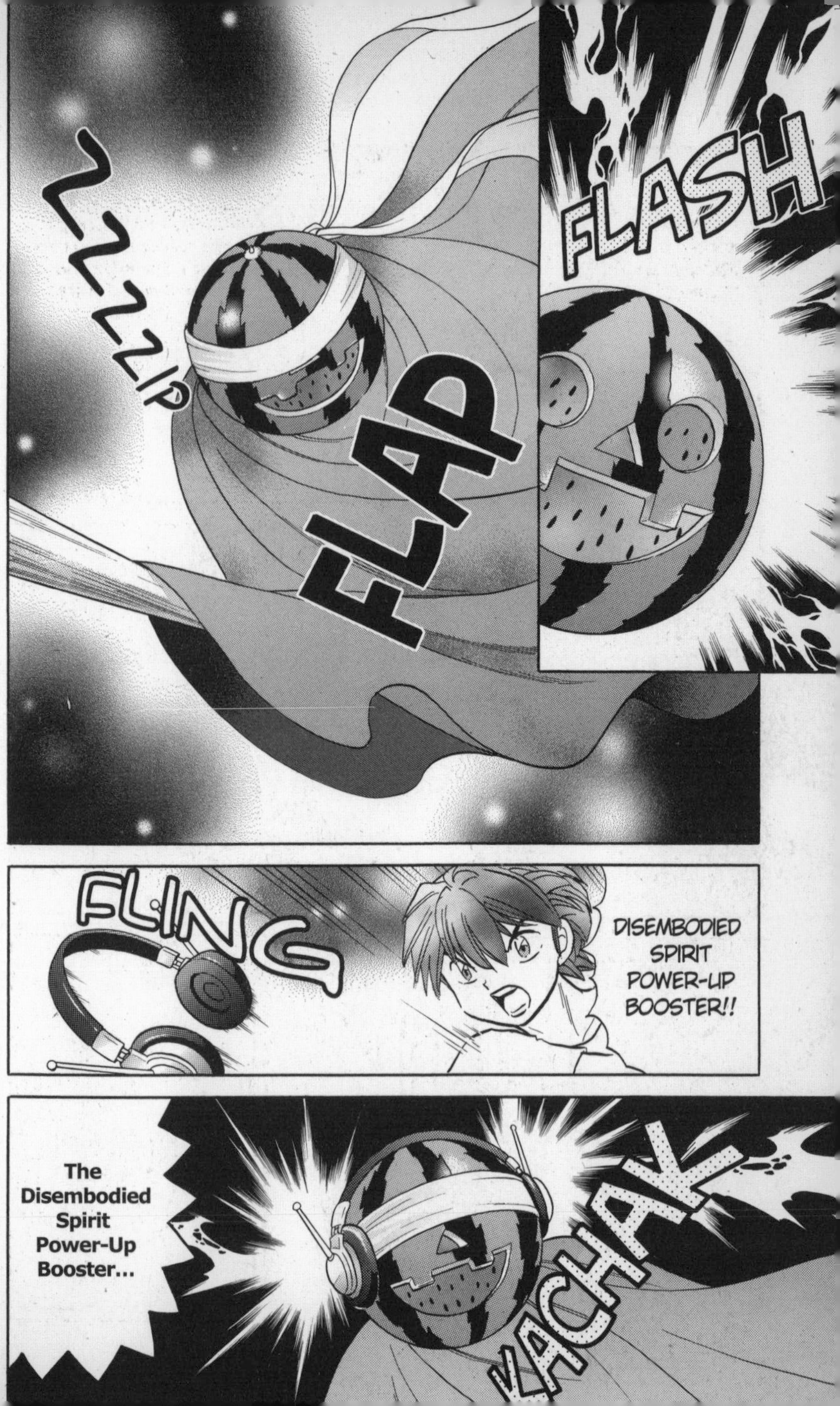
FLASH
ZZZZZIP
FLAP
DISEMBODIED SPIRIT POWER-UP BOOSTER!!
FLING
KACHAK
The Disembodied Spirit Power-Up Booster...

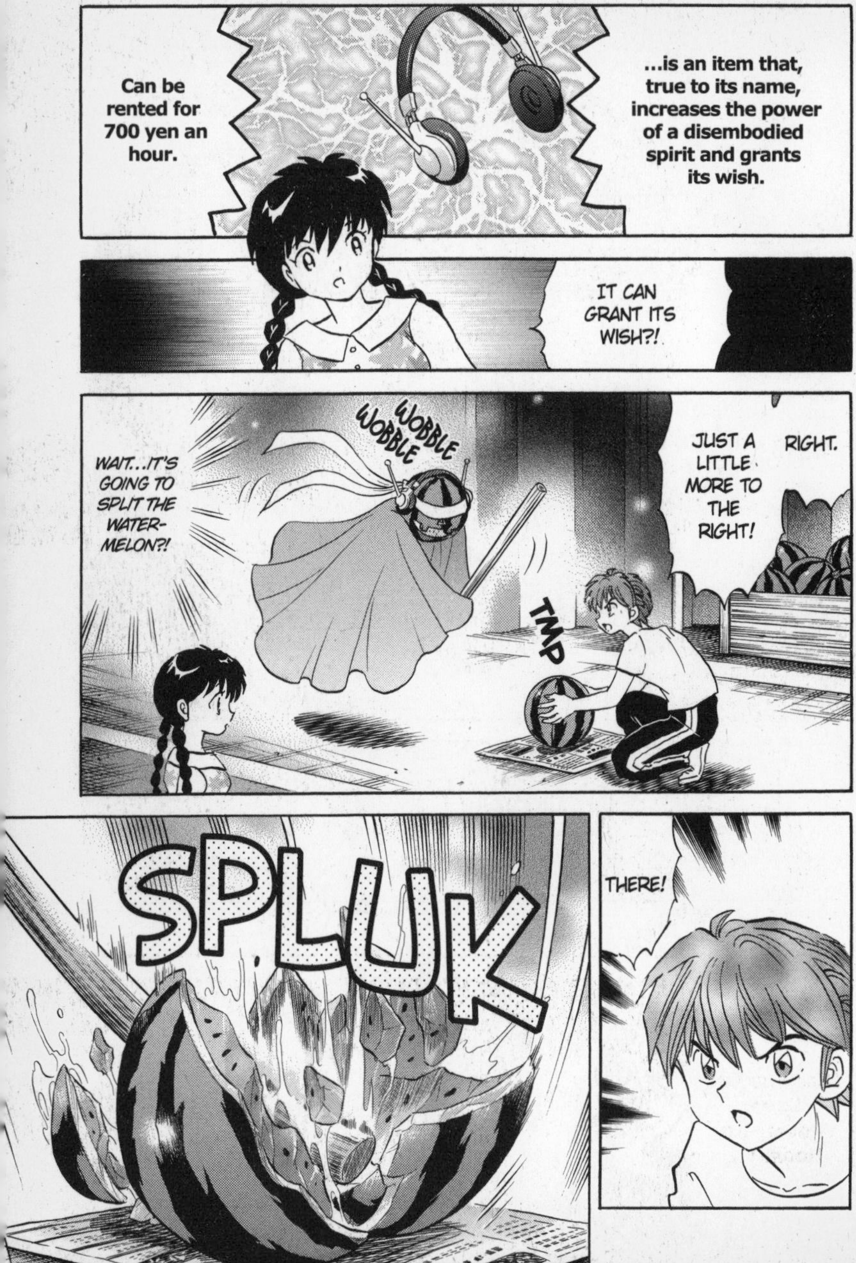
...is an item that, true to its name, increases the power of a disembodied spirit and grants its wish.
Can be rented for 700 yen an hour.
IT CAN GRANT ITS WISH?!
RIGHT.
JUST A LITTLE MORE TO THE RIGHT!
WOBBLE WOBBLE
TMP
WAIT...IT'S GOING TO SPLIT THE WATER-MELON?!
THERE!
SPLUK

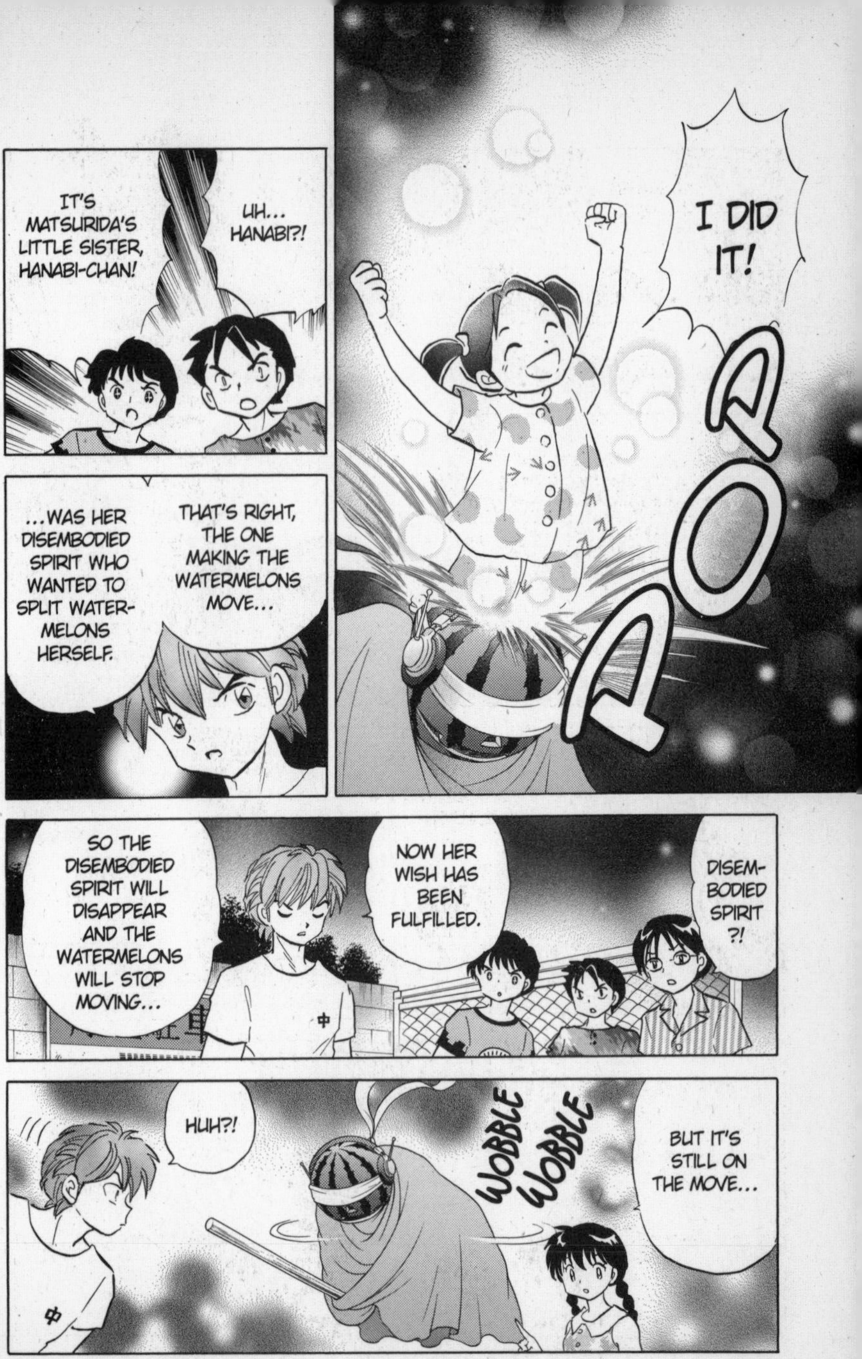
I DID IT!
POP
UH... HANABI?!
IT'S MATSURIDA'S LITTLE SISTER, HANABI-CHAN!
THAT'S RIGHT, THE ONE MAKING THE WATERMELONS MOVE...
...WAS HER DISEMBODIED SPIRIT WHO WANTED TO SPLIT WATER-MELONS HERSELF.
DISEM-BODIED SPIRIT?!
NOW HER WISH HAS BEEN FULFILLED.
SO THE DISEMBODIED SPIRIT WILL DISAPPEAR AND THE WATERMELONS WILL STOP MOVING...
BUT IT'S STILL ON THE MOVE...
WOBBLE WOBBLE
HUH?!